The Challenge of Legal Pluralism

Within the Latin American context, legal pluralism is often depicted as a dichotomy between customary law and national law. In addition, the use of customary law alongside national law is frequently portrayed as a vehicle of resistance.

This book argues that, because ordinary Indians are not positively biased in favor of customary law per se, a heterogeneity of legal practices can be observed on a daily basis, which consequently undermines the commonly held view of customary law as a "counter-hegemonic strategy," even if, on other socio-geographical levels, this thinking in terms of resistance holds true. Based on qualitative research, the work analyzes how internal conflicts among indigenous inhabitants of the Ecuadorian highlands are being settled in a situation of formal legal pluralism, and what can be learned from this in terms of Indian–state relationships. It is shown that, on a local level, the phenomenological dimension of legal pluralism can be termed "interlegality." On a macro level, ontological assumptions underscore that legal pluralism is still seen as a dichotomy between customary and national law.

Multidisciplinary in nature, the book will be of interest to academics and researchers working in the areas of Legal Pluralism, Cultural Anthropology, and Latin American Studies.

Marc Simon Thomas is a researcher in the Montaigne Centre for Judicial Administration and Conflict Resolution, Utrecht University, the Netherlands. His research and publications are focused on dispute settlement, legal anthropology, and legal pluralism.

Cultural Diversity and Law

Series Editor: Prakash Shah, School of Law, Queen Mary University of London, UK

Around the world, most states are faced with difficult issues arising out of cultural diversity in their territories. Within the legal field, such issues span across matters of private law through to public and constitutional law. At international level too there is now considerable jurisprudence regarding ethnic, religious, and cultural diversity. In addition, there are several layers of legal control – from communal and religious regulation to state and international regulation. This multiplicity of norm setting has been variously termed legal pluralism, inter-legality or internormativity and provides a fascinating lens for academic analysis that links up to cultural diversity in new and interesting ways. The umbrella of cultural diversity encompasses various population groups throughout the world ranging from national, ethnic, religious, or indigenous groupings. This series particularly welcomes work that is of comparative interest, concerning various state jurisdictions as well as different population groups.

Also in the series

Legal Pluralism in the Holy City
Competing Courts, Forum Shopping, and Institutional Dynamics in Jerusalem
Ido Shahar
ISBN 978-1-4094-1052-2

Muslim Families, Politics and the Law
A Legal Industry in Multicultural Britain
Ralph Grillo
ISBN 978-1-4724-5121-7

State and Legal Practice in the Caucasus
Anthropological Perspectives on Law and Politics
Edited by Stéphane Voell and Iwona Kaliszewska
ISBN 978-1-4724-4690-9

Declarations of Interdependence
A Legal Pluralist Approach to Indigenous Rights
Kirsten Anker
ISBN 978-1-4094-4737-5

The Challenge of Legal Pluralism

Local dispute settlement and the Indian–state relationship in Ecuador

Marc Simon Thomas

LONDON AND NEW YORK

First published 2017
by Routledge
2 Park Square, Milton Park, Abingdon, Oxon OX14 4RN

and by Routledge
711 Third Avenue, New York, NY 10017

Routledge is an imprint of the Taylor & Francis Group, an informa business

© 2017 Marc Simon Thomas

The right of Marc Simon Thomas to be identified as author of this work has been asserted by him in accordance with sections 77 and 78 of the Copyright, Designs and Patents Act 1988.

All rights reserved. No part of this book may be reprinted or reproduced or utilised in any form or by any electronic, mechanical, or other means, now known or hereafter invented, including photocopying and recording, or in any information storage or retrieval system, without permission in writing from the publishers.

Trademark notice: Product or corporate names may be trademarks or registered trademarks, and are used only for identification and explanation without intent to infringe.

British Library Cataloguing in Publication Data
A catalogue record for this book is available from the British Library

Library of Congress Cataloging in Publication Data
Names: Thomas, Marc Simon, author.
Title: The challenge of legal pluralism : local dispute settlement and the Indian-State relationship in Ecuador / Marc Simon Thomas.
Description: New York : Routledge, 2016. | Series: Cultural diversity and law
Identifiers: LCCN 2016007309| ISBN 9781472480576 (hb) | ISBN 9781315614380 (ebook)
Subjects: LCSH: Legal polycentricity--Ecuador. | Indigenous peoples--Legal status, laws, etc.--Ecuador. | Dispute resolution (Law)--Ecuador. | Customary law–Ecuador.
Classification: LCC KHK315 .T485 2016 | DDC 347.866/0908998--dc23
LC record available at http://lccn.loc.gov/2016007309

ISBN: 978-1-4724-8057-6 (hbk)
ISBN: 978-1-315-61438-0 (ebk)

Typeset in Times New Roman
by Taylor & Francis Books

Contents

Acknowledgments vi
List of abbreviations viii

1 An introductory overview 1
2 Legal pluralism, multiculturalism, and the state 20
3 Legal pluralism in Ecuador 47
4 The parish of Zumbahua: Cohesion and conflict 75
5 Conflicts, authorities, and procedures 106
6 Interlegality at the *teniente político*'s office 140
7 Trouble in Tigua 159
8 The La Cocha-Guantópolo murder case 185
9 Conclusion 212

Bibliography 232
Index 247

Acknowledgments

This book has only been possible because of the varied assistance provided to me by many different people. Mentioning all of them would be impossible, so I will limit myself here to mentioning those whose help was especially crucial to the enterprise I've undertaken.

First and foremost, I would like to thank those Ecuadorians living in Quito, Puembo, Latacunga, Pujílí, and Zumbahua for their kindness and trust, and for sharing their knowledge and experience with me. In the parish of Zumbahua, I am specifically indebted to the residents in and around the communities of Guantópolo, La Cocha, and Tigua, and of the village of Zumbahua, for letting me be a part of their daily life, fiestas, and dispute settlements. For example, it was an honor to be part of the inner circle at the wedding in Guantópolo on August 29, 2010, as described in Chapter 4. With regard to the settlement of local disputes, "Rosita" and "Miguel," and their relatives deserve special mention, given that their case was the basis of Chapter 6 of this book. I owe many thanks to the *cabildos* of Guantópolo and La Cocha, Alfredo Toaquiza in Tigua, members of the Junta Parroquial in Zumbahua, and Teniente Político Jaime Rodrigo Pallo for sharing their stories with me, and for allowing me to do archival research in their *libros de actas* and other files. Special thanks are due also to "Sergio," as well as his son, his sister, and his mother who – besides providing a lot of valuable data and facilitating contacts – arranged housing for me during my four-month stay in Zumbahua.

In Pujílí I would like to thank Judge Edwin Palma Herrera and his employees for their help during my visits to the Civil Court, and for allowing me to view court files. In a similar vein, I am grateful for the help I received from the judges of the Criminal Courts in Latacunga (specifically Judge José Luis Segovia from the Juzgado Tercero de lo Penal de Cotopaxi) and their employees. At the Fiscalía, I could not have done important archival research on the La Cocha–Guantópolo murder case without help from Diego Mogro Muñoz and his assistant. I also am thankful to Miriam Umajinga for her help at the Fiscalía Indígena. I am equally in debt for the assistance I received from staff at the FUDEKI law firm and the indigenous-rights organization MICC. At the library of the Casa de la Cultura, I was touched by the help

I received from Julián Tucumbi, librarian and *indígena*, as he proudly introduced himself. When I visited the capital of the Cotopaxi province, I usually stayed at Hostal Tiana, where I always felt very welcome. It was there that I met Jean Brown, who offered invaluable insights regarding life in Ecuador. I owe a special debt of gratitude to Carlos Poveda Moreno, once a judge, now a lawyer, as well as a teacher at the Universidad Andina Simón Bolívar in Quito. Dear Carlos, I greatly appreciate our numerous discussions regarding the challenge of legal pluralism at your house and office, and at the university. And I consider it an honor to have you as a personal friend.

In Quito, I would like to thank the staff of CODENPE and CONAIE, DINAPIN, the Constitutional Court, the Ministry of Justice, Abya-Yala, and FLACSO. I especially want to single out my friend and colleague, the legal anthropologist Fernando García. He not only put me on the track of the 2002 La Cocha murder case when I visited FLACSO for the first time in June 2007, but has supplied me with a steady stream of stimulating ideas, both through his own writings and during many personal conversations. It was in August 2010 that I met Jean Colvin and her husband in their apartment in Quito. I am grateful to them for introducing me to the Toaquiza case, which forms the core of Chapter 7.

In the Netherlands, I want to thank my former colleagues at both CEDLA in Amsterdam and the Department of Cultural Anthropology in Utrecht, especially Prof. Michel Baud and Prof. Patrick Eisenlohr. Thanks also to Arij Ouweneel, who stimulated my initial interest in Ecuador back when I was one of his students at CEDLA in 2006–2007. My present colleagues at the "Montaigne Centre" for Judicial Administration and Conflict Resolution provided me the academic stimulus to finalize this book.

The research underlying this book profited in many ways from comments by and discussions with colleagues I met at conferences or communicated with via email. In particular I would like to thank Maarten Bavinck, Susan Berk-Seligson, Victoria Chenaut, Jean Colvin, Armando Guevara Gil, Manfred Hinz, Miriam Künkler, Lars Leer, Wibo van Rossum, Oswaldo Ruiz Chiriboga, Esther Sanchez Botero, Yüksel Sezgin, Ido Shahar, and Janine Ubink. I owe special thanks to Prof. André Hoekema for insights he has shared with me over the course of many years on the topic of interlegality.

This book is a rewritten and updated version of my PhD dissertation (Simon Thomas 2013) which I defended successfully on October 23, 2013, in Utrecht, which in its turn originated from my Master's research (Simon Thomas 2009). It could not have been written without the exceptionally thorough work of Robert Forstag, who edited the English and translated much of the Spanish material of that dissertation. I also thank the editors of Ashgate Publishing, nowadays Routledge, Anna Dolan, Alison Kirk, and others, for their help and guidance during the book's editorial and publication process.

Finally, I owe an immeasurable debt of gratitude to my wife Charlotte, and my daughters Carlijn and Floor for being there for me during the entire course of this project. I dedicate this book to them.

List of abbreviations

Alianza PAÍS	Alianza Patria Altiva y Soberana – Alliance for Proud and Sovereign Nation
CEDLA	Centro de Estudios Latinoamericanos y del Caribe – Centre for Latin American Research and Documentation
CODENPE	Consejo de Desarrollo de las Nacionalidades y Pueblos del Ecuador – Council for the Development of Nationalities and Indigenous Groups in Ecuador
CONAIE	Confederación de Coordinación de las Nacionalidades Indígenas del Ecuador – Confederation of Indigenous Nationalities of Ecuador
CONESUP	Consejo Nacional de Educación Superior – National Council for Higher Education
CONFENAIE	Confederación de Nacionalidades Indígenas de la Amazonia Ecuatoriana – Confederation of the Ecuadorian Amazon
DINAPIN	Dirección Nacional de Defensa de los Pueblos Indígenas – National Organization for the Defense of Indigenous People
ECUARUNARI	"Ecuador Runacunapac Riccharimui" Confederación de los Pueblos de Nacionalidad Kichwa del Ecuador – "Awakening of the Ecuadorian Indian" Confederation of the People of the Kichwa Nationality
FEI	Federación Ecuatoriana de Indios – Federation of Ecuadorian Indians
FEINE	Consejo de Pueblos y Organizaciones Indígenas Evangélicas del Ecuador – Ecuadorian Federation of Evangelical Churches
FENOC	Federación Nacional de Organizaciones Campesinas – National Federation of Peasant Organizations
FENOCIN	Confederación Nacional de Organizaciones Campesinas, Indígenas y Negras – National Federation of Peasant, Indigenous, and Black Organizations

List of abbreviations   ix

FICI	Federación Indígena y Campesino de Imbabura – Indigenous and Peasant Federation of Imbabura
FLACSO	Facultad Latinoamericana de Ciencias Sociales (Sede Ecuador) – Latin American Faculty on Social Sciences (Ecuador Office)
FOIN	Federación de Organizaciones Indígenas del Napo – Federation of Indigenous Napo Organizations
FUDEKI	Fundación Defensoría Kichwa de Cotopaxi
IISL	Oñati International Institute for Sociology of Law
ILO	International Labor Organization
IMF	International Monetary Fund
INEFAN	Instituto Ecuatoriano Forestal de Áreas Naturales y Vida Silvestre – Ecuador Forestry Institute for Natural Areas and Wildlife
MICC	Movimiento Indígena y Campesino de Cotopaxi – Indigenous and Rural Movement of Cotopaxi
MICH	Movimiento Indígena de Chimborazo – Indigenous Movement of Chimborazo
MUPP	Movimiento de Unidad Plurinacional Pachakutik – Pachakutik Movement for Multinational Unity
NALACS	Netherlands Association for Latin American and Caribbean Studies
NBI	Necesidades Básicas Insatisfechas (unsatisfied basic needs)
OPIP	Organización de Pueblos Indígenas de Pastaza – Organization of the Indigenous Pastaza Peoples
OSG	Organización de Segundo Grado – Second-Degree Organization
OTG	Organización de Tercer Grado – Organization of the Third Degree
PDBA	Political Database of the Americas
RELAJU	Red Latinoamericana de Antropología Jurídica – Network of Legal Anthropology in Latin America
UN	United Nations
UNDRIP	United Nations Declaration on the Rights of Indigenous Peoples
UNOCAT	Unión de Organizaciones y Cabildos de Tigua – Union of Indigenous Organizations and Communities of Tigua
UNOCIC	Unión de Organizaciones y Comunidades Indígenas de La Cocha – Union of Indigenous Organizations and Communities of La Cocha
UNOCIZ	Unión de Organizaciones y Comunidades Indígenas de Zumbahua – Union of Indigenous Organizations and Communities of Zumbahua

1 An introductory overview

No somos ángeles: introduction to this book

The first time I heard someone mention that some of the subjects of my research might "not be angels" was in August 2010, when I attended the biannual RELAJU meeting in Lima, Peru.[1] I received this word of warning from a lawyer who, in presenting his views on the contemporary situation of legal pluralism in Ecuador, argued that not every single member of a local indigenous authority was as fair, honest, and impartial as they were sometimes depicted.[2] He stated that some local leaders "*no son ángeles*" ("are not angels") in a presentation on the pros and cons of customary law. Basically, he was arguing that, because of an insufficient system of accountability, customary law – or at least those who administer it – can often result in biased conduct. Because of this, he argued that the recognition of customary law be as limited as possible. I partially agree with his observation, but I thoroughly disagree with the conclusion he drew from it. And so did most of the audience that was attending his presentation.

The second time I heard a similar statement was in a totally different setting. I was seated next to the *teniente político* in the remote Andean village of Zumbahua, observing a local trial. In addition to myself and the *teniente político*, his secretary, a police officer, the parties involved, and several *dirigentes* (local indigenous leaders) of neighboring communities were present in his small office. The conflict that had to be settled had to do with marital infidelity and a physical altercation between spouses.[3] While persuading the parties in that local conflict to reconcile, one *dirigente* stated that "*nadie somos santos*" (literally: "none of us is a saint," meaning that nobody is perfect). Basically he was downplaying the tensions over what was actually at stake by arguing

---

1 RELAJU: Red Latinoamericana de Antropología Jurídica (Network of Legal Anthropology in Latin America).
2 It was a Colombian lawyer who made this observation during a session on the coordination between national law and customary law at a RELAJU congress in August 2010, Lima, Peru.
3 This trial of what I have dubbed the "Rosita vs. Miguel case" will be extensively discussed and analyzed in Chapter 6.

that making mistakes was part of being human. And so was – he pointed out – making peace following a conflict. As such he was giving expression to a fundamental value of local customary law: reconciliation. Neither I nor anyone else present disagreed with his reasoning.

Although referring indirectly to the same phenomenon, it is clear that legal pluralism does not mean the same thing to both the lawyer and the *dirigente*. The lawyer should be seen here as a representative of national law. In a way he was formulating Ecuador's unofficial – but nevertheless frequently practiced – political and juridical position regarding the relationship between customary and national law: although its use is constitutionally recognized, its shortcomings can hardly be overemphasized and its actual scope is in fact severely limited.[4] The first example is therefore illustrative of how the challenge of implementing formal legal pluralism in the absence of coordinating rules (harmonizing both legal systems) is often faced. For many of the parties involved (for example, scholars, jurists, politicians, and even some indigenous leaders), the debate concerning legal pluralism is fundamentally about individual rights vs. collective rights. In this view, the essential question of the debate concerns which cases customary law can be applied to, by whom, and when – *within* national and international law. Legal pluralism is thus understood as a jurisprudential process, and there are particular ontological assumptions which underlie such an understanding.[5]

The *dirigente* in the second vignette above represents the phenomenological dimension of legal pluralism. One should bear in mind that, although the *teniente político* of Zumbahua in the example is a state official, he in fact settles most conflicts presented to him according to customary norms and procedures. A state official applying customary law suggests that, at least in daily practice, there is a certain fluidity between the two legal systems. This is reflected by the *dirigente* in the second example. Contrary to the highlighted differences between customary law and national law, and the problems regarding their harmonization indicated by the lawyer, the second example reflects a more nuanced daily reality. What we see in the two vignettes above is a difference between legal pluralism seen as a jurisprudential process and legal pluralism experienced as an empirical reality.

Objectives and research question

Legal pluralism is generally understood as "the presence in a social field of more than one legal order" (J. Griffiths 1986: 1), which can be described and

4   Some Ecuadorian jurists go even further in their rejection of customary law, as reflected in the following example that I came across in the magazine En Marcha (2010: 3): "'Customary law' is a delusion of good-for-nothing anthropologists and political opportunists, and is a notion that has unfortunately fallen into the hands of lawyers who want to make a career out of the pursuit of 'indigenous justice'."
5   What I mean by "ontological assumptions," is law as a set of universal principles, codified through the positive law of the state (Goodale 2009: 32). In other words, the term refers to "the law on the books."

analyzed both as situational and as a process. In the Ecuadorian context, this means that the existence of customary law alongside national law is both a fact and an ongoing process, which has to be seen in the context of the relationship between indigenous people and the state. In accordance with Moore's "semi-autonomous social fields" (Moore 1978), legal pluralism involves the dialectical and mutually constitutive relationship between customary law and national law (Merry 1988: 880), considering that this relationship is not power-neutral (Sieder 1997). Studying legal pluralism involves conducting legal-anthropological research, while taking historically changing legal and political power structures into account.

Along with Africa and Asia, Latin America is heavily represented in the literature on legal pluralism. Within the Latin American context, legal pluralism is often depicted as a dichotomy between customary law and national law. In addition, the use of customary law *alongside* national law is frequently portrayed as a vehicle of resistance – that is, a strategy of indigenous people to use their "traditional" norms and practices to protect their autonomy against encroachment of the state.[6] In the words of Sieder (1997: 10): "Legal pluralism is [...] understood as a relation of dominance and of resistance." It is far from evident, however, if this is the case *wherever* legal pluralism is present. An analytical approach that views legal pluralism as consisting of two distinct legal systems must be empirically verified rather than assumed *a priori*.

An important argument that this book will make is that indigenous people in Ecuador do not always prefer customary law to national law. On the contrary, these people are typically very well aware of the option of turning to national law when the latter is likely to result in outcomes more favorable to them. Therefore, viewing customary law solely as a "counter-hegemonic strategy" does not adequately explain the heterogeneity observed in the legal practices of ordinary Indians. Thus, in cases involving internal conflicts, such individuals sometimes use customary law, at other times turn to national law, and in still other cases make use of both legal systems. Yet such a characterization obscures a much more fundamental point: more often than not, rural Indians do not even distinguish between the two different systems. By this I mean that, on a micro level, their options are not always that clearly distinct, and consequently their everyday lived experience of legal pluralism is not that of a dichotomy. The present volume will show that the way in which legal pluralism is experienced depends on who is applying or talking about customary law and under what circumstances. In other words, legal pluralism has different meanings at different socio-geographical levels.

---

6   I have placed the word "traditional" in quotation marks because the indigenous norms and practices, or customary law, are not traditional in the sense of static or authentic. Customary law is highly flexible and changeable, develops by means of daily practice, and is to a large extent shaped by its context. See Chapter 2 for an extensive discussion of customary law.

Drawing on de Sousa Santos' notion of "interlegality," this study underscores the notion that the daily practice of legal pluralism in the Andean highlands is not one of clearly separated legal systems and corresponding authorities, but rather that of "different legal spaces superimposed, interpenetrated, and mixed" (de Sousa Santos 2002: 437). Consequently, this book rejects the idea that, in a situation of legal pluralism, everybody makes the kind of conscious and rational choices referred to in the legal anthropological literature as "forum shopping" (K. von Benda-Beckmann 1981). Portraying legal pluralism as a dichotomy is far too simplistic. Instead, the options ordinary people have for settling their conflicts seem to exist on a continuum. This observation is not new; de Sousa Santos (2002), A. Griffiths (2002), Hoekema (2004), Sieder (2001), Sierra (1995a, 1995b), and von Benda-Beckmann and von Benda-Beckmann (2006) to name just a few, have already shown that "the posited division between 'customary law' and 'state law' [is] in fact a legal fiction" (Sieder 2001: 211). The new contribution that the present study makes is in providing insight into how, and why, people make use of the possibilities provided to them by a situation of *formal* legal pluralism (that is, a situation in which the Ecuadorian Constitution recognizes customary law alongside national law).

But just as important as the notion of interlegality on a local level is recognition of the fact that, on other socio-geographical levels, legal pluralism is also often posited as a dichotomy. Thus, on a macro level, a strong distinction between customary law and national law is frequently drawn. We will see that, in the view of some local indigenous leaders, provincial and national jurists and politicians, and the national indigenous movement, there is a very real division between customary law and national law. Such a division has recently become manifest because Ecuador has constitutionally recognized customary law while failing to develop rules defining the proper scope of jurisdiction of customary law in relation to national law. It is this legal void that is of specific interest in the present study. The view of those who believe there is a dichotomy in the application of the two systems can be seen as an example of law-on-the-books, as opposed to law-in-action. They treat a situation of legal pluralism as if it were an analytical framework of two different legal systems, a conceptualization which flies in the face of how the interplay of the two systems is experienced by highland Indians.

This book will show that legal pluralism does not mean the same thing to all people. To this end, three detailed case studies will describe how legal pluralism works in daily practice in Ecuador, a culturally diverse country which recently has constitutionally recognized the use of customary law alongside national law. By providing an empirical understanding of such a situation, this book aims to gain empirical insight into how a situation of *formal* legal pluralism in which coordinating rules are absent works in daily practice for Ecuadorian Indians living in the Andean highlands. Additionally, it strives to use these insights to make a contribution to the understanding of legal pluralism in general.

Research setting

Ecuador is one of the smallest countries in Latin America. The chain of the Andes Mountains divides the country into three different zones: the coast, the highlands, and the eastern or "Amazon" region. Ecuador has a population of 13.5 million people. Roughly one-third of the population is considered indigenous; the other part of the population consists of whites, mestizos, and Afro-Ecuadorians.[7] The indigenous population consists of more than ten major groups (called "nationalities") with even more subgroups, and a variety of different languages.[8] The indigenous peoples of the nation are categorized in terms of their residence in one of the three areas of the country. The highland Kichwa Indians are the largest indigenous group, and the above example of the *dirigente* originated among their Panzaleos subgroup.

As is the case in most Latin American societies, Ecuador has been multicultural in its composition (that is, different cultures and groups, with different customs) since colonization, and therefore it has had experience with legal pluralism for nearly five hundred years. Ecuador has dealt politically with its cultural diversity in a variety of different ways, alternately employing assimilationist, integrationist, and – most recently – multicultural models. However, for centuries, ethnic difference did not play an important role in the country's politics, or in its legal and administrative arrangements. Struggles between indigenous people and power holders could most usefully be classified as class struggles. Past legal disputes over economic and political differences thus typically concerned working conditions or access to land and other natural resources, rather than "indigenous rights," this latter notion only having emerged during the past thirty years (Pallares 2002). As a result of the recent emergence of an Indian resistance movement in the country,[9] a new constitution was proclaimed in 1998 in which Ecuador legally acknowledged its cultural diversity.[10]

Several explanations have been proffered to explain the development of this stronger ethnic consciousness and concomitant indigenous activism. Yashar (2005) argues that contemporary "changes in citizenship regimes," accompanied

---

7   Of course, this is a simplistic way of picturing the nuanced reality. The ethnographic landscape is far more complex and also variable over time.
8   See for example http://www.conaie.org/ (accessed April 16, 2013) on the different "*nacionalidades*" and "*pueblos.*"
9   Resistance in the present context is seen as organized political protest, and thus can be viewed as one end of a spectrum, while at the other end one finds "gestures of tacit refusal" (Comaroff & Comaroff 2012: 393). Abu-Lughod (1990) also distinguishes between resistance as peasant insurgency and revolution vs. local and everyday resistance.
10   As such, Ecuador is not unique. A series of Latin American countries have acknowledged their cultural diversity since 1972. These countries include Argentina (1994), Bolivia (1994), Brazil (1988), Colombia (1991), Costa Rica (1977), Ecuador (1998 and 2008), Guatemala (1985), Mexico (1992), Nicaragua (1986), Panama (1972 and 1983), Paraguay (1992), Peru (1993), and Venezuela (1999); Chile modified its *Ley Indígena* in 1993 (Assies 2000b: 3, note 2; Sieder 2002: 4).

by the development of a "political associational space" and pre-existing "trans-community networks," politicized indigenous people. Van Cott (2005), on the other hand, sees the decisive factor in this transformation as the crisis of the traditional political parties and the new political space resulting from the decline of class identities and disparities. Additionally, Sieder (2002) cites the development of international jurisprudence, which increasingly characterized the rights of indigenous peoples as "human rights." In this respect, ILO Convention 169 is considered the most important international instrument.[11] All of these explanations should be seen in relation to the structural adjustments policy and the regnant neoliberalism of the 1990s. Assies (2000b: 3) argues that Indian resistance has been driven by a combination of political liberalization, economic restructuring, and state reform. However, other researchers, such as Baud (2009), Becker (2008), Brysk (2000), and Korovkin (2001) point instead to a long history of indigenous activism (especially in the Andean highlands) in order to explain its recent dramatic eruption in Ecuador. Thus, we cannot understand present-day indigenous activism without taking into account a wide range of historical, political, economical, and international legal circumstances.

The ways Ecuador has been dealing politically with its cultural diversity are reflected in the manifestations of legal pluralism over the past five centuries. It was only in 1998 that a policy of formal legal pluralism followed that of legal monism, which had been dominant for centuries. From a long-lasting situation of *de facto* legal pluralism (in which Spanish or national law was considered the only officially applicable law, and customary law was tolerated to a certain extent), a situation of *de jure* legal pluralism recently developed. It is largely because of the efforts of the Ecuadorian national indigenous movement CONAIE that,[12] as a reflection of Ecuador's acceptance of cultural and ethnic diversity, the 1998 Constitution recognized the use of indigenous customary law along with national law, thus bringing formal legal pluralism into being. After five centuries of merely *de facto* legal pluralism, this was truly a watershed development.

The 1998 Constitution was passed a number of years after similar reforms in Bolivia (1994), Colombia (1991), and Peru (1993), and it can be justly said that it included more extensive formal recognition of customary law than most other Latin American countries (Andolina 2003: 724). However, in what seems like a vindication of the notion of "the dialectics of progress," this innovative legislation is enforced very inconsistently (Simon Thomas 2009: 39). For example, so-called coordinating rules (that is, rules that would define the personal, territorial, and material jurisdiction of both forms of law) have never been approved, and no case law regarding such differentiation has yet been developed. It seems as if the Ecuadorian state formally "endorsed" customary law (for

---

11 International Labor Organization (ILO) Indigenous and Tribal Peoples Convention, 1989, No. 169.
12 CONAIE: Confederación de Coordinación de las Nacionalidades Indígenas del Ecuador (Confederation of Indigenous Nationalities of Ecuador).

political reasons), while doing nothing to support it, and that it even tried in subtle ways to undermine it (Tamanaha 2008: 50). The Correa administration's critical attitude towards customary law can be seen as an example of this phenomenon.

In his introduction to the edited volume *The Challenge of Diversity*, Willem Assies pointed to the necessity of "further study of the relationship between new legislation and concrete practices" (Assies 2000a: ix). He specifically addressed the implementation of formal legal pluralism. Several scholars have taken up that challenge, among them Charles Hale (2002) and Rachel Sieder (2002). Most research on these neoliberal constitutional changes, however, took place when the winds of neoliberalism were still blowing strong. With the leftist president Rafael Correa in power since 2007, it is interesting to see how this continuing challenge of diversity in Ecuador has evolved after a shift in the political winds. As in the case of the legal and political debates over the jurisdictional scope granted to customary law, tensions can be detected regarding other indigenous agendas which have been recognized in the 1998 Constitution and its successor, the Montecristi Constitution of 2008.[13] In other words, the recent new policies aimed at reversing neoliberalism (Becker 2011a) call for an analytical update on the relationship between progressive constitutions and actual practices. By using the lens of formal legal pluralism, the second aim of this study is to interpret Ecuador's redefinition as a multi-cultural country, a struggle that reflects the current tense relationship between Ecuadorian Indians and the state.

Research question

The aim of this book is to provide an understanding of diversity in contemporary Ecuador through an emphasis on the nation's situation of formal legal pluralism in the absence of coordinating rules. It is within this absence of rules that would define the personal, territorial, and material jurisdiction of both customary law and national law (what I call a "legal void") that a legal anthropological analysis of the daily practice of conflict settlement is provided. The fieldwork for this research was conducted in the parish of Zumbahua in the Andean highlands. As mentioned before, the overall aim of this study is twofold. First, it seeks to provide a description of the daily practice of formal legal pluralism. Second, it aims to provide insight into that practice in terms of multiculturalism and the Indian–state relationship.

The fundamental research question of this study is as follows: how are internal conflicts being settled in the parish of Zumbahua, and what does this teach us about Ecuador's indigenous people in relation to the state? This broad research question will be answered by addressing four secondary questions. The first of these emphasizes the historical context. How has legal pluralism been

---

13 For example, the recognition of indigenous languages, or the recognition of indigenous rights to natural resources (Becker 2011a).

8 *An introductory overview*

treated over the centuries, and how has the situation of *formal* legal pluralism come into being? The second question is multifaceted, and takes the legal/political context into account. How is the situation of formal legal pluralism treated nowadays, who are the parties defining the application of legal pluralism, and what can be said about the process of developing coordinating rules? The third question concerns the specific locale where the fieldwork for this study was conducted. What are the characteristics, internal conflicts, and procedures available to settle conflicts within the parish of Zumbahua? Finally, the fourth secondary question concerns the historical, legal, and political context with the locality: what does formal legal pluralism mean in the parish of Zumbahua, and how does its existence affect residents there?

Research design and methodology

This book is based on qualitative research. It concerns the ways ordinary rural Indians solve their internal conflicts on a daily basis. As such, this study falls within the genre of legal anthropological research on dispute settlement, with an emphasis on customary law and legal pluralism. At the same time, it forms a part of extensive research done in Latin America on the changing relationship between indigenous populations and the state. This research is multidisciplinary in nature, in that it involves contributions from anthropologists, Latin American specialists, and legal scholars.

This book contains three case studies, each of them concerning an internal conflict that was resolved by one of the authorities available to the residents of Zumbahua. I have chosen this method because the comparative examination of legal systems constitutes a particularly suitable framework for conducting a case study, since such studies include detailed descriptions of the disputes and their outcomes, drawn from both observation and documentation (DeWalt & DeWalt 2002: 182). This research strategy, as Yin (2003: 11–14) calls it, allows not only coverage of a wide range of contextual conditions, but also forces the researcher to use a mixture of different data-collection techniques. In my own case, this mixture included archival research, participant observation, informal conversation, and interviewing. In order to prevent my selection of cases from distorting the outcome of this study, I tried to compare these cases with other cases concerning similar disputes as much as possible. In Chapter 6, for example, I cite several cases that were settled at the *teniente político*'s office to illustrate the daily practice at his office, although the chapter itself is largely based on the Rosita vs. Miguel case. The three cases which form the core of this book are each described, interpreted, and analyzed in separate chapters.

The locality of this study is the parish of Zumbahua, Pujilí canton, Cotopaxi province, Ecuador. The parish of Zumbahua is located in the west Andean ridge of the Ecuadorian highlands, and was a hacienda for centuries before becoming a civil parish in 1972. This meant that, historically, the inhabitants were subordinate in power to the *hacendado* (hacienda owner) under circumstances in which state authority was relatively absent. However, power relations irreversible changed when the hacienda was abolished, and the state (for example, national law and its courts) gradually acquired a greater presence and accessibility in the region. This change in turn had an impact on the definition and resolution of internal conflicts. The people living in the parish are so-called *campesinos*,[14] a term often translated in the anthropological literature as "peasants," but which, in a contemporary Ecuadorian context, simply refers to "rural residents."[15] *Campesinos* lead an existence based on subsistence farming and other activities, and they are economically poor. Poverty is the main reason for the high level of migration among *campesinos*. And finally, as the literature shows (for example, Colloredo-Mansfeld 2009a; Jackson 2002), rural residents of the Andean highlands are famous for their internal disputes.

The main subjects of this study (that is, the people living in the parish of Zumbahua) belong to the Panzaleos subgroup of the Kichwa nationality, according to the classification of CONAIE. This national indigenous movement classifies the indigenous population in terms of nationalities ("*nacionalidades*") and subgroups ("*pueblos*"). This "indigeneity" is another important characteristic of the people who live in Zumbahua.[16] Being indigenous (a category that is negotiated by both individual and collective subjects) to a large extent defines their relationship to the state and in particular it determines the range of available authorities and procedures for settling internal conflicts. The construction of ethnic categories is a crucial element in Latin America's historical development. Who is and who is not indigenous and what it means (or meant) to be indigenous is highly variable, context-specific, and has changed over time, as the scholarly literature has emphasized (Canessa 2012: 10; see also: Canessa 2006; Chaves & Zambrano 2006; de la Cadena 2000; Jackson & Warren 2005; Pallares 2002).[17] This characterization stands in stark contrast to how CONAIE seems to essentialize indigeneity in a way that portrays indigenous culture as some sort of fixed and timeless phenomenon. On a local level, the Kichwa language, the community as a place, and local norms and practices appear to be the most important markers of "indigenous" identification (see also Cervone 2012: 14–17; Colloredo-Mansfeld 2009a: 76–80).

14 See Ouweneel (1993) for a theoretical discussion of the concept of "peasants" in Latin America.
15 "Peasants," according to Kottak (2008: 168), are small-scale agriculturalists, who produce crops to feed themselves and have rent obligations to landlords and the state. The aspect of rent for land is nowadays not that significant for the people living in Zumbahua, and while the majority of the residents are farmers, some earn their livelihood via other pursuits.
16 Postero (2007: 11) argues that this is specifically the case regarding people living in the Andean highlands, who were engaged with colonizing institutions of a religious, political, and economic nature over the course of several centuries.
17 According to Goldstein (2012: 273, note 6) "indigenous" in the Andean highlands is a category of racial identification which has replaced the more derogatory category of "indio."

From the colonial period onwards, a complex interplay of ethnic and racial labeling took shape that led to a long and varied process of inter-ethnic negotiations. This dynamic process led to constant interpretation and reinterpretation of Indian–state relationships. An important component of these relationships was the way the use of local customary law developed. These developments in turn have shaped the contemporary *de facto* ways that indigenous people settle their disputes. The 1998 Constitution, and its successor, the Montecristi Constitution, in which the multicultural nature of the state and subsequently legal pluralism was formally recognized, can be considered a provisional breach of the changing Indian–state relationship in Ecuador. To a large extent, these constitutional changes shape the *de jure* ways indigenous people can nowadays solve their internal conflicts. It is this dynamic interplay of historically changing social, legal, and political circumstances that shaped the context for the fieldwork conducted in the parish of Zumbahua. Therefore, Zumbahua, even though not necessarily representative of all Andean parishes, offers important insight into routine dispute settlement and, as such, into the Indian–state relationship in contemporary Ecuador.

Fieldwork was done during the course of two months in 2009 and six months in 2010.[18] My research was facilitated by the fact that I had conducted previous fieldwork on the same topic and in the same area in 2007.[19] Basically, I continued and expanded that earlier fieldwork from the point where I had left it off. Since this book is largely based on three case studies concerning dispute settlements, the combination of ethnography and archival research is essential for demonstrating the linkages between such legal cases and social reality (Merry 2002: 137). But the most important anthropological aspect of the fieldwork was "being there," which basically meant gathering information through building rapport with residents of the parish and carefully observing events that took place there that involved the resolution of conflicts (Bernard 2006: 368–369; DeWalt & DeWalt 2002: 40–45). Weaving myself into the social context of the parish in this way was absolutely essential for obtaining what Geertz (1973) calls "thick" data.

During these eight months of fieldwork, I lived and worked in Quito, Puembo, Latacunga, and Zumbahua. While in Quito, I conducted research in libraries and universities, and also obtained research materials from major bookstores. The sources for this research include published books and articles (that is, on the subjects of customary law or legal pluralism in Ecuador, or on contextual issues concerning the parish of Zumbahua), as well as primary sources such as government documents and newspaper articles. I also visited the Constitutional Court three times to attend public hearings, went to CONAIE headquarters and the offices of CODENPE a couple of times,[20]

---

18 September–October 2009 and July–December 2010.
19 This earlier fieldwork was done in May–July 2007. See Simon Thomas (2009: 9–14) for methodological details.
20 CODENPE: Consejo de Desarrollo de las Nacionalidades y Pueblos del Ecuador (Council for the Development of Nationalities and Peoples of Ecuador).

and visited the Ministry of Justice and the *Asamblea Nacional* to observe sessions and talk to people who worked and had business there. Puembo is a small and quiet village, situated in the valley east of Quito, where I stayed with my wife and children from September to December in 2010, and from where I traveled to "the field" on a weekly basis.[21] In Latacunga (the capital and administrative center of Cotopaxi province), I spent a lot of time at the Court of Justice, the Fiscalía and the Fiscalía Indígena,[22] where I observed, talked to people, and conducted archival research. Latacunga is the home of the offices of the indigenous OTG MICC and the law firm Fundación Defensoría Kichwa de Cotopaxi (FUDEKI),[23] as well as other law firms, and I visited each of these places more than once. From Latacunga I could easily drive to Pujilí (the administrative center of the canton with the same name), where I did my research at the Civil Court. In Zumbahua, the *teniente político*'s office, the police station, and the office of the Junta Parroquial were of special interest to me. And so, of course were other communities of the parish, especially those of La Cocha, Guantópolo, and Tigua, which I visited frequently and where I conducted a great deal of archival research.

Methodology

An anthropologist using archival legal texts, such as court records, faces a challenging situation: "in order to make sense of these records, [he or she] has to ground them in an ethnography of the surrounding community. This includes an analysis of its major actors and its changing political, economic, social, and cultural terrain over [...] time" (Merry 2002: 128).

Written material on legal cases, such as that which I found in files at courts and the Fiscalías, and in the *libros de actas* of the *teniente político* and of several communities, provided me the primary sources I needed to get an accurate overview of the wide range of different kinds of disputes and their subsequent solutions. Bernard (2006: 448–450) notes the advantages of archival research (for example, it is non-reactive – meaning that you can take your time conducting it, and you can study data that otherwise would be difficult to gather) and its disadvantages (that is, like any other data, they are not infallible, and some disputes go unreported). I most definitely found this to be the case. At the four criminal courts of the Court of Justice in Latacunga, I was granted access to all of the files that I requested. However, in practice it proved

---

21 This meant that four days in Zumbahua or Latacunga were followed by three days at home. On a number of occasions, my wife and two daughters accompanied me on my field trips.
22 Fiscalía Provincial de Cotopaxi (Public Prosecutor of the Cotopaxi province) and Fiscalía de Asuntos Indígenas de Cotopaxi (Public Prosecutor for Indigenous Affairs in the Cotopaxi province).
23 OTG: Organización de Tercer Grado (Organization of the Third Degree); MICC: Movimiento Indígena y Campesino de Cotopaxi (Indigenous and Rural Movement of Cotopaxi).

impossible for me to conduct thoroughly structured archival research within the time constraints of this study.[24] What I did instead was read through parts of the archive which I randomly selected, and I relied on judges and other people working at the courts to draw my attention to cases that concerned indigenous people. During at least ten visits at the Court of Justice, I examined more than 120 files, conducting an in-depth analysis on eight of them. Basically, this meant that I was not able to get exact figures, but that I did manage to identify several cases concerning people living in Zumbuhua, and thus was able to get a fairly good idea of the kinds of cases that were typically brought to the criminal courts in Latacunga.

I faced similar obstacles at the Civil Court in Pujilí. Although the Pujilí court deals with fewer cases than the criminal courts in Latacunga, it did not even have an accessible computerized filing system. At the Fiscalía in Latacunga, I discovered that every public prosecutor had his own secretary, who was responsible for keeping his own files up to date, a circumstance which made it difficult for me to obtain the kind of data I was looking for. That is why, when I conducted research at the Fiscalía, I only read through the file concerning the La Cocha-Guantópolo murder case (see Chapter 8), which contained more than 600 pages. At the Fiscalía Indígena, I was able to examine the registration book and I was given access to all of the files that I requested. Over the course of three days, I read through several files. Once I identified relevant cases, I received all the help I requested at each of these offices. I was provided a desk of my own to read through the files, and I was allowed to copy anything I wanted. If there was no nearby copy shop (as was the case in Pujilí), I took pictures of every page in the files that seemed relevant to me. I ended up photographing seventeen files that were interesting enough to be analyzed further. At the Fiscalía, the file of the homicide case I was investigating contained several disks with copies of TV documentaries and other videos, and I was allowed to make digital copies of these video files as well.

In the parish of Zumbahua, I encountered a similarly helpful attitude on the part of the authorities, but since there were no copy machines in the parish, I only had the option of photographing files page by page, or simply writing out the relevant parts. Both of these techniques were time consuming, and provided me a unique opportunity to ask questions of the authorities about the cases I was researching. I ended up photographing thirty-four *actas*. At the *teniente político*'s office, I was able to do all the research I wanted on the six handwritten *libros de denuncias* and *libro de actas* available. At the

24 I was specifically interested in cases concerning residents of the parish of Zumbahua, but because files were organized by name, date, and a couple of other criteria, but *not* by place of residence, this proved to be an impossible task. A complicating factor was the fact that the archives at the courts contained files which dated back to the 1990s, and no combined or linked database exists (that is, each court has its own, stand-alone, computerized filing system, and each handles over 1,000 cases per year).

police station, the officers shared files with me that had been compiled over the past year. In the communities of Guantópolo and Tigua, two former chairmen of the local *cabildos* (village counsils) allowed me to inspect *libros de actas* from the period 1998–2010.

Thus, archival research, in combination with the collection and analysis of other primary and secondary written sources, provided me a comprehensive overview of the wide range of disputes and their subsequent solutions that have taken place in the parish of Zumbahua over the last fifteen years or so (see Chapter 5). It was especially the information gathered through the archives of the courts, the Fiscalías, the police, and the *teniente político* that provided new insight into the resolution of internal conflicts. My previous impression that there has not been much qualitative research on the litigation of indigenous people's internal disputes in these institutions was confirmed. Conversely, there has been a great deal of research on internal conflicts on the basis of the *libros de actas* of indigenous communities (for example, Brandt & Valdivia 2006, 2007; Valdivia & González Luna 2009; Vintimilla et al. 2007), including Zumbahua.[25] The data reported in these studies proved very helpful to me, since I could compare them with my own findings.

In addition to archival research, I made use of several other data-collecting methods. Participant observation, which refers to the researcher taking part in daily activities as one means of learning the explicit and tacit aspects of life routines (DeWalt & DeWalt 2002: 1) took place on numerous occasions (for example, at courts, Fiscalías, and the *teniente político*'s office, as well as at private homes, weddings, and fiestas). I had informal conversations almost every day about many different topics with anybody who was willing to talk to me. I conducted semi-structured interviews with judges and other employees of the courts, and with public prosecutors, lawyers, policemen, the *teniente político* in Zumbahua, members of the Junta Parroquial, and with *dirigentes* in several communities of the parish. All conversations and interviews were conducted in Spanish. Some of the interviews were audio-taped, and I took notes on them when possible. Every day upon arriving home (sometimes the following day) I processed these notes, as well as the data that I had collected, on my laptop. These field notes, together with the data found in the archives (that is, copies, photographs, and notes on file) have been the most important sources of information for this book. Additionally, the use of different data-collection methods allowed me to cross-validate my conclusions by comparing the different kinds of data I collected (that is, triangulation of research methods (Boeije 2010: 176–177; DeWalt & DeWalt 2002: 102)).

---

25 Brandt, Valdivia, González Luna, and Vintimilla conducted primarily quantitative research on conflicts by analyzing the *actas* in 133 indigenous communities, including the Guantópolo community in the parish of Zumbahua. They essentially counted and described the conflicts that were referred to in these *actas*. Their research was not entirely quantitative since they also asked *dirigentes* to reflect on the kind of disputes that took place within their communities.

The researcher

As DeWalt and DeWalt (2002: 81) state:

> the "quality" of ethnography will vary depending on the personal characteristics of ethnographers, their training and experience, and perhaps also their theoretical orientation. As interpretive anthropology makes clear, all of us bring biases, predisposition, and hang-ups to the field with us and we cannot completely escape these as we view other cultures.

That is why I have made rigorous efforts to identify my own biases. I hold degrees in law, cultural anthropology, and Latin American studies, and I have also received training in legal anthropology through elective courses, workshops, and international conferences designed primarily for socio-legal scholars.[26] That is why I was able, once in the field, to read (literally) the juridical texts as a jurist, and also "read" (figuratively) what actually happened in the field as an anthropologist, and to subsequently better understand the significance of these findings.

One might argue that thorough theoretical knowledge involves the risk of bias arising once the empirical research is undertaken. Such theoretical knowledge might influence the researcher's observation, accounts, and analyses. To a certain extent this might be the case, but to conduct legal anthropological fieldwork in the absence of any theoretical framework is even worse, since such a course of action would involve the risk of wasting a lot of time over already-covered ground (Bernard 2006: 96). Frankly, most of the time I did not think of any theoretical debate whatsoever, since this was not the level on which I interacted with most of my informants. On several other occasions, on the other hand, being well-informed beforehand turned out to be very handy indeed.[27] In a more practical sense, the fact that I could present myself as a lawyer with some basic knowledge of the Ecuadorian juridical systems

---

26 I obtained my law degree at the University of Leiden in 1992, my BSc in Cultural Anthropology at the University of Utrecht in 2006, and my MA in Latin America studies at CEDLA (Centre for Latin American Research and Documentation, Amsterdam) in 2008. I have taken additional courses on "Law in Developing Countries" at the Van Vollenhoven Institute in Leiden in 2004, on "Anthropology of Law" at the Erasmus University of Rotterdam in 2005, and on "Living Realities in Legal Pluralism" taught by members of the Commission on Legal Pluralism in 2011. I participated in the four-day workshop "Legal Pluralism and Democracy" held the Oñati International Institute for Sociology of Law (IISL) in Spain in 2010. Additionally, I have presented papers at international conferences in Norway (2010), The Netherlands (2010, 2012, 2013), Peru (2010) (RELAJU), Spain (2011) (IISL), California (2011) (Law & Society Association), and South Africa (2011) (Commission on Legal Pluralism).
27 For example, when I was discussing the Ecuadorian situation of formal legal pluralism in the absence of coordinating rules with judges, public prosecutors, lawyers, and indigenous leaders, it proved advantageous to be able to discuss both legal matters and cultural matters in a Latin American context. Legal pluralism and the rights of indigenous people are hotly debated issues in Ecuador. I would not have been able to interact as I did with these informants without my theoretical background.

and the perceived problems regarding the situation of formal legal pluralism provided me a relatively easy access to law firms, courts, and Fiscalías of a kind generally not enjoyed by researchers of a different professional background.

Another bias that I am aware of is that of my being male. I fully acknowledge that the gender of the researcher in the field has several consequences (for example, that it limits your access to certain influences, that it influences how you perceive others, and that it influences how others perceive you) (Bernard 2006: 373–374; DeWalt & DeWalt 2002: 83–86). Although women occasionally do appear in this book (for example, as a party in a dispute, a *dirigente*, a lawyer, a judge, or a politician), most subjects in this study are men. This has resulted, at least in part, from how I as a male researcher acted in the field and was looked upon by others. On the other hand, the juridical system in Ecuador is dominated by men, and so are most indigenous local authorities. By no means would I suggest that women play no role at all in either of these contexts. It is just that men play an overwhelmingly dominant role, and this study simply reflects this state of affairs.[28]

I've already mentioned how my particular background enabled me to present myself as both a lawyer and an anthropologist interested in the Ecuadorian legal system, and especially in the phenomenon of legal pluralism within that system. To others (for example, residents of Zumbahua or indigenous leaders) I presented myself primarily as an anthropologist interested in customary law in relation to national law. Both were true but, right from the start of my fieldwork, I sensed that the particular skills and interests I emphasized often determined the kind of information that I was provided. I had no problem with changing my role according to the circumstances that presented themselves because doing so did not involve violating the basic rules of informed consent (that is, informants were aware that they were subjects in my research, they knew what the research was about, and they were able to choose whether or not to participate) (DeWalt & DeWalt 2002: 198–199).

In a way, the topic of my research (that is, legal pluralism) forced me to talk to a wide range of people about closely related issues like customary law and national law, their interaction, and also about politics, economics, state–society relations (for example, discrimination), and other topics. In order to understand what legal pluralism actually meant to people, I talked to as many different informants as possible. Rabinow (2007) has compellingly shown how he went through different chronological phases in his fieldwork, according to the knowledge and experience of his informants vis-à-vis the research he was conducting, in order to "establish the grounds for a dialogue" (Rabinow 2007: 161). In my own case, I discussed law, customary law, and legal pluralism with persons from a wide variety of backgrounds and education, from taxi drivers,

---

28 Interesting research on the role of women in relation to legal pluralism in Ecuador has been undertaken by Valdivia (2009), Sieder and Sierra (2010), and UN Women (2011).

market vendors, and hostel operators to scholars, attorneys, prosecutors, judges, and indigenous authorities. With each of my informants, I to some extent formed an "intersubjective construction [...] of communication" (Rabinow 2007: 155), meaning that, while we were communicating, we were interpreting each other's words within the framework of our own "set of assumptions, experiences, or traditions," while simultaneously modifying these biases.

Proceeding in this fashion taught me two important things. First, on an analytical level, it led me to understand that legal pluralism does not mean the same thing to all people. When I conducted earlier research on legal pluralism in Ecuador in 2007, I did a case study on the La Cocha murder case of 2002 (Simon Thomas 2009). I now realize that, at that time, I was overly attached to a restrictive conception of legal pluralism (that is, the concept of legal pluralism I had been reading about in scholarly literature).[29] In other words, I thought of legal pluralism in terms of being a dichotomy. After conducting longer periods of fieldwork in 2009 and 2010, especially in the parish of Zumbahua, and talking to a wider range of different people, I was able to understand the relationship between legal pluralism and its wider historical, socio-geographical, and current context at a deeper level. This led me not only to see my earlier research as mainly reflecting only one side of the story, but also allowed me to realize that the blurred daily reality of settling disputes is best understood in terms of the concept of "interlegality."[30] This concept best explains the way the *dirigente* at the beginning of this chapter started with mixed notions of good and bad, and why the *teniente político* mixed elements of customary law with national law. Second, on an emotional level, I realized that my opinion on customary law had changed. At first, I had been uncritically in favor of it, attracted by its emphasis on reconciliation, compensation, and restitution, instead of on meting out punishment. Over time, however, I began to realize that customary law, like any legal system, has its drawbacks, and is not immune from criticism. This is illustrated by the fact that its interpretation and administration can vary among people living in the same community, and also because customary law can sometimes increase tensions instead of restoring harmony. The lawyer who was introduced at the beginning of this chapter therefore rightly sensed that customary law can be contaminated by bias.

29 Basically, the court files of that case; numerous newspaper and other articles; and interviews with the former judge Carlos Poveda, the indigenous leader Lourdes Tibán, and with other involved parties were the main sources of that study. Since the actual case had taken place five years prior to the time I conducted my research, any participation or observation on that specific case was impossible and time limits restricted me to a high concentration of participant observation on the settlement of other disputes in the parish of Zumbahua.
30 "Interlegality" refers to how ordinary people experience legal pluralism in daily life. It is the "intersubjective, or phenomenological dimension of legal pluralism" (de Sousa Santos 2002: 97). See also Chapter 2 for an extended discussion of the concept.

Ethics

My changed attitude towards customary law sometimes put me in a difficult situation. Since legal pluralism and the rights of indigenous people (including their customary law) are hotly debated issues in Ecuador, I was often asked to give my opinion. I knew that I had to confine myself to my role as researcher, and thus remain as neutral and detached as possible (DeWalt & DeWalt 2002: 41), but this was never easy to do. Whether in the presence of a diehard protagonist of indigenous rights and customary law, or a hardline jurist defending legal monism, if either of them started to interrogate me on my position in the collective vs. individual rights debate or what I really thought of Ecuador's actual situation of formal legal pluralism, I had to avoid revealing my own views and biases. At such times, it once again helped that I could either position myself as an anthropologist (doing research on law) or as a lawyer (doing qualitative research). I tried to explain that I was able to look at such issues as a relative outsider, which allowed me take different views into account.[31] However, while holding strong views, at the same time these informants expressed a real concern about the issues we were discussing. It therefore sometimes bothered me that I was not completely honest about my feelings regarding the subject I was researching.

Every participant in research has the right to privacy (DeWalt & DeWalt 2002: 202), so I have decided to protect the anonymity of the subjects of my study as much as possible. I am fully aware of the fact that at times (for example, while I was doing research in the archives) I was given access to knowledge of legal cases of great consequence for the people involved. I have therefore, on a case-by-case basis, carefully considered the impact of the production of knowledge on my informants and others involved in these cases (Starr & Goodale 2002: 2). On the other hand, since some of the cases described in this book are a matter of public record, it does not make much sense to conceal the identity of certain people involved. There is no point in protecting the confidentiality of people (for example, "public figures" like national indigenous leaders) or institutions whose identity and activities are a matter of public record. For this reason, public figures like politicians, published authors, and public officials (for example, judges, public prosecutors, *teniente políticos*) will be referred to by their real names, as will the organizations that they work for. Subjects whose real names have previously appeared in other publications will also be identified accordingly. All other

---

31 I would typically say that I saw positive as well as negative elements in the use of customary law. But it would not have been prudent for me to say that essentializing culture and customary law, closing one's eyes to the negative sides of customary law, or overplaying one's "culture cards" in a legal or political debate would probably end up harming the rights of ordinary indigenous people. Nor could I say that I felt that people caricaturing customary law, having prejudices about it, or denigrating it, was for me the equivalent of rank prejudice. On those occasions, I decided that it was wise not to be too forthright.

informants and subjects appearing in the cases I analyze will be referred to by first-name-only pseudonyms, or by generic descriptions like "an ex-*dirigente*." Readers familiar with the events and institutions described may be able to discern the identity of these individuals. However, I am satisfied that I have protected the anonymity of my informants to the fullest extent possible.

Finally, I am aware of the fact that legal anthropological research tends to produce knowledge that is strongly determined by local power structures (Starr & Goodale 2002: 2–3). In reference to research on internal conflicts in indigenous communities, Becker (2010b) asks whether highlighting divisions does harm to the struggle for equal rights and autonomy. More specifically, it could be asked if writing about disputes might harm communities, which to a certain extent are vulnerable already, or if doing so might disturb often fragile power structures. Colloredo-Mansfeld (2009a: 146) argues that "turning a blind eye to internal fights will not do." This is because, according to him, plurality rather than unity has not only been typical for indigenous communities, but has also been a key factor to the success of indigenous movements in Ecuador. In line with this argument, I decided to tell the stories about local internal conflicts and the political controversy some of these cases caused on a national level as fairly as possible. I decided to do so because I believe that the challenge of legal pluralism (by which all of my informants are influenced, or are concerned with) should not be understood as primarily a jurisprudential process. I think it matters to describe, analyze, and understand it as an empirical reality – a reality of which conflicts form a substantial part.

Outline of the book

The structure of this book is straightforward. The first part is theoretical, contextual, and descriptive in nature, while the second part has an almost completely empirical character. After this introduction, Chapter 2 deals with the theoretical concepts that constitute the framework of the present study. Customary law, legal pluralism, and the derived concepts of interlegality and "forum shopping" are introduced and explored. So are the state, Indian–state relationships, multiculturalism, the dilemma of collective vs. individual rights, sovereignty, and subsidiarity. Chapter 3 provides an overview of legal pluralism in Ecuador. Starting with a historical summary featuring developments during the "long nineteenth century" and the land reforms in the twentieth century, that chapter discusses recent constitutional changes. Special attention is given to articles in the 1998 and 2008 Constitutions that explicitly recognize legal pluralism. These constitutions will be compared, and the chapter ends with a discussion of the challenge of coordinating customary law and national law. Chapter 4 provides the reader an introduction to the parish of Zumbahua: its history, socio-political geography, and daily life. Cohesion and conflict are the guiding themes, and all this is told by means of an account of a wedding and subsequent celebration. Chapter 5 is completely dedicated to conflicts, authorities, and procedures in Zumbahua. Starting with a brief theoretical section on understanding disputes, this chapter provides a description of the variety of conflicts and types of conflict resolution in the parish. Then the different local and provincial authorities are discussed in order to grapple with the fundamental question of who local residents turn to in order to get their internal conflicts settled.

The first case study is described and analyzed in Chapter 6. The daily routine at the *teniente político*'s office in Zumbahua is portrayed within the context of the Rosita vs. Miguel case, which is an internal conflict that was dealt with locally, and that is told in three different stages. This case will serve as a vehicle for analyzing the ambiguous juridical role of the *teniente político*, whose functioning is illustrative of interlegality (that is, the way highland Indians perceive legal pluralism). The second case study, the Toaquiza vs. the community case, forms the core of Chapter 7. Here, we will see how a local conflict in the Tigua community (home of the famous Tiguan style *art naïf* paintings) becomes transformed when it is brought before the Court of Justice in Latacunga. This case is also told in three stages: the charge, the verdict, and the appeal. Emphasis is placed on how the national courts of Ecuador dealt with that matter. As such, it is used to highlight the differences between customary law and national law processes. It also shows that, in the national legal system, cases concerning indigenous people are often restricted to the question of whether or not a dispute can be considered an "internal conflict" (which is a constitutional term, the practical scope of which remains under dispute).[32] Chapter 8 is dedicated to the La Cocha–Guantópolo murder case. Here too, a local case ends up in a national court. A homicide which was initially adjudicated by the *cabildo* of the La Cocha community became subject of a trial in the provincial Court of Justice and eventually in the Constitutional Court in Quito. The "internal" aspect of the case has not only been legally debated, but also has become part of a political controversy regarding the contemporary situation of legal pluralism. It will be shown that, on a macro level, legal pluralism is consistently depicted as a dichotomy. In the final chapter of this book, theory and empiricism are brought together and the general research question is answered.

---

32 Both the 1998 Constitution (article 191, section 4) and the Montecristi Constitution of 2008 (article 171) use the term *conflictos internos* ("internal conflicts") to describe disputes that could be settled according to customary law, but neither of them provides a satisfactory definition of that term, and this ambiguity fuels theoretical and practical debates about its actual meaning.

2 Legal pluralism, multiculturalism, and the state

Introduction

The central aim of this book is to provide insight into two phenomena: the living reality of legal pluralism in Ecuador, and the contemporary relationship between the indigenous people and the state. In other words, legal pluralism will serve as an empirical lens through which Ecuador's "multinationalism" will be examined.[1] The goal of the present chapter is to explore the theoretical debates surrounding this book's main concepts: customary law, legal pluralism, the state, and multiculturalism.

In order to understand how customary law works in daily practice, one has to take rules and processes, as well as the historical, social, and political context into consideration. These factors will be addressed in a brief literature review of customary law. Additionally, this chapter argues that it is impossible to consider customary law apart from its context (and especially apart from its relationship with national law). To fully grasp what customary law is about, one should always study it in relation to national law (that is, one has to study the situation of legal pluralism). The study of customary law and legal pluralism have both evolved over time. It will be shown that, beginning in the 1970s, debates among scholars have for the most part focused on the proper scope and boundaries of the concept of "law" and legal pluralism. Nowadays, however, the study of legal pluralism in Latin America concentrates on a combination of history and ethnography within the framework of political power structures.

All of this has led to a characterization of the state as the guardian of national law. This chapter builds on the work of those who conceptualized the state in different ways, with an emphasis on Chatterjee's (2004) notion of a "political society." The overview presented here will shed light on the relationship between Ecuadorian indigenous people and the state, which, in the case of the Andean highlands, can broadly be characterized as absent. Finally, this theoretical framework takes proper account of multiculturalism.

---

1 Since 2008, Ecuador constitutionally recognized the nation being "*intercultural*" and "*plurinacional*" (intercultural and multinational).

It will be shown that this concept is used in many ways. Two distinct viewpoints regarding how multiculturalism should be preserved (that is, the politics of recognition, and the politics of redistribution) will be discussed. This will be followed by a discussion of the anthropological understanding of sovereignty and the related idea of decentralization in the context of neoliberal reforms. Within the framework of a consideration of these issues, the relationship between customary law and national law is discussed in terms of both a "top-down" and "bottom-up" dynamic. It will be shown that, in implementing legal pluralism, Ecuador has not yet succeeded in finding a middle ground between a deeply rooted legal monism, on the one hand, and cultural relativism, on the other.

Customary law

Customary law is generally understood to mean a set of unwritten, flexible, local, and obligatory norms and practices of a particular community or group of people.[2] The limited sphere of such norms and practices makes them different from national laws, which govern all inhabitants of a country.[3] These norms and practices also differ from normative rules that exist within smaller social units like the family.[4] Additionally, customary law can exist anywhere (that is, in Western and non-Western societies) and can be applied by any self-defined group of people (for example, ethnic, indigenous, religious, etc.). Because the subjects of this book are the indigenous people living in the Ecuadorian highlands, some prefer to use the compound term "*indigenous* customary law" to characterize their specific form of customary law. However, for readability

---

2 The term "customary law" itself has been subject to dispute. Some scholars prefer the following alternative terms to "customary law": traditional law, indigenous law, and folk law, as well as the Spanish terms *derecho indígena, derecho consuetudinario, derecho originario, justicia indígena,* or *justicia tradicional* (Simon Thomas 2009: 20).
3 In this book, the term "national law" is understood as the rules and principles generated and used by state organizations (von Benda-Beckmann & von Benda-Beckmann 2006: 15). Its basic characteristics (that is, written, general, and certain rules) contradict those of customary law. Western, positive law refers to the theory of law from the perspective of the legal scholar Hans Kelsen (de Sousa Santos 2002: 5; von Benda-Beckmann & von Benda-Beckmann 2006: 13).
4 Those who oppose according customary law the status of bonafide law, like the jurist Brian Tamanaha, point to this somewhat vague boundary to support their position. Tamanaha (1993: 193), while recognizing the rule-making and enforcing power of social institutions (for example, universities, community associations, little-league baseball, and even family), points out that the forms of social control they exercise can hardly be called "law." That is why Hoekema (2004: 10) draws a helpful distinction between "functional groups" (for example, unions or banks) and small-scale communities. Functional groups by definition have narrow goals, and thus bind their members in limited ways. It is for this reason that Hoekema refers to the obligations imposed by functional groups in terms of "group norms" rather than "customary law."

purposes,[5] as well as for substantive reasons,[6] I will continue to use the shorter term "customary law." The following common characteristics of customary law emerge from a comprehensive review of the literature:[7]

- Customary law, contrary to Western positive law, is neither an autonomous sphere of action nor a specialty of some more broadly applied law. Instead, it regulates a wide range of spheres of social life: marriage, parenthood, inheritance, collective land tenure, conflict settlement, while also providing principles and mechanisms for social regulation and public order.
- It has a major oral component. Rhetoric, persuasion, and argumentation play an important role, and emphasis is on hearing all parties involved. The use of extended discussions and dialogue is crucial for resolving cases in a satisfactory manner. Conversely, written records are seldom used.
- It is strongly focused on reconciliation, and tends to place greater emphasis on compensation and restitution (monetary or otherwise) to the victim than on meting out punishment to offenders.
- Depending on the circumstances, customary law can be applied by a wide range of authorities, including family members, village elders, *cabildos*, and tribunals. Decisions by *cabildos* and tribunals are often made in consultation with the community in order to attain as wide a consensus as possible.
- Customary law is flexible, evolving through daily practice. Although it is often looked at as static or rooted in the past (a vision often propagated by indigenous leaders themselves as a strategy to defend their autonomy)

---

5   In Simon Thomas (2009: 20–21), I have dealt more extensively with the question of whether to use the term "indigenous customary law" or "customary law." My main argument there was that the term "customary law" does not completely cover the norms and practices of indigenous peoples. "Indigenous law" would appear to be an adequate translation of the Spanish terms *derecho indígena, justicia indígena*, etc. However, this term has undesirable essentialist and ethnocentric connotations that fetishize or reify "authentic" custom or tradition, and which thus fail to capture its flexible character. Therefore, I argued in favor of the compound term "indigenous customary law," while continuing to use the more manageable "customary law."
6   "*Indigenous* customary law" might suggest a traditional or authentic kind of customary law. In reference to Guatemala, Sieder (2002) has suggested that the increasing use of customary law since the 1990s suggests a "re-invention of tradition." The increased use of customary law in Ecuador by indigenous authorities since the formal recognition of legal pluralism in 1998 can be seen in a similar way.
7   This open-ended and non-cumulative enumeration is based on an extensive ethnographic literature on customary law in Latin America. Some prominent examples of this work include the following: Assies (2001); Brandt and Valdivia (2006, 2007); Chávez and García (2004), García (2002), Giraudo (2008), Goodale (2009), Guevara Gil (2011), Herrera (2011), Ilaquiche (2004a, 2004b), Nader (1990), Ochoa García (2002), Orellana Halkyer (2004), Perafán Simmonds (1995), Serrano Peréz (2002), Sieder (1997), Sieder and Sierra (2010); Simon Thomas (2009, 2013), Tibán (2007), Tibán and Ilaquiche (2004, 2008), Valdivia and González Luna (2009), van de Sandt (2007), Vintimilla et al. (2007).

this certainly is not the case. In fact, customary law is highly changeable, and is to a considerable extent shaped by its context. Therefore, the (re)invention of certain customs or norms is not uncommon.
- Customary law is not only about norms, but also concerns agreements regarding practices that are being worked out in instances when norms have been violated. Sometimes even the choice of the local authorities by litigants and the procedures used by these authorities constitute important aspects of customary law.
- Finally, it is neither uniform nor fixed. Norms and practices can even vary between neighboring communities.

At times, the fact that customary law has been practiced over the course of many generations has been adduced in support of its legitimacy (ASIES 1995: 7, cited in Sieder 1997: 8), but I disagree with this latter criterion. Customary law, like Western positive law, is a social construction (Geertz 1983), and therefore in principle it is subject to changes over time. I am in agreement with the assertion of Sieder (1997: 8–9) that customary law's legitimacy should not be merely assumed, and needs instead to be empirically established. Any such empirical examination of customary law will also reveal exceptions and contradictions to the characteristics listed above. For example, in the Ecuadorian Andes, many cases heard by indigenous authorities are written down in *libros de actas*. Therefore, the list of characteristics should not be seen as restrictive. Instead, its purpose is to provide a general idea of customary law in all its varied facets, and especially to understand it in contrast to national law.[8]

A number of caveats should be taken into account in characterizing customary law. The first of these concerns the assumption that customary law is a perfectly fair and harmonious system. Research shows that this is not always the case. It is true that, as mentioned above, customary law focuses on reconciliation, compensation, and restitution. This means that apologies are often required and that sanctions are often imposed that are directly related to the damage that has been done. For example, if the head of a family is injured in a fight, the offender might be ordered by an indigenous authority to take over his work in the fields. The resolution of a conflict often affects not only the parties involved, but their families and sometimes the community as a whole as well. This communal aspect of customary law serves to guarantee that agreements are reached and that follow-up is ensured (Handy 2004: 553–557; Sieder 1998: 107–109; Sieder & Sierra 2010: 17–18; Yrigoyen Fajardo 2000: 203). But this does not mean that customary law always prevents partiality, gender

---

8   Obviously, the task of defining customary law involves a number of challenges. This task becomes even harder if one takes into account that different parties (for example, legal anthropologists, legal practitioners, state officials, politicians, indigenous leaders, and indigenous movements) each have their own classificatory agenda. That is why it is important to always keep in mind *who* is doing the characterization.

bias, or discrimination (Nader 2002; Sieder & Sierra 2010: 19), as pointed out by the lawyer cited in the introduction of this book.

Furthermore, although it is considered important that customary law be recognized as obligatory by the majority of the community that it governs, this does not guarantee harmonious intra-communal relations (Sieder & Sierra 2010: 18–19). Because customary law is neither fixed nor uniform, there may be different or competing versions of it; not only among different communities but even within them. Because "any indigenous community will be riddled with conflicts" (Jackson 2002: 120), its customary law is invariably contested within the community itself, and thus reflects local tensions (Sieder & Sierra 2010: 4). To summarize these warnings, which will be reiterated throughout this book, customary law should not be idealized.

Studying customary law

Let us now turn to an examination of how customary law has been studied. Three different paradigms can be distinguished: rule-centered, process-oriented, and pluralist. The foundation for legal anthropology's development was laid by – among others – the jurist and historian Henry Maine and the sociologist Emile Durkheim. Both of these men had (as was common at the end of the nineteenth century) a sociocultural evolutionary view regarding legal conceptions. Maine stated that one's legal situation originally was determined by place in the family (*ius sanguinus*), and later was negotiated by oneself (*ius soli*) in modern society (de la Peña 2002: 52–56; Maine 1894 [1861] cited in Moore 2005: 20–23). Durkheim's approach to the evolution of law was different. He argued that, in traditional societies, law served to prevent deviant behavior, and that it constituted a repressive force, while justice was enacted by the community itself. In modern societies, on the contrary, the law's aim was to be restrictive, and it tried to anticipate potential conflicts. The field of law thus became professionalized (de la Peña 2002: 56–59; Moore 2005: 40–44). The distinction between communal, repressive rules and individual, restrictive rules constitutes a component of some present-day descriptions of customary law; especially when it is opposed to Western, positive law.

Bronislaw Malinowski, one of the most prominent early legal ethnographers (Moore 2005), distanced himself from Durkheim's ideas of law. Malinowski (1985 [1926]) argued that, in every society, repressive and restrictive rules existed simultaneously. Throughout his study on norms and practices in the Trobiand Islands, he emphasized themes like reciprocity, social pressure, and tradition, the same adjectives employed by some contemporary researchers of customary law. According to Malinowski, all societies have some kind of law, although he introduced a division of norms with and without a formal authority that served as their guarantors. One of the founding fathers of structural-functionalism, Alfred Reginald Radcliffe-Brown, took as his point of departure the notion that solidarity and norms together defined equilibrium in society. He held that norms were guaranteed by the use of coercive force, applied by a tribunal or specialized body, and that the aim of sanctions was to restore balance (Collier 1995: 47; de la Peña 2002: 62–63). In contrast to Malinowski, Radcliffe-Brown concluded that some "simpler" societies had no law (Nader 2002: 85). It was, however, Malinowski's view that every society could be said to have some sort of law, and this became the predominant assumption for future generations of researchers studying law in primitive societies (Nader 2002: 86).

Viewed in retrospect, Malinowski and Radcliffe-Brown were mainly concerned with whether traditional societies could be considered to have laws. Among their followers, a new debate arose around the question of how to study customary law. The first theoretical conceptualization in this regard posited the existence of general rules which applied to everyone, and which aimed at the maintenance of order in a society. Their research concentrated more on authorities and institutions and less on social processes. Conflicts were considered deviant behavior, and through analyzing the decisions of authorities and institutions, in combination with the power they exercise, one could – according to this view – infer the underlying rule. This line of thought regarding customary law, which prevailed during the first half of the last century, is called the normative paradigm (Sierra & Chenaut 2002: 116–123) or rule-centered paradigm (Comaroff & Roberts 1981). Beginning in the 1940s, this view was criticized on the grounds that it appeared to overestimate the importance of authorities and institutions.[9]

Thus, a second paradigm, which arose in the 1940s and fell out of favor in the 1960s, considered disputes to constitute normal rather than exceptional social behavior. This view held that, when analyzing norms and conflicts, one should pay careful attention to the arguments of, the negotiations between, and the compromises of the concerned parties, instead of focusing mainly on authorities or institutions (Sierra & Chenaut 2002: 123–129). Thus, conflicts and their resolution became the focus of legal anthropology. The joint work of the jurist Llewellyn and the anthropologist Hoebel can be regarded as one of the first studies conducted according to this second paradigm (Gulliver 1997 [1969]: 13–14; Nader 2002: 9–10). The work of Llewellyn and Hoebel was followed by several major studies (for example, Bohannan 1989 [1957]; Gluckman 1955;[10] Nader 1997; and Pospisil 1958). Pospisil, studying the Kapauku in New Guinea, stated that it was not "the abstract rule that affects

---

9   Such an overemphasis led the anthropologist Sir Edward Evans-Pritchard, for example, to declare that the Nuer of the Southern Sudan did not have laws (Comaroff & Roberts 1981: 9). Dissatisfaction with the characterization of such societies as "lawless" prompted later scholars to shift their focus to the study of disputes (A. Griffiths 2002: 292).
10 Bohannan and Gluckman achieved prominence as a result of the so-called the "Bohannan-Gluckmann controversy." Bohannan (1989 [1957]) stated that, although no formal law existed in traditional societies, these societies did have tribunals that resolved conflicts. But, because it was impossible to describe such tribunals in Western legal terms, he used local-oriented (*emic*) terminology to describe customary law among the Tiv in Nigeria. In contrast, Gluckman (1955) had no trouble describing "tribal" law with Western-oriented terminology (*etic*)

the Kapauku people, but the actual decision of the headman" (1958: 255), thus emphasizing *process*, rather than *rules*.[11]

Eventually, this second, process-oriented paradigm (Comaroff & Roberts 1981) for the study of disputes came under attack. Specifically, critics held that studying the settlement of disputes alone was too limited. Among other things, this meant that if one studied problem cases, one also had to study "non-problematic" cases in order to get a complete picture of everyday life. As Holleman (1973: 599) stated:

> In the study of substantive law and its practice, and in a field of law in which litigation is rare, a fieldworker relying mainly on a case method focused upon actual [problematic] cases may get a skewed idea of the accepted principles and regularities in this particular field [...] The [non-problematic] case then becomes a necessary check on the [problematic] case, rather than the other way around.[12]

More importantly, in the 1970s, legal anthropologists began to advocate shifting the focus of research "to the description and analysis of *behavior* connected with *disputing*" (Just 1992: 374; emphasis in original). An integration of the two paradigms was sought, one in which the broader context would also be taken into account (Nader & Todd 1978) (that is, a shift from rules *or* processes, via rules *and* processes, to rules and processes *within* their social, cultural, and political context).

Another trend that began in the 1970s was the development within legal anthropology of a growing awareness that customary law contained cultural elements, was not independent of other social systems, and could not be considered separately from the state in which it functioned (Collier 1995; Just 1992; Nader 1990; Starr & Collier 1989). The legal anthropologist Sally Falk Moore, with her concept of semi-autonomous social fields, provided a compelling analysis of this relationship between customary law and the state. She argued that a small "social field" is capable of internally generating rules, customs, and symbols, but that this same social field "is vulnerable to rules and decisions and other forces emanating from the larger world by which it is surrounded" (Moore 1978: 55). It is this vulnerability that makes it semi-autonomous. To

---

    which he used to characterize the system of law of the Barot in the nation then known as Rhodesia.
11 It can be said that the twentieth century as a whole saw a gradual shift from engagement with the question of whether customary law could be considered law, to how to study it. While early legal anthropologists based most of their findings on informal interviews with indigenous leaders, Llewellyn and Hoebel initiated a trend in the early 1940s of studying disputes in a way that emphasized process.
12 Holleman (1973) uses the rather unwieldy terms "trouble-cases" and "trouble-less cases" to distinguish between problematic cases (that is, those cases in which a dyadic disagreement becomes transformed into a triadic process) and cases which were resolved without the mediation of a third party, because they did not lead to a grievance or disagreement (see Chapter 5).

this must be added the fact that the parties functioning in such a field could themselves hypothetically mobilize state law, or threaten to do so (see for example Sierra 1995b). This too has its impact on any social field's internal capacity to make rules. On the other hand, the social field does have the means to induce or coerce compliance (Moore 1978: 56). In a way, these fields do have some sort of autonomy, because "the various processes that make internally generated rules effective are often also the immediate forces that dictate the mode of compliance or noncompliance to state-made rules" (Moore 1978: 57). Moore's concept, although hardly immune from criticism, is nowadays often cited to explain customary law's flexible and adaptive character, and to provide insight into the concept of "legality."

Thus, instead of asking *what* customary law is, one should instead ask *how* customary law is used at a particular time and place. First and foremost, such a task requires an examination of customary law in relation to national law. After all, in most societies, the use of customary law is strongly related to national law in that it is used *instead of* or *in addition to* national law. The concept of more than one normative system functioning simultaneously is called legal pluralism. Like customary law, legal pluralism is a highly contested issue. In addition to legal anthropologists, socio-legal researchers, juridical practitioners, and stakeholders have over the course of many years been engaged in a fierce debate regarding the content and range of legal pluralism. The following section will provide an overview of how the concept of legal pluralism has been treated in the literature during the past forty years. It will show that the heart of the debates on the concept of legal pluralism nowadays is related to the dynamics of power and social change.

Legal anthropology and pluralism

During the first half of the twentieth century, the new discipline of legal anthropology generally, and its study of customary law specifically, was mainly limited to the examination of small-scale, closed, "untouched" societies. The colonial state and its representatives, as well as the successor independent republics, were for the most part disregarded (K. von Benda-Beckmann 2001). This began to change in the 1970s, when the concept of legal pluralism became fashionable. It is generally agreed that this latter concept was first introduced in 1971, in two papers published in a book edited by Gilissen (1971b): *Le pluralisme Juridique* (K. von Benda-Beckmann 2001; Woodman 1998). Although the first essay in this collection (Gilissen 1971a) does not present a definition of the term itself, it does introduce the idea that various types of legal systems exist and that, in certain circumstances, this entails some sort of contact among them. The second essay (Vanderlinden 1971: 20) identifies an important quality of legal pluralism, namely the fact that it enables "different legal mechanisms [to be] applicable to an identical situation." This insight draws attention to another important point: different legal systems applying to different situations should not be labeled "legal pluralism" but instead "plurality of law." Hooker (1975) added that legal pluralism required the *interaction*, rather than the mere *coexistence*, of two or more different legal systems.

For the past twenty-five years, subsequent debates on the concept of legal pluralism focused on two theoretical issues (A. Griffiths 2002; J. Griffiths 1986; Merry 1988; F. von Benda-Beckmann 2002; von Benda-Beckmann & von Benda-Beckmann 2006; Woodman 1998). The first concerns the scope of the term "law." On the one hand, so-called "*étatists*" (K. von Benda-Beckmann 2001: 23) have a centralistic perspective on law, believing that only written national law should be considered as falling within the formal normative order, a tenet that causes them to reject legal pluralism as a concept. "Legal pluralists," on the other hand, challenge the claim that national law is exclusive in nature. Legal pluralists hold a decentralist view of law which allows them to recognize the phenomenon of legal pluralism as legitimate. I agree with Hoekema (2004: 7), who states that this controversy mainly concerns a juridical dilemma. The reason why *étatists* (who are for the most part legal scholars) reject the concept of legal pluralism in relation to customary law, is that the characteristics of customary law violate the requirements of positive law (that is, codification in writing, generality, and relative inflexibility). This raises the question of how to deal with legal pluralism. Legal pluralists, on the other hand, address the fundamentally different question of how legal pluralism works in practice.

The second debate involves demarcating legal pluralism's proper sphere. As such, it is closely related to the above-mentioned discussion about the scope of the term "law," and involves the distinction between "weak" (J. Griffiths 1986: 8) or "state law" legal pluralism (Woodman 1998: 34) on the one hand, and "strong" (J. Griffiths 1986) or "deep" (Woodman 1998) legal pluralism on the other. The first type of legal pluralism is the result of the recognition of one legal system (for example, customary law) by another one – usually that of the state. The second type consists of two or more separate and distinct legal systems. According to some (for example, John Griffiths (1986)), the first type of legal pluralism does not offer an adequate analytical framework because of the previously defined relationship between customary law and national law. Others, like Woodman (1998) or Franz von Benda-Beckmann (2002), argue that such a binary distinction between legal monism and legal pluralism cannot be made. If the aforementioned arguments of contact (Gilissen 1971a) and interaction (Hooker 1975), or Moore's concept of semi-autonomous social fields are taken seriously, then it must be concluded that different normative orders do not have clearly delineated boundaries (Woodman 1998: 51). This means that it should not matter whether or not legal pluralism is recognized by the state. In this connection, it would seem important to conduct research on pluralism both within a legal system and between legal systems.

Such conceptual discussions seem to have recently lost some of their relevance. The main focus of research in legal anthropology has shifted to the interaction between customary law and national law, or more precisely, to "the dialectic, mutually constitutive relationship between state law and other normative orders" (Merry 1988: 880). By exploring this relationship, Merry attempts to explain how on the one hand national law penetrates and restructures customary law, and on the other hand how customary law resists and circumvents such penetration (Merry 1988: 881). However, any notion of this mutually constitutive relationship being one of equals should be rejected out of hand. According to Sieder (1997: 10), "legal pluralism is better understood as a relation of dominance and of resistance." As a consequence, the use of customary law is considered a form of resistance, a strategy of indigenous people for obtaining and retaining their autonomy, and for safeguarding it against the hegemony of national law and the state (Collier 1995; Merry 1988: 878; Sieder 1998: 105–106).

We have thus far seen that researchers have for the most part viewed legal pluralism as involving the coexistence of two different legal systems. Although the interaction between the two systems (with all its dynamics of a context containing unequal power relations, etc.) is generally recognized, the meaning of legal pluralism is rather fixed. By this I mean that, according to most of the literature explored thus far, the interaction does not fundamentally influence the content of both systems. To simplify: system A interacts with system B, and the outcome is A+, or B+. There seems to be no room for something new, like a combined system AB, or a completely new system C. The coexistence of two different legal systems is depicted as a jurisprudential process, leaving little room for a description of what legal pluralism *does* in practice (Goodale 2009: 32; Oomen 2005: 25). Thus, the question becomes how to theorize and analyze legal pluralism as it is understood in daily reality. Boaventura de Sousa Santos' (2002) notion of "interlegality" proves useful in this regard.

Interlegality

It is the above-mentioned empirical gap that led de Sousa Santos (2002: 97) to ask questions that refer to "the impact of legal plurality on the legal experiences, perceptions and consciousness of the individuals […] living under conditions of legal plurality." His answer can be found in the understanding of what he calls "interlegality," which essentially refers to a situation where there is a perception of two different legal systems mixed to such an extent that they have resulted in the creation of a new system. Or paraphrasing Hoekema (2004: 23), interlegality is not just an accumulation of distinct elements, but instead constitutes a *new* hybrid legal order.

How can we understand interlegality more profoundly? Let us return to the focus on the relationship between customary law and national law – specifically, the fact that they are mutually constitutive, as well as unequal in terms of their relative power. In such a relationship, one tends to view the state, its national law, and its agents (that is, legislators, judges, etc.) as an independent variable. In daily practice, however, this is far from the case because the state, its legal system, and its agents appear to be dependent on external factors as well. That is why de Sousa Santos (2002: 94) calls for "bring[ing] the state back in[to]" the study of legal pluralism.[13] The state and its policies towards law in general and customary law specifically, provides an additional component of the wider context within which legal pluralism should be studied. Additionally, another contextual issue that should be integrated into the study of legal pluralism is the historical circumstances in which legal pluralism arises (de Sousa Santos 2002; Nader 2002: 12). It is for this reason that the study of legal pluralism currently combines ethnography and history within the framework of political power structures. The present book reflects this approach.

Nonetheless, the study of legal pluralism risks falling into the trap of treating customary and national law as separate entities that merely exist in the same political space.[14] De Sousa Santos argues that this does not reflect how people experience legal pluralism in daily life. Instead, he contends, the experienced reality is that of "different legal spaces superimposed, interpenetrated, and mixed in [people's] minds, as much as in [people's] actions." He labels this experienced reality "interlegality" (de Sousa Santos 2002: 437). Interlegality thus refers to how ordinary people experience law in daily life. It is the "intersubjective, or phenomenological dimension of legal pluralism" (de Sousa Santos 2002: 97). De Sousa Santos is credited with creating the term (Hoekema 2004: 23; Simon Thomas 2009: 5), since he first introduced it in 1987 (de Sousa Santos 1987). We will later examine how several distinguished legal anthropologists have taken up his conceptualization of how different forms of legality exist simultaneously and in interrelated forms.

Sierra (1995b, 2004), for example, agrees that customary law and national law should not be viewed as two separate and mutually exclusive legal systems, arguing instead that legal pluralism should be seen as heterogeneous and mutually constitutive. Referring to de Sousa Santos' notion of interlegality, she shows that what people do in daily practice could be described as a *bricolage* (that is, do-it-yourself-handicraft). Goldstein (2012: 30) uses the term "legal *bricolage*."[15] Depending on the context, the power relationships at stake, and

---

13 Although de Sousa Santos does not refer to Skocpol (1985) directly, since he has put the phrase "bring[ing] the state back in[to]" within quotation marks, I assume that he is indirectly referencing his work.
14 Jackson and Warren (2005: 563) even stated that "[national] and customary law are *always* opposed in the literature [my emphasis]." They cite research conducted by Sierra (1995a) in support of their argument that this "dichotomy between law and custom dissolves in actual situations." Sierra (1995a: 117) contends that, in the case of the Nahuas in Mexico, one could speak of "a multifaceted characteristic of law, in which official and customary law enable a range of different possibilities" to settle conflicts (see also Sierra 2004: 43–47).
15 It is unclear here if Sierra is alluding to Lévi-Strauss' (1972: 16–33) use of *bricolage* in his book *The Savage Mind*. According to Lévi-Strauss (1972: 17), *bricolage* refers to the process in which a worker (the *bricoleur*) constructs or creates something by using "whatever is at hand." Goldstein (2012: 30) cites Lévi-Strauss when he introduces the term "legal *bricolage*," but does not reference either Sierra's (2004) use of *bricolage* or de Sousa Santos' (2002) concept of interlegality.

degree of access to authorities, indigenous people have recourse to different legal systems, and this leads to a mixing of norms and procedures in daily practice (Sierra 2004: 43–44). Additionally, Hoekema (2003, 2004, 2005) and his students,[16] characterize interlegality as a process (that is, the above-described "mixing" itself) and emphasize the mixed outcomes in which it results. Interlegality, according to Hoekema (2004: 18–24) provides a new legal order, in that it constitutes an intermingling of concrete norms, as well as an adoption of values which accompany these norms and endow them with meaning.

Others, like Goldstein (2012), Goodale (2009), and Cervone (2012) even seem to reject the notion of legal pluralism (because of its empirical shortcomings in the Latin American context) in favor of interlegality (Goldstein 2012: 33, 200–202; Goodale 2009: 33, 78–79).[17] I think that this is going too far, because I specifically disagree with the assumption that interlegality equals legal pluralism in all instances. In my view, legal pluralism has a different meaning at different socio-geographic levels. Therefore, I agree that the empirical reality at the local level is highly complex and nuanced. This being the case, the notion of interlegality proves to be very helpful in describing and interpreting legal pluralism's daily complexity. And that is what I believe de Sousa Santos meant in the first place when he characterized interlegality as the *phenomenological* dimension of legal pluralism. On the other hand, one cannot deny the fact that the existence of legal pluralism beyond the local level (for example, on a national, more political level) is still seen and treated as a dichotomy.

Forum shopping

A situation in which there are no clear and firm boundaries between two or more legal systems provides the opportunity for deliberately selecting one of them, a phenomenon described in the literature as "forum shopping." This concept was introduced into legal anthropology by Keebet von Benda-Beckmann (1981: 117) as follows: "I shall speak of 'forum shopping' [...] because disputants have a choice between different institutions, and they base their choice on what they hope the outcome of the dispute will be, however vague or ill-founded their expectations may be." Since her introduction of the concept more than thirty years ago, fairly uncritical references to it have appeared in dozens of anthropological studies of legal pluralism. On the one hand, this suggests that the concept is both simple and powerful, and thus easy to use. When people can choose among different authorities or systems, it is only natural that they will tend to select the one that they feel best serves their own interests. On the other hand, the unquestioning embrace of the term seems to reflect a lack of interest in the

---

16   See for example Herrera (2011) and Orellana Halkyer (2004).
17   Goldstein (2012) and Goodale (2009) write about Bolivia, while Cervone (2012) specifically focuses on the Ecuadorian highlands.

questions of how and why people engage in such behavior (Shahar 2013). The present section attempts to fill this void by explaining what forum shopping is in order to provide a theoretical basis for determining whether it can be used as an analytical tool that might provide insight into the daily practice of formal legal pluralism in Ecuador.

Keebet von Benda-Beckmann (1981: 117) acknowledges having introduced the term "forum shopping" based on an analogy with private international law. According to private international law,[18] forum shopping refers to the choice one of the parties makes between two or more courts that have the power to consider the case at hand. This choice is based on the assumption that the chosen court is likely to consider that case in a way that is biased in favor of the party making the choice.[19] The actual practice of such choice-making behavior, however, is not uncontested (Fawcett & Carruthers 2008; Stikwerda 2012). Shahar (2013) shows that legal scholars who study forum shopping as a symptom of conflicts between legal systems tend to be critical of this phenomenon. Similar "anti-forum shopping" legal sentiments can be recognized in Ecuador too,[20] especially among legal practitioners criticizing the situation of formal legal pluralism. It should be noted that forum shopping in this strictly legal context involves a high degree of intentional and opportunistic behavior.

Contrary to such a purely legal point of view, a socio-legal or legal anthropological point of view provides the tools to understand at a deeper level what forum shopping actually does. It proves that forum shopping does not involve a strictly rational choice that takes place within a situation of different legal forums operating on same level playing field. The decision-making process is often far more complex than just "a simple outcome of a rational deliberation of pros and cons" (Shahar 2013). Legal anthropological research shows that forum shopping practices are embedded in social, cultural, and political contexts that render legal scholars' voluntary rational choice assumptions invalid (Shahar 2013). As a matter of fact, it was Keebet von Benda-Beckmann (1981: 143) herself who, more than thirty years ago, suggested for example that "social control at the village level" influenced people's choice-making behavior. Therefore, we need to acknowledge that forum shopping might not be possible under all circumstances.[21]

18 Private international law is a set of rules that determines which legal system or which authority in a certain country applies to a given dispute when such a dispute has an "international" element.
19 Fawcett and Carruthers (2008: 32) define forum shopping as "the claimant seeking to sue in the country with the law most favorable to him." Stikwerda (2012: 214) writes about "forum-shopping" or "forum-tourism" in unflattering terms.
20 See for example Brandt and Valdivia (2007: 153) who write about "the problem of 'forum shopping'."
21 The same fine distinction can be drawn regarding closely related phenomena like "idiom shopping" (Spiertz 1986) or "discourse shopping" (Biezeveld 2004). "Idiom shopping," as explained by Spiertz (1986), basically refers to the strategy that people employ when they frame some of their arguments in terms of customary law and others in terms of national law, depending on which authority is

When Keebet von Benda-Beckmann coined the term "forum shopping," she simultaneously introduced the phenomenon of "shopping forums." "Not only do parties shop," she wrote, "but the forums involved use disputes for their own, mainly political, ends too" (K. von Benda-Beckmann 1981: 117). The institutions that she studied displayed a tendency to "acquire and manipulate disputes from which they expect to gain political advantage, or to fend off disputes [...] which they fear will threaten their interests" (K. von Benda-Beckmann 1981: 117). The argument that authorities tend to be selective in the kinds of disputes they agree to hear (K. von Benda-Beckmann 2003: 238) has been supported by other authors as well (Hoekema 2003; Spiertz 1986; von Benda-Beckmann & von Benda-Beckmann 2006). The cases that are analyzed later in this book will also show that local authorities in the Ecuadorian parish of Zumbahua tend to be selective to a certain extent, and that political considerations may at times underlie this selectivity. As a matter of fact, the case studies presented in this book tend to be more illustrative of the idea of "shopping forums" than of "forum shopping."

Bringing the state in

If one considers legal pluralism in terms of dominance and resistance, and views customary law as a strategy aimed at countering state hegemony, then the phenomenon becomes a way of understanding socio-political processes. On the one hand, legal pluralism appears to be a lens through which society's power relationships can be viewed. Yet, at the same time, legal pluralism is shaped by these selfsame power relationships (Oomen 2005: 18). One of the key role players within the interplay of legal pluralism and the dynamic of power relationships is the state. The state should be considered a dependent variable. What this means is that the state and its policies, according to de Sousa Santos (2002) provide one of the contexts in which legal pluralism can fruitfully be studied. It is for this reason that we must now clarify what we mean when we refer to "the state."

After Skocpol (1985) "brought the state back in," the state once again emerged as a topic of interest in the social sciences (Hansen & Stepputat 2001: 1). The conceptualization of the state reflected in this book follows that of Clark and Becker (2007: 5) who in turn build on findings derived from the essays in Hansen and Stepputat (2001). According to Hansen and Stepputat, the state should not be seen as ahistorical, and it should also be denaturalized (that is, the idea here being that the state is not an embodiment of sovereignty, and can thus take many forms and ambiguities). While the state manifests

> handling their case, and which vocabulary is thought to be appropriate and likely to be effective. Biezeveld (2004), however, shows that not only legal arguments, but arguments based on history, politics, and power, are used in the same way as well. She contends that people show "enormous creativity in the way they seek to employ these different kinds of discourse" (Biezeveld 2004: 138), and consequently she introduces the concept of "discourse shopping."

itself in different ways in different places, it can be said to possess distinct general characteristics. The "myth of the state" as a regulator of social order and stability, and the everyday practices within the state, both merit close study. The state should not be seen as monolithic, but as a series of institutions and sites. As Hansen and Stepputat (2001) put it, the state should be seen as shot through with ambiguities and contradictions. For example, there is a huge difference between what a *teniente político* (a state representative at the local level) says and does, compared to the rhetoric and actions of the national government.

The analytical concept of the state presented here is derived from Philip Abrams' (1988) deconstruction of the state in theoretical terms. He contends that the state includes both a state system and a state idea (while he tends to embrace the state as an idea rather than as a system (Abrams 1988: 75)). On the one hand, we have the actual functioning of the state (that is, "a palpable nexus of practice and institutional structure centered in government") and on the other hand the way it is perceived by society (that is, the "public reification" of it) (Abrams 1988: 82). Just as socio-legal scholars are used to dealing with the gap between "law in the books" and "law in action," socio-political scholars seem to recognize a gap between the claims of the state and state functioning in daily reality.[22]

The state can take many different forms. Hansen and Stepputat (2001) see the state as a set of both concrete and real institutions, on the one hand, and of illusory entities, on the other. They argue that the state sometimes manifests itself locally and personally, and at other times at great distance and impersonally. Finally, they contend that the state can be both constructive and destructive (Hansen & Stepputat 2001: 5–8), that states are in a continuous process of construction, and that this construction takes place through "languages of stateness" that are both practical and symbolic in nature.[23] A combination of two of their languages of stateness which specifically relate to

22 As explained by Clark and Becker (2007: 5) and by Hansen and Stepputat (2001: 3–4) this view of the state constitutes something of a midpoint between Gramsci's position on power, government, and authority and that of Foucault. Both of the cited studies show that, in Gramsci's understanding, state power emerged as hegemony armed by coercion. Gramsci emphasizes the state's political, unstable, partial, and always violent character. According to Foucault, on the other hand, power is not concentrated in the state, but is inherent in every social relationship. Therefore, the state could be considered not to be the source of power, but the effect of it. The state stands apart from and above society. This book shares this balanced approach to the state.
23 Hansen and Stepputat (2001: 7–8) distinguish between three "practical languages of governance" and three "symbolic languages of authority". The former are: 1) monopolization of violence through visible military and police forces, 2) knowledge of the population in terms of its size, occupational profile, etc., and 3) the development and management of the national economy. The latter are: 1) the institutionalization of law and legal discourse, 2) the materialization of the state in buildings, monuments, etc., and 3) the nationalization of a history and shared community.

law are particularly useful for the present study. What they call a "practical language of governance," as it is used by the state, involves the monopolization of violence (for example, by *de facto* visible police forces or the existence of prisons). A "symbolic language of authority" that is used concerns "the institutionalization of law and legal discourse as the authoritative language of the state and the medium through which the state acquires discursive presence and authority" (Hansen & Stepputat 2001: 8). This description refers to the state's *de jure* ability to kill, punish, and discipline by making the rules (that is, laws) and to its ability to enforce obedience to said rules by setting up the whole complex of apparatuses, institutions, and regulations responsible for their application. Thus, in its process of construction, the state defines legislation, and administration of justice.

This process of construction gives rise to the following questions: What are the limits of the state? And how does the state relate to other political actors, like relatively powerless indigenous people? For the purposes of understanding what this means in terms of the present study, Chatterjee (2004) proves to be especially helpful. He points to the difficult relationship between state and civil society in India, and extends his findings to "most of the world" (by which he means the developing world). He identifies two different forms of citizenship: formal and real (Chatterjee 2004: 4). We have "a *formal* structure of the state as given by the constitution and the laws [and] all of society is civil society; everyone is a citizen with equal rights and therefore to be regarded as a member of civil society" (Chatterjee 2004: 38). But he goes on to say that this is not how things work in *reality*. In the developing world, poor people are not always fully included in the state, even if they aren't completely excluded either. But, within the territorial jurisdiction of the state, these people "have to be both looked after and controlled by various governmental agencies" (Chatterjee 2004: 38). As a result, such individuals are brought into a certain political relationship with the state. The complex relationship between the state and its agents, on the one hand, and the poor and powerless on the other hand, mean that the latter live in a "political society" (Chatterjee 2004: 40). It is within this political society that most political mobilization takes place, and it is there that the state has to obtain and maintain its legitimacy as guardian of its citizens' wellbeing. Therefore, political society becomes "a site of negotiation and contestation" (Chatterjee 2004: 74), opened up by the activities of state agents aimed at the poor.

As Baud (2009: 21–22) explains, Chatterjee draws attention to three important points: 1) a lot of politics is constructed locally; 2) this is done in direct response to the state; and 3) "its outcome should be considered the result of the historical development of political society on a local and regional level, as well as of structures and ideologies of the state." This historical and dialectical perspective allows us to analyze the state as a series of institutions and sites (fragmented and internally contradictory, as was argued above) where conflicts are constantly negotiated from above as well as from below. Subordinate people (in this study, rural indigenous people) are not only passive subjects vis-à-vis the state and its policies, but instead play an active role. This, however, does not occur as a result of direct contact between those who govern and those who are governed, but through so-called mediators (Chatterjee 2004: 64).

For Chatterjee, the site where this negotiation and contestation takes place is above all a sphere dominated by informal *de facto* sovereignties (that is, the mediators). In one of Chatterjee's examples, it is a local slumlord (representing those who illegally have occupied land in order to build their slum dwellings), who conducts clandestine negotiations with a representative of a government electricity company over the provision of (and payment for) electricity to the community. The negotiated outcome, albeit established through a newly set up collective association, likely would not have been achieved if the slum dwellers had acted legally, and had they been empowered to make individual arrangements. In this example, Chatterjee (2004: 56) draws particular attention to the "entire set of paralegal arrangements" that constitutes the basis of that specific outcome. He also argues that, because of the illegal actions that are negotiated and the paralegal spheres in which the mediation takes place, political society also has its dark side. Thus, once local power-holders have become mediators, they can easily develop "their own entrenched interests within the power structure" (Chatterjee 2004: 67).

What Chatterjee basically argues is that the relationship between those who govern and those who are governed cannot always be seen as a one-on-one relation between the state and members of civil society. Specifically, when matters involve large groups of poor and marginalized people who do not form a part of civil society, the state (or rather state agencies) must, according to Chatterjee, descend from their ivory tower "to the terrain of political society, in order to renew their legitimacy as providers of wellbeing, and there confront their political demands" (Chatterjee 2004: 41). "Governmental administration has to follow a different logic from that of the normal relations of the state with citizens in civil society," according to Chatterjee (2004: 135). State agencies must thus negotiate with representatives of groups of the poor and marginalized (that is, mediators) in order to govern. As a consequence, Chatterjee (2004: 4) states, *real* citizenship is not so much constituted by a top-down governance, but should rather be seen from the bottom up, as a "politics of the governed."

Indian–state relations

Chatterjee's reflections on the nature of the state, its representatives, and the nature of citizenship are especially applicable to the Indian–state relationship in Latin America. In scholarly literature on state–society relations in Latin America, the issue of whether we could speak of a strong or a weak state appears to be of interest. "Postcolonial Latin American states have long cycled through weakness and strength," as Colloredo-Mansfeld (2009b: 89) has written. Therefore, the impact of recent constitutional reforms and the adoption of neoliberal reforms, with their concomitant decentralization policies, are hotly debated. Does this all imply a restriction or an extension of the reach of the state? To answer this question, a few remarks as to what a state (whether weak or strong) *is* are in order. According to Migdal (1988) the main issue here is the ability of state leaders to use the agencies of the state to get citizens to do what they want them to do. Strong states are those that are highly capable of completing this task, while weak states are relatively incapable of doing so. Focusing merely on the direct impact of states on societies, however, would give a partial view of the relations between peoples and states, and would miss important aspects of why some states are more capable than others. Societies also affect states. A central argument of Migdal is that the capacity of states (or their incapacity, as the case may be) and especially their ability to implement social policies, is closely related to the structure of the societies that they govern. In a way, this is similar to what Chatterjee (2004: 4) sees as two different manifestations of citizenship, "the formal and the real," where the real is constituted solely by "the governed." The ineffectiveness of state leaders who have faced impenetrable barriers to state predominance has stemmed from the nature of the societies they have confronted (for example, from the resistance of local indigenous leaders or the rural elite, through their various social organizations).

In the Latin American context, this leads to distinct views on the effect of what Van Cott (2000) has called "constitutional transformations" on the capacity of the state. Some argue that these transformations have weakened the role of the state, contending that decentralization has impeded democratization, reinforcing local power elites, clientelist politics, unequal access to law, and new forms of incorporation (Assies 2001: 12; Sieder 2002: 8). Others argue that the decentralization policies have actually extended the territorial outreach of the state, in that they have increased its power to intervene in many spheres that were previously semi-autonomous (Assies 2000b: 12). It is clear that the reforms both imposed new constraints and provided new opportunities for indigenous people.

Within Latin America, Ecuador constitutes an interesting case. With an economy that was principally organized around the hacienda system for centuries, the state remained at a certain distance; especially for rural indigenous people living in the Andean highlands. Until the agrarian reforms of the twentieth century,[24] these persons had a relationship with local landholders, rather than with the state. This meant that national law remained largely inaccessible for indigenous people, on the one hand, and that some space for autonomy and the use of customary law was provided, on the other. However, when the occasion arose, rural Indians would seek the intervention of higher state authorities to resolve local matters (Baud 1993; Platt 1982; Stern 1982). These triangular relationships between indigenous people, local power-holders, and the state changed in the second half of the twentieth century. The main

---

24 Ley de Comunas of 1937, and subsequent land reforms in 1964 and 1973 (see Chapter 3).

reasons for the change were the agrarian reforms and constitutional transformations. But whether we can speak of *fundamental* changes in a weak or strong state is a matter of debate. Perhaps it is more appropriate to look at the developments as a continuing negotiation and contestation (Chatterjee 2004) between the Ecuadorian state and its indigenous population. In relation to their indigenous populations, states like Ecuador oscillate between weakness and strength (Dembour 2001).

Multiculturalism

Similar to what can be drawn from this book's discussion of the term "legal pluralism," one has to distinguish between *multicultural* as a mere adjective that describes either an objective condition of plurality or the composition of a place or society, and *multiculturalism* as a political project, an effort of liberal democratic governments to accept and embrace ethnic differences (Cowan 2006: 12; Postero 2007: 13). Especially regarding the latter, there is a growing amount of literature, mainly in political philosophy, but in other sciences as well. These writings appear to support the view of Castles (2000: 5, cited in Vertovec 2001: 3) that multiculturalism fundamentally involves "abandoning the myth of homogeneous and monocultural nation-states" and "recognizing rights to cultural maintenance and community formation." In policy terms, multiculturalism frames the public institutional sphere (for example, procedures, representations, and laws). From a legal point of view, multiculturalism concerns the question of how to deal with individual rights vs. collective rights. And in terms of the context of this book, Ecuador has always been multicultural in its composition, but has only recently come to recognize this pluralism politically as well as legally, and it is now struggling with the question of how to translate this recognition into practice.

A number of different phrases have been used to express the degree of cultural diversity present: "multicultural constitutionalism" (Van Cott 2000), "neoliberal multiculturalism" and "state-sponsored multiculturalism" (Postero 2007: 13), or "interculturality." However, what multiculturalism in essence stands for is the recognition of marginalized groups, ensuring their individual rights as citizens, and in some cases granting collective rights to entire groups. In Latin America, this means above all the recognition of "indigenous rights." As this book has shown, since the 1980s more than ten Latin American states have formally endorsed various forms of multiculturalism in order to give formal expression to the multicultural character of their composition. Part of their goal was to overcome past histories of subordinated segregation, forced integration, and assimilationist policies (Assies 2000b: 4). The fundamental question in this regard has to do with the definitive shape that this recent recognition will take. Or, more specifically: how can the formal recognition of legal pluralism be put into practice?

Acceptance of the multicultural nature of society thus calls for changes in the legal arrangements of such a society (Parekh 2000: 2), and political theorists struggle with the question of how this might happen. Following Nancy

Postero (2007), two different theoretical approaches to that question can be distinguished: those in favor of a politics of recognition (for example, Gutmann 1994) and those advocating a politics of redistribution (for example, Rawls 1971). The first group argues in line with Taylor's view (Taylor 1994) that social recognition of minority cultures is essential to one's identity and self-worth, and that failure of recognition can gravely damage both. In this line of thinking, the emphasis is on the cultural nature of injustice, and cultural domination is seen as a form of oppression that requires state intervention. One critic of such a viewpoint is Benhabib (2002), who argues that it is based on an essentialized notion of culture. Turner (1993: 412) contends that such a notion:

> risks essentializing the idea of cultures as separate entities by overemphasizing their boundedness and distinctness; it risks overemphasizing the internal homogeneity of cultures in terms that potentially legitimize repressive demands for communal conformity; and by treating cultures as badges of group identity, it tends to fetishize them in ways that put them beyond the reach of critical analysis.

Benhabib (2002: 4–5) warns that this kind of adherence to a "reductionist sociology of culture" hobbles our thinking about the injustices suffered by groups.

The second, earlier line of thought suggested that true equality requires a transformation of the political and economic structure of society. Or as Almeida et al. (2005) have argued regarding the Ecuadorian context, diversity has gone beyond simple questions of ethnicity, since dominant sectors keep a hold on (economical, natural, and political) resources and consequently are enabled to retain power. The focus, according those in favor of a politics of redistribution, should be on the socioeconomic rather than cultural aspect of injustice. In reality, however, a strict distinction between the politics of recognition and the politics of redistribution cannot be maintained, since both are closely related (Parekh 2000: 2). One cannot separate cultural demands from economic capacity. Nor can one separate economic power from culturally meaningful frameworks (Postero 2007: 14). To put it simply, recognizing multiculturalism without a concomitant redistribution of at least some power does not work; the politics of recognition and the politics of redistribution should be integrated. In a case study on Bolivia, Postero's main argument is that, while cultural diversity to a certain extent has been recognized, the frustrations with failures to make substantial changes in redistributing resources are a key component of current social unrest in that country (Postero 2007: 15).[25]

---

25 In a way, this is similar to what I have recently argued regarding the use of customary law in Ecuador. As a result of the attempt by indigenous authorities to enforce the constitutional promise of coordinating rules, the struggle over jurisdiction tends to clearly delineate boundaries. Concomitantly, this struggle tends to intensify the use of indigenous customary law (Simon Thomas 2012).

Collective rights vs. individual rights

Arrangements regarding pluralism that should be made between state and society are reflected in what this book calls the dilemma of individual rights vs. collective rights. In this connection, Koenig and de Guchteneire (2007: 5) write: "The [...] dilemma is how to reconcile the recognition of minorities as groups with the concept of human rights, which focuses on the rights of the individual person." In the context of this book, the question would be formulated as follows: to what extent can, or should, customary law (which is collective in nature) meet generally accepted human rights standards (which are individual in nature)?

An obvious starting point for answering that question is Kymlicka's (1995) extensively cited, and often contested, distinction between "external protections" and "internal restrictions." But such an approach would obscure the fact that not everybody regards the individual rights vs. collective rights issue as a dilemma. At one end of the spectrum, one can find a strictly juridical point of view, which advocates the rejection of collective rights, according to the principle that universal human rights only apply to individuals. At the other end, Stavenhagen (2002) and others argue that the recognition of special group rights are a necessary condition for enjoying individual human rights. They consider collective rights to be instrumental to the realization of individual rights (Assies et al. 2000: 302). Such a notion is based on the contention that individual human rights cannot be fully enjoyed by subordinated groups like indigenous peoples.

To return to a theoretical reflection on the above-mentioned dilemma, Kymlicka (1995) draws a distinction between external protections and internal restrictions. This corresponds to Taylor stating that liberalism fails to recognize the crucial role culture plays in determining the self. Contrary to Taylor, Kymlicka attempts to find a solution within the boundaries of liberalism. Framing his arguments as a critique of Rawls (1971), Kymlicka argues that, from a liberal point of view, collective rights in the sense of external protection can be accepted. In his view, group interests equal individual interests. Conversely, internal restrictions (that is, those that involve a claim of a group against its own members, intended to protect the group from internal dissent) cannot be justified. Kymlicka does not accept that the interests of the group overrule those of the individual in such cases.

Kymlicka's view has had its detractors. One line of criticism has to do with the fact that problems arise when the line between external protections and internal restrictions becomes blurred (Modood 2007: 29).[26] A second problem arises when a "liberal society is confronted with anti-liberal views which reveal that liberalism itself is but one of several possible perspectives"

---

26 As a matter of fact, Kymlicka admits this himself, citing the collective land rights of indigenous people as a group protection (Kymlicka 1995: 42–44). In his view, the collectivity of land rights should be respected, even when this would restrict the possibility of individual members selling their plots.

(Eriksen 2002: 148). Such proves to be the case when human rights are confronted with customary law. The problem with Kymlicka's argument is that it requires indigenous people and their customary law to be internally liberal (Assies et al. 2006: 39; Tamanaha 2008: 56), and this does not always apply. The case studies presented in this book will confirm that customary law has a non-liberal orientation, in contrast to human rights, which enact liberal norms that protect individual autonomy, liberty, bodily integrity, and so on. When this is taken into account, Kymlicka's rejection of internal restrictions becomes problematic, especially when it is put in practice.[27] If human rights are applied as literally and as fully as possible, there would hardly be any space left for the use of customary law. This is why I would argue that some freedom of action should be accorded customary law – without, of course, falling into the trap of cultural relativism.

A third line of criticism is the notion of a "reductionist sociology of culture" (Benhabib 2002: 4). Basically, Kymlicka has been called to task for defining cultures as being static, distinct, and bounded entities. Thus, just like Taylor, he is accused of holding an essentialist view of culture. As will be shown later in this book, this line of criticism makes absolute sense in the Ecuadorian context if one looks at the daily practice of customary law. As argued before, the line between customary law and national law is quite blurred in practice. In addition, customary law (specifically its punitive measures) varies to some extent among different communities. Furthermore, there is typically a certain amount of discord *within* indigenous communities regarding the sanctions imposed by customary law in particular locales. Thus, any general statement regarding customary law and its punitive measures risks the trap of essentialism. One cannot speak of customary law in general being compatible or incompatible with the protection of human rights. Instead, one must answer such a question by examining how customary law is used at a particular time and place.

Finally, Kymlicka has also been criticized for treating ethnic and religious groups differently, and for treating "natives" and immigrants differently (Modood 2007). In addition, he has also been called to task for failing to notice that there are considerable power differences within groups or cultures, and that a lot of these differences are gendered (Okin 1999).[28] The former criticism is not especially salient in the Ecuadorian context, while the latter is. Specifically, power differences within indigenous communities (for example, between different families, or between those with close connections to indigenous movements

---

27 This is made clear by Assies et al. (2000: 303), when they argue: "If self-governing collectives are not granted any sanctioning capacity *vis-à-vis* their members, they hardly can sustain their self-government in practice."
28 In this book, I do not delve into gender issues relating to customary law. Such a topic deserves a book of its own. However, I do acknowledge that there are indeed power differences within customary law between men and women. For more on this subject, see Valdivia and González Luna (2009), Sieder and Sierra (2010), and UN Women (2011).

and those without such connections) help determine the forms that customary law assumes in practice. Two of the case studies presented in this book (the Tigua and La Cocha-Guantópolo cases) are illustrations of this. What Okin (1999) rhetorically asks in a title of one of her books (*Is Multiculturalism Bad for Women?*) could be rephrased as follows: is formal legal pluralism bad for indigenous people? In some cases (for example, the lawyer's warning in this book's introduction that the use of customary law is subject to bias) one could well respond in the affirmative.[29] These constitute examples of Chatterjee's (2004: 67) dark side of political society.

Kymlicka's liberal theory regarding external protections and internal restrictions is not a sufficient condition for adequately organizing a multicultural society, and neither are the two extreme positions (that is, a strictly juridical point of view that rejects any legal pluralism, or the unconditional embracing of it by cultural relativists). What would fit the bill in this regard? Parekh has at least hinted at a possible answer. He states that acceptance of differences requires more than changes in the legal arrangements of society. "Respect for them requires changes in attitudes and ways of thought as well" (Parekh 2000: 2). Sieder (2002: 13), in an analysis of the Latin American context, also calls for an "open, equal intercultural dialogue." Thus, it is not just formal recognition that makes a multicultural society truly work. Knowledge of and respect for other cultures is necessary as well.[30] As regards the actual acceptance of formal legal pluralism, this implies that "the full recognition of [customary law] will involve a profound adjustment of legal thinking and practice" (Sieder 2002: 13) and that differences "should be the subject of dialogue rather than being resolved through legal means" (Assies et al. 2000: 304).

Sovereignty and subsidiarity

In relation to a policy of institutional restructuring (which is, as previously stated, the second distinct meaning of the term "multiculturalism"), the subject of cultural diversity or multiculturalism challenges the historical construction of the sovereign, representative nation-state. The state, as we have seen, includes both a state system and a state idea (Abrams 1988). In addition, the state can take different forms, while state construction takes place through "languages of stateness" (Hansen & Stepputat 2001). A state's citizens are not

---

29 For example, I have argued elsewhere that one of the consequences of the contemporary legal void in Ecuador's situation of formal legal pluralism, in combination with the above-mentioned intensified use of customary law, tends to be an aggravation of punitive measures by some indigenous authorities (Simon Thomas 2012).
30 And this interest in "the other" has to go beyond a "boutique multiculturalism," a recognition of the legitimacy of other cultures, but a rejection of it at a point where "some value at its center generates an act that offends against the canons of civilized decency" (Fish 1997: 378).

reactive automata, but instead play an active role in it, not directly but through so-called mediators (Chatterjee 2004). In the Latin American context, this has led to a debate as to whether a state can be considered weak or strong, and whether a formal recognition of multiculturalism has changed this. However, one could just as well frame this discussion in terms of a question of whether the state is present or absent (Clark & Becker 2007: 6; Colloredo-Mansfeld 2009a: 19). This is especially relevant in remote rural areas like the Andean highlands.

Within a specifically Latin American context, the foregoing considerations are important for an anthropological understanding of the concept of sovereignty in the context of late twentieth century decentralization policies carried out under the banner of neoliberalism.[31] In Latin America, neoliberalism is both an economic doctrine and a cultural project (Assies et al. 2000: 297). The debt crisis in the early 1980s eventually paved the way for the World Bank and the International Monetary Fund (IMF) to put pressure on Latin American governments to carry out structural adjustment reforms. Basically, this meant decreasing the state's social responsibilities and redefining its participation in national economies. Practically speaking, this involved the elimination of subsidized public services (for example, water, electricity, and transportation), as well as the delegation of certain responsibilities (for example, political and fiscal responsibilities) to local administrations (Cervone 2012: 236). These economic reforms galvanized Indian resistance, which eventually resulted in constitutional reforms embracing (at least formally) the multicultural nature of the state. Decentralization, in this sense, can be seen both as part of a strategy aimed at reducing the role of the public sector and as a way of carrying out democratization that contributes to the empowerment of the subordinate indigenous population (Assies 2000b: 10). As a result of this process, local governments attained a greater degree of autonomy.

The formal recognition of legal pluralism (including the right granted to indigenous authorities to administer justice) could be seen in the light of the decentralization policy of the Ecuadorian government (Assies 2000b; Wilson 2008). However, as indicated in the introduction of this book, with the formal recognition of legal pluralism in the absence of coordinating rules, the Ecuadorian state in fact did nothing more than formalize *de facto* indigenous practices. Because coordinating rules have not been developed, the real extent to which the indigenous authorities and the use of customary law have been recognized is still unclear. It is the contention of Koenig and de Guchteneire (2007) that this is what the dilemma of individual rights vs. collective rights is

---

31 "Sovereignty" from an anthropological point of view has to do with *de facto* sovereignty. This not only includes the "ability to kill, punish, and discipline with impunity" (Hansen & Stepputat 2006: 295), but extends to the "monopoly to decide not only who is included and excluded from the political community, but also what order, security and normal life consists of, and what measures should be taken to restore them when these principles are threatened (including, in the last resort, the power to decide matters of life or death)" (Sieder 2011: 162).

really about in real terms. One might say that this decentralization of administrative affairs implies a fragmentation of juridical authority as well as an extension of *de facto* application of customary law. To understand what such a fragmentation and extension in daily practice is really about, one consequently has to take a local perspective.

As will be shown in the historical overview in Chapter 3, the actual day-to-day governance of the country (that is, *de facto* sovereignty) was previously divided among different authorities in rural areas. The presence of the state has in fact been very limited in these areas, both during colonial times and following independence. As Hansen and Stepputat (2006: 295) point out: "Although effective legal sovereignty is always an unattainable ideal, it is particularly tenuous in many postcolonial societies where sovereign power historically was distributed among many forms of local authority." With the formal recognition of legal pluralism, this previously existing situation of *de facto* deferred sovereignty became legalized.

Decentralization of legal jurisdiction in the absence of rules harmonizing the differential application of national and customary law raises questions about the role of national law, especially in cases in which the different legal systems threaten to clash with one another. In broader terms, it seems pertinent to ask whether decentralization implies a restriction or an extension of the reach of state power. According to Van Cott (2008: 4) a process of decentralization can be characterized either by a "top-down" or "bottom-up" dynamic. In the former case, decentralization is initiated and designed by the state, and local authorities are only given the power the state wants to grant them (de Benoist 1999). In the latter case, it is the local or regional level that determines when a given legal matter needs to be referred to the national courts for adjudication. Van Cott argues (2008: 4) that Ecuador employs a mixture of both approaches. I would add that, as regards the decentralization of administrative affairs, local and regional indigenous populations typically take the lead in making such determinations.

One could even argue that, given the longstanding lack of presence of formal juridical systems in the nation's rural areas, as well as an increased indigenous protection of the ability to adjudicate legal conflicts, "decentralization" is really not an appropriate label. Instead, the principle of "subsidiarity" seems to be a more accurate term. Subsidiarity in this sense means that legal matters are being handled by the lowest-level authorities that can claim jurisdiction (de Benoist 1999). These authorities resolve the conflicts as much as they possibly can, and they accept responsibility for their own decisions. The state only has a subsidiary function, stepping in to adjudicate disputes that cannot be resolved at the local level. In this conceptualization, it is the lower-level authority that delegates tasks and responsibilities to the state. However, as will be shown in the case study of a homicide presented in Chapter 8, the state always reserves the right to intervene in any given legal matter. In a way, local authorities (acting as mediators) are in constant negotiation with state representatives (that is, judges, public prosecutors, the *teniente politico*, and the police) (Chatterjee 2004) over the actual scope of customary law's jurisdiction.

Conclusion

It is clear that customary law as an object of legal anthropological research has undergone a number of paradigmatic changes over the years, but that it is now seen as a local system of rules and processes operating within a social, cultural, and political context. Originally studied as an autonomous legal system, since the 1970s a consensus has emerged among scholars that it should be studied in relation to national law. Legal pluralism has now become the most widely accepted concept. Legal pluralism has itself been subject to theoretical controversies, but by the end of the twentieth century legal pluralism was commonly construed (at least in Latin American studies) as the dialectical and mutually constitutive relationship between customary law and national law, with the accompanying caveat that such a relationship was not "power neutral." Therefore, the study of that relationship must include the application of ethnography within the framework of historically changing power structures. At the same time, it remains the case that legal pluralism is often understood as the coexistence of two different normative systems within the same social field. This understanding hinders a thorough analysis of what legal pluralism *does* in daily practice. De Sousa Santos' concept of "interlegality," as a phenomenological counterpart of legal pluralism, proves to be helpful in this regard.

When studying legal pluralism and interlegality, one has to take contextual circumstances into account, especially the state, national law, and state agents. If one wants to understand how states interact with their populations (especially with their subordinate populations) the concept of political society, with its mediators acting in paralegal spheres, as explained by Chatterjee (2004), proves to be appropriate for analyzing the Indian–state relationship in Ecuador. In the Andean highlands, the state (historically seen) has been rather absent. This absence raises the question of whether the Ecuadorian state should be characterized as strong or weak state – a common distinction in scholarly literature on state–society relations in Latin America. Here too, Chatterjee proves to be a useful reference, with his argument that a political society is a site of ongoing negotiation and debate.

In conclusion, the process of multiculturalism (as it has played out in Ecuador since the late twentieth century) means that marginalized groups are formally recognized by ensuring their individual rights and also by in some cases granting them collective rights. Part of this process meant that the use of customary law has been constitutionally recognized. However, coordinating rules to make national law and customary law compatible have not yet been enacted, and this has led to tension between Indians and the state. Basically, this is because, although multiculturalism has been recognized on paper, actual power has not yet been redistributed. Formal recognition has not been integrated with formal redistribution. In terms of the dilemma of collective rights vs. individual rights, Ecuador has not yet been able to find a balance between still persistent notions of legal monism and a cultural relativist-like position regarding legal pluralism.

The idea of coping with such a dilemma by making a distinction between external protections and internal restrictions has not withstood critical scrutiny, and nowadays a more gradual process of mutual dialogue and understanding is proposed to cope with such a dilemma. The lived reality of legal pluralism as interlegality might illuminate this proposed dialogue. In most cases, ordinary Indians and their local authorities appear to be able to settle their internal conflicts in the absence of the state. In other words, this means that the practice of local sovereignty based on the principle of subsidiarity is still expedient. Formal recognition of legal pluralism, as part of a decentralization policy, seems to empower indigenous people. However, the state reserves the right to intervene in what it considers exceptional cases. These "bottom up" and "top down" dynamics do not so much show a strengthening or a weakening of the position of either the Indians or the state, but instead suggest an interdependent relationship between those parties.

3 Legal pluralism in Ecuador

Introduction

Merry (1995: 20) has written that the law not only "provides a place to contest relations of power, but also determines the terms of the contest." And this appears to be especially true in the Ecuadorian context, in which the recognition of customary law recently has become a highly debated political issue. As such, this situation is not a whole lot different from that in other countries in the region with important indigenous populations. However, if one compares the Latin American situation with other parts of the world, like Asia and Africa, certain differences do emerge. In the former Dutch East Indies, for example, *adat* was applied by Dutch governmental institutions (J. Griffiths 1986; Hoekema 2003; K. von Benda-Beckmann 2001) and in colonial Ghana, local traditional leaders were given some governmental recognition by the British rulers (Lund 2008; Ubink 2008). These are but two examples in which customary law was accorded formal recognition many decades before the same phenomenon occurred in Ecuador.[1] It is beyond the scope of this book to elaborate on the ins and outs of this difference, but the historic indifference (an attitude that has changed only recently) is striking indeed.

This chapter provides an overview of how customary law has been treated politically and legally over the past five centuries in Ecuador. It shows that, although the situation has varied somewhat during the five centuries since the Spanish conquest, Ecuador has a long history of *de facto* legal pluralism. During colonialism, a segregationist political model was employed in which the use of customary law – although not formally recognized – was to a certain extent tolerated, as long as it did not frustrate the interests of the Spanish Crown. Segregationism was replaced by an assimilationist model when Ecuador became an independent Republic in 1830, and this in turn was replaced by an integrationist model in the early 1900s. Although these distinct political

---

1 Hoekema (2003: 186–188) rightly distinguishes between two kinds of formal recognition: 1) incorporation, referring to the empowerment, within the dominant state law, of a specific indigenous practice or authority which settles disputes, like *adat* in Indonesia and traditional leaders in Ghana, and 2) recognition, as, for example, in the Ecuadorian Constitution of 1998.

models treat customary law and its relationship with national law differently, they have in common their formal support of juridical monism, and thus a rejection of legal pluralism. It is only since 1998, in a neoliberal era that featured state-supported decentralization, that the country has constitutionally recognized the use of customary law alongside national law.

Internal conflicts in the Andean region have over the centuries frequently been resolved by indigenous authorities. Because of a relative absence of state authority, internal conflicts were typically settled within communities, or by a *hacendado* or other local power holder, with formal courts resorted to only on rare occasions. This is confirmed by scholarly writings related to this topic, some of which have been used as sources for this chapter. In sum, there have always been internal conflicts which one way or another have been settled by making use of distinct normative systems and different authorities. In other words, people have always made use of a situation of real legal pluralism. From that standpoint, the recent formal recognition of legal pluralism could be seen as a confirmation of what has been regular practice for centuries. However, this new situation of formal legal pluralism has given rise to new conflicts. The present chapter will attempt to provide some historical perspective in order to better appreciate how the current situation arose.

When customary law was constitutionally recognized in 1998, a situation of formal or *de jure* legal pluralism came into being. With this recognition, a politically and legally sensitive debate regarding the scope of customary law began. From the very start, it was unclear when, where, and which cases indigenous authorities were allowed to adjudicate. Actually, this debate on what I call "the challenge of legal pluralism" was put on the agenda at the very moment that the Constitution of 1998 was put into force. This is because it stated, while remaining rather vague on the actual scope of the recognition, that the law should develop rules which would make both legal systems compatible. Although this promise was repeated in the new Constitution of 2008 (or "the Montecristi Constitution," named after the town in the Manabí province where the constituent assembly convened), no such coordinating rules have yet been developed. As a result, there is still no agreement on the proper scope to be granted to indigenous authorities for the administration of customary law, resulting in a situation of legal uncertainty (Simon Thomas 2012).

While touching briefly on the colonial period and the "long nineteenth century," in which the hacienda system maintained its dominant position in the countryside while the state remained relatively absent, the first part of this chapter emphasizes the land reforms in the twentieth century because of their significance for the autonomy of rural indigenous communities in relation to customary and national law. After all, it is in the *comunas* (the number of which expanded after the Agrarian Reform laws in 1964 and 1973) where a *cabildo* is now formally allowed to adjudicate in accordance with customary law.[2]

2   The legal construction of a *comuna* was introduced in the Ley de Comunas of 1937.

Therefore, the second part of this chapter focuses on the actual period of formal legal pluralism, paying special attention to the two constitutions and to several efforts in the early 2000s to reach agreement regarding coordinating rules. This chapter's final section is on the recent campaign, led by Pachakutik assemblywoman Lourdes Tibán, to secure agreement on coordinating rules under the Montecristi Constitution.

Historical overview

A situation of *de facto* legal pluralism has existed since colonial times. When the Spanish colonized the territory now known as Ecuador, they enacted special legislation that introduced the concept of two separate *Repúblicas* and then politically reorganized the peoples and the lands of their newly conquered territory. According to the concept of two *Repúblicas*, the Spanish first introduced special legislation that legally and administratively divided the people who lived in the countryside – whom they called "*indios*" – from those who lived in cities and towns. Thus, there was the *República de Españoles* (that is, the Spanish and their descendants who lived in the urban areas) and the *República de Indios* (that is, those who lived in the countryside, whether of indigenous or Spanish origin). Second, after the Spanish settlement was solidly established, from the second half of the sixteenth century on, the Spanish began to legalize (collective) land tenure of the *indios*, for both economic and political reasons (Ouweneel & Hoekstra 1993: 114). In the Andes, this meant that existing extensive settlements were transformed into so-called *reducciones*, or connected centers, under the control of one *cabildo*.

In line with the strategy of indirect rule, such *cabildos* were composed of *curacas*, members of the ancient, hereditary indigenous elite. In addition to their role in securing tax revenues, these *curacas* were provided a limited territorial jurisdiction (Korovkin 2001: 44), in which they were allowed to adjudicate certain local conflicts (while cases involving major offenses and infractions had to be handed over to the Spanish authorities). This informal recognition of customary law was limited to a sphere that did not violate the laws imposed by the Spanish, which did not affect the official religion and which did not exercise an impact upon the colonial, economic, and political order (Ouweneel & Hoekstra 1993: 112; Yrigoyen Fajardo 2000: 204). In this manner, a situation of real legal pluralism came into being.

It was in this context that indigenous people in the *República de Indios* developed strategies to make use of the situation of *de facto* legal pluralism. Sometimes they resorted to their local customary law (if necessary, inventing or reinventing it) and sometimes they instead resorted to colonial law. Spanish colonialism, which was characterized by a strong juridical formalism, assigned all inhabitants certain rights. Among other things, this meant that rural indigenous people could resort to Spanish law in cases of disputes, just like anyone else. And so they did, as the occasion arose (Baud 1993: 190; Benton 2002 cited in Tamanaha 2008). As shown by Platt (1982), in what is now called Bolivia, indigenous leaders turned to the Spanish Crown with legal property titles by which they tried to defend their lands from dispossession. But the *indios* did not only use their juridical rights to combat colonial exploitation. When they could, they also used such rights to settle internal disputes (Stern 1982: 132). As Cervone (2012: 167) rightly remarks, there have been signs of interlegality (that is, indigenous actors incorporating the discourse of "law") since the early days of colonialism.

The "long nineteenth century"[3]

The colonial model of segregation was replaced by an assimilationist model beginning in the 1830s, when Ecuador became an independent republic and sought to put an end to any kind of separately defined "indigenous world." The colonial division into two *Repúblicas* was abolished, and a process of building a single unified nation (meaning one people, one culture, and one normative system) began (Assies et al. 2000: 305; Yrigoyen Fajardo 2000: 206–207). However, especially during the early years of the new republic, hierarchies that were characteristic of the colonial period remained intact, local elites held their power in many (rural) regions, and forms of colonial *indio* tribute remained (Crain 1990). In other words, the memories of the *pacto de reciprocidad* (Platt 1982: 40), or Colonial Contract (Ouweneel 2012) lived on. Although there are obviously considerable differences in time and place, it is fair to say that local power relations only really started to change after the abolition of the tributary system in 1857.

One of the main purposes of the nascent independent republic was to continue the transformation of traditional agriculture. Based on a policy of promoting exports, haciendas were given preference over small self-supporting farms. Communal land tenure had already been abolished during the period of Simon Bolívar's *Gran Colombia* (1819–1831) (Baud 1993: 192), and when Ecuador enacted its first organizational laws in 1830, it introduced the office of the *teniente político*, whose the most important, albeit hidden, agenda was to break the existing local rural elite's power, in particular that of the *curacas* (Guerrero 1989). This turned out to be an effective strategy, and the abolishing of tribute payments in 1857, along with a relative state absence from the countryside, resulted in the gradual replacement of the *curacas* by the "holy trinity" (as the rural power of the hacienda owners, the Catholic Church, and the *teniente político* was informally referred to). Thus, from a state–Indian perspective, the rural indigenous people primarily had to deal with the holy trinity, and the state was still relatively absent.

From a juridical perspective, this meant that *de facto* legal pluralism came under pressure, but did not fade away. Besides holding political responsibilities, this *teniente político* was assigned a juridical role of adjudicating minor

---

3 The "long nineteenth century" in the Ecuadorian context refers to the period following the era of colonialism to the early twentieth century.

offenses in indigenous communities. Although one of the results of this new office was that customary law became illegal, many rural indigenous communities continued to practice customary law. Furthermore, even *tenientes políticos* did not always follow the letter of the law, and thus applied both customary law and national law. Thus, as in the colonial period, a situation of real legal pluralism prevailed for rural indigenous people. At the same time, such people no longer enjoyed the juridical protection of colonial law, and they now had to cope with the power of the holy trinity in the context of a generally absent state.

This political indifference towards rural indigenous people seemed to change at the end of the nineteenth century. Starting with Eloy Alfaro's Liberal Revolution in 1895, an integrationist political model gained ascendance. Because of strong demands for land and other claims on the part of "free" agriculturists, combined with other demands related to the salaries and working conditions of *peons* on haciendas, in Ecuador an intellectual, "political current [...] arose in defense of the indigenous population in a more or less well-intentioned effort to give [indigenous] heritage a place in [politics]" (Baud 2009: 25). This movement was known as *indigenismo*. Baud also shows that this movement was initially opposed to the conservative, exclusionary politics of the nineteenth century, and as such it pressed for liberal, legal reforms with respect to the rights of the indigenous rural population. Examples of these reforms are the 1899 Regulation of the Debt System,[4] and the 1918 Reform of the Day Laborer Law.[5] The former intended to put an end to the *de facto* situation of slavery to which the *concertaje* system in some cases had led (Baud 2007: 79), while the latter introduced an eight-hour workday, outlawed debtors' prison, and abolished the inheritance of parental debts (Clark & Becker 2007: 9–10). Not all these efforts proved to be successful. In fact, in many respects the hacienda system survived until the 1964 agrarian reform. Yet these changes did affect the political and legal resources available to the rural indigenous people (Baud 2007; Clark & Becker 2007; Crain 1990). It is fair to say that, in general, the haciendas kept their dominant position while the state was kept at a distance. But if one takes a closer look, there are signs of an "interaction between various social and political spheres" (Baud 2007: 88), that challenged the simplified notion of a dichotomy between rural local power holders on the one side, and the state on the other. And this interaction obviously affected the situation of real legal pluralism, and especially that of interlegality.

The liberal period (1895–1925) marked a time of relative political stability (Clark 2007: 89). This changed in 1925, when the military and members of the middle class overthrew the Gonzalo Córdova administration (the last in a succession of liberal governments), triggering a period of political instability and frequent changes of government during the following two decades. This

4 Reglamentación del Concertaje.
5 Reforma de la Ley de Jornaleros.

situation of political instability coincided with the Great Depression of the late 1920s and 1930s. Although this economic crisis hit Indians who lived in rural areas especially hard, the rapid succession of governments provided them some important political opportunities (Clark 2007: 90). One of the primary gains in social legislation during this era was the 1937 Ley de Comunidades Indígenas y Montuvias (often shortened to Ley de Comunas) which extended legal recognition of political units to Indian communities.

Land reforms in the twentieth century

The 1937 Ley de Comunas, and the corresponding Judicial Statute of Rural Communities,[6] invited rural communities of more than fifty people to form small political-administrative units called *comunas*. In certain parts of the country, indigenous people quickly embraced this *comuna* structure and subsequently their numbers increased (Becker 1999: 531), while in other areas they did not. This law should be seen in the context of several other regulations that were instituted in order to resolve the "Indian problem" (that is, integrating Indians into the modernizing project of the liberal state) once and for all. Its intention, therefore, was not to protect traditional community structures, or to grant indigenous communities more autonomy over local affairs. Instead, the 1937 law sought to impose a set of standardized political institutions and government structures on rural areas. It intended to homogenize rural communities in Ecuador (Becker 1999; Lucero 2003; Striffler 2002; Yashar 2005). According to existing law in those days, only provinces, cantons, and *parroquias* were recognized as political units, and small indigenous communities were not. Thus, in order to facilitate more state influence in such communities, they were invited to become part of the political-administrative apparatus of the state. Among other things, the law allowed *comuna* members to elect a *cabildo* in order to manage local affairs, and to hold property collectively. But at the same time, a *comuna* was linked to the local administration of the *parroquia* and the *teniente político*, through whom the central state anticipated and increased its influence.

As Becker (1999), Clark (2007), and others observe, a lot of "free" indigenous communities indeed recognized that registering themselves as *comunas* would in fact undermine their autonomy.[7] That is why many of them rejected the opportunity this law offered. However, a small number of such communities obtained the status of *comuna*. And, although the Ley de Comunas only applied to "free" indigenous communities, but not to those formally linked to haciendas, the latter tried to make use of this law as well. These communities sought to achieve a status which offered them more autonomy. Some communities succeeded in this endeavor (see for example Clark 2007), but most

6   Estatuto Jurídico de las Comunidades Campesinas.
7   "Free" indigenous communities is a term that is often used for those Andean communities that were not formally bound to a hacienda.

did not. As will be shown in the next chapter, the indigenous workers at the hacienda of Zumbahua, the region which is the focus of this book, provide an example of a hacienda that tried to obtain the status of *comuna*, but failed to do so.

Although the Ley de Comunas provided new legal possibilities for rural indigenous communities, the full opportunities offered by this law were not realized until the 1964 and 1973 land reforms, which weakened the power of the holy trinity and thus increased the possibilities for local autonomy. During the 1940s and 1950s, relatively little had changed in the Andean highlands of Ecuador. Most haciendas remained intact, and so did their traditional and obligatory rural labor arrangements like *huasipungo* and the *yanapo* system.[8] In other words, rural life in those years was dominated by haciendas, within which small titles had been granted to indigenous households, thus creating an internal small-scale agriculture (*minifundio*) system (Waters 2007; Yashar 2005). Beginning in the 1950s, economic, political, and ideological conditions began to change in Ecuador (Waters 2007: 124–129). As a result of the development of an industrial sector and an import substitution policy, urbanization increased, which eventually affected the rural sector. In short, a system that had for many years been characterized by subsistence farming and an almost exclusively internal market was by the 1950s marching steadily toward modernization.

The 1964 Agrarian Reform Law was designed to eliminate ancient forms of labor relations and to revitalize the production process with more modern and productive farms.[9] The military regime at that time concluded that economic development required replacing the hacienda system. Consequently, this land reform abolished the *huasipungo* and *yanapo* system, and *huasipungueros* were to be granted (or sold) land in proportion to time served on the hacienda. Primarily, the 1964 Agrarian Reform Law promised civil rights by attempting to reorganize material and political power relations in the countryside (Waters 2007; Yashar 2005). After this agrarian reform legislation abolished the *huasipungo* system and gave some indigenous persons back their land, there was a virtual explosion in the number of *comunas* in certain areas (Becker 1999). For example, in 1972 the hacienda of Zumbahua was abolished and the *parroquia* of Zumbahua was established.

The 1973 land reform provided more social rights for rural inhabitants (Yashar 2005: 91–92). With social programs (land redistribution, rural development, schooling, etc.) General Guillermo Rodríguez Lara's government

8 *Huasipungo* is a system of land–labor exchange. The tenant farmers (*huasipungueros*) lived and worked on the hacienda in exchange for small subsistence plots (*huasipungos*). They did the yearly routine jobs. The *yanapo* system concerned workers (*yanapos*) who lived in neighboring "free" communities, and who did the seasonal jobs. *Huasipungueros* and *yanapos* were not the only ones working on a hacienda. They were accompanied by for example *arrimados, peones, empleados,* and *arrendatorios* (de Zaldívar 2012: 41, note 13).
9 Ley de Reforma Agraria y Colonización.

increased the state's presence in the local communities on the one hand, and instituted a more serious form of land redistribution on the other. Although the land reforms were often criticized for not going far enough (Baud 2009: 30), they had a significant impact, especially in the Andean highlands. The fact that only organized and officially recognized indigenous communities could benefit from the programs resulted in an increase in the number of *comunas*. The land reforms provided these communities secure land titles, increased their access to the state, and marked the end of the holy trinity that had for all intents and purposes governed them. However, the state soon backed away from the social rights provisions that it promised, leaving a poor rural indigenous population struggling for survival on their small plots of land. In the end, the state had promised more than it could actually deliver (Yashar 2005: 95–98).

Thus, the 1964 and 1973 land reforms led to large-scale organization of rural indigenous people in accordance with the community model that had been introduced in 1937. The corporatist land reforms granted them new social and civil rights. However, although this meant that they attained formally equal status, they in fact continued to be denied equal access to state, resources, and land. The land reforms, combined with the state's continuing weak control over the countryside, also created a space in which indigenous communities could secure more local autonomy in order to sustain and strengthen customary law (Lyons 2001: 24; Yashar 2005: 95). Korovkin (2001: 51–52) points to an increasing use of customary law in the case of internal conflicts by both *cabildos* and *asambleas generales*. Nevertheless, the twentieth century's integrationist model supported juridical monism, thus limiting any official recognition of legal pluralism. As a result, rural indigenous people remained in a subordinate position.

Constitutional changes in 1998

Thus, during the "long nineteenth century," as well as during most of the twentieth century, the situation of real legal pluralism remained unchanged. What can be called a certain political indifference towards the countryside until the end of the nineteenth century changed in some respects during the twentieth century. However, legal pluralism did not become part of the political agenda until the end of the twentieth century. For centuries, the Spanish Crown and subsequently the independent state exercised a limited degree of control in the countryside, while never having a direct impact on the use of customary law. In 1998 however, the Ecuadorian state constitutionally recognized legal pluralism. This raises the question as to why the state chose to do so.

One explanation can be found in the state itself. At the end of the twentieth century, it became clear that the relatively weak control of the Ecuadorian state over the countryside, in combination with the politically and legally subordinated position of rural indigenous people, had become a problem. Some scholars, like Van Cott (2000), have convincingly shown that the

Ecuadorian state was overly centralized and inefficient. Additionally, judiciaries throughout the nation were weak and politically compromised. Dealing with this weakness has thus been one of the principal challenges of the nation. The solution was found in a decentralization policy. Administrative decentralization was also encouraged by international development agencies like the World Bank. Neoliberals saw it as a strategy to reduce the role of the public sector and to enhance civil society (Wilson 2008). Others viewed decentralization as a strategy for democratization that would contribute to the empowerment of the disenfranchised (Assies 2000b: 10). The formal recognition of legal pluralism in Ecuador has to be seen in the light of this decentralization policy (Simon Thomas 2012).

Another explanation can be found in the emergence of the national indigenous movement CONAIE onto the political stage. Although CONAIE initially focused on socioeconomic issues, it eventually shifted its focus "from peasant struggles to Indian resistance," and recognition of *de facto* autonomy of the rural indigenous population (and subsequently of their customary law) became one of its most important demands in the 1990s. What should be kept in mind in this context are two external factors that emboldened CONAIE. First, constitutional reform processes took place in several countries in Latin America during the last fifteen years of the twentieth century, and these countries also recognized – at least in principle – the multicultural nature of the region. Developments in Ecuador were part of this larger pattern. Second, important international jurisprudence had developed, which increasingly characterized the rights of indigenous peoples as human rights. In this respect, ILO Convention 169 is considered the most important international instrument. The Draft United Nations Declaration on the Rights of Indigenous Peoples is also important in this connection.[10] Before continuing to discuss the constitutional changes, a brief discussion of Ecuador's recent politics in relation to CONAIE will facilitate a better understanding of these changes.

CONAIE

CONAIE's history, achievements, and relationship to the state, as well as the influence of leftist political parties, unions, and the Catholic church, and a comparison of the resulting dynamic to similar indigenous movements in the region, has been thoroughly described by many others, including Andolina (2003), Brysk (2000), Korovkin (2001), Pallares (2002), Selverston-Scher (2001), Van Cott (2005), and Yashar (2005). In line with the scope of the present study, this chapter is therefore limited to a broad overview of this national indigenous movement's emergence within a strictly Ecuadorian context, emphasizing its present impact, with brief digressions on its specific role with regard to legal pluralism.

---

10 At that time, the United Nations Declaration on the Rights of Indigenous Peoples (UNDRIP), which was adopted by the United Nations General Assembly in 2007, was still a draft.

With regard to the emergence of Ecuador's indigenous movements, an appropriate point of departure can be found in the first half of the twentieth century. Although there were sporadic instances of rural indigenous people rebelling against hacienda owners and other local power holders since the time of the Spanish conquest, the first attempt by indigenous people to conduct an organized protest occurred on a Cayambe hacienda in 1926 (Van Cott 2005: 102–103). In the mid-1940s, Andean peasants organized as rural workers in a network of unions, the FEI.[11] This federation's *raison d'être* can be found in the discrepancy between the state's promises of modern rural relations (as enshrined, for example, in the 1937 Ley de Comunas) and the daily reality of feudalistic relations between hacienda administrators and their workers. It has been emphasized that the FEI was led by mostly non-indigenous people, although some local indigenous leaders also participated in its founding.[12] Nevertheless, the founding of the organization constitutes an important milestone, because it marked the very first time that indigenous communities were linked on a national level, and it thus served as a basis for future organizing in the 1960s and 1970s.

Drawing on pre-existing rural organizations whose intended aim was to secure land rights and equal treatment of all peasants (an unfulfilled promise of the 1964 land reforms) the Andean ECUARUNARI was founded in 1972.[13] During the 1960s, more and more peasants began to organize in the countryside, for example in FEI or later in FENOC.[14] Initially, their demands had emerged as isolated grievances of, for example, recently formed *comunas* that had been denied equal access to resources. This eventually scaled up to provincial organizations, which in turn played a leading role in uniting rural indigenous inhabitants of the Ecuadorian Andes by founding the ECUARUNARI. From the start, this federation's agenda was dominated by land reform struggles and other class-based debates. However in the 1980s more ethnicity-based issues, like the right to bi-lingual education, gained importance. This was one factor that led ECUARUNARI into close collaboration with its Amazonian counterpart.

Just like ECUARUNARI, CONFENAIE in the Amazon emerged for the purpose of defending local autonomy and demanding equal rights of inclusion.[15] However, the latter organization arose within a different historical context. Life in the Andean highlands had been dominated by haciendas and other

---

11 FEI: Federación Ecuatoriana de Indios (Federation of Ecuadorian Indians).
12 For example, Agustín Vega from the Tigua hacienda (Becker 2007: 177); see also Chapter 7 of this book.
13 ECUARUNARI: "Ecuador Runacunapac Riccharimui" Confederación de los Pueblos de Nacionalidad Kichwa del Ecuador ("Awakening of the Ecuadorian Indian" Confederation of the People of the Kichwa Nationality).
14 FENOC: Federación Nacional de Organizaciones Campesinas (National Federation of Peasant Organizations).
15 CONFENAIE: Confederación de Nacionalidades Indígenas de la Amazonia Ecuatoriana (Confederation of the Ecuadorian Amazon).

power holders, while the state actively sought to incorporate and control indigenous communities. The indigenous people living in the Amazon, on the other hand, had enjoyed far greater autonomy for centuries. Yet this changed radically in the mid-twentieth century. Because of an increasing demand for natural resources (like oil) and concomitant state interference, as well as state-encouraged rural migration from the Andes to the Amazon in order to relieve pressures for land reform in the highlands, the Amazon Indians began to experience a high degree of state control in the 1960s. These changes forced them to organize. At first, Amazonian Indians only organized politically at a local level (for example, into organizations like FOIN and OPIP).[16] But in 1980, CONFENAIE came into being as a regional federation.

Ultimately, with its origin in these two different regional organizations, CONAIE was founded in 1986. After spending several years working out common positions on controversial issues, ECUARUNARI and CONFENAIE, now united in CONAIE, decided that they represented nationalities, each with their own language, history, and worldview, and that they were living in a country that should recognize its multinational character. According to its website,[17] CONAIE's main objectives are to consolidate the indigenous nationalities and other groups in Ecuador; to fight for land, education, cultural identity, and dignity; and to combat the oppression of the state, the church, and colonialism.

One of the reasons why CONAIE eventually became an influential political player was that its regional organizations have traditionally maintained strong ties with their provincial and local branches (Mijeski & Beck 2011).[18] A good example of such a branch of CONAIE is MICC in the province Cotopaxi. The OTG MICC was established in Latacunga in 1978, and it currently has more than twenty local departments.[19] With regard to its size and organization, MICC is comparable to its sister organizations FICI (in the province of Imbabura) and MICH (in the province of Chimborazo).[20] Such OTGs

16 FOIN: Federación de Organizaciones Indígenas del Napo (Federation of Indigenous Napo Organizations); OPIP: Organización de Pueblos Indígenas de Pastaza (Organization of the Indigenous Pastaza Peoples).
17 See: http://www.conaie.org/sobre-nosotros/que-es-la-conaie (accessed September 6, 2012).
18 Administratively, CONAIE is modeled on the country's political organization, while remaining faithful to its cultural roots. Culturally, the indigenous population is divided into *nacionalidades, pueblos,* and *comunidades.* For example, the La Cocha *comunidad* in the parish of Zumbahua belongs to the Panzaleos *pueblo*, which in turn belongs to the Andean Kichwa nationality. Similarly, such communities within a parish or canton are administratively organized in OSGs (for example, UNOCIC in La Cocha, or the UNOCAT in Tigua), which form a part of larger OTGs on a provincial level (for example, MICC in Cotopaxi). The Andean OTGs are organized within the regional ECUARUNARI, which is in turn part of the national CONAIE (Almeida et al. 2005: 45; Ilaquiche 2001a: 111–112; Tibán 2001b: 51).
19 Website MICC: http://micc.nativeweb.org/ (accessed September 11, 2012).
20 FICI: Federación Indígena y Campesino de Imbabura (Indigenous and Peasant Federation of Imbabura); MICH: Movimiento Indígena de Chimborazo (Indigenous Movement of Chimborazo).

serve a double function. On the one hand, they are the eyes and ears for ECUARUNARI and CONAIE and, as a consequence, they are able to influence national indigenous policy. On the other hand, they serve to translate and execute top-down orders at a local level. MICC is considered to be one of the most representative and loyal branches of CONAIE (Colvin 2004; Martínez Novo 2004: 237),[21] mainly because it has firm ties with its local OSGs,[22] and also because prominent indigenous leaders have emerged from its ranks. These include Cesar Umajinga (prefect of the Cotopaxi province), Lourdes Tibán, and Raúl Ilaquiche. Consequently, MICC's influence is far reaching.[23]

With the emergence of CONAIE, the indigenous struggle for equal rights began in earnest. Despite political promises, by the end of the 1980s practically nothing had changed. As a result, CONAIE staged a series of high-profile protests. What began with hunger strikes and peaceful marches culminated in June 1990 in a "National Indian Uprising" that involved ten days of street protests,[24] the occupation of churches, and strategic roadblocks. And again, contrary to promises made by the national government in reaction to that protest, nothing really changed in favor of the indigenous people. That is why, in April 1992, during the year marking the 500th anniversary of the arrival of Columbus in the Americas, a two-week protest march of thousands of indigenous activists from both the Amazon and the highlands to Quito was undertaken.[25] As stated by Yashar (2005: 147), in these years, CONAIE showed its power of mobilization. In 1994, it demonstrated its negotiating power by influencing the final text of a new law on agrarian reform.

After years of protest, CONAIE entered national politics in 1996, and its appearance on the political scene was instrumental in the promulgation of a new Constitution in 1998. CONAIE entered an alliance with the MUPP, or Pachakutik Party.[26] CONAIE had advocated the holding of a constitutional assembly as early as 1994. With Pachakutik's eight seats in the National Congress (of which one seat was given to Luis Macas, former president of CONAIE), their chances of achieving this goal increased considerably. Its overall aim was a constitutional guarantee of the rights of indigenous people, plus the recognition of Ecuador as a multinational state. Such a Constituent Assembly was approved by referendum in 1997. In national elections in November of that same year, Pachakutik obtained seven out of seventy seats.

21 Colvin (2004: 23) pictures MICC as one of the most active and aggressive indigenous organizations in the country.
22 OSG: Organizacíon de Segundo Grado (Second-Degree Organization).
23 For example, its involvement in the La Cocha murder case of 2002, and in the La Cocha-Guantópolo murder case of 2010 (see Chapter 7).
24 This uprising was more than the "typical" peasant mobilization demanding land and credits. Its significance lay in the fact that it was the first *national* mobilization of indigenous people (Yashar 2005: 146).
25 See Whitten et al. (1997) for details of that protest march.
26 MUPP: Movimiento de Unidad Plurinacional Pachakutik (Pachakutik Movement for Multinational Unity).

By May 1998, the Assembly had drafted a new constitution. The demand for a multinational state, however, was not complied with, and they had to settle for the terms "multicultural and multi-ethnic." But they did achieve recognition of several collective rights that effectively constituted their vision of multiculturalism. In the new constitution of August 10, 1998, among the recognition of other collective rights, customary law was formally recognized.

In spite of an impressive first showing of Pachakutik, the following years witnessed a decline in electoral support for CONAIE. In 2002, the party regained a certain prominence as a result of its alliance with Colonel Lucio Gutiérrez. As mentioned before, two indigenous leaders, Nina Pacari and Luis Macas, briefly served in the cabinet of President Gutiérrez in 2003. But soon, the cooperation became strained and the ministers linked to CONAIE ended up resigning, leaving CONAIE in a weakened position (Mijeski & Beck 2011: 130). What followed was a continuing electoral decline. A reason for this could be found in CONAIE's excessive focus on expanding its political space, rather than prioritizing the needs of the local indigenous communities. The October 2006 elections showed that voter support for the organization had virtually disappeared. This is not to say that it ceased to have any political role at that point. However, the above-described course of events clearly shows not only the vulnerability of indigenous agendas, but also the problems of indigenous parties which are not yet fully developed (Baud 2009: 32).

CONAIE received a new lease on life in 2006. The leftist, or post-neoliberal Rafael Correa had won the presidential elections. CONAIE provided what could be called a moderate level of support for Correa during his campaign. As a result, Correa embraced several of CONAIE's proposals, including calling for the election of a new Constituent Assembly shortly after he took office in 2007. The subsequent elections in September of that same year resulted in Pachakutik winning only four out of a total of 130 seats. Despite this disappointment, CONAIE managed to secure the implementation of some important items of its agenda. For example, one of its longstanding demands for constitutional recognition of the multinational character of Ecuador was finally achieved in the 2008 Montecristi Constitution. So was their appeal to secure official status for the Kichwa language. Additionally, several references to *sumac kawsay* (Kichwa for "a better life") were made in the Montecristi Constitution. Promises with regard to water rights and other natural resources were also made, and the recognition of the use of customary law was once again affirmed.

It of course remains to be seen whether the Correa administration keeps its promises and implements the promised policies. In this context, the protests organized by CONAIE against a new mining law in September 2009, which led to violent clashes between indigenous demonstrators and the police, can be considered a bad omen. In response to these events, forums have been established in order to stimulate discussion between indigenous representatives and the government. This process failed as a result of the withdrawal of the indigenous representatives from the process. In March 2010, the mining law was upheld by the Constitutional Court.[27] President Correa's water privatization plans, which led to nationwide protests in 2010, also provided no grounds for hope. One of these protests resulted in forty injuries and the death of an indigenous leader (*El Comercio* 2009). These events seem to show that President Correa is turning his back on his promises to safeguard indigenous rights. Similarly discouraging have been Correa's blunt statements regarding the use of customary law.[28] This turn of events has resulted in a rather tense relationship between CONAIE and the Correa administration (Becker 2011a; Mijeski & Beck 2011).

This fragile relationship also points to an often overlooked fact regarding CONAIE: that it lacks the internal coherence commonly attributed to it. To begin with, CONAIE, although often presented as such, is not the sole national indigenous movement (Lucero 2003: 32). It is said that CONAIE's local and regional affiliates represent 70 percent to 80 percent of the total indigenous population (Van Cott 2005: 108), and that its counterparts, FEINE and FENOCIN, represent the rest.[29] As previously pointed out, CONAIE has its roots in two different regional federations, and this is something that compromises its internal cohesion as well. As Selverston-Scher (2001: 125–126) has shown, any uniformly positive picture of CONAIE is thoroughly unrealistic. The organization is wracked by internal strife and by conflicts between "traditional" and "modern" practices which impede its development. Differences between the Andean and the Amazon indigenous groups constantly cause strain within the movement. And, as she adds, because the CONAIE leadership is focused on expanding its political space, it strategically does not always prioritize the needs of the local indigenous communities. In the words of Baud (2009: 35), political success "also widened the gap between the leadership and the grass roots." It is clear that CONAIE has suffered a certain fragmentation and loss of its potential strength in recent years (de Zaldívar 2012: 16). Part of this dynamic has involved the emergence of internal differences of opinion within the organization. As will become clear in the discussion of the La Cocha-Guantópolo murder case in Chapter 8, one such difference of opinion concerns the issue of the proper jurisdiction to be granted indigenous authorities for the administration of customary law. Although the point of view of CONAIE, their regional federations, and their

---

27 See Ecuadorian Constitutional Court ruling 001–10-SIN-CC, March 18, 2010, http://ecuador.justia.com/nacionales/resoluciones/resolucion-que-conoce-e-inicia-el-proce dimiento-dispuesto-por-la-corte-constitucional-mediante-sentencia-no-001–10-sin-c c-emitida-el-18-de-marzo-de-2010-y-publicada-en-el-suplemento-del-ro-no-176- de-21-de-abril-de-2010/gdoc/ (accessed September 12, 2012).
28 See Chapter 8 (the *Todo es político* section), where President Correa – among other things – calls customary law "monstrous" (El Vistazo 2010).
29 FEINE: Consejo de Pueblos y Organizaciones Indígenas Evangélicas del Ecuador (Ecuadorian Federation of Evangelical Churches); FENOCIN: Confederación Nacional de Organizaciones Campesinas, Indígenas y Negras (National Federation of Peasant, Indigenous, and Black Organizations).

provincial branches seems to be clear and unanimous, at a grass-roots level, some internal differences emerged in that specific case.

The Constitution of 1998

In terms of the multicultural character of the state, articles 1, 83, and 84 in the Constitution of 1998 are particularly noteworthy. In article 1, Ecuador is defined as a *"pluricultural y multiétnico"* ("multicultural and multi-ethnic") state. Although CONAIE unsuccessfully advocated the nation being characterized as *"plurinacional,"* the definition of Ecuador as "multicultural" in nature can be considered an important break with the past. Article 83 introduces the indigenous population as (self-defined) "nationalities," and article 84 promises a preservation and further development of some sort of indigenous autonomy in section 7, as part of a broader recognition and guarantee of several group rights.[30] Additionally, article 191, section 4, is of interest to this book, because it specifically concerns the use of customary law:

> Article 191 (4). The authorities of the indigenous peoples shall exercise the functions of justice [and] apply their own norms and procedures for the solution of internal conflicts, in accordance with their customs or customary law, as long as these latter are not contrary to the Constitution and the laws. The law shall make such functions compatible with the national system [translation: Yrigoyen Fajardo (2000: 220)].[31]

This constitutional recognition of customary law is an essential amendment vis-à-vis the former tradition of legal monism combined with real legal pluralism. Despite the fact that this Ecuadorian constitution was passed a number of years after similar reforms in neighboring countries, its text is considered to be more progressive (Andolina 2003: 724). However, it is also vaguely formulated. For example, its subjects are "indigenous peoples," without specifying who exactly is – or is not – indigenous. The same could be said about the "authorities." Who gets to define who these authorities are? Is it the state, or the indigenous communities themselves? And then there is the troubling use of the term "internal conflicts." Does this refer to the territorial dimension (where?), to the personal dimension (who?), or to the material dimension (what?) of the conflicts?

---

30 See for the full text of the 1998 Constitution (both in Spanish and in English): http://pdba.georgetown.edu/constitutions/Ecuador/ecuador98.html (accessed December 11, 2012).
31 *Artículo 191 (4) Las autoridades de los pueblos indígenas ejercerán funciones de justicia, aplicando normas y procedimientos propios para la solución de conflictos internos de conformidad con sus costumbres o derecho consuetudinario, siempre que no sean contrarios a la Constitución y las leyes. La ley hará compatibles aquellas funciones con las del sistema judicial nacional.*

This hazy character of the constitutional text gives rise to debate over customary law's range. So does the restriction that these practices should not contradict the constitution or other legislation. In addition, international law requires that customary law not violate individual human rights (Yrigoyen Fajardo 2000: 209–214). Assies (2003: 171), in the context of his review of the Colombian Constitutional Court's doctrine on the scope of customary law, considered rightly that "the full application of all laws would reduce autonomy to mere rhetoric." If the formal recognition is taken seriously, one has to be receptive to customary law's fundamental differences in relation to national law. That is why the Colombian Constitutional Court refers to a "genuine intercultural consensus [that] exists regarding these rights" (Sánchez Botero 2000: 224).[32] It is an attractive idea that such is also the underlying reason why article 191, section 4 of the Ecuadorian constitution states that the law shall make these practices compatible with the national judicial system. However, contrary to this regulation, neither permissive law nor coordinating rules have been developed in the years following 1998.

At the same time that the new constitution was approved, Ecuador also ratified ILO Convention 169. This convention states that the rights of indigenous peoples (with the tell-tale final "s") to land and natural resources are essential to their material and cultural survival. In addition, it declares that indigenous peoples are entitled to exercise control over their own institutions, within the framework of the states in which they live. It also requires states to respect customary law as long as the latter does not violate human rights. Since Ecuador has a so-called monist legal tradition that dictates that ratified international law be incorporated into national law, ILO Convention 169 has the force of domestic law since its ratification in 1998. Nevertheless, the convention is not really accepted in practice, either by the government or by society. Reports of violation of the law by the state are limited, and indigenous organizations rarely apply it (García 2005: 167).

So, it seems as if the Ecuadorian state formally "endorsed" customary law for political reasons, while doing nothing to support it, and even tried in subtle ways to undermine it, either by not living up to the regulations of ILO Convention 169, or by not delivering what it promised in the constitution. Pursuant to the regulation in article 191 of the 1998 Constitution, which includes a call for a law that would make national law and customary law compatible, two serious initiatives have been taken. However, neither of these attempts to harmonize the two systems succeeded. The first was vetoed by President Gustavo Noboa in January 2003, and the second was declared unlawful by Congress that same month. Both of these initiatives will now be discussed.

32 The doctrine developed by the Colombian Constitutional Court provides an excellent example of the use of jurisprudence to modify existing law. Its case law "maximizes the autonomy of indigenous communities and respects [...] their ways of doing justice without embracing an unconditional cultural relativism" (Assies 2003: 179). See Assies (2003) and Sánchez Botero (2000) for a detailed discussion of the Colombian Constitutional Courts' verdicts.

Lack of coordinating rules

In September 1998, almost immediately after the new constitution became effective, CONAIE started a project that aimed at harmonizing differences within customary law, as well as between customary law and national law. The project's main purpose was to secure the application of the constitutional recognition of customary law. This project was approved by the Commission on Indigenous and Ethnic Affairs of the National Congress,[33] which at regular intervals was kept informed about its progress. During the project, CONAIE asked for and received assistance from several professionals and college graduates, indigenous as well as non-indigenous. Finally, this resulted in a bill called the Law Enabling the Exercise of the Collective Rights of Indigenous Peoples that,[34] when it was presented before the National Congress on November 14, 2001, enjoyed an extraordinary degree of political and social support. Subsequently, this bill was discussed on two occasions by the full Congress. Several amendments were included, and after lengthy negotiations among legal specialists of all parties, the National Congress decided to submit the final text to the president in late 2002. The rules for enacting legislation in effect at that time gave President Noboa the choice of either approving the bill's complete text, or exercising a full or partial veto (García 2005: 155).

After three weeks, on January 8, 2003, the president vetoed CONAIE's bill. He did so by just sending an official note to the National Congress. García (2005) provides a detailed critique with respect to this veto's content. Briefly, the president's arguments are not only inconsistent with the Constitution, but also clearly show his ethnocentrism. Because of Noboa's veto, further development of a multicultural and multi-ethnic state was dealt a severe setback. In practice, this meant the definite end of that bill, and with it the end of the most serious attempt so far to develop coordinating rules (García 2005: 155–159; García & Sandoval 2007: 49).

A second bill, the Law on Coordination and Distribution of Jurisdiction in the Administration of Justice,[35] has a similar history. This project also resulted from article 191, section 4 of the Constitution, was financed by the Fondo Derecho y Justicia and was supervised by ProJusticia and the World Bank. The developers, from the Universidad Simón Bolívar, had been assisted by indigenous organizations, legal scholars, judges, and high-ranking officials. A draft was published as well in *Justicia Indígena en el Ecuador* (Trujillo et al. 2001) and in *Justicia Indígena: Aportes para un debate* (Salgado Álvarez 2002).[36] This bill constituted a compromise between a legislative solution and the possibility

---

33 Comisión de Asuntos Indígenas y Otras Etnias.
34 Ley de Ejercicio de los Derechos Colectivos de los Pueblos Indígenas.
35 Ley de Compatibilización y de Distribución de Competencias en la Administración de Justicia.
36 Both studies discuss and comment on the draft bill. Both Assies (2003: 179–181) and Hoekema (2003: 213–216) commented on it after its final rejection.

for jurisprudence to be developed. In a way, it can be read as a wish list of what should constitute the ideal relationship between customary law and national law (Berk-Seligson 2006). The bill stated that it would be impossible to cope in advance with all potential internal conflicts between customary law and national law, or between customary law and human rights. That is why it argued for solutions on a case-by-case basis. Reflecting their close observation of the development of case law in the neighboring country of Colombia, they stated that, in general, constitutional restrictions should not be applied too strictly, because doing so would reduce the recognition of cultural diversity to mere rhetoric (Trujillo et al. 2001: 20–22).

On November 27, 2002, the final text of this second bill was presented to the National Congress. That same day, the chairman sent it on to the Special Committee on Civil and Penal Law,[37] which had a great deal of experience and knowledge on bills and amendments on public and penal law, but without these same skills in reference to customary law. Following a long delay, the bill was sent to the Committee on Indigenous and Ethnic Affairs (García 2005: 159). This latter committee approved the text. But by then, the Civil and Penal Law Committee had already formulated a list that contained thirty different criticisms of the bill, and therefore it declared the bill unlawful and dismissed any further discussion of it. Just as in the case of Noboa's veto of the previous bill, this second bill's treatment reflected the lack of legal space and political will to act in accordance with article 191, section 4, of the Constitution. Thus, legal monism prevailed over legal pluralism (García 2005: 155–156).

In essence, these two failures do not necessarily represent crushing defeats in terms of the process of making the two systems compatible. This is because rules defining customary law's proper place in a situation of formal legal pluralism do not have to result from legislation. Such rules could also be based on jurisprudence or social norms. However, no jurisprudence aimed at harmonizing rules has yet evolved in Ecuador. In the early years of the twenty-first century, several potentially relevant cases were ruled upon, among them the 2002 La Cocha murder. Yet these cases, while establishing important legal precedents in general terms, provided no harmonizing rules (García 2005; Simon Thomas 2009). Neither did two initiatives taken by FLACSO in cooperation with ProJusticia,[38] or another initiative undertaken by FLACSO to analyze the results of the implementation of ILO Convention 169 (García & Sandoval 2007; Simon Thomas 2009: 45–46). Thus, just as politicians failed to develop coordinating rules, so did jurists and scholars.

---

37 Comisión Especializada Permanente de lo Civil y Penal.
38 FLACSO: Facultad Latinoamericana de Ciencias Sociales (Sede Ecuador) (Latin American Faculty on Social Sciences [Ecuador Office]). Nevertheless, these initiatives have resulted in two interesting legal ethnographies on customary law (García 2002; Chávez & García 2004).

The Montecristi Constitution

Since the Constitution of 1998 was ratified under the Jamil Mahuad administration, five different presidents have held office in Ecuador, each with a slightly different agenda regarding indigenous people. Although President Mahuad initially placed a high priority on the concerns of indigenous people and established CODENPE (Lucero 2007: 218), the nation's economic problems at the end of the twentieth century consumed his energies for most of the sixteen months he held office. His proposed measures to deal with the dramatic economic situation met with strong opposition, and subsequent massive protests in 1998 and 1999 (in which CONAIE played an important role) forced him to resign in January 2000. CONAIE, together with the military led by Colonel Lucio Gutiérrez and the jurist Carlos Solórzano, formed the "national salvation junta," which was soon replaced by Mahuad's vice-president, Noboa. Concessions to the broad indigenous program were few (Jameson 2011), as illustrated by the way Noboa vetoed the bill called the Law Enabling the Exercise of the Collective Rights of Indigenous Peoples.

Gutiérrez won elections held at the end of 2002, once again in alliance with CONAIE and the military. In January 2003 he was installed as president, and he named two indigenous persons to important cabinet posts: Nina Pacari (foreign minister) and Luís Macas (minister of agriculture). But at the same time, Gutiérrez had, without consulting his indigenous partners, agreed on economic measures in consultation with the IMF that had an especially dire impact on the nation's indigenous population. As a result, the cooperation with Pachakutik and CONAIE came to an end. Pacari and Macas resigned, and the indigenous movement was once again in the opposition. In April 2005, Gutiérrez was replaced by Alfredo Palacio. Although the indigenous movement was still fragmented after its ill-fated political adventure, the Palacio administration provided them some new opportunities. The young minister of economy, Rafael Correa seemed to be particularly supportive of earlier positions that had been taken by the indigenous movement, and he positioned himself as a critic of neoliberal policies. Correa was forced to resign in August 2005, but his brief stint as a cabinet minister eventually catapulted him to the presidency in January 2007 (Jameson 2011; Lucero 2007).

Correa proposed holding elections for a constitutional assembly as soon as he took office. His proposal won a massive 82 percent "yes" vote, and in September 2007 his *Alianza PAÍS* obtained eighty of the 130 seats in the constitutional assembly,[39] which eventually drafted the Montecristi Constitution of 2008.[40] Correa's preferred tactic of holding referenda on key national issues seems to have been effective in enacting reforms. However, given his

---

[39] Alianza PAÍS: Patria Altiva y Soberana (Alliance for Proud and Sovereign Nation)

[40] See for the full text of the Montecristi Constitution (both in Spanish and in English): http://pdba.georgetown.edu/constitutions/ecuador/ecuador.html (accessed December 11, 2012).

mixed record on indigenous affairs during his five-and-a-half years in office (as of the date of this writing), it remains to be seen if he will be able to create enduring transformations – or, indeed, if he even has the will do to so (Conaghan 2008; Kennemore & Weeks 2011).

Correa's relationship with the indigenous movements has steadily deteriorated (Becker 2011a; Mijeski & Beck 2011). The window of opportunity to expand indigenous rights that seemed to have opened in the first months of his presidency has apparently closed. As will be shown in Chapter 7 on the La Cocha-Guantópolo murder case, this became clear in the most recent round of discussions on the personal, territorial, and material applicability of customary law. President Correa clearly showed that he is not a supporter of extending the juridical autonomy of indigenous authorities.

The new Constitution of 2008 not only recognized Ecuador as an "intercultural and multinational" country in article 1, but also reaffirmed the situation of formal legal pluralism in the nation. In article 57, indigenous communities are guaranteed several collective rights, such as the right "to keep and develop their own forms of peaceful coexistence and social organization, and to create and exercise authority in their legally recognized territories and ancestrally owned community lands" (section 9), and "to create, develop, apply and practice their own legal system or common law" (section 10).[41] Additionally, article 167, which is about the power to administer justice by "other bodies [...] provided for by the Constitution," paves the way for article 171, which is specifically about the recognition of legal pluralism.[42]

> Article 171. The authorities of the indigenous communities, peoples, and nations shall perform jurisdictional duties, on the basis of their ancestral traditions and their own system of law, within their own territories, with a guarantee for the participation of, and decision-making by, women. The authorities shall apply their own standards and procedures for the settlement of internal disputes, as long as said procedures are not contrary to the Constitution, or to human rights enshrined in international instruments.
>
> The State shall guarantee that the decisions of indigenous jurisdiction are observed by public institutions and authorities. These decisions shall be subject to the monitoring of their constitutionality. The law shall establish mechanisms for coordination and cooperation between indigenous jurisdiction and regular jurisdiction [translation: PDBA and author].[43]

---

41 Translations: Political Database of the Americas (PDBA).
42 It is Heading IV of the Montecristi Constitution that regulates the participation in and organization of public power, and its fourth chapter concerns judiciary and customary law (Función Judicial y Justicia Indígena), differentiating between ordinary justice (*justicia ordinaria*) and customary law. Only article 171 is dedicated to the use of customary law by indigenous authorities.
43 The original of article 171 reads as follows: *Las autoridades de las comunidades, pueblos y nacionalidades indígenas ejercerán funciones jurisdiccionales, con base en sus tradiciones ancestrales y su derecho propio, dentro de su ámbito territorial, con*

In line with article 171 of the Montecristi Constitution, two new laws that address customary law and legal pluralism were enacted in October 2009: the Organic Code on the Judiciary,[44] and the Law on Jurisdictional Guarantees and Constitutional Control.[45]

The two constitutions compared

If one takes the design of the new constitution as a starting point, then it seems as if this document assigns more weight to legal pluralism than its predecessor. Thus, while the 1998 Constitution only references customary law in a chapter on the judicial branch, the Montecristi Constitution includes an entire chapter on collective rights for communities, peoples, and nationalities (article 57), and also addresses indigenous rights in a chapter on the judicial branch (articles 167 and 171). In addition, the recognition of the right to apply customary law by indigenous authorities is confirmed in the Organic Code on the Judiciary in articles 7 and 17. The relationship between customary law and national law is also one of the subjects that the Organic Code on the Judiciary deals with in articles 343 and 344.[46] Thus, despite the fact that their formulations suffer from a certain vagueness, both the new

---

garantía de participación y decisión de las mujeres. Las autoridades aplicarán normas y procedimientos propios para la solución de sus conflictos internos, y que no sean contrarios a la Constitución y a los derechos humanos reconocidos en instrumentos internacionales. El Estado garantizará que las decisiones de la jurisdicción indígena sean respetadas por las instituciones y autoridades públicas. Dichas decisiones estarán sujetas al control de constitucionalidad. La ley establecerá los mecanismos de coordinación y cooperación entre la jurisdicción indígena y la jurisdicción ordinaria.

44 See: http://www.oas.org/juridico/MLA/sp/ecu/sp_ecu-int-text-cofj.pdf (accessed December 11, 2012). The Organic Code on the Judiciary (Código Orgánico de la Función Judicial) is about the structure of the judiciary, and the powers and functions of its jurisdictional, administrative, auxiliary, and autonomous bodies (article 2).

45 Ley Organica de Garantías Jurisdiccionales y Control Constitucional, see: http://www.oas.org/juridico/PDFs/mesicic4_ecu_org2.pdf (accessed December 11, 2012).

46 Article 343 reads as follows: *Las autoridades de las comunidades, pueblos y nacionalidades indígenas ejercerán funciones jurisdiccionales, con base en sus tradiciones ancestrales y su derecho propio o consuetudinario, dentro de su ámbito territorial, con garantía de participación y decisión de las mujeres. Las autoridades aplicarán normas y procedimientos propios para la solución de sus conflictos internos, y que no sean contrarios a la Constitución y a los derechos humanos reconocidos en instrumentos internacionales. No se podrá alegar derecho propio o consuetudinario para justificar o dejar de sancionar la violación de derechos de las mujeres.* (The authorities of indigenous peoples, communities, and nationalities exercise jurisdictional functions, based on their ancestral traditions and their own customary law, within their own territory, and with guarantees for participation and decision-making for women. The authorities shall implement their own rules and procedures to settle internal conflicts, and which are not contrary to the Constitution and internationally recognized human rights. Customary law may not be invoked to justify or fail to punish the violation of women's rights [author's translation]).

constitution and the accompanying code give greater weight to legal pluralism than the 1998 Constitution did.

Article 344 (c) of the Organic Code on the Judiciary, which constitutes an elaboration of the *ne bis in idem* principle ("double jeopardy" rule),[47] formulated in article 76 (section 7, letter i) of the Montecristi Constitution, deserves special mention. Although Ecuador had previously recognized the right not to be subjected to a new trial for the same alleged crime,[48] it had never been explicitly mentioned in relation to customary law in any previous constitution. With the verdict of Judge Carlos Poveda in the La Cocha murder case of 2002 in mind (Simon Thomas 2009),[49] articles 76 (section 7, letter i) of the Montecristi Constitution and 344 (c) of the Organic Code on the Judiciary can thus be seen as nothing less than watershed events.

The second new law related to the Montecristi Constitution, the Law on Jurisdictional Guarantees and Constitutional Control, provides citizens a series of legal guarantees for the purpose of ensuring the effective implementation of their constitutional rights. Of specific interest to the present study is the so-called "extraordinary action of protection" according to the decisions of indigenous authorities (see articles 65 and 66 of the Law on Jurisdictional Guarantees and Constitutional Control).[50] While according a maximum degree of autonomy to indigenous authorities, article 66 of this Law on Jurisdictional Guarantees and Constitutional Control also refers to some basic legal rules and procedures that such an authority is required to comply with. These include the right to have court decisions based on an intercultural interpretation of the conflict at hand (article 66, section 1), the right to due process (article 66, section 4), the right to an interpreter if necessary (article 66, section 5), and the right to ask for a second opinion on how customary law has been applied in a certain case by an expert (for example: a legal anthropologist). In addition, should any conflict regarding jurisdiction arise between indigenous and state authorities, the Law on Jurisdictional Guarantees and Constitutional

---

47 Article 344 is divided into five sections: a) *diversidad* (diversity), b) *igualdad* (equality), c) *non bis in idem* ("double jeopardy" rule), d) *pro jurisdicción indígena* (pro-indigenous jurisdiction), and e) *interpretación intercultural* (intercultural interpretation).

48 See for example article 8, section 4 of the American Convention on Human Rights (a treaty which was ratified by Ecuador on August 12, 1977); article 5 of the Código de Procedimiento Penal (Criminal Procedure Code) and article 24 (section 16) of the 1998 Constitution.

49 In the La Cocha murder case of 2002 (see Chapter 7) three indigenous persons suspected of homicide were initially tried by indigenous authorities before the individuals in question were also named, not long afterward, as suspects in a criminal investigation conducted by the public prosecutor in Latacunga. In the subsequent Criminal Court's verdict, Judge Carlos Poveda argued that, according to the "double jeopardy" rule, he was not competent to adjudicate this case a second time. Therefore he declared the public prosecutor's investigation invalid. However, upon appeal, the Court of Justice referred the case back to another judge, who finally did sentence the three individuals involved.

50 "*Acción extraordinaria de protección contra decisiones de la justicia indígena.*"

Control charges the Constitutional Court with the responsibility to settle such conflicts. Thus, the only institution that is competent to review indigenous authorities' (juridical) decisions is the Constitutional Court. Such an extraordinary protective action can be initiated by any individual who believes that his or her constitutional rights have been affected by an indigenous authorities' decision.

The Montecristi Constitution is in some respects, however, just as vague as its 1998 predecessor. For example, with respect to the territory where indigenous authorities are to hold jurisdiction, it mentions "[their] own territories" (article 171) and "their legally recognized territories and ancestrally owned community lands" (article 57, section 9), but fails to specifically define these territories. The same can be said regarding the material dimension of the recognition of legal pluralism, given that the Montecristi Constitution employs the question-begging phrase "internal disputes" (article 171), without further explanation. Third, there is vagueness as regards the identity of potential litigants who can have recourse to customary law, leaving unanswered not only whether only indigenous persons enjoy such a right, but also the fundamental question of what constitutes "an indigenous person."

Finally, echoing the 1998 document, the Montecristi Constitution calls in article 171 for the development of mechanisms (for example, additional law or jurisprudence) to be developed in order to allow for the co-existence of customary law and national law. However, no such harmonization has yet occurred – either through new law or new jurisprudence (García 2009a, 2010a).[51] In this legal as well as political process, President Correa's view of customary law should not be underestimated. He recently called customary law "monstrous" (*El Vistazo* 2010),[52] proclaimed on national television that customary law is subordinate to national law and declared that, in cases involving criminal acts, (indigenous) perpetrators should be tried by national courts (Caselli 2010).[53] In light of such a presidential declaration, the recently proposed Law of Coordination and Cooperation between Customary Law and National Law,[54] with which the next section deals, is of particular interest.

---

51 García (2010a) mentions seven cases of the Constitutional Court involving indigenous people, elaborating on just two of them: Caso 0027–009-AN, the indigenous university Amawtay Wasi vs. CONESUP (Consejo Nacional de Educación Superior – National Council for Higher Education of Ecuador), and Caso 008–09–11-IN / 0011–09-IN, CONAIE vs. the National Assembly because of a proposed mining law. These cases have provided interesting legal precedents in general terms, but have not led to the development of harmonizing rules.
52 "*Justicia indígena es una monstruosidad*" ("Customary law is monstrous"), said President Correa in an interview on May 26 for the magazine *El Vistazo*.
53 President Correa did so on May 22, 2010. He has also called the events "a degrading spectacle," and stated, "For God's sake, this is torture, this is barbaric."
54 Ley de Coordinación entre los sistemas de derecho indígena y el sistema de derecho ordinario.

70 *Legal pluralism in Ecuador*

Taking up the challenge of coordination

A governmental project to develop the coordinating law envisioned in article 171 of the Montecristi Constitution was launched in October 2008. Originally planned in three stages,[55] this effort, led by the Ministry of Justice and Human Rights and the Ministry of Cultural Heritage,[56] in cooperation with the United Nations, has only concluded its first phase. The political implications of the La Cocha-Guantópolo murder case in May 2010 led to a temporary shelving of the project that same year (García 2010b). It should be pointed out that the previously cited quotes of President Correa regarding customary law being "monstrous" and "barbaric" were uttered in the context of his reaction to the adjudication and sentencing of five suspects of that homicide by the indigenous authorities in La Cocha. In addition, Ecuador's Ministry of Justice and Human Rights probably thought it would be wise not to let this politically sensitive case frustrate the process of developing a coordinating law.

In reaction to this delay, Lourdes Tibán of the Pachakutik Party spearheaded an effort to draft such a coordination law. Their project was submitted to the National Assembly in February 2010,[57] and since then has been debated by the Special Committee on Justice and State Structure and other offices on a number of occasions.[58] The project was granted official status in January 2011, and eventually this led to a final report intended to serve as the basis for a first round of debate by the National Assembly of December 19, 2011.[59] This debate finally took place in May 2012, when the National Assembly reiterated the need for such a coordinating law, while also stating the advisability of both consulting indigenous communities themselves for their views on the subject, and of institutionalizing customary law and harmonization processes.[60] It is unclear how long this process of securing the enactment of a coordinating law will take but, given the fact that the extensive legislative

---

55 Phase one was meant to contain the writing of a concept bill, the second phase was to include consultation with regional and local indigenous movements, and the bill itself was to be introduced during phase three (García 2010b).
56 Ministerio de Justicia y Derechos Humanos and Ministerio Coordinador de Patrimonio Cultural.
57 It was submitted on February 1, 2010; Oficio No. AN-LTG-0043–10.
58 Comisión Especializada de Justicia y Estructura del Estado.
59 See Informe Para Primer Debate; http://clavero.derechosindigenas.org/wp-content/uploads/2011/10/ECUADOR-Informe-JusticiaInd%C3%ADgena.pdf (accessed August 30, 2012) for an earlier version of the draft law of July 27, 2011. The final version has been approved on December 19, 2011; Oficio No. 715-CEPJEE-P; see http://documentacion.Asambleanacional.gov.ec/alfresco/d/d/workspace/SpacesStore/7804fdcb-62d8-44b8-bd6a-1a861dbd9f0e/ Ley%20Org%C3% A1nica%20de%20Coor dinaci%C3%B3n%20y%20Cooperaci%C3%B3n%20 entre%20la%20Justicia%20Ind %C3%ADgena%20y%20la%20Justicia%20Ordinaria (accessed September 4, 2012).
60 See http://ecuadorinmediato.com/index.php?module=Noticias&func=news_user_view &id=173654&umt=proyecto_ley_organica_coordinacion_y_cooperacion_entre_justi cia_indigena_y_ordinaria_paso_primer_debate (accessed August 30, 2012).

procedure required for it to pass has only just begun,[61] it is my assumption that it will take at least two to three years.

An explanatory memorandum of the draft law was released to the public on December 19, 2011. The law itself consists of only eleven articles and four chapters. However, these are preceded by twenty-one pages of justification and explanation in the explanatory memorandum. For example, the memorandum indicates that the draft law is based on articles 1, 57, and 171 of the Montecristi Constitution. In addition, both the United Nations Declaration on the rights of Indigenous Peoples of 2007 and ILO Convention 169 are also cited. Additionally, references to scholarly literature are provided. Finally, the accompanying text provides a list of twenty-four cooperating ministries and other indigenous organizations who have worked together to edit the final text, in order to underscore its broad support. The main point of the explanatory memorandum, however, is an elaboration of the competences of indigenous authorities, which I have earlier called the material, territorial, and personal dimensions of the recognition of customary law.[62]

With regard to the material dimension, the memorandum explains that indigenous authorities are competent to settle any conflict that destabilizes the harmony of a given community.[63] The definition of an indigenous authority is prescribed in articles of the draft law. In order to be considered an authority, a person must have his or her roots in the community, and exercise a high degree of authority there. It does not mention anything about indigenous authorities' accountability, so the lawyer we met at the start of this book probably will not be satisfied with the draft law so far. Neither does the draft law limit the competence of indigenous authorities as regards either the type (that is, penal or civil) or severity of the case (that is, infractions or crimes).[64] Just like the Montecristi Constitution, the draft law uses the phrase "internal conflicts" without defining what these are, and then adds that such conflicts must take place within a "territory which is commonly inhabited by indigenous peoples."[65] The explanatory memorandum explains that this phrase was intended to be

---

61 See http://www.asambleanacional.gov.ec/tramite-de-las-leyes.html (accessed September 4, 2012) to get an idea of the legislative procedure of the National Assembly.
62 See also the explanatory memorandum of an earlier draft of July 27, 2011, http://clavero.derechosindigenas.org/wp-content/uploads/2011/10/ECUADOR-Informe-JusticiaInd%C3%ADgena.pdf (accessed August 30, 2012).
63 "*Todos los conflictos que atenten contra la armonía de la comuna, comunidad, pueblo o nacionalidad a la que pertenecen,*" article 5 of the Draft Law of Coordination and Cooperation between Customary Law and National Law of December 19, 2011.
64 In an earlier draft of July 27, 2001 some conflicts were excepted, including cases like genocide, those involving the internal or external security of the state, and those involving conflicts over paternity or alimony. In the final version of December 19, 2011, such exceptions are mentioned only in the explanatory memorandum.
65 "*espacio o area habitualmente ocupado por la comuna.*"

consistent with the jurisprudence of the Inter-American Court of Human Rights in not limiting the territorial definition to geography alone.[66] I will not be surprised if both the territorial and the material dimensions prove to be contentious issues in the upcoming debates regarding this proposed legislation.

A previous version of the draft law, dated July 27, 2011 refers to several examples of how to deal with the personal dimension (for example, if a conflict occurs between an indigenous person and a non-indigenous person, if one denies being an indigenous person, etc.). The final version of December 19, 2011 lacks such an elaboration. It only states in article 6 that any jurisdictional conflict that arises between an indigenous and state authority has to be resolved by the Constitutional Court, in accordance with article 144 (section 1) of the Law on Jurisdictional Guarantees and Constitutional Control. It seems to me that the draft law tries to avoid the trap of addressing the seemingly endless number of possible conflicts over jurisdiction,[67] instead leaving this matter to future case law. Finally, in article 11, the draft law prescribes that both customary law and national law embrace the reciprocity principle in order to coexist by, for example, providing assistance with regard to investigations, judgments, or execution of decisions.

Berk-Seligson (2006) characterized an earlier bill, the draft law on Coordination and Distribution of Jurisdiction in the Administration of Justice of 2002, as a "wish list." I myself would describe the draft law of 2011 as highly politicized. First of all, the initial process was put on hold by the Ministry of Justice after the indigenous assemblywoman Lourdes Tibán of the Pachakutik Party initiated this draft. Second, with regard to its content, while using almost the same vague terms as the constitution does regarding the subject of legal pluralism, it does not put any restrictions on its material and territorial dimension. In addition, possible conflicts over the personal dimension are left for the Constitutional Court to resolve. Given that this is just a draft written for the first round of debate, I can understand the strategy of "bidding high." However, such a gambit involves the risk that its advocates will not simply get less than what they ask for, but will be left entirely empty-handed. Moreover, as will become clear in the chapter on the La Cocha-Guantópolo murder case of 2010, this draft law must be seen in the context of recent controversial

66 The memorandum is referring here to the Inter-American Court of Human Rights of November 28, 2007 Case of the Saramaka People vs. Suriname: http://www.forestpeoples.org/sites/fpp/files/ publication/2010/09/surinameiachrsaramakajudgmentnov07eng.pdf (accessed September 5, 2012).
67 Petronilo Flores, in a presentation on the coordination and cooperation between national law and customary law at the VII Congreso Internacional Relaju (Red Latinoamericana de Antropología Jurídica) "Un reto para nuestras sociedades: Identidades, Interculturalidad, Pluralismo Jurídico y Derechos Colectivos," August 2–6, 2010, Lima, Peru, distinguished between 1) indigenous people and non-indigenous people, 2) within or without indigenous territory, and 3) affecting or not indigenous peoples' rights. He identified twelve possible different conflicts. I think that, with a little bit of creativity, one can easily generate additional possibilities. This is probably why the draft law was purposely worded in such vague terms.

indigenous trials. Taking all of this into consideration, and given the contemporary political context, I think it is fair to say that the approval of this draft law is far from assured.[68]

Conclusion

After five centuries of real legal pluralism, Ecuador finally recognized a situation of formal legal pluralism in the Constitution of 1998. As is the case elsewhere in Latin America, the constitutional changes in Ecuador have been considered progressive. In practice, this means that the use of customary law by indigenous authorities in cases involving internal conflicts has been broadly recognized in rather vague terms, but also that the coordinating rules needed to facilitate this right have not been developed. Additionally, Ecuador's innovative legislation on the recognition of legal pluralism is enforced very inconsistently by the judiciary. This did not change after 2008, when the Montecristi Constitution reaffirmed the recognition of formal legal pluralism and once again called for coordinating rules. Apart from a highly politicized draft law initiated by Lourdes Tibán, nothing has changed.

Thus, what actually has happened is that a *de facto* centuries' old practice received *de jure* recognition in 1998. This in itself can be considered a victory for indigenous peoples. However, because this formal recognition has not resulted in significant changes on the ground, its practical value is limited. The failure to devise coordinating rules has led to legal uncertainty for indigenous people regarding the use of customary law in cases involving internal conflicts, as well as increasing political tensions about this use. It should be recalled in this connection that the use of customary law in the countryside, albeit either formally restricted (during colonization) or even forbidden (during the era of legal monism), has informally been tolerated over the course of five centuries. Therefore, the use of customary law has always depended on the autonomy provided to local indigenous authorities by other power holders (that is, the Spanish, the *hacendado*, the *teniente político*, or the Church), and the actual scope of local sovereignty has thus always been

---

68 The question then becomes: what should a draft coordination law consist of to get approval? Or, in broader terms: what should an ideal coordination law look like? Trujillo et al. (2001) and Salgado Álvarez (2002) have already discussed and commented on the draft of the Law on Coordination and Distribution of Jurisdiction in the Administration of Justice of 2002. A similar analysis has been given here regarding the Tibán draft law. Although references have been made to the doctrine developed by the Colombian Constitutional Court (Assies 2003; Hoekema 2003), the *communis opinio* is that legislation should be developed (see also Simon Thomas 2009: 48–49 for an overview of such opinions). I doubt if this will be effective in practice (Simon Thomas 2009: 77). I agree with Díaz-Polanco (2009) that it is paradoxical to include something as flexible and profoundly local in nature as customary law within national, written law. I therefore do not think that developing a coordination law would prove viable. Instead, I am looking forward to a doctrine that will be developed by the Ecuadorian Constitutional Court.

legally uncertain. One might have expected all this to change after the use of customary law was constitutionally recognized. The next chapters in this book will show that this is not the case. Instead, the fact that the personal, territorial, and material scope of the situation of formal legal pluralism remains unclear to some extent leaves ordinary people at the mercy of local power holders. The question arises as to what effect all this will have on the ability of indigenous people to resolve their conflicts. Yet another important question that arises concerns the effect of recent constitutional changes on different kinds of conflicts and the role of authorities. The fact that such questions remain shows that recent developments cannot truly be said to constitute a major breakthrough in the struggle for legal recognition of customary law.

The legal and/or political solution for this undesirable situation continues to seem far off. As I see it, the Ecuadorian state formally endorsed the concept of customary law as part of its neoliberal doctrine and decentralization policy, while doing nothing to support it in practice, and the recognition of customary law also does not form an integral part of the political program of the leftist Correa administration. What all this means for indigenous people living in the parish of Zumbahua in daily practice will be illustrated and analyzed in the following chapters.

4 The parish of Zumbahua
Cohesion and conflict

Fiesta in Zumbahua – part I

It was still dark as we approached the house of the bride's family. We were warmly welcomed by about twenty to thirty people, among them a few young men who were so drunk that they could hardly stand up straight. That Sunday morning, Sergio, his sixteen-year-old son José, a couple of family members whom we had picked up on our way out of the village, and I had just arrived from Zumbahua. We had set out at 4:15 am and, after a ten-minute drive, Sergio showed me where to park my pickup truck on the side of the road. While I was trying to figure out exactly where we were, Sergio and his family members were already descending the slope just north of the road, down through the fields, and toward a small settlement which is part of a community called Guantópolo. A few roosters were crowing but, other than the lone lit house we were heading to, all the homes in the community were dark, and their inhabitants were all asleep.

I had been told that there was going to be a big party in Zumbahua. A couple of days before, Sergio had invited me to the wedding. He had also showed me an invitation to a baptism to be held on that same day, which (so Sergio explained) was a popular day for celebrations. I was excited about attending my first fiesta in Zumbahua as an "insider." My expectation that this was going to be a really big event had been confirmed once again the day before: the weekly Saturday market had ended slightly earlier than usual, and Plaza Rumiñahui, the main square in the center of Zumbahua, was cleaned somewhat more thoroughly than usual. After the plaza had been swept and the leftovers of market day removed, three platforms of scaffolding pipes and wooden boards were set up where bands would play the following day. But before the "public" party at the plaza started in the afternoon, on this Sunday morning people were preparing for their own ceremonies and celebrations at home and at the town's church. In order to not miss any of the upcoming events, we had to get up around 4:00 am. In addition, because of the crowded schedule, I had been asked to serve as a chauffeur for Sergio and his relatives (which I was certainly happy to do).

We were led into one of the two rooms of the brick house. Women were seated on the ground. José and another boy sat on a double bed (in which three small children were still asleep). The father of the bride sat on a chair, while Sergio and I were seated on a small wooden bench. Some other family members and godparents were seated in an adjoining room,[1] either on the ground or beside a second double bed. Everybody was decked out in their Sunday best. Some of the men were wearing striped red and blue – or solid red – ponchos made of thick wool, while others sported more Western-style clothes. The women wore colorful skirts and stockings that matched their beautiful blouses and shawls, and all had their hair tied back into a single braid. All of the men and women were wearing some form of headgear, whether a baseball cap (a few men and all the boys) or (in most instances) traditional Ecuadorian Andes hats.[2] As soon as everyone was seated, breakfast was served: a bowl of chicken soup, followed by a plate of noodles with some vegetables and a boiled egg. The few leftovers were carefully collected by some of the guests. While we were eating and chatting, the three small children I had seen sleeping in the bed when I arrived woke up – along with two other children and two teenagers hidden beneath the blankets – and suddenly jumped out of the bed. After they hastily gobbled up their food, we all left.

As dawn broke, I could now see some pigs and chickens scratching around, the lights of all of the nearby houses were on, and the drunk men outside, who all reeked of alcohol, were hanging on to one another to keep themselves from staggering or falling. All of us, about forty people now, started to climb the slope back to the main road, which ran from Latacunga to the Pacific Coast, through the parish of Zumbahua. As soon as we reached the car, those who had accompanied me and Sergio from the start decided to come with us, while the others, including the bride, continued walking to a nearby sector of the same community of Guantópolo. Because the main road meandered uphill with a lot of curves, and those who were walking had taken a straight line through the fields, we arrived at the neighboring settlement, where the groom's parents lived, at almost the same time. Although the young couple had been

1   Other than one's first-degree blood relatives, godparents are the most important persons connected to children in traditional Ecuadorian social organization (Simon Thomas 2009: 55). The children–parents–godparents triad can best be characterized as a kind of co-parenthood. Grandparents can also be godparents, but one could easily ask someone else to fulfill that function also. For example, any married couple that is economically solvent, and that has a close relationship with one or both of the birth parents, can be asked to be godparents. In the province of Cotopaxi, there have been godparents with over ninety godchildren (Naranjo 1996: 140–143; Tenesaca 1995: 296–298; Weismantel 1988: 53). Nowadays, foreign godparents (mainly from European countries or the United States) are increasingly common, because such individuals are assumed to be wealthy.
2   These were black, brown, and green fedoras decorated for this special occasion with a peacock feather. Colvin (2004: 68) shows, using paintings as evidence, that during hacienda times men, women, and children wore white, broad-brimmed hats. She argues (Bielenberg 1995 in Colvin 2004: 68, note 16) that, after the Agrarian Reforms in the 1960s, people wanted different clothing and therefore changed to fedora hats.

living together for a while in Quito, where they both worked, they had decided to marry in the parish where they both had been born, and where their parents still lived. I was told that the couple had decided to marry in a "traditional" way in Zumbahua mainly to comply with the wishes of the groom's father.

This tradition prescribes a formal meeting between the bride and groom's extended families (Bonaldi 2010: 97). So, when we arrived at the house of the groom's parents, our group of forty people was welcomed by an equally large group comprising the groom's extended family. This cordial welcome was accompanied by a hearty breakfast that featured vegetable soup, chicken, rice, and potatoes. And here too, I was embraced by a couple of drunk men. The reception was held outside the house, and the guests ate their meals while standing. Since I had already had breakfast less than one hour before, I only ate a bowl of soup, which I mainly used to warm my hands, which were chilled by a stiff morning wind as I enjoyed a beautiful view of the extensive *páramos* (natural high-altitude grasslands) of the parish. Meanwhile, within a courtyard between the adobe and brick buildings of the settlement, the parents of both the bride and groom were seated on a bench, while the couple themselves knelt before them after removing their headgear in order to receive parental counsel. Since I had grown accustomed to Andean people always wearing some kind of hat, seeing the couple without any head covering came as something of a surprise.[3]

After this, Sergio and I, together with some close relatives of the bride and groom, had the honor of being invited into the family's house. The couple had to get dressed for the ceremony, which required that the groom and his father and the bride and her mother wear matching clothes. These outfits were unpacked in front of the assembled guests. The bride and her mother both dressed in a black velvet skirt, grey stockings, black shoes, light-blue blouses, pink sweaters and green shawls. The female attendants present tied back the long black hair of each of the women into a single braid wrapped tightly in a pink, striped ribbon. These same attendants assisted both of them in putting on their various ornaments, and in outfitting them with identical new brown hats. The groom and his father were dressed in light blue shirts, dark blue sweaters, grey pants, black shoes, and black hats. After getting dressed, the four of them went back to the inner space where they were seated, accompanied by the two other parents at both ends of the bench. There, before the assembled guests, a traditional cleansing ritual was performed by a shaman in the indigenous language Kichwa. After these elements of the traditional marriage ceremony were completed, everybody hurried back to the road to be taken by car to the Catholic church of Zumbahua, where mass was scheduled to start some ten minutes later.

3   More than twenty years ago, Weismantel (1988: 7) described the older generation accusing the younger of being "naked" or "skinned" when the latter went out in public without a poncho and a hat. Wearing a poncho is not so common anymore, and not everybody wears a traditional Andean hat (some wear a baseball cap, or a round sailor's hat instead). But very few people in the Ecuadorian Andes wear no headgear at all.

Because we were in a hurry, and only a few cars were available to transport all the guests, I took as many people as possible with me. I managed to pack a total of eighteen people into my car (using the trunk as well), including the bride and the groom. As fast as I could with that many people on board, I drove back to Zumbahua, and arrived at the church on Plaza Rumiñahui just in time. The church was overflowing with people. During this special mass, three sacraments of the Church were performed. Ten children, ranging from one to six years old, were baptized. Since this mass was only going to last one hour, the ceremonies were hastily performed one after another. For the wedding ceremonies, the couples sat solemnly together, heads bowed, and after the priest recited the mass, a cloth cord was placed around the bride and groom's shoulders, symbolizing their spiritual union. For the baptismal ceremonies, the godparents were all asked to simultaneously step forward with their godchildren in order to present them at the font, before returning them to their biological mothers. The number of ceremonies made it clear why the town of Zumbahua was all abuzz. A foretaste of the fiesta was provided when, at 9:00 am sharp, the three newlywed couples and their families left the church, followed by the ten small children with their families. Rice and coins were thrown in the air, and several hired musicians performed. In the processions, each of the families celebrating a marriage, preceded by the band they had hired, walked back to their houses. Sergio and I decided to join the family we had been with earlier that morning. When we made our second visit to the groom's family (this time to give presents) I was offered my third bowl of soup that morning.

After consulting with Sergio, I had already decided what to give the newlyweds. Because Sergio indicated that they would likely be overloaded with liquor and trousseau, and because, like almost everybody else coming from this area, they were likely very poor, I decided to give them cash. This turned out to be a good choice. When I handed over a sealed envelope with the money inside, it was thankfully received by the bride, who quickly placed it in one of her inside pockets. And Sergio's expectations about the majority of the presents proved to be right too. I had never seen such a load of quilts, blankets, and other domestic utensils given a bride and groom. I had also never seen so much liquor being given to anyone. Beer, wine, and other alcohol would prove to play a major role during the festivities that afternoon – as it always did in celebrations in the Ecuadorian highlands, as I repeatedly discovered during the course of my fieldwork.

The above narrative is for the most part based on field notes I wrote on Sunday, August 28, 2010 (the day of the fiesta) and on the following days. It shows that society in Zumbahua is a "normal" society where people work, fall in love, marry, party, and most of the time just live their lives. On the other hand, the description of the wedding (and its fiesta, as will become clear later) raises several issues (for example, poverty, migration, alcohol) which underlie many of the internal conflicts this book is about. This chapter will provide some relevant background information on the history, the socio-political geography, and the – often conflictive – life in the parish.

Zumbahua has an important market on Saturdays. It also has a clinic, schools, a tourist site, and is located on a major road that connects the highlands with the coast. This means that Zumbahua is fairly well connected to its surrounding region. Still, many think of the town as a remote place.[4] It also has a long history of being a hacienda. In fact, Zumbahua has only been a parish for forty years. The fact that the town had functioned as a hacienda for more than three centuries means that there was a long-standing pattern of unequal power relations between those who owned the land and those who worked on it. This dynamic has led to the current existence of a large number of *minifundios* (Martínez Novo 2004: 245), which in turn can be seen as one of the causes of poverty and migration.

This chapter will, among other things, portray the difficulty of life in the rural parish of Zumbahua. The means of living there are simple, people are poor, and the physical and social infrastructure is minimal. Sometimes these features of life there serve to unite the inhabitants against outside forces (for example, the hacienda owners or the state). At other times, the difficult conditions cause residents of the parish to turn against one another. The main purpose of this chapter is to portray the delicate balance between cohesion and conflict that prevails among Zumbahuans. These two themes will be analyzed in this chapter's final section, using theoretical insights on community life from Colloredo-Mansfeld (2009a), Ouweneel (1993), and Radcliffe and Westwood (1996), while their transformation over time in the Zumbahuan context will be explored on the basis of research conducted by Becker (2007) and Weismantel (1988). The most important contribution of this chapter, however, is that it will serve as a prelude to both the next chapter on internal conflicts and their settlement, and to the three case studies that follow. These case studies will show the extent to which the scope of the conflict, the parties involved, and the arguments used have all changed as a result of recent changes in the socio-cultural life of the region within the national political context.

Zumbahua: past and present

The parish of Zumbahua is situated at 1° southern latitude, approximately between 3,450 and 4,400 meters above sea level,[5] at the west side of the west Andean ridge, the *Cordillera Occidental*, in Ecuador. From Latacunga, the province's capital, it takes two hours by bus to get to Zumbahua.[6] The bus takes the main road (the *Transversal Central*, E30) from Latacunga (at 2,750

---

4   Remote in the sense of how Radcliffe and Westwood (1996: 110) picture such places: "in a 'common-sense' way as backward, uneducated and poor, reliant upon help from outside."
5   Based on two topographical maps, obtained at the Instituto Geográfico-Militar del Ecuador in Quito: Mapa Pilaló (Pilaló) CT-ÑIII-E3c, 3891-III-SW, and Mapa Laguna de Quilotoa (Pilaló) CT-ÑIII-E3a, 3891-III-NW.
6   Although nowadays Latacunga is only two hours away by bus, Weismantel (1988: 48) notes that: "in living memory it was an arduous two-day trek, with a long, cold

meters above sea level) west to the lower-lying towns of La Maná and Quevedo. This road ends at the coastal towns of Portoviejo and Manta, and as such it is one of the few roads that links Ecuador's Pacific coast with the Sierra. Starting at Latacunga, the bus soon crosses the town of Pujilí (at 2,870 meters above sea level), which is the capital of the canton with the same name, and then it usually makes a short stop in Cuatro Esquinas, a suburb of Pujilí where most passengers take the opportunity to buy some bread at its regionally renowned bakery. Then the bus starts to meander uphill into the *páramos*.

At the beginning of the ascent, the slopes of the west Andean ridge look like a huge, green and grey patchwork quilt. In the lower areas, the small plots of land are divided by pathways, fences, or bushes. But as the bus proceeds still further uphill, one sees the fences change into hedges of agave, and once the bus reaches the highest altitudes, these hedges of agave suddenly become hedges of cactuses (in those cases in which there are any hedges at all). During the first half hour of the ride, one can see several houses or small settlements near the road, with all of the buildings made of concrete blocks. Once in the *páramos*, however, there are hardly any buildings left, other than a few scattered huts or barns (called *chaquiwasis* in Kichwa) built on the slope of a hillside. These *chaquiwasis* (meaning "small house" in Kichwa) are constructed of adobe and wood sticks, with a roof of *páramo* grass. One can also see a small settlement, but, for the most part, the area the bus is driving through looks uninhabited. One can easily spot ten times more llamas and donkeys along the road than human beings. However, taking into account the many times that the bus driver is asked to stop somewhere in the middle of nowhere to let people (usually with loads of belongings) get off the bus, the *páramos* can be safely said to be inhabited. Then, after about one hour and a half, first the bus passes Tigua Chimbacucho (at 4,100 meters above sea level, and home town of the well-known *art naïf* Tiguan painters) and then Guantópolo (at 3,700 meters above sea level), both *comunas* belonging to the parish of Zumbahua, before it finally reaches the village of Zumbahua.

Actually, most buses do not stop in the village of Zumbahua itself, because the center of the town is situated some hundred meters down the main road. Instead, the buses make a short stop at a small settlement known as El Campamento, located slightly farther uphill, near the road. These buses continue their journey to Piló, La Maná, Quevedo, and even further to the Pacific coast. Only those buses heading further north (to Quilotoa, Chugchilan, Sigchos, and then eastward, via Saquisilí back to Latacunga) stop in Zumbahua.[7] The settlement of El Campamento is far better equipped to handle the daily stream of trucks, buses, vans, and cars (and their passengers). It is a "traffic-stop" development of small shops, restaurants, a public bathroom, and a gasoline

night spent in the *páramos* of Tigua." The asphalted road through Zumbahua dates from 1946 (Jácome 2009: 335).
7 In a number of popular travel guides, this route is called the "Quilotoa loop."

station (which sells only diesel and regular unleaded gas, Extra).[8] Since the traffic mainly moves people and products between the Sierra and the coast, and to a lesser degree to and from the parish, the characterization of Weismantel (1988: 54) more than twenty years ago still holds true today: "[It] is not a road *to* Zumbahua, but a road *through* it."

History

What Zumbahua is today can be traced back to the beginning of the seventeenth century, when a hacienda was established. It is not known whether this area was inhabited in pre-colonial times (Weismantel 1988: 60). Jácome (2009: 15–17), however, refers to residents of the canton of Pujilí (of which the parish of Zumbahua nowadays forms a part) in earlier times, but since the town of Pujilí and its surroundings are situated in a significantly different ecological zone (at 2,870 meters above sea level) from that of Zumbahua (at 3,700 meters), I am inclined to agree with Weismantel's assumption that the latter area was for the most part uninhabited before the arrival of the Spanish colonists. It was with the introduction of herds of sheep that the highlands in general, and Zumbahua specifically, came into their own as important agricultural areas.

From the time of its founding in 1639, the hacienda of Zumbahua included peasants who worked the land. Like haciendas in general, the Zumbahua hacienda needed workers.[9] As a result, a new population settled where none had previously existed. Mainly, such workers were recruited from elsewhere. Thus, even though Zumbahua's contemporary image is that of a "traditional" indigenous community, its "very existence [...] may be an artifact of the colonial period" (Weismantel 1988: 62). One might even view it as the product of an early form of (economic) migration (see also Kyle 2000: 21–22). Depending on their size, such communities were called *comunidades, lugares,* or *departamentos*. In the 1700s the hacienda expanded until it bordered the

---

8 As is the case in most rural areas in Ecuador, premium unleaded gas, Super, is not available, indicating that it is mostly trucks, buses, and vans, rather than cars, that utilize the road.

9 Initially, when the Spaniards arrived in the Andes, they settled in already existing towns in the Inter-Andean Valley. But with the passage of time they moved up into the two *Cordilleras* to expand their business from trading to agriculture and stock breeding. Legally, they had to comply with rules that had granted *indios* certain land rights, so they were forced to establish their haciendas in the more remote areas. Haciendas obviously needed workers and it was these workers that formed the new settlement. Mainly, such workers were recruited from elsewhere. *Hacendados* were not able to give their workers a lot in cash, so they instead compensated them with small land titles (*huasipungo*), which were meant for their household subsistence. Most workers that came to a hacienda stayed there all their lives; mainly due to a inheritable debt system between a hacienda and its workers (*concertaje*). Workers residing on the hacienda did the yearly routine jobs, while the seasonal jobs were done by workers that were hired from neighboring "free" indigenous communities (*yanaperos*).

neighboring ones of Tigua and Chugchilán. However, some "free" communities, such as Apagua in the northwest (from which workers were hired to do seasonal jobs) survived into the twentieth century (Weismantel 1988: 62). After the Spaniards were ousted, during the years of the *República de Gran Colombia* (1819–1830), the parish of Zumbahua became part of the *departamento* of Quito. Neither the province of Cotopaxi, nor the canton of Pujilí, of which it nowadays forms a part, existed in the first half of the nineteenth century.

The province of Cotopaxi was founded in 1851,[10] and the hacienda of Zumbahua was recognized (being part of Pujilí, which had become a canton in 1852) as a civil parish in 1861. However, after a couple of years, Zumbahua lost this status and reverted to the category of an ecclesiastical parish (Jácome 2009: 45–46). In 1908, the government expropriated the hacienda of Zumbahua and officially transferred it to the Junta Central de Asistencia Pública.[11] Subsequently, this public body rented the hacienda out to landlords for eight-year periods. In turn, these landlords transferred their responsibilities to *mayordomos* and *mayorales* (that is, field foremen and supervisors respectively) (Becker 2007; Weismantel 1988; for a similar case, see Clark 2007: 97–99).[12] As indicated briefly in the previous chapter, the relationship between the hacienda and its communities could be characterized as unequal, one in which the hacienda was the more powerful party, but in which the communities were not entirely impotent. One way in which the community could exercise its power was by rebellion. Weismantel (1988: 69–71) discusses examples of such rebellion in the Zumbahuan parish in the twentieth century.

As shown in the previous chapter, another time-honored strategy of the peasants was to seek the intervention of higher state authorities to resolve problems they had with the hacienda. Becker (2007) describes conflicts between workers and the Zumbahua hacienda that arose during the 1930s and 1940s. These disputes were essentially about working conditions and payment. With the nearest *teniente político* in the parish of Pilaló, five hours away on horseback (Becker 2007: 162),[13] the indigenous workers on the hacienda managed to secure legal assistance from Gonzalo Oleas, a socialist lawyer based in

---

10 That same year, on October 9, it changed its name to Provincia de León, after Vicente León, a lawyer and philanthropist, who donated his fortune to education. Latacunga became the capital of this province – and nowadays its main plaza is still named after the lawyer. In 1938, the province changed its name back to Cotopaxi, in accordance with the Ecuadorian preference for giving provinces geographically relevant names (Jácome 2009: 45).

11 Junta Central de Asistencia Pública (Public Assistance Coordinating Body) is a government agency that administered state-owned haciendas (Becker 2007: 162; Becker 2011b: 243; Weismantel 1988: 65).

12 *Mayordomos* (field foremen) passed down the orders from the hacienda owner and/or his administrator to the *mayorales* and the workers, and organized the labor and workforce. *Mayorales* (supervisors), often *huasipungueros,* who enjoyed a certain elevated status, supervised the work in the fields (de Zaldívar 2012: 61).

13 Pilaló is situated 38 kilometers down the road to the West; nowadays it takes a bus ride of about an hour to get there.

Quito (Becker 2011b). With his support, they finally succeeded in having most of their demands met. They did so by resorting to national law. In one particular case in 1943, they even tried to get recognized as a *comuna* (on the basis of the Ley de Comunas), but that request was declined.

As a result of the land reform laws of 1964, the hacienda of Zumbahua was finally redistributed, and the land was divided among the workers. However, it was not until June 16, 1972 that Zumbahua regained its status as a civil parish (Jácome 2009: 66–67; Martínez Novo 2004; Weismantel 1988; 68–69). However, the transition from one large landowner into several individual landowners, and from one into several power holders, was certainly not peaceful. First, the actual disbanding of the hacienda must have been extremely violent. The exact sequence of events remains unclear (Martínez Novo 2004: 244; Weismantel 1988: 68), but it is known that the hacienda buildings were destroyed, as can be seen today in what is now called Parque Central Condor Cocha. Second, a number of internal tensions erupted within the community. Until the demise of the hacienda, La Cocha had been the most important community within it, comprising several *lugares* and *comunidades* (Weismantel 1988: 52). Given this powerful position, La Cocha also sought to acquire the status of civil parish in the early 1970s (Umajinga 1995: 255) (either superseding, or alongside, the parish of Zumbahua). This request was denied. As a consequence, a certain rivalry between La Cocha and its neighboring communities developed that, to a certain extent, can still be observed even today (Noroña Salcedo 2006; Weismantel 1988: 52). Finally, tensions have also emerged at the family level. This occurred because the process of land division appeared to have been somewhat unfair, or at any rate chaotic. One could say that the former local elite seized its opportunity to regain its power. By quickly buying up some properties, some former *mayordomos* and *mayorales*, or local *curacas*, proved to be savvier operators than the *huasipungueros* (that is, those who worked and lived on the hacienda) and *yanaperos* (that is, those who worked on the hacienda, but did not live on it). This resulted in an unequal division of land among the former hacienda workers (Noroña Salcedo 2006: 7; Umajinga 1995: 254; Weismantel 1988: 69). Conflicts over local power, as well as over land tenure, still exist today.

In 2007, Zumbahua became the center of national and international attention when, on January 14, the new president Rafael Correa was symbolically inaugurated by the indigenous population on the Plaza Rumiñahui (Martínez Novo 2014).[14] At the central plaza, President Correa was flanked by two of his counterparts: Evo Morales of Bolivia and Hugo Chávez of Venezuela,[15] both of whom arrived via the international airport of Latacunga. It was César Umajinga,

---

14 President Correa did not choose Zumbahua by chance. He lived in the parish for almost a year in 1986, when he did volunteer work as a teacher for the Salesian Order while he was a student at the Universidad Católica de Santiago de Guayaquil.
15 The Tiguan *art naïf* artist Alfredo Toaquiza portrayed the three presidents in a painting, which I saw available for purchase in 2010 at the art gallery in Tigua.

originally from Zumbahua (de Zaldívar 2012: 90, note 6), but now prefect of the province of Cotopaxi, and member of the Pachakutik Party, who handed Correa a *bastón de mando* (a ceremonial staff that symbolizes power over a group of people) to legitimize his authority.[16] There was also a Catholic mass, and some traditional cleansing rituals were performed. At this ceremony, President Correa told the indigenous crowd that he would never fail them (BBC News 2007; *El Comercio* 2007; Jácome 2009: 68; *El Universo* 2007). According to the CONAIE, in the end he did not keep this promise. That is why that organization symbolically revoked the granting of the *bastón de mando* at a gathering – again at the Plaza Rumiñahui in Zumbahua – on April 23, 2011 (*El Universo* 2011b).

Sociopolitical geography

Province, canton, and parish

The parish of Zumbahua is situated in the province of Cotopaxi. Based on the data of the census of 2010,[17] it has about 409,000 inhabitants, of which 23 percent identify as "indigenous." The province is named after the 5,897-meter high volcano of Cotopaxi, and is situated in the country's center. To the north of it lies the province of Pichincha: the political center of the nation, in which Quito – the capital of Ecuador – is located. South of Cotopaxi is the province of Tungurahua, with Ambato as its administrative center. Cotopaxi itself is a predominantly rural province. Its administrative capital Latacunga, situated on the Pan American Highway that connects Quito with the South, is somewhat smaller than many provincial capitals of the Sierra. Although it has an international airport, a central bus terminal, some commercial enterprises, and a market on Tuesdays and Saturdays, Latacunga is not as important a regional economic center as either Quito or Ambato. Weismantel (1988: 56) writes, "instead of acting as a market for goods and labor produced by rural areas in the province, […] Latacunga instead is dependent on its rural hinterlands as a market for the goods and services it can provide." As was shown in the previous chapter, Latacunga houses a Court of Justice with several (criminal) courts, the Fiscalía Provincial de Cotopaxi, the Fiscalía de Asuntos Indígenas de Cotopaxi, as well as dozens of small law offices.

Administratively, the province of Cotopaxi is divided into seven cantons.[18] The parish of Zumbahua falls within the jurisdiction of the Pujilí canton, with about 69,000 inhabitants (according to the census of 2010).[19] The capital

16 For video of the event, see http://www.youtube.com/watch?v=AWUv7RiJM3k (accessed July 25, 2012).
17 See: Resultados del Censo 2010 de población y vivienda en el Ecuador, Fascículo Provincial Cotopaxi, http://www.inec.gob.ec/cpv/descargables/fasciculos_provincia les/cotopaxi.pdf (accessed July 17, 2012).
18 Latacunga, La Maná, Pangua, Pujilí, Salcedo, Saquisilí, and Sigchos.
19 See: http://www.inec.gob.ec/cpv/?TB_iframe=true&height=450&width=800%20rel= slbox (accessed July 17, 2012).

of this canton, the town of Pujilí, lies about 12 kilometers to the west of Latacunga, located in the Inter-Andean Valley. The aforementioned important road from Latacunga to La Maná, Quevedo, and further to the Pacific Coast, runs through it. Along with other major canton-capitals in the Inter-Andean Valley, like Saquisilí and Salcedo, Pujilí is primarily a market town; the markets are held on Wednesdays and Sundays, so as not to conflict with the markets held in Latacunga. As one of the few canton-capitals in the province, Pujilí has a Civil Court.[20]

The canton of Pujilí is divided into seven parishes: Matriz, Angamarca, El Tingo (La Esperanza), Guangaje, La Victoria, Pilaló, and Zumbahua (which is the name of both the parish and its administrative seat, the latter popularly known as *el centro* (the center)). The parish of Zumbahua covers about 171 square kilometers, and is situated approximately 70 kilometers west of Latacunga. Because it is situated at an altitude between 3,400 and 4,100 meters above sea level, climate, depending on the season, is cold and dry (summer),[21] or chilly, gray, and rainy (winter). Spectacular views that comprise both peaks and valleys measuring several hundred meters are commonplace. Because of cultivation and erosion, almost no trees are left. The population of Zumbahua's parish is about 12,500,[22] of which the majority can be called *campesinos* (as explained earlier: small-scale agriculturalists). The most important crops of these small farmers are barley, potatoes, and beans. The most common livestock are sheep, llamas, and goats. The majority of the population considers themselves part of the Panzaleos people of the Kichwa nationality. Their mother tongue is Kichwa shimi, with Spanish being their second most spoken language (Simon Thomas 2009: 54).

Initially, in 1972, the parish had only two *comunas* (Zumbahua and La Cocha). Nowadays, the parish consists of eleven *comunas*, including Guantópolo, Ponce Quilotoa, and Tigua Chimbacucho, each of them governed by its own *cabildo*.[23] Just as Ecuadorian provinces are governed by *prefectos* (governors, or prefects), and cantons are governed by *jefes políticos* (political chiefs, or mayors), parishes are administered by Juntas Parroquiales, or parish boards. The institution of the Junta Parroquial was created by the Constitution of 1998,[24] and was actually put in place in 2000 (de Zaldívar 2012: 287, note 6; Jácome 2009: 68). Before this time, the *teniente político* played a more

---

20 Almost all courts in the Cotopaxi province are situated in the capital Latacunga. Besides Pujilí, only Saquisili, Pangua, La Maná, and Salcedo have a Civil Court (http://www.cortesuprema.gov.ec /corte/pais.php, accessed March 25, 2010).
21 Temperature fluctuates between 6 and 12 degrees Celsius. Temperatures are lowest during the month of August (Umajinga 1995: 248; Weismantel 1988: 43).
22 See: http://www.eruditos.net/mediawiki/index.php?title=Poblaci%C3%B3n_de_la_ Parroquia_ Zumbahua (accessed July 17, 2012) and Simon Thomas (2009: 86, note 90).
23 The eleven communities are: Chami, Guantopolo, La Cocha, Michacalá, Ponce-Quilotoa, Saraugsha, Talalag Yanaturo, Tigua Chimbacucho, Tigua Rumichaca, Yanashpa, and Yanaturo (Jácome 2009: 295; Plan de Desarrollo 2006).
24 Article 235 of the Constitution of 1998.

important role in the administration of the parish. The jurisdiction and responsibilities of a Junta Parroquial nowadays are defined in article 267 of the Montecristi Constitution and in the Ley Orgánica de las Juntas Parroquiales Rurales (Organic Law of the Junta Parroquial), and basically concern issues such as parish development and its land use, physical infrastructure, facilities, and public spaces of the parish, and the rural parish road network, all of these in consultation with provincial and other governments. A Junta Parroquial does not play any (official) role in *"asuntos judiciales"* ("juridical affairs"), like the settlement of internal conflicts,[25] these being functions of either the *teniente político* or the *cabildos*.

The village

Once one gets off the bus at El Campamento, it is a steep descent of about one hundred meters to get to the village of Zumbahua (at 3,500 meters above sea level). When I visited Zumbahua for the first time, in August 2007, this distance had to be negotiated on a muddy and slippery footpath. By 2010, however, a concrete staircase had been put in place, one of a number of improvements instituted in recent years. At the bottom of this stairway, one takes the road to the right, passing the brand new Millennium School on the right hand side, and the small *teniente político*'s office on the left, which leads to the main town square, Plaza Rumiñahui. While walking into the town, one might see some small children playing in front of their houses, women doing their washing outside in a *mila* (concrete washbasin, usually built at the side of a house), and some rooting pigs, scratching chickens, and sleeping dogs along the road. Depending on the day, one might also see schoolchildren in their uniforms exercising on the sports field of the school (or several parked small trucks and vans belonging to stallholders or customers of the weekly market). But, whatever the day, one cannot possibly miss the small stalls where women are selling candies or food (mostly French fries and eggs), alongside the road and especially at Plaza Tupac. For tourists, there is a sign that reads "Food- and handicraft market (Saturdays)," which shows the way to both Quilotoa (14 km further onwards) and Tigua (12 km back).

Unless one arrives on a Saturday morning, Zumbahua gives the impression of being something of a ghost town. Other than a few women, small children, and elderly men, there is hardly anybody in the streets during the daytime. The few shops one can discern are closed. Other than some small trucks coming to or leaving the village, or the buses that drive through the center every half hour or so as part of their "Quilotoa loop," there is hardly any traffic. The few tourists that come to Zumbahua usually manage to arrange transportation to Quilotoa Lake as soon as they can. One cannot blame them. With its ugly, vast, and generally empty Plaza Rumiñahui, with its minimal number of paved streets (the rest being muddy or dusty, depending on the time of the

---

25 Interview with the secretary of the Junta Parroquial on October 21, 2010.

year), and with most houses and buildings closed, the place isn't exactly a tourist mecca.

However, if one takes the time to hang out for a few hours – or, better yet, to linger there for a couple of days or more – one gets a better idea of how this parish center functions. To give just a few examples, because the village of Zumbahua is the administrative seat of the parish, the Junta Parroquial has an office here. The town is also home to the *teniente político*'s office, a police station, a Catholic church, a cemetery, and a clinic. Actually, this clinic is the only one of its kind in this (mainly indigenous) part of Cotopaxi province, and therefore it is of regional importance (Vintimilla et al. 2007: 72). This facility not only serves residents from this and the neighboring parishes, it also treats those who have been injured by the all-too-frequent car and bus accidents that occur on the main road through town.[26] In or near the main plaza, one can also find several offices offering short-term or long-term loans, a bank, and an office of the Registro Civil. Zumbahua also has a carpenter's workshop, a blacksmith, and a small construction shop. There are three hostels, a couple of restaurants, and a great many small shops selling a wide variety of merchandise, from liquor, beer, and wine, cigarettes, prepaid Porta phone cards, dry food, and gas, to simple gifts, crockery, and fedora-style hats. And of course, there are several tailors, shoemakers, and hairdressers. As a matter of fact, in nearly every private home in the town, someone is selling, making, or repairing something. But, since these informal businesses for most owners are part-time ventures, most of the roll-down shutters are down, and front doors are closed during weekdays. And if they open, it is often only for few hours at the end of the day, when there is somewhat more traffic and people on the streets, and some young men are playing their daily game of soccer or volleyball at a paved playing field next to the church.

The scene is dramatically different on Saturday mornings, when the weekly market at the Plaza Rumiñahui is held. On these market days, almost everybody opens their door and/or puts a stall in front of their house, in order to try to earn some modest additional income. On Saturdays, every restaurant in town (I counted six of them, while during weekdays only Restaurant Zumbahua is open) serves its *menú del día* ("daily special"), usually consisting of rice, chicken, potatoes, and vegetables, from as early as 6:00 am. Actually, some market-related activities typically begin on Friday afternoon, when the stalls are put in place and the first market vendors arrive. The Saturday markets attract buyers and sellers from the entire region, a fact that is reflected in the variety of food that is sold. Raw fish from the coast can be bought from men who display their merchandise on the back of their pickup trucks, and fruit such as bananas, lemons, and avocados from the (tropical) lowlands, and

---

26 For example on Monday morning, August 16, 2010, when at 3:00 am a bus lost control and tumbled some hundred meters down a hill near Apagua. Seven passengers were killed and seventeen were injured and treated at the clinic (*El Comercio* 2010n). That night, I was awakened by the sirens of the ambulances.

corn, onions, carrots, tomatoes, sweet peppers, lettuce, broccoli, and potatoes originating from different ecological zones of the highlands can be bought at stalls on the plaza. And of course, there is also meat and bread for sale. Several times it crossed my mind how the offerings at the Saturday market could be adduced as evidence of how a vertical *ayllu* in the early days could have been self-sustaining.[27]

In addition to fresh food, dry food like rice, noodles, herbs and spices, oil, and canned sardines is also sold at the market. Clothes, shoes, hats, tools, furniture, CDs, and fancy cell-phone covers are also displayed. The northwest part of the plaza is used as a small eating area. There one can sit and eat soup with toasted corn, rice with chicken, and other local dishes. Pigs, sheep, goats, and llamas are traded either in the town's streets, or at a side-market held in an open area next to the cemetery and the hospital. On market days, the village of Zumbahua is packed with people and parked vehicles, and music blares from loudspeakers that are hung from the lampposts around the plaza. But because a market day starts at dawn, it usually ends by early afternoon. At that time, merchandise is packed up, any lingering drunken men are directed home or to their vehicles, stalls are dismantled, and finally, the plaza is swept clean. The town then sinks back into its typical sleepy haze – a tranquility that will only be broken by the following market day (unless, that is, a fiesta is scheduled for Sunday).

So far, one might well get the idea that time stands still in Zumbahua. But this is a case where appearances are deceiving because, albeit at a slow pace, Zumbahua is indeed evolving. For example, if one looks at the 2002 photo of the village on Google Earth,[28] and then compares it with a photo from 2012, a lot of improvements can be noticed. In ten years, the number of buildings almost doubled (including the police station, the building in which the Junta Parroquial runs its office, the Millennium School, and several houses, among them Sergio's house, in which I stayed for several months), and while in 2002 only Plaza Rumiñahui and the road through the center were paved, now almost every street of the blocks adjacent to plaza is also paved. As a matter of fact, while I was doing fieldwork in 2010, road workers were completing the surfacing of two of the town's streets. It is indisputable that the involvement of the Correa administration has played a role in this development. For example, it was the government that initiated the building of the Millennium School. Zumbahua has electricity, but lacks a system of drinking water (people instead place large blue water basins on the top of their houses). Residents who need to make a phone call can go to one of the several Porta

---

27 An *ayllu*, the Kichwa word for community (Radcliffe & Westwood 1996: 108), which dates back to the pre-colonial period, is a unique characteristic of human settlement in the Andes. An *ayllu* in those days could be seen as a community based on kinship (*ius sanguinus*) whose means of sustaining life was agriculture. Such an *ayllu* in the Andes had a vertical structure, comprising different heights having different climates, and therefore featuring different crops.

28 Date image January 16, 2002.

phone centers in the village. These are rarely used, however, because almost everybody has a cell phone.[29]

Weismantel (1988: 54) observed back in the 1980s that "the entire [village], which seems so empty and desolate, is in fact undergoing a period of change and growth. Most of the buildings in it are less than ten years old, and new construction is under way." She predicted that "if economic conditions were to improve, the [village] could rapidly blossom." As far as I can observe, Zumbahua still is – slowly – improving, even though it can hardly be said to be "blossoming." However, the fact that it is situated near the main road from Latacunga to the Pacific Coast, and that it has a regionally important function with its market on Saturdays, its school, and its clinic, means that Zumbahua nowadays is not as isolated and underdeveloped as it was previously. At the same time, the village (and in fact the whole parish) has to cope with some serious threats like poverty and migration, basically due to lacking secondary education facilities and work opportunities, and a growing shortage of agricultural lands. In other words, the economic improvement that Weismantel hoped for has not transpired. As a consequence, the younger generation increasingly moves to cities like Ambato, Quito, and Guayaquil, or even leaves Ecuador in search of better economic opportunities, while leaving the elderly and children behind.

Comunas

In addition to the village just described, the parish of Zumbahua consists of eleven *comunas* or communities. These communities can in turn be divided into several *sectores*. As mentioned in the previous chapter, the territorial unit of the *comuna* was devised in 1937 when the Ley de Comunas was enacted. In Zumbahua, the first two *comunas* (Zumbahua and La Cocha) were created in 1972, following the abolishment of the hacienda. Other *departamentos, lugares*, or *comunidade* changed their status to that of *comunas* in the following years. The communities of Guantópolo and Talatag can easily be reached because they are situated near the main road from Latacunga to the coast. Other communities, however, are less easily accessible, because there is no paved road that leads to them. The community of Michacalá lacks any access road at all. For this reason, the design of such a road was identified in the 2006 Development Plan of the Junta Parroquial, as a high priority.[30] Most *comunas* consist of a small central settlement with a plaza, several houses, a community hall, a church, and sometimes a school or even a cemetery. But most inhabitants of such a *comuna* live in dispersed settlements in the rural

---

29 Residents of Zumbahua exclusively use Porta prepaid cards, because the other major cell provider in Ecuador, Movistar, provides no coverage in the region.
30 See: http://www.cotopaxi.gov.ec/archivos/Menu/PlanZumbahua.pdf (accessed October 5, 2012). This plan was also provided to me by the secretary of the Junta Parroquial on October 11, 2010.

hinterlands. Therefore, geographical boundaries between communities are not easy to identify, and for most residents, these boundaries are of little importance. Boundaries do become significant, however, when conflicts over resources arise (Weismantel 1988: 52).

The case of the community of Ponce-Quilotoa, as has been described by Noroña Salcedo (2006) involved a conflict over resources. Ponce-Quilotoa is the most recent community accorded legal recognition. It is situated in an area known mainly for the volcanic Lake Quilotoa, a nationally and internationally visited natural attraction. That is why, for residents near the lake, tourism is, along with agriculture and livestock breeding, a major source of income. For some families, tourism provides 50 percent of their income. And, in order to insure that these tourism-generated incomes would benefit only those in their community (and not the whole parish), they opted in 2002 to become a *comuna* (that is, before they were part of the La Cocha community). As such, they were able to administratively manage their own affairs, and this in turn provided them during those years the much-needed legal status with regard to Ecuador's Park Service INEFAN,[31] with which they had an argument about who should be in control of the lake and its area. INEFAN wanted the lake to become part of an Ecological Reserve Management Plan, which included the stipulation that people were not allowed to live within two kilometers of it. After obtaining their legal status, the inhabitants of Ponce-Quilotoa were able to come to an agreement with the Ecuadorian National Park Service.

Nowadays, families engaged in tourism earn a modest income from operating small shops, restaurants, and hostels, by providing guided tours, and from the sale of their "Tigua-like" *art naïf* paintings. This modest tourist industry annoys the residents of La Cocha, including Zumbahuans (who still believe that Lake Quilotoa falls within their territory). This is because those few tourists who venture into the area typically drive through Zumbahua without visiting its shops, restaurants, and hostels. The painters living in Tigua are also unhappy, because they often lose business to the artists of Ponce-Quilotoa. However, those who are annoyed are also well aware that, without the volcanic Lake Quilotoa and the tourist facilities that the people from Ponce-Quilotoa have developed, there would be even less tourism in the region than there is at present. As a matter of fact, tourism to the volcano has increased since the resurfacing of the road from Zumbahua to the crater lake in 2010.

Páramos

For most Ecuadorians, high places like Zumbahua are *puro páramo* (the high Andean meadows in its purest form), a region characterized by one of the *dirigentes* of La Cocha as, "*una zona fría*" ("a cold area").[32] Actually, *páramos*

---

31 INEFAN: Instituto Ecuatoriano Forestal de Áreas Naturales y Vida Silvestre (Ecuador Forestry Institute for Natural Areas and Wildlife).
32 Interview on November 13, 2010.

are much more diverse than such a simplification suggests (Hess 1990). Differences in altitude, soil, and climate (temperature, rainfall, and wind) produce a variety of micro-climates and micro-ecosystems, resulting in the *páramos* being far from homogeneous.[33] The residents of Zumbahua themselves broadly define two zones,[34] determined primarily by altitude. The lowlands (between 3,400 and 3,900 meters above sea level) are agricultural and residential. The vast plains at an altitude between 3,900 and 4,400 meters above sea level are considered to constitute the real *páramo*, and about half of the parish lands fall within this latter zone.

It is in this higher region that the vast and picturesque grasslands can be found, and where cattle graze. Nomadic pastoralism (which in that region takes the form of residents tilling the fields during the day and returning to their homes in the evening) can be found in the parish. A peculiar characteristic of the Zumbahuan region is a redistribution method in which those living in lower-lying areas entrust their animals to those who live and work in the higher areas. In return, the former "pay" for the latter's products with their crops. Although the grasslands are not cultivated, they are in fact controlled to a certain degree (for example, by systematically burning off grasses in order to facilitate new growth). Add to this the fact that the grazing livestock not only provides wool, milk, and meat, but also a means of transportation (that is, llamas), as well as manure that can be used to enrich the soil in the lower zone. Therefore, the high *páramos* – considered by some an uninhabitable area – in fact are an important and heavily utilized zone (Hess 1990; Umajinga 1995: 248–249; Weismantel 1988: 40–49). Nowadays, the *páramos* are even used to attract tourists, either as a scenario of guided walks among beautiful scenery, or as camping grounds.[35]

However, this higher zone of the *páramo* is threatened by the ascent of the agriculture of the lower zone (Hess 1990). This upward expansion of the agricultural frontier has occurred for a number of different reasons. The principal cause has been population pressure.[36] As population density grew,

---

33 For example, there is a great difference between *páramos* of the *Corderilla Occidental* (west Andean ridge), and the *Corderilla Central*. The former has a rougher topography, it receives less rain, and it is more densely populated. As a result, it is dominated by small-scale agriculture (*minifundio*) and high-altitude pastoralism.

34 A similar division into two zones is made by Cañadas (1983 in Hess 1990: 335), who classifies the *páramos* into "*subpáramos*" between 3,200 and 3,900 meters above sea level, and "*páramos*" between 3,900 and 4,700 meters above sea level (4,700 meters is the snowline).

35 Some residents of Zumbahua designed a small brochure, meant to attract tourists to come and stay in their village, which was handed out to tourists who got off the bus in El Campamento. I also saw several copies at a hostel in Latacunga. Among other things (a good hostel, good food, the weekly market, etc.), this brochure extols the *caminatas por las montañas mas admiradas del mundo* (most beautiful mountain trails in the world).

36 Another important local case was the previously mentioned Ponce-Quilotoa vs. INEFAN. In order to obtain their status as a *comuna* situated near the crater lake,

higher yields were needed, and therefore more land needed to be cultivated. In addition, the ongoing division of family plots of land (basically as a result of inheritance practices) also led to an increasing demand for more land. In Zumbahua, it is common for small plots of land to be given to children (sometimes at the time that they marry), but when the parents are working a plot of land that is so small that it cannot reasonably be shared, the logical alternative is to move to higher ground. The expansion of the road system and technical improvements (for example, the use of tractors) (Hess 1990), and the increased use of fertilizer, subsequently facilitated the conversion of high *páramo* into agricultural land. For some time now, the combination of population growth (resulting in the division of agricultural land into ever smaller plots of land) and the decrease of higher zone *páramo*, has reached its limits, consequently putting pressure on the population of the parish.

Fiesta in Zumbahua – part II

Now let us return to the newlyweds, whom we last saw at the reception at the groom's house. Between 1:00 and 2:00 pm on the Sunday of the wedding, every celebrating family and their guests gathered at the Plaza Rumiñahui in Zumbahua. Three different bands installed their equipment on the three stages. Each of these bands, which played popular Latin music, proceeded to perform in turn, to which some in the crowd danced while others ate, drank, and generally had a good time. Along the four sides of the plaza, dozens of small stalls were set up where villagers sold food, candy, beer, and wine. The predominant color of the merchandise of the stalls was yellow (that is, the color of the boxes of bottles of Pilsener beer, one of the nation's most popular). Half-liter bottles were sold for one dollar, as were one-liter cartons of wine. The streets surrounding the plaza were packed with trucks and cars, which had transported guests from the entire region and beyond to the fiesta. I estimated the crowd to number about 2,000. The three bands (which were hired by the three different families of the newly wedded couples) would alternate every half hour or so, and every time it was a band's turn to play, the lead singer of the band announced who they were playing for, lauding "their" bride and groom in particular. Crowds shifted from stage to stage, according to the band that was playing. Thus, what might have appeared to an outsider as one giant fiesta actually was a pastiche of different families from different communities (but all living in the same parish) each having its own party simultaneously in the main plaza of Zumbahua.

During the fiesta, most of those in attendance were in the plaza, either dancing to the music of one of the bands, or chatting with one other. And

> it was necessary that a certain number of people actually live near that lake. That is why, even though the grasslands near the lake were more appropriate for pasturage, the community ordered several families to go and live on these lands, and to try to make them agriculturally viable.

drinking, of course. Nearly everyone was holding a bottle of beer or liquor (mostly *aguardiente*, a potent spirit made from raw sugar cane) or a carton of wine and a small plastic cup. Custom prescribes that, when you are in a conversation with someone, or if you want to start chatting with someone, you offer him or her a sip from your own bottle, poured out into the cup you are carrying. The other person in turn is supposed to respond to this gesture by offering you a cup from his own bottle or carton. You are supposed to drink nearly the entire contents of that cup and then pour any remaining drops on the ground as an offering to *Pachamama* (Mother Earth). This drinking ritual is not only taken very seriously as a custom; in addition, it has the practical consequence of accustoming participants to drink large quantities of beer, liquor, and wine within a short time span. It is therefore no surprise that, after a couple of hours of partying, some people get very drunk. But besides some men who staggered about, the atmosphere remained festive: the bands continued to play, the sun was shining, and everybody was having a good time.

At the height of the fiesta, at about 4:00 pm, however, some small scuffles broke out at different places at almost the same time, and the atmosphere changed instantly. It was mostly young men who were involved in these fights. Maybe it was because they had drunk too much, maybe they were just bored, maybe it was about a girl. In no time these small fights spread like wildfire across the plaza. All of a sudden, it seemed like *only* young men were at the fiesta (which definitely was not true). Like a wave, a group of about hundred young men moved from one corner of the plaza to the other and back, pushing the other guests aside. Music stopped, and everybody turned to watch the fighting. Of course, as a well-informed researcher, I was aware of tensions among people living in the Ecuadorian Andes in general: rivalries within families or between families; within or between settlements, communities, or parishes; between people living in remote sectors and people living within the larger villages; between those who had left the region as economic emigrants (and who occasionally returned home) and those who had stayed in the countryside. Yet it had never crossed my mind that I would become a spectator of such an enormous free-for-all. Both the scope and intensity of the fighting really took me aback.

That is why I hurried immediately to a more quiet side of Plaza Rumiñahui, climbed a low wall, and proceeded to observe the unfolding events. Most of the young men were only pulling each other's clothes, pushing one another, and shouting. Only a few were actually hitting or punching. I also spotted the groom, no longer wearing his new sweater, and with the sleeves of his shirt rolled up, ready to join the fray. Luckily, he was restrained by some of his relatives. But then, in the center of the crowd, I saw some arms swing beer bottles. And then I heard screaming. It was at that point that several men and women moved in to separate the warring parties. Peace was quickly restored and the resulting damage could clearly be seen. The ground was littered with broken bottles, and several young men were bleeding heavily from their heads and faces. It was an unpleasant sight, but everybody was still on his feet. The injured were quickly taken away to be attended to, after which the atmosphere seemed to relax a bit. When, after a few minutes, the band started to play again, the fiesta soon continued as if nothing had happened.

People started dancing and drinking again, and although it was the end of the afternoon, and the temperature would soon drop, only a few people left. The majority of the celebrants stayed and continued partying. More and more men got drunk: some ended up crying and some just fell asleep. When, at around 6:30 pm, the mother of the groom was graciously but firmly summoned to go home (because she was almost unconscious from drinking), I decided that it was time to leave. When I came home, Sergio already had fallen asleep on his bed, but I myself was unable to fall sleep until 11:00 pm when the music finally stopped. When I woke up early the next morning, I had a terrible headache. This, however, did not stop me from going back immediately to Plaza Rumiñahui, to see what it looked like after the previous day's festivities. I was struck by the fact that everything seemed to have returned to normal. The stalls and their merchandise had been removed by their owners, the three stages were gone, the waste cleared, and the plaza swept clean. Everyone I subsequently spoke to who had been at the event, including Sergio, agreed that it had been a wonderful party.

The wedding, and the events that took place during the public party at Plaza Rumiñahui afterward, are illustrative of two different phenomena: cohesion and conflict. Literally, a wedding is a formal union of two people. The accompanying ceremonies at the bride and groom's houses could be seen as the sealing of an alliance between two families and their closest friends. Meals were only for family, close friends, and honored guests (Douglas 1975: 256) while, during the fiesta bonds with friends were affirmed, made, or even broken. As will be shown further on, fiestas in the Andean highlands as such can be considered rituals of existing social relationships (Cervone 2010: 102). The wedding and the fiesta are thus examples of cohesion. The fight that took place in the afternoon, on the other hand, reflects tensions that exist within the parish. Such fights among young men are by no means uncommon during Andean fiestas. I myself have personally witnessed many such fights at fiestas during my fieldwork, as well as elsewhere during village festivals at different places around the world. But what particularly struck me on this occasion was that some men and women stepped in to restore the peace. The breakup of the fight could thus be viewed as an illustration of cohesion. However, bystanders do not always succeed in restoring the peace, as will be shown in one of the following chapters, in which two similar conflicts resulted in fatalities, and led to subsequent legal trials in order to identify and punish the offenders.

Life in the parish

Poverty

As one can deduce from the preceding sections: life in the parish of Zumbahua is not easy. It is certainly possible to acclimate oneself to the physical hardships of the geography and climate of the parish. However, its socio-economic circumstances and prospects are far more difficult to deal with. Poverty and inequality continue to be the main challenge for Ecuador as a whole, according to the World Bank.[37] About 35 percent of Ecuadorians live in poverty, and about 10 percent live in extreme poverty. This problem is more severe in rural areas.[38] According to Ecuador's own figures (based on the census of 2010),[39] things are improving, but the World Bank data cannot be refuted. According to the census of 2010, 47.8 percent of the population of Cotopaxi province lives in poverty (according to the NBI indicator,[40] the figure is 51.6 percent). The Plan de Desarrollo (2006) provides NBI figures for the parish of Zumbahua as such: poverty 98.7 percent, and extreme poverty 88.6 percent. In other words, the means of living in the parish of Zumbahua are simple, people are poor, and support services and infrastructure is minimal. There is hardly any work, and agriculture alone, even when supplemented by raising livestock, does not provide more than bare sustenance for much of the population.

Take Diego, for example. He does not have a job, and the profits from the hostel that he manages are negligible. At times, he secures temporary employment (for example, his job collecting data for the national census of 2010). But actually his only hope for regular income would be a permanent full-time job that might be assigned to him by the Correa government, as a reward for his help during Correa's first presidential campaign in 2007. Meanwhile, he has his regular living costs for basic essentials like food, housing, and clothing. According to Western standards, these might not seem all that high but, all together, these are significant expenses for someone whose income hovers near the poverty line – which is $1.25 per day,[41] according to the World Bank. To give just a few examples: the cheapest Porta prepaid telephone card costs $3.00, a full tank of gas used for cooking and a hot shower costs $1.25 (in addition to a $50.00 deposit), the monthly electricity bill is about $3.00, a one-way ticket to Latacunga costs $1.50, and if Diego is invited to a wedding or baptism, he has to buy presents as well. Then there are the annual costs for the education of his two sons. I helped him out with these latter expenses, in exchange for his help during my fieldwork.

And one must keep in mind that Diego lives in the more financially stable part of the parish (that is, in the village) (see also Weismantel 1988). It can

37 See: http://www.worldbank.org/en/country/ecuador (accessed July 23, 2012).
38 See: http://web.worldbank.org/WBSITE/EXTERNAL/TOPICS/EXTPOVERTY/EXTPA/0, contentMDK:20207570~isCURL:Y~menuPK:435735~pagePK:148956~piPK:216618~theSitePK:430367,00.html (accessed July 23, 2012).
39 See: http://www.desarrollosocial.gob.ec/wp-content/uploads/2011/05/Evolución-y-Situa ción-de-la-Pobreza-en-Ecuador-Dic-2010-pp.pdf (accessed July 23, 2012). These figures show that poverty has decreased from 49.9 percent in 2003 to 32.8 percent in 2010, and that extreme poverty has decreased from 26.6 percent (2003) to 13.1 percent (2010).
40 NBI stands for *necesidades básicas insatisfechas* (unsatisfied basic needs, such needs being defined as housing, health, education, and work).
41 All quoted prices are in US dollars, unless otherwise indicated.

therefore be assumed that he knew better times before the economic hardship that he was experiencing while I was living with him. His house has electricity, tiles on the floor, and an inside bathroom. This is more than some of his neighbors have. And compared to residents living in the more rural communities, these represent downright luxuries. For example, many rural homes do not have electricity,[42] and consist of no more than two small rooms and a dirt floor. But the most pressing concern of rural residents is the declining productivity of their land. One reason for this has been, according to Weismantel (1988), the abolishment of the hacienda, which made Zumbahuan inhabitants more dependent on cash (after having previously relied on their relationship with the hacienda and agricultural activity as ways to survive).[43] This dependence only grew in the following years, to some extent as a result of neoliberal reforms (Noroña Salcedo 2006: 5). Basically, this means that, from the start, small-scale farmers have lacked sufficient capital to invest and the market for their products did not increase. Therefore, profit margins have always been low. Those who had been able to obtain a small piece of land in the early 1970s were able to meet their needs and to sell a little surplus, but they did not exactly make a fortune.[44] Another reason for disappointing profits has been the rapid fragmentation of land among subsequent generations.[45] As a result, it is still more difficult for farmers to rely on (commercial) agriculture alone to support a household. This is why rural residents have to make use of other strategies to survive.

Migration

People living in the parish of Zumbahua make use of a number of different strategies for survival, either alone or in combination. To start with, they cultivate crops for their own consumption. They barter crops and other goods among themselves (a strategy also reflected in the *compadrazgo* system). They also redistribute goods, products, or services (for example, when people entrust their herds to those who live and work in the higher *páramos*, or when they do communal work). And, of course, they bring their merchandise to the market (in the narrow sense of the weekly market in the village, as well as in

---

42 The Plan de Desarollo (2006) mentions that only 56 percent of the houses in the parish have electricity.
43 Weismantel (1988: 73–74) has shown that, during the times of the hacienda, the peasants did not have much need for cash. They instead functioned in an "economic system in which goods, services and land could be exchanged without the use of money." Once they were on their own, they had hardly any money to invest. In the years Weismantel was doing her research, cash was still so scarce that its actual worth in the region was less than its face value.
44 Products sold at the local weekly market of Zumbahua do not usually comprise more than 10 percent of the harvest (Noroña Salcedo 2006: 6; Sánchez-Parga 2002: 32).
45 The majority of the small-scale farmers own less than five hectares (Plan de Desarollo 2006).

the broader sense of the regional/national/global capitalist economy). As explained in the previous section, agriculture alone is not enough for most rural inhabitants to survive. That is why they also engage in other economic activities like wage-labor relationships. A lot of the men I have spoken to, or whose personal data I came across in files, are so-called *jornaleros*, or day laborers. These persons either work on the land (doing seasonal work), or in construction. However, since there is not nearly enough work in Zumbahua for its residents, people are forced to migrate – which is not at all uncommon in Ecuador as a whole. As Kyle (2000: 17) points out, "Migration has never been a sideshow in the Andean region."[46] Weismantel (1988: 192, 1997: 30; see also Martínez Novo (2004: 245)) shows that this applies to Zumbahua as well.[47] The lack of sufficient economic opportunities, however, is not the only reason for migration.[48] Education is another important factor. Since Zumbahua (and its region) lacks a secondary school, children are forced to go elsewhere (for example, Latacunga) to obtain a proper education. Thus, many young persons and adults, and men and women (see also Sánchez-Parga 2002: 29–43), migrate temporarily or permanently, both within Ecuador and to other countries.

According to the World Bank, more than one million people have migrated from Ecuador to the United States, Spain,[49] Italy, neighboring countries, and elsewhere,[50] resulting in remittances becoming a substantial source of income (although remittances have decreased in recent years because of the global economic crisis).[51] In a highly detailed report, FLACSO (2006) estimates the

---

46 Kyle (2000: 18–19) states that there have been two broad periods of historical migration in Ecuador. The first, a long period of migration of persons forced and regulated by the Spanish to live in *reduccíones* (that is, connected, or concentrated centers, which were designed by the Spanish colonial rulers to reduce the existing extended settlements, mainly for reasons of control), provides a good illustration. The second migration, which occurred during the twentieth century, can be characterized by three trends: 1) from the highlands to the coast to do seasonal work at banana and cacao plantations; 2) from the highlands to the Amazon; and 3) increasing movement to larger cities since the 1960s.
47 Weismantel (1988: 191–192, 1997: 30) mentions men who found construction work in Quito beginning in the early 1970s, as well as men working on sugar plantations near the coast since the early 1960s.
48 Jokisch and Pribilsky (2002: 82) indicate that there has often been a close interrelationship between poverty and migration.
49 Prior to the late 1990s, transnational migration from Ecuador primarily was directed to the United States (Kyle 2000). From the late 1990s on, however, this changed into a "new migration" to Europe, mostly to Spain, but also to The Netherlands and other countries (Jokisch & Pribilsky 2002).
50 See: http://siteresources.worldbank.org/INTPROSPECTS/Resources/334934-1199807908806/Ecuador.pdf (accessed July 24, 2012).
51 With the global economic crisis starting in 2008, it has become increasingly difficult for many migrants abroad to send money back home. Many of them have a hard time supporting themselves in their new homes, and are in no position to send remittances back to their families in Ecuador. Significantly, the Correa administration has embarked on a plan to encourage transnational migrants to return home.

number of transnational migrants at 1.5 million, of whom 1.5 percent come from the province of Cotopaxi[52] (which translates into a total of 20,000 persons). It is thus no surprise that there are Zumbahuans who have left Ecuador. On several different occasions, I heard the story of twenty men now supposedly working in construction in the Netherlands. A more reliable story was told me by a man named Hector,[53] who said he had done construction work in Stockholm for a couple of years. This same man reported that he traveled through Europe working as a street musician. I obtained even more trustworthy data from the archives of the Civil Court in Pujilí regarding expatriates living in Madrid, Milan, and Azerbaijan who were parties in legal cases in Ecuador.[54]

However, migration within Ecuador, whether temporary or permanent, is far more common than emigration to other countries for those born in Zumbahua parish (Jácome 2009: 109–119; Plan de Desarrollo 2006; Umajinga 1995: 264). Migration is typically referred to as a problem (Plan de Desarrollo 2006; Umajinga 1995), as if communities are at risk of disintegration as a result of some of their residents moving away. Colloredo-Mansfeld (2009a: 29), on the other hand, observes that this is not necessarily the case. On the contrary, migrants' bonds with families and places of origin tend to remain strong, and the general pattern among those who leave is to make return visits as soon as possible (see also Taussig 1978). These observations are in line with what I have personally witnessed. The wedding ceremonies described at the beginning of this chapter provide an excellent example. First, many of the guests returned home for the fiesta. Second, the bride and groom themselves returned to the latter's hometown of Zumbahua for the wedding. On other occasions, such as All Saints Day, and on All Souls Day, I also witnessed many people returning home to celebrate with their family.[55] However, the overall consensus of those who have remained in Zumbahua is that both national and international migration is problematic. Many whom I spoke with feel that migration negatively influences behavior and morals, especially among the younger generations. In the words of a member of the Junta Parroquial,[56] migrants become "*aculturados*" (that is, they lose their distinct local identity and culture). The examples he adduces

---

52 Based on data of the census of 2001, which asked respondents if they had lived in other countries during the last five years; see: http://www.rlc.fao.org/es/desarrollo/mujer/docs/ ecuador/cap03.pdf (accessed July 24, 2012).
53 Informal conversation I had with Hector and Sergio on August 16, 2010.
54 I came across these cases while I was doing archival research at the Civil Court in Pujilí on October 19, 2010.
55 I was struck on these days by the sight of several taxis parked in the streets of the village. These belonged to men who had left Zumbahua to become taxi drivers in larger towns or cities (for example, Latacunga, Ambato, or Quito) and who for this occasion had used their regular source of income to return home for a couple of days.
56 Interview I had on October 21, 2010, at the office of the Junta Parroquial.

are migrants who wear Western-style clothes, disrespect leaders and the elderly, and who display more violent behavior.[57]

Fiestas and drinking

A policeman once confided to me without a trace of irony, as a characterization of life in Zumbahua, that "a boy holding a girl's hands could be seen as sufficient reason to organize a fiesta."[58] "Sure," Sergio would confirm happily to me more than once. "We might be poor, but we will always find a reason to party." Fiestas and celebrations, of which weddings and baptisms are among the most important (Bonaldi 2010: 95), play a significant role in the social life of the parish. Fiestas like Corpus Christi,[59] Christmas Eve, New Year's Day, and the Feast of Epiphany (that is, thirteen days after Christmas), are among the most popular yearly events (Bonaldi 2010; Colvin 2004; Weismantel 1988). Most of these events, since they are of Catholic provenance, include a mass, and then there is of course also music, traditional (that is, masked, and/or costumed) dancing, and sometimes even the highly popular bullfighting. Everyone from the village or community and surrounding areas, men and women, young and old, joins in the eating, drinking, and dancing. The most important persons at such events are the *priostes* (that is hosts and/or sponsors). These individuals are usually designated a year in advance, and assigned responsibility for planning, organizing, and financing the fiesta (Cervone 2010: 103–104; Colvin 2004: 83). Besides these yearly "public" fiestas, more "private" ones (usually rites of passage like baptisms and weddings), occur frequently as well. At these more private affairs, the members of the host family also tend to be the most important persons at the party.

When anthropologists study fiestas in the Andean context, they often focus on power relations (Cervone 2010; Guerrero 1991; Taussig 1978). Fiestas, in these studies, are conceptualized as "ritual moments [which] are converted into a ritualization of the existing power relations between the social actors who participate in them" (Cervone 2010: 102). This ritualization of existing power relations does not always proceed smoothly (Taussig 1978), and this may be one of the reasons why fighting often breaks out at such events. I think it is fair to say that nowadays, gatherings like annual fiestas, baptisms and weddings, or even important communal meetings, also serve as a stimulus

---

57 Whether migration and increasing violence actually are that directly connected can certainly be disputed, but at least this is the opinion of many residents of Zumbahua, as is the view that migrants fall under bad influences. Zumbahuans have a rather essentialist view of culture, as reflected in their frequent use of the term "*aculturar.*" Taussig (1978), on the contrary, has argued that the encounter during fiestas of migrants and those that stayed behind, should rather be seen as a form of integration, albeit an integration accompanied by tensions.
58 Interview on October 28, 2010.
59 The Junta Parroquial even promotes the Corpus Christi fiesta by hanging posters in the village and surrounding areas weeks in advance.

for migrants to return home. It is on those occasions that they see relatives, *padrinos*, friends, and other community members, and at which relationships with them are made, renewed, or broken. In addition, power relationships (for example, questions as to who will have the honor of being a *prioste*, who performs the dances, where and when (Cervone 2010), or how the host family pays for the event) manifest themselves. But since such a large number of community members have migrated, fiestas and other events also serve as a bonding mechanism. The renewal or reinforcement of ties occurs during the chatting, dancing, eating, and drinking at the fiestas, each of which acts in a way that is also highly ritualized.

Take for instance the issue of drinking. Consumption of alcohol is an integral part of every fiesta in the Andes. Weismantel (1988: 8, 1991: 873) has argued that in Zumbahua, where reciprocity and redistribution play such a critical role in the creation and maintenance of social ties, both gifts of food and drinking rituals are important. Douglas (1975: 256) has shown that, while meals are restricted to family, close friends, and honored guests, people drink together who know one another far less intimately. Yet certain criteria also apply as to who might constitute an appropriate drinking companion. Douglas (1987: 8–12) notes that drinking alcohol, while serving other purposes as well, is an extremely important feature in the production and reproduction of identities. In line with this thought, Weismantel (1988: 136) observes that "for men, drinking […] is an inescapable part of social life." This does not mean that one should lose sight of the negative side effects of excessive drinking. Drinking and drunkenness should be treated as social and health concerns. One cannot ignore that in Zumbahua (and sadly in a lot of places elsewhere around the globe) drinking, or more specifically, drunken men, is a factor related to domestic violence (Weismantel 1988: 182). Almost all of my informants confirmed this relationship, and some of them (like the *teniente político*, members of the Junta Parroquial, policemen, *dirigentes*, and ordinary Indians) also saw a relationship between drinking and vandalism, fighting, and other violent crimes (see also Weismantel (1997: 15)). And because drinking is so often associated with violence, Ecuador has since 2010 had stricter laws regulating the sale of alcohol.[60] Anthropologists, however, do not necessarily treat alcohol as problem. Since "celebrating is normal, and […] in most cultures alcohol is a normal adjunct to celebration" (Douglas 1987: 3–4), they try not to moralize alcohol use, or think of it in primarily medical or legal terms. Anthropologists also do not necessarily think of drunkenness as a problem, since it is a phenomenon that is "an expression of culture because it is socially learned and patterned, and varies in structure and function from society to society" (Wilson 2005: 13).

---

60 This law prohibits bars and restaurants from serving alcoholic drinks after midnight Monday through Friday, or after 2:00 am Friday and Saturday. The law also stipulates that shops are allowed to sell alcohol only until 10:00 pm and prohibits the sale of alcohol on Sundays.

At several occasions during the course of my fieldwork, I had to learn how to view alcohol differently from the way I had learned to as a result of my own cultural background. An example of how I had to learn to think in new ways occurred when I attended my first fiesta in Zumbahua parish. It was during a week of celebrations in the community of La Cocha, where I attended a Friday afternoon bullfight.[61] While standing behind a rather rickety fence watching several men and one bull in the arena, I got into a conversation with two male spectators. After we spoke for a while, one of the men offered me his glass with some of his beer. Because this is not done where I come from, I did not know how to thank him politely, and since we happened to be standing near a stall where beer was being sold, I decided to buy a few bottles. I handed the bottles out to my new friends, keeping one for myself, and after having made a toast, I took a large swig of beer. To my surprise, this caused great confusion, ending in the other men laughing at me in a friendly way. They quickly explained to me – the ignorant anthropologist – the ritual of the mutual exchange of drinks, the gulping down of nearly the entire contents, and offering what is left over to *Pachamama*. Later, I became more aware of the details of this ritual (that is, who is offering what to who, who offers first and how much and, of course, the importance of who the *priostes* drink with). I thus learned that drinking in Zumbahua at a fiesta, to use the words of Douglas (1987: 4), is "a social act, performed in a recognized social context."

It is obvious that when a group of people drink, some of them are likely to get drunk. At the fiestas in Zumbahua, but also during the Mama Negra festival in Latacunga, or during the annual cantonal celebration in Pujilí, I saw several people – mostly men, but some women too – become very drunk indeed.[62] Such individuals usually end up crying, which typically serves as a signal for their relatives to more or less gently push them away from the party scene. I have also seen several drunk men just fall asleep, either while leaning against a wall or while sitting on the pavement (see also Weismantel 1991). Onlookers do not seem especially bothered by such scenes. As Weismantel (1988: 182) observes: "As long as men restrict their drinking [and drunkenness] to fiestas and market days, [...] it falls within the scope of acceptable male behavior." However, some men do not always seem to be able to handle alcohol in a positive way, given the frequent skirmishes and more serious fights that occur, some of which even result in fatalities (two such cases will be discussed later in this book). Fiestas and drinking thus appear to be one cause for some of the conflicts described here, but also of the cohesion among people living within the parish, and between them and their brethren who have migrated.

61 On August 13, 2010.
62 Weismantel (1988: 136, 1991: 865) observed that it is elderly women who tend to be more willing to drink, with younger women with children less willing to do so. This is consistent with my own observations (that is, almost every small stall where beer and wine was sold during the fiesta on August 28, 2010, was manned by younger women, who were selling rather than drinking the alcoholic beverages).

Conclusion

"Cohesion and conflict" is the very fitting subtitle of the present chapter, which has essentially been a broad introduction to life in a parish in the Andean highlands of Ecuador, which has dealt with the important issues of poverty and migration, and which has portrayed the fighting and bonding that can be observed during fiestas. The parish in question was a hacienda until forty years ago and thus still reflects that legacy, while at the same time it has been influenced in more recent decades (as shown in the previous chapter) by an increasingly active state presence, new indigenous movements, and changing political and legal attitudes regarding diversity and pluralism.

Following Ouweneel (1993: 406), this book acknowledges that rural Andean communities are not only defined by the legal entity of the *comuna*, but should also be seen as a symbolic construction that represents a strategy to deal with internal and external changes, threats, and conflicts. Such a rural community can thus also be defined as a "current of structural power in [its] own right," rather than as a "merely defensive outcome of distant forces [for example, colonialism]" (Colloredo-Mansfeld 2009a: 6). Additionally, because of its residents' juridical bond to a place, they tend to share the same set of ideas regarding land, tenure, land distribution, and the rights and obligations regarding use of the land. It is therefore obvious that the *comuneros*' sense of community is strongly attached to the land. And it is through a series of practices like fiestas that a community makes reference to itself and to the physical location where it resides (Radcliffe & Westwood 1996: 108). Thus, land, land tenure, etc., define the "haves" and the "have-nots," as well as who belongs to "us" or "them," and so do fiestas. At the same time, it should be appreciated that the boundaries between these categories are dynamic, contested, and multi-faceted (Ouweneel 1993; Radcliffe & Westwood 1996; Weismantel 1991).

In the parish of Zumbahua, until 1972, most of the land was owned by the state. The people who worked on the land (that is, the *huasipungueros* and the *yanaperos*) were tied to it as well (that is, through their property of small plots of land and/or their relationship to the landlords). With the abandoning of the hacienda, the land was distributed among the workers, albeit not equally. As Weismantel (1988: 69) has pointed out, the unequal division of land after the abolition of the hacienda remained, and wide disparities in the size of landholdings still exist. This created distinct classes of possessors and dispossessed. Yet both of these groups had an unmistakable feeling of connection to the land and the place. I once got into a heated conversation with some young *jornaleros* who insisted on being labeled "Zumbahuans," rather than Panzaleos,[63] and thus expressed a clear "us and them" mental construct. It is especially those who still live in Zumbahua who manifest such a strong connection. Yet even migrants, who typically make return visits to Ecuador,

---

63 Conversation I had with a group of young *jornaleros* about life in the parish at Restaurant Zumbahua on August 7, 2007.

also display this same connection. For example, while living in Quito, the young couple introduced at the beginning of this chapter decided to marry in the parish where they were born and where their parents still lived. At other celebrations and fiestas as well, the number of people returning home is significant. However, as shown before, some (cultural) tensions between those who stayed and those who left, but who occasionally returned, cannot be ignored. Such a phenomenon poses something of a challenge to the boundaries between "us" and "them."

Thus, the parish of Zumbahua consists of elements related to Anderson's (2006) "imagined communities," while it also consists of everyday community business (Colloredo-Mansfeld 2009a: 19–20), some of which leads to internal conflict. This means that its inhabitants sometimes form a united front against outsiders. On the other hand, there is certainly no absence of internal conflict, and keeping this reality in mind acts as a healthy antidote against the "romantic view of rural, indigenous communities as cohesive and consensus-based totalities" (Jackson 2002: 120). This is what Colloredo-Mansfeld (2009a: 210) has beautifully captured in his phrase "fighting like a community," which has two meanings: "taking on outsiders" and "fighting among one another," while taking into account that the dividing lines between people or groups (that is, between insiders and outsiders) are far from rigid. An individual can just as easily agree as disagree with others on a particular point. The same thing happens among groups of people. In addition, opinions change over time. There appears to be a fine line between cohesion and conflict, the distinctiveness of which depends on time, place, issue, and persons involved, as well as on changes in such circumstances. Conflicts emerge from a certain situation, but as the situation changes, the nature of the conflict can fundamentally change. How this happens in practice will be shown in more detail in the next chapter's section on understanding disputes.

It is interesting to observe how cohesion and conflict have changed over time. Because the present book is not historical in nature, it has to rely on others who have previously engaged in research about Zumbahua. Marc Becker, for example, conducted an archival study on struggles for land rights in the 1930s and 1940s in the Ecuadorian Andes in general, and in the parish of Zumbahua specifically (Becker 2007, 2011b). Basically, he writes about workers on the Zumbahua hacienda, and their disputes with the hacienda owner over working conditions and wages. It is possible to read his narrative as an example of the community fighting an outsider. However, the hacienda owner's defense was that in a particular case, according to him, there were just "two rebellious Indians, who, calling themselves leaders [...] foment[ed] disorder, [and] constitute[d] a bad example for others" (Becker 2007: 172). The landlord thus suggested that these individuals did not represent the whole work force. This might have been nothing more than a strategic argument of the landlord, but Becker (2007: 175), in second instance, also suggests that this landlord could have been right, because it remained unclear who those fomenting the rebellion exactly were. Although the individuals in question often petitioned in the name of all peons at Zumbahua, they tended to monopolize the discourse and rarely mentioned other names. At certain points, it was unclear whether they truly represented all indigenous workers or instead simply pressed their own personal agenda and economic interests.

Mary Weismantel, who conducted anthropological research on food and gender in the parish of Zumbahua in the early 1980s, also shows examples of both cohesion and conflict. Several times she refers to celebrations and fiestas, and the drinking associated with such events. Because Weismantel was conducting her research not long after the hacienda system was abolished, she places a great deal of emphasis on the legacy of that institution. She states that, under that system, the power relationship between "white" employees (that is, *mayordomos*) and "Indian" peons had been quite structured (thus suggesting an us-against-them situation) and that relationships between indigenous rural workers became tense soon after the abolition of the hacienda.[64] She describes a dispute in the village of Zumbahua in 1983 between two groups of citizens, which she uses to illustrate tensions between more traditional residents and more modern, younger inhabitants of the parish (Weismantel 1988: 77–82). This exemplifies a transition from (imagined) cohesion that supposedly existed during the hacienda era into the conflicts that later emerged. In addition, it illustrates that the present-day fear of "*aculturacion*" – as expressed by those who nowadays (still) live in Zumbahua – was present thirty years ago.

More recently, the 1998 Constitution and the Monecristi Constitution of 2008 have had their influence on cohesion and the resolution of internal conflicts. These constitutional changes, especially with regard to the indigenous rights of rural people, have not gone unnoticed in Zumbahua. As will become clear in the following chapters on the settlement of internal conflicts (note that this term itself is a creation of the 1998 Constitution), the constitutional recognition of legal pluralism has influenced the processes of settlement. For example, references to articles 191 of the 1998 Constitution or 171 of the Montecristi Constitution have become increasingly common in defenses of the right to use customary law.[65] However, the lack of coordinating rules seems to have had an impact on the settlement of a number of disputes. It will be shown that, in certain cases, especially those in which the competence of indigenous authorities is at stake, the question regarding jurisdiction (that is, who is allowed to adjudicate a given legal matter) seems to have become even more relevant than the actual dispute itself. As such, poverty,

---

64 Martínez Novo (2004: 244) describes *huasipugueros* as being more privileged than *yanaperos*, since they already owned small plots of land.
65 This could be considered an example of "interlegality," in the sense of the process of the mixing of elements of different legal systems (see also the section on interlegality in the previous chapter).

migration, the presence of the state, and the power of indigenous movements are far from the only important factors that affect the daily life – with its mix of cohesion and conflict – of the residents of Zumbahua. The constitutional recognition of legal pluralism is also critically important in this respect.

5 Conflicts, authorities, and procedures

Introduction

Becker's and Weismantel's research on Zumbahua focuses on conflicts between the community and the hacienda, as well as on tensions (whether economic or ethical) within the community. It is striking that, during the timeframe covered by them, the state was not a subject in these conflicts.[1] In a way, the opportunities of the people living in Zumbahua to settle their disputes seemed to be limited to their own locality within a context involving the relative absence of the state. With regard to contemporary internal conflicts, this book will show that not much has changed over the past thirty years. Although from an outsider's point of view, rural and indigenous life seems characterized by a high degree of harmony, the actual daily reality remains that of people involved in disputes about money, land, relationships, and other matters. What has changed recently are the kinds of authorities these people have recourse to in order to settle any conflicts that may arise. These increased options have resulted from the contemporary situation of formal legal pluralism.

This chapter is about conflicts in Zumbahua, and the wide range of authorities that can be resorted to in order to settle said conflicts. Before delving into the local reality, this chapter starts with a short theoretical section on understanding disputes. A section then follows on conflicts in Zumbahua, in which an analytical distinction is made between so-called "family norms" and "community norms." The former concern family affairs and sexual violence, while the latter concern property, violent crime, and breaching social norms. It will be shown that such distinctions in fact are often rather arbitrary, given that the people of Zumbahua do not categorize their conflicts in such a way, and also because their disputes tend to be multifaceted. For Zumbahuans, a more important distinction when it comes to conflict resolution has to do with the authorities that are resorted to. This section will show that the particular circumstances of a given conflict will determine which authority is considered capable of settling the problem.

---

1   In the example discussed in Becker (2007), the state was involved, but only as an *object*.

The present chapter focuses on the available authorities (and their procedures) in the parish of Zumbahua. It will be seen that clear and firm rules regarding the capability of each available authority cannot be distinguished (see also García 2002: 72–75). One of the main reasons for this indistinctness is the lack of rules that define the personal, territorial, and material jurisdiction of customary law in relation to national law. For example, in instances of family disputes, one sometimes turns to a *cabildo* and other times to the *teniente político*. In instances involving sexual violence, on the other hand, plaintiffs often prefer to recur to the Civil Court in Pujilí. In cases involving "community norms" (for example, conflicts over land), disputants may resort to either indigenous authorities or to the provincial court. In this connection, it should also be borne in mind that, in addition to the *availability* of legal venues, there is the important factor of *favorability* that determines such choices (that is, a party's perception of which authority is likely to provide a favorable outcome to their case).

Even as regards the limited issue of the jurisdiction of indigenous authorities, there are no clear rules. Generally, jurisdiction is determined by *where* the conflict took place and the seriousness of the conflict. Concerning domestic problems, parents, grandparents, or godparents often become involved. Authorities dealing with problems on the community level, on the other hand, are *cabildos, asambleas generales,* or OSGs (Brandt & Valdivia 2007; García 2002: 31–41; Ilaquiche 2004b: 60–62). However, the lack of a clear distinction between such domestic problems and community problems can often make it difficult to determine jurisdiction. With the characteristics of customary law in mind, it is obvious that these unclear boundaries between the competences of indigenous authorities result from customary law's flexibility. Strictly speaking, only national law provides clear procedures to determine which court holds jurisdiction in a given conflict. What results, as the remainder of this chapter will show, is a highly complex and nuanced picture when it comes to conflict resolution in Zumbahua.

Understanding disputes

As stated in this book's theoretical chapter, since the 1940s the focus of legal anthropological research has been on studying disputes. For many years, the primary question of concern had to do with whether "primitive" societies could be considered to function under some kind of rule of law. Some seventy years ago, the research focus shifted to the matter of how to study customary law. Disputes were regarded as the most reliable sources of knowledge concerning unwritten rules inherent in the legal systems under study. Scholars such as Llewellyn, Hoebel, and Pospisil believed that, by studying disputes, a methodological answer could be found to the question of how to study oral legal orders in the non-Western world. The analysis of "problem-cases" became a standard for conducting legal anthropological research. From the early 1960s on, the focus of study of such cases shifted from an interest in the rules and dispute settlement institutions to an interest in the behavior connected to disputing and the reasons for disputes. As such, the study of disputes became a key for understanding social relations in action (Caplan 1995: 1; Comaroff & Roberts 1981: 249; Snyder 1981: 143–144; K. von Benda-Beckmann 2003: 235–236).

Another shift occurred more recently, involving moving from a narrow view of disputes as a means of settling disagreements (that is, "dispute" equals "trial"), to a broader view that encompasses the initial grievance, the trial, and the final outcome of the case (that is, "dispute" equals "social process"). From the 1980s on, researchers believed that, broadly speaking, disputes followed different phases. Snyder (1981: 147), for example, recognized the pre-conflict or grievance stage, the conflict stage, and the dispute stage, as three phases of the dispute process. Felstiner et al. (1980–81) went further, identifying the following aspects of conflict preceding the actual trial: "naming" (that is, characterizing a particular experience as injurious); "blaming" (during which a perceived injurious experience becomes transformed into a grievance); and "claiming" (involving the voicing of a grievance to the person or entity believed to be responsible, and the requesting of some remedy). In the "claiming" phase, the grievance becomes transformed into a dyadic disagreement. Felstiner et al. (1980–81) emphasized the transitions among these phases. Such transformations are caused by, and have consequences for, the parties involved, the scope of the conflict, and the entities adjudicating disputes.[2] These transformations lead to a further development, in which the dyadic disagreement evolves into a triadic process. This broader view of dispute processes takes into account not only the strategic behavior of the disputing, but also of the adjudicating institutions. This has resulted in a fundamental change in how courts and other authorities were viewed. Their role in settling disputes was no longer taken for granted (K. von Benda-Beckmann 2003: 236) and they, as well as the parties involved in the conflict, now had to be seen as objects as well as subjects in the different phases of dispute processes.

While the above-mentioned authors emphasize the different phases preceding the settlement of a dispute, Keebet von Benda-Beckmann (2003: 238) argues that the dispute process should not be considered to be over after the final ruling has been issued. She in fact takes up a point previously made by Felstiner et al. (1980–81: 639), namely that "there is always a residuum of attitudes, learned techniques, and sensitivities that will, consciously or unconsciously, color later conflict." They also argued that any given dispute might continue even after a settlement, or that the end of one dispute might lead in turn to a new grievance.

---

2   In their article, Felstiner et al. (1980: 639–649) differentiate among: 1) the identity and the number of parties involved, 2) the scope of the conflict, 3) the choice of an audience and/or institution, 4) the objectives sought, 5) the prevailing ideology, 6) influence of reference groups, 7) the representatives and officials involved, and 8) the dispute institutions involved. The authors emphasize that it is not possible to present subjects (what is being transformed) and agents (who do the transformation) by means of a simple matrix, since every factor can be construed as both.

This means that the expectation that disputes be resolved can lead to a harmony that is overly idealistic (Colson 1995; K. von Benda-Beckmann 2003). Keebet von Benda-Beckmann (2003: 238) consequently argues that the transformation process enters a new phase when a dispute is settled by a court or another authority and (together with the parties involved) returns to the social environment from which it originated. It is in this old (or more often: changed) social setting where the real outcome of the settlement is negotiated. Thus, one can not only distinguish a pre-trial and a trial phase in the disputing process, but also a post-trial phase.[3]

Just as Kritzer (2011: 4) views the "naming–blaming–claiming" schema as an abstraction of a more complex reality, I think that this counts for the "pre-trial–trial–post-trial" model as well. Different phases overlap, and parties and institutions easily switch between being an object or a subject during the whole process. This is especially the case in a legal pluralistic context, where the co-existence of two different (and at times competing) legal systems can make things more complicated. One can think of the possibility of "forum shopping" and "shopping forums" during the pre-trial phase; but forum shopping can just as easily occur during the trial or the post-trial phase. For example, it is not uncommon for a situation involving a specific settlement employing customary law that is disputed by indigenous people themselves to result in recourse to national law by one of the parties.[4] In addition, as will be shown in Chapter 8, while in some instances a dispute may be considered settled according to customary law, there is always a possibility of violation of the "double jeopardy" rule by national law.

In sum, disputes provide information about more than just law: they also provide a lens through which social relationships may be better observed. In addition, studying disputes is not only about trials, it is about disputing processes – including the pre-trial and the post-trial phase – in which law plays a role. In other words, in contemporary legal anthropology research, disputes do not primarily serve as a means to understand law, but rather provide an insight into dispute processes, the behavior of human beings involved in the dispute, and the role of law in its resolution. The overall aim of this book is to show how formal legal pluralism works in daily practice, and how disputes are resolved under such a system. Therefore, the scope of this research is mainly on disputes in the narrow sense. After all, it is during the trial phase that both legal systems are most likely to clash. Let us now turn to what kind of initially dyadic disagreements are asserted publicly, and which can thus become objects of trials in the Zumbahuan setting.

---

3   This distinction was suggested by Keebet von Benda-Beckmann in her lecture on dispute management, during the International Course on Legal Pluralism *Living Realities of Legal Pluralism*, held by the Commission on Legal Pluralism in Cape Town, South Africa (September 4–7, 2011).
4   See for example *acta* May 5, 2002, La Cocha, but also Jackson and Warren (2005: 563).

110 *Conflicts, authorities, and procedures*

Conflict and conflict resolution in Zumbahua

Most Zumbahuan "conflicts" or "problems" (both terms are used in local discussions of legal disputes) are just as common and varied as almost anywhere else. Homicides also occasionally occur. The bulk of the disputes are directly or indirectly related to the characteristics of life in an indigenous community and its contextual challenges, as described in the preceding chapter: scarcity of land, poverty, excessive drinking, migration, and so on. But whatever their cause, all disputes can be traced back to a violation of the standards or values within the parish. The purpose of this section is to provide insight into the variety of disputes that occur in the parish of Zumbahua. It is based on interviews, archival research, and the literature. Its focus is on disputes in the trial phase, but some attention will be paid to the violation of community norms as well.

The basic social values of reciprocity, solidarity, and collectivity are the guiding principles of customary law in Andean communities. Therefore, the most important umbrella norms are *ama lulla* (do not lie), *ama shua* (do not steal), and *ama killa* (do not be lazy) (Colloredo-Mansfeld 2002; García 2002: 41; Ilaquiche 2004b: 30; Yumbay 2007). It has been said that these basic norms have applied since the time of the Incas (Colloredo-Mansfeld 2002), but this does not imply that their subsequent lines of action are unchangeable, "traditional," or "authentic." Basic features of customary law are its flexibility, changeability, and adaptiveness. This means that the norms that are being applied in Zumbahua are subject to change. Through work, travel, or any kind of day-to-day businesses, people come into contact with the outside world. Almost anyone in Zumbahua has some sort of contact with people living in cities (inside or outside Ecuador): 93 percent of residents listen to the radio every day and 70 percent watch television (Brandt & Valdivia 2007: 46). This means that a wide range of ideas about individuality, gender, human rights, and other important issues have reached Zumbahua as well. As a result, when people talk about and deal with the norms that guide their lives, there is a constant tension between notions of tradition and modernity (Brandt & Valdivia 2007: 14).

Family affairs

When asked about possible conflicts, most of my informants refer to issues within their families. Whether it is the *teniente político*, a police officer, a member of the Junta Parroquial, a *dirigente* of a *cabildo*, my friend Sergio, "the man on the street," or a well-informed outsider like Jean Colvin, everybody refers – in different words – to "conflicts within the family." Some persons refer to "physical violence" or "aggression against women." Many such crimes are never reported, and thus they sometimes do not appear in *actas* or other legal records. Nevertheless, they do occur frequently. Since domestic violence is a very sensitive issue among the Kichwa (Berk-Seligson 2006: 15), Jean Colvin has typified them as "silent crimes."[5] "Family affairs," however, are not only about aggression against women. The term encompasses a far greater range of behavior, including separation of couples, divorce, and adultery (see the next chapter's Rosita vs. Miguel case). So is the disobedience of children and theft among relatives. A typical kind of family conflict concerns broken marriage commitments.

Cases I came across in different *libros de actas* concern a wide range of quarrels between family members, most of them between spouses. For example, there are references to a man "physically attacking his wife with a knife";[6] and a couple "physically attacking each other."[7] The most severe case was one concerning the death of a woman "who was being tortured by her own husband."[8] There were also references to adultery.[9] Family conflicts can occur not only between spouses, but also between siblings. One case I came across concerned a quarrel between a brother and a sister over an inheritance that resulted in the latter being hospitalized.[10] Not all cases of family members having a difference of opinion or not getting along together end up being serious family conflicts. A good example of this involves Sergio, who separated from his wife a couple of years ago, but still gets along with her quite well, especially when it comes to matters involving the wellbeing and education of their two children.[11]

Brandt and Valdivia (2006) confirm that family conflicts involving psychological or physical abuse are the most common problem in the Andean highlands.[12] Most of these cases concern the conduct of a husband towards his wife. Fewer cases concern sexual assaults. And some cases involve women assaulting their husbands. Such cases may also have to do with the physical abuse of parents toward children, or *vice versa*. Fights between siblings have also been recorded (Brandt & Valdivia 2006: 133). Other types of problems within the family that were noted by Brandt and Valdivia (2006) involved the separation of couples, divorce, and infidelity. Still other cases had to do with husbands or wives running away from home, adoption, inheritance, and the failure of men to pay alimony following a divorce.

Sexual violence

A particular form of family conflicts is sexual violence. The most common forms of sexual violence involve cases of rape, as well as cases of a young

5 Interview with Jean Colvin on August 24, 2010.
6 "*Maltrata físico [...] con una arma blanca a su esposa*," *Libro de actas* Guantópolo, January 1, 2008.
7 "*Maltrata físico tanto al uno al otro*," *Libro de actas*, Guantópolo, January 3, 2008.
8 "[Q]*uien fue torturado por el propio esposo*," *Libro de actas*, Guantópolo, November 5 and 6, 2002 (see also Vintimilla et al. 2007: 77).
9 *Libro de actas*, Guantópolo, October 30, 2008.
10 Interview with a *dirigente* in Guantópolo, on November 14, 2010.
11 During the countless conversations I had with Sergio, he shared personal information with me about his life.
12 The research contained 802 different cases of which 122 (15.2 percent) concerned *violencia familiar* (Brandt & Valdivia 2006: 140).

woman being made pregnant by a boyfriend, and the biological father denying paternity. Most of these cases are handled within the community (Brandt & Valdivia 2006: 30, 133; García 2002: 30, 2009a: 129). A typical dyadic disagreement – between the pregnant woman and her lover – thus soon becomes a triadic process. Parents, family elders, or even *dirigentes* typically come into the picture at some point.[13] Although they usually succeed in settling the dispute by negotiation or mediation, some cases reach the formal legal system, and thus have to be settled at the Civil Court in Pujilí. In a formal lawsuit, these cases usually end up in a dispute over alimony. This is because denying fatherhood as such is not an offense, but the obligation to pay alimony can be enforced by civil law.

While doing research in the archives of the Civil Court in Pujilí, I came across two such lawsuits concerning alimony in relation to incidents of sexual violence which had taken place in the parish of Zumbahua.[14] In the first case, a twenty-five year old unmarried woman with a baby daughter went to the civil judge in Pujilí on January 9, 2009. She wanted the presumed biological father of the girl to pay monthly alimony of $100, because "he had completely forgotten about living costs, clothing, medicines, etc., etc."[15] She had brought this written suit as a plaintiff to the judge with help from an attorney.[16] She demanded that the man recognize his paternity and pay child support. The man, however, denied paternity and refused any financial responsibility whatsoever to the woman and her daughter. To resolve the paternity question, the man was summoned by the judge to undergo a DNA-test at the Ecuadorian Red Cross. The test proved that the defendant was indeed the girl's father. More than six months later, the judge ordered the man to pay a monthly alimony of $35 to the girl's mother. Another case, which involved a twenty-three year old man, seemed a lot more straightforward. Together with his attorney, he tried to counter the claim of a paternity suit of a woman for the lump sum of $1,200 by arguing he "never knew of a child for whom I bore responsibility" and that he never recognized the child in any Civil Registry or before any other authority.[17] He thus argued that there were no grounds for the claim, and he offered to take a DNA test to prove that he was not the father. At the time of this writing, this case was still being tried, so no decision can be presented. However, these two cases of sexual violence illustrate the unpredictability of such cases. They also illustrate the aforementioned

---

13 Interview with a former *dirigente* in Tigua, on October 28, 2010.
14 Caso 2009–371 and Caso 2009–10/2009–377, Juzgado Quinto de lo Civil, Pujilí.
15 "[S]e*ha olvidado por complete de los alimentos, vestuario, medicinas, etc., etc.*," Caso 2009–371, Juzgado Quinto de lo Civil, Pujilí.
16 One does not need an attorney in order to represent a party to a case that only involves alimony (Ley Reformatoria al Titulo V, Libro II del Código de la Niñez y Adolescencia). However, because this case was also about the recognition of paternity, the woman had to have a representative.
17 "[N]*unca tuve conocimiento de la existencia de un hijo bajo mi responsabilidad*," Caso 2009–10/2009–377, Juzgado Quinto de lo Civil, Pujilí.

difference between notions of tradition (settlement within the community) and modernity (a DNA test).

Property

Problems concerning property, possession, or ownership are the second most common source of disputes. Almost all of my informants in the parish of Zumbahua related stories of robberies that they knew of. According to García (2002: 30) violation of the norms related to property concern theft of inanimate possessions or animals; disputes over land, borders, or the settlement of individual or collective debts; or vandalism. It seems obvious that there can be other sources of property disputes. For example, when people mention "robberies," they typically refer to petty-theft, burglary, or robbery. A "robbery" (*robo* in Spanish) can thus refer to the theft of a gas-tank,[18] or to a hold-up or pickpocketing of tourists.[19] And disputes over land might refer to a disagreement over property boundaries, but just as easily it can refer to a dispute over a right of way, or over livestock destroying crops. In fact, any number of issues can result in a property dispute. However, in the following paragraphs I will give some examples of the more typical kinds of property disputes. One could say that the norms mentioned in the previous two sections basically concern socalled "family norms" and that, with the introduction of problems concerning property, "community norms" are being dealt with.[20]

Many of the instances of theft reported to me were related by my informants to unemployment. Some of them even related theft to migration and

---

18 *Archivo de las denuncias en general, Teniente Político* of Zumbahua, October 16, 2010.
19 Interview with police officer in Zumbahua, October 28, 2010.
20 The literature has categorized local norms in a number of different ways. For example, Brandt and Valdivia (2007; see also Vintimilla et al. 2007: 74) distinguish between so-called "family norms" and "community norms." Family norms cover topics such as what is a family, who belongs to a family, and the rights and obligations of each family member. Concerning the latter, different norms count for fathers, mothers, children, grandparents, and others. Family norms also concern which problems or conflicts should be solved within the family or by (an) outsider(s). And finally, family norms concern the rights and obligations of living together. Community norms, on the other hand, cover a wide range of rules concerning the community: who belongs to it, rights and obligations, how members of a community should live together, and what to do should conflicts arise. Basically, Brandt and Valdivia used this difference for purposes related to their quantitative research. One frequently used distinction in the Ecuadorian Andes has been suggested by Fernando García (2002: 30, 2009: 129; also used in Brandt & Valdivia 2006: 30). García employs the following categories: family disputes, sexual violence, violation of social norms, property disputes, and life-threatening conflicts. This categorization, based on his own ethnographic research, fits into my own findings, based on interviews with informants and research in *actas* and legal files. That is why I draw heavily on García's work in my attempt to unravel the diversity of potential and actual disputes in the parish of Zumbahua.

subsequent changes in attitude. Early in the course of my research, when I explained to my friend Sergio what my study involved, he said that I probably would be interested in the large number of robberies that take place in Zumbahua, which he saw as closely connected to the high rate of unemployment in the region.[21] I had a similar experience with a police officer. When I went to the police station for the first time, mainly to introduce myself and to explain the purpose of my research, the officer on duty did not hesitate to point out to me that theft has its roots in poverty and unemployment. He added that most instances of theft were committed by minors who, as a result of difficult economic circumstances, were often forced to migrate to nearby towns to search for work, and who only returned to their community on weekends.[22] Two months later, when I had an interview with one of the members of the Junta Parroquial of Zumbahua, this "problem" of migration of mostly young people was explained to me. Migration, according to this official, causes the problem of "acculturation" (that is, adapting one's conduct and values to a culture different from the one that a person was raised in). Basically he argued that, when people live and work in nearby towns, sooner or later their behavior and attitudes change (for example, wearing Western instead of "traditional" clothes or embracing different standards and values). This informant felt that, due to immigration, those migrants lost their respect for local, "traditional" norms, and thus became susceptible to committing theft.[23] On the whole, my informants not only suggested a direct relationship between poverty and theft, but also an indirect link between migration and crime.

Several cases concerned damage or destruction of material possessions, territory, crops, or animals (Brandt & Valdivia 2006: 128). Many of these instances resulted from accidents (for example, traffic accidents; or livestock eating or damaging neighbors' crops while crossing fields). However, sometimes the destruction clearly appeared to be intentional (for example, resulting from rivalry between neighbors or different families). An appropriate illustration of these kinds of cases is related by Nancy Wiltink (2005: 192). She describes a case of some inhabitants of the community of Quilotoa who, afraid of losing some additional income as tourist-guides or as hostel owners, vandalized road signs that were placed on a popular walk from the lake, and which directed tourists to a hostel in a neighboring community. A second large group of cases concerns disputes over territory or boundaries. Brandt and Valdivia (2006: 140) recorded that almost 11 percent of all cases under research were related to either damage and destruction or disputes over land.[24] This picture is confirmed by what I found in the archives of the Civil Court in Pujilí. Most

---

21 Informal conversation with Sergio on August 14, 2010.
22 Conversation with police officer on August 20, 2010.
23 Interview with member of the Junta Parroquial in Zumbahua on October 21, 2010.
24 I came across several examples of disputes over land in *actas* (for example, in the *libro de actas* of Guantópolo).

likely, the majority of such cases are related to the scarcity of arable land in the highlands.

Violent crime

Although not as frequently mentioned as family conflicts or robberies, violent crime is by no means infrequent in the parish of Zumbahua.[25] There are numerous instances of fights, and of physical or verbal attacks registered in the *Archivos de las denuncias en general* of the *teniente político*.[26] Violent crime is also commonly reported to the Fiscal Indígena's office.[27] Most of my informants related violent crime to excessive drinking,[28] especially at parties.[29] Another common class of complaints involved merely the threat of violence.[30] As will be shown in Chapter 8, in connection with the La Cocha-Guantópolo murder case, some such threats are actually carried out.

Most cases of violent crime concern fistfights in which no weapons are used. In those instances in which weapons are used, they are usually what people come across during the fight: a rock, a bottle, or a piece of wood. In a fight I witnessed during a wedding-party at the central Plaza in Zumbahua, broken bottles were used, and during the fight in La Cocha in 2002 that caused the death of Maly Latacunga, a rock, a pipe, and a screwdriver were used. Such weapons often result in injuries requiring medical treatment, and the resulting doctors' bills become the object of litigation. If the parties to the dispute cannot resolve the disagreement by themselves, a *cabildo* or the *teniente político* has to decide who is responsible for paying the bill.[31] And if a dispute arises regarding the validity of injuries or doctor's bills, one can go to a Fiscal Indígena to obtain officially stamped medical certificates.[32]

---

25 For the purpose of this chapter I will stretch García's restricted description of *conflictos contra la vida* (conflicts aimed at one's life) (García 2002: 30). He defines such conflicts as those related to murder or attempted murder, suicide, and fatal traffic accidents. I am also including fights and assaults in the public sphere (otherwise it would be a so-called "family affair") within this category.
26 See for example: *Archivo de las denuncias en general, Teniente Político* of Zumbahua, October 10, 2010, or November 6, 2010.
27 Archival research conducted at the Fiscal Indígena's office on November 24, 2010.
28 Alcohol-related violence seems to be not only a contemporary issue. Korovkin (2001: 51) notes that in the 1950s and 1960s, fighting in relation to drinking provided *tenientes políticos* (in the canton of Otovalo) "an apparently unending source of unpaid labor."
29 Interview with a police officer in Zumbahua on October 28, 2010, and with an ex-*dirigente* of Guantópolo on November 1, 2010. See also Brandt and Valdivia (2006: 133–134).
30 *Archivo de las denuncias en general, Teniente Político* of Zumbahua, August 1, 2010.
31 See for example *libro de actas* Guantópolo, August 19, 2002.
32 Interview at the Fiscal Indígena's office in Latacunga, November 24, 2010.

Social norms

This last group of norms concerns a wide range of mostly communal or public rights and obligations (Brandt & Valdivia 2006: 30; García 2002: 30, 2009a: 129; Vintimilla et al. 2007: 93). A lot of these social norms directly touch upon the basic local social values of reciprocity, solidarity, and collectivity. According to these values, one should accept one's responsibilities, refrain from fighting, not cause trouble, not destroy the natural environment, and not vandalize communal property.[33] It is here that the contrast with national law is most obvious. For example, local norms hold that one should not gossip, slander, or engage in witchcraft.[34] Residents are also enjoined to respect authorities, to do communal work, and to consider presenting themselves as candidates for a public function such as *asesor* ("adviser") or *dirigente*. In turn, advisors and *dirigentes* are expected to fulfill their responsibilities.

A lot of these norms consist of unwritten *costumbres* (customs), which are informal rules aimed at enforcing customary law. Written rules, on the other hand, consist of covenants or regulations of OTGs like the MICC in Latacunga and OSGs like the UNOCIC in La Cocha or the UNOCAT in Tigua,[35] as well as regulations enforced, or fines imposed, by local authorities. For example, the Junta Parroquial of Zumbahua has a written set of rules regarding the weekly Saturday market posted on the door of its office, next to a set of rules regulating the registration of teams for a local sporting event. The *cabildo* of Guantópolo has an extended list of obligations and agreements on various issues, from collective harvesting to participation in indigenous protest marches. Such rules are an example of what was referred to in Chapter 2 as the composite social, political, and legal nature of customary law (Harper 2011: 17).[36] It is the existence of these social norms that make the above-mentioned tension between notions of tradition and modernity (Brandt & Valdivia 2007: 14) most visible.

Coincidence of conflicts

Finally, it is important to note that many incidents involve more than one of the previously mentioned elements. This miscellaneous category contains a

---

33 In Zumbahua, for example, it is forbidden to fight in the streets or otherwise disturb public order. Most of the time, such fights are caused by excessive drinking during parties, so the fight during the wedding party at the main square in Zumbahua, as was described in the previous chapter, provides a good illustration of such a disturbance.
34 See for example *Archivo de las denuncias en general, teniente político* of Zumbahua, October 23, 2010, when someone complains that she has been accused of being a witch.
35 UNOCIC: Unión de Organizaciones y Comunidades Indígenas de La Cocha (Union of Indigenous Organizations and Communities of La Cocha); UNOCAT: Unión de Organizaciones y Cabildos de Tigua (Union of Indigenous Organizations and Communities of Tigua).
36 See for example the rules regarding the *Asociación de Mujeres* (Women's Association) in Guantópolo; *libro de actas* March 12, 2003.

wide variety of crimes and infractions, as became clear to me when I examined both police files in Zumbahua and the *libros de actas* at the *teniente político*'s office. To name just a few examples: counterfeit banknotes, traffic accidents, driving without a license, or selling and drinking alcohol on Sundays. An illustrative example of coincidence of conflicts is provided by the next chapter's Rosita vs. Miguel case, in which the parties initially resorted to the *teniente político* because of the commission of a violent crime: a fight that caused injuries requiring medical treatment. Rosita and Miguel wanted the *teniente político* to resolve the issue of who was responsible for the costs of treatment. Each party blamed the other for having started the fight which had caused the injuries, and therefore they each held the other responsible for the medical costs. This conflict thus seemed to primarily revolve around a financial issue. However, it soon emerged that the fight occurred because each of the parties' spouses had had an extramarital relationship with one another. Rosita's husband had been unfaithful with Miguel's wife. Thus, a family conflict was also involved. In addition, the affair and resulting fight had caused some serious tension between the two extended families – yet another issue that needed to be addressed.

Such coincidence of conflicts proves that the kinds of distinctions made in the above sections, however useful they are as an analytical tool, can in fact prove to be rather arbitrary. So is the distinction between "family norms" and "community norms" (Brandt & Valdivia 2007; Valdivia & González Luna 2009), between written and unwritten norms (Brandt & Valdivia 2007), and between severe cases and minor cases. Any combination of family conflicts, property disputes, violent crime, and violation of community norms can occur. All these distinctions are arbitrary because the people of Zumbahua do not categorize their conflicts in such ways. In fact, if they make any distinction at all, it is on the basis of authorities that adjudicate (or might adjudicate) particular conflicts. As will be shown in the following chapters, authorities often categorize cases in terms of the kind of conflict, the parties involved, and where, when, and under what circumstances it transpired. All of this serves to reiterate an important point made in the previous chapter: that conflicts in Zumbahua are difficult to classify in simple terms. This is one of the main reasons why a comparison with national law is so difficult. Local Zumbahuan conflicts, or customary law, do not differentiate between civil law and penal law, or between serious crimes and less serious misdemeanors or infractions.[37] All this is another way of saying that conflicts in Zumbahua cover a broad range of social life.

Local authorities

Family

If one studies customary law, its norms and practices, one can hardly ignore the family's role as an authority. This is because a lot of initially dyadic

---

37 Article 10, Código Penal (Penal Code).

disagreements, mostly family disputes, are settled *within* the family itself. This results in some people (some of my informants and some scholars alike) considering the family as the lowest-level authority. The conflicts within a family concern a wide range of issues, from insults between spouses, to alcohol abuse, to getting a divorce. Because the majority of such conflicts are sensitive issues (see also Berk-Seligson 2006), people in Zumbahua tend to settle them in the private sphere. Family authorities include parents, grandparents, family elders, or even godparents (Brandt & Valdivia 2007: 100; Ilaquiche 2004b; 61). In an earlier publication, Brandt and Valdivia (2006: 145) even draw a distinction between the nuclear family and the extended family, showing that almost three times as many people attempt to resolve family issues within the nuclear family. Both the nature of the disputes and the settlements reached are highly varied in nature. Thus, conflicts might involve a mutually acceptable agreement, a simple lecture from an adult to a minor or, in more serious cases, the imposition of punishments such as the lecture of an elder or even corporal punishment and/or "purifying" rituals.[38] It is only when an internal family dispute cannot be solved *within* the family, either because it involves an especially serious matter, or because it continually recurs, that the parties involved turn to a communal authority like a *cabildo* (Berk-Seligson 2006; Brandt & Valdivia 2007: 100; Vintimilla et al. 2007: 96).[39] It is for this reason that a *cabildo* is generally considered more broadly to be the lowest-level authority, at least when it comes to administering justice. To paraphrase García (2002: 31–33), a family provides good advice, and the community judges and sentences.

The cabildo *and the* asamblea general

Broadly speaking, when conflicts cannot be resolved in the private sphere, or when problems are considered to be beyond the family's capacity to cope with them, one turns to a *cabildo* or to an *asamblea general*. Basically, a *cabildo* deals with conflicts that concern only individual parties, and an *asamblea general* handles conflicts that concern the community. Thus, a *cabildo* addresses family matters, conflicts between neighbors (for example disputes over land) and instances of petty theft. An *asamblea general*, on the other hand, adjudicates matters involving adultery, violence, more serious theft, or the violation of social norms. The intervention of an *asamblea general* is also called upon in cases of recidivism. Thus, if one has already been indicted twice by a *cabildo*, the third offense will be adjudicated by an *asamblea general*. In instances involving the most serious crimes (for example, murder), OSGs (like the UNOCAT in Tigua, or the UNOCIC in La Cocha) or even an OTG (like the

---

38 As was explained to me by several informants during formal and informal conversations. An example of a mutual agreement in case of a divorce was provided by Sergio.
39 Interview with a former *dirigente* of the Tigua community on October 28, 2010.

MICC in the Cotopaxi province) can be called upon to assist.[40] Indigenous authorities like a *cabildo*, an *asamblea general*, an OSG, and an OTG should not be confused with locally existing Juntas del Campesinado (often referred to by residents as "Juntas Campesinas"), a kind of rural police, specialized in identifying and punishing livestock robbers.[41] The former are formal entities, while the latter are loosely constituted groups formed at the local level (Berk-Seligson 2006; Vintimilla 2003), may even be illegal (*El Comercio* 2010k), and are openly criticized for taking justice into their own hands. To my knowledge, such Juntas Campesinas do not operate in the parish of Zumbahua. The formal indigenous authorities, on the other hand, do.

A *cabildo* consists of a chairman, a deputy chairman, a secretary, a treasurer, a delegate, and several ordinary members. Each officer is chosen for a term of two years. Only "decent" community members qualify for service on the *cabildo*. Specific requirements are as follows: minimum age of eighteen, being well known in the community, and primary level education. The secretary is required to know how to read and write in both Spanish and Kichwa (because during trials both Spanish and Kichwa are spoken, but the *actas* must be recorded in Spanish). Furthermore, one has to have demonstrated one's abilities, honesty, experience, and leadership. And of course, the secretary must be thoroughly versed in local practices and customs. A *cabildo* member also has to know how to apply them. Members are also expected to be receptive to the advice and intervention of former *dirigentes* and the elderly (Becker 1999: 541; Ilaquiche 2004b: 63–64; Weismantel 1988: 52–53).

An *asamblea general* is a body comprising both *cabildo* members and other community representatives. More specifically, when a *cabildo* is consulted, it is usually the chairman or the secretary who settles the conflict. In the case of an *asamblea general*, it is the *cabildo* in collaboration with the community that decides.

A *cabildo* and an *asamblea general* apply customary law. This means that they are guided by the basic social values of reciprocity, solidarity, and collectivity, with their most important umbrella norms being *ama lulla* (do not lie), *ama shua* (do not steal), and *ama killa* (do not be lazy). When a particular conflict has "civil law" characteristics, resolution is to be found by means of a consensus of members that leads to a reconciliation between the parties. For

---

40 Brandt and Valdivia (2006: 29), Brandt and Valdivia (2007: 113–117), and Cervone (2012) even mention OSGs and OTGs applying customary law on their own, but this is not common practice in the parish of Zumbahua, as far as I can tell.
41 Juntas Campesinas are groups of rural citizens (*mestizos* and/or *indígenas*) who patrol the countryside in order to chase and punish robbers, especially livestock robbers. They are feared for their brutality. They are criticized openly for using objectionable practices like blackmailing and extortion. Unlike customary law, the practices of the Juntas Campesinas are not aimed at compensation or reconciliation, but at punishment. For more information see the following: Berk-Seligson (2006), *El Comercio* (2010i), *El Comercio* (2010j), *El Comercio* (2010k), Vintimilla (2003).

example, in the Rosita vs. Miguel case, a part of the conflict concerned infidelity, and this was settled by an agreement in which the two unfaithful individuals had to promise not to see or to call each other again in the near future, and to publicly apologize to their spouses. On the other hand, when a conflict has "penal law" characteristics,[42] most of the sentences imposed have elements of compensation or restitution. In the Rosita vs. Miguel case, it was agreed that Miguel had to pay Rosita's costs. In other words, as regards that aspect of the conflict that concerned the physical fight, the damage caused by the injuries (that is, the doctor's bills) had to be reimbursed.

The main objective of the settlement of a dispute according to customary law is to maintain or repair harmony, thus creating a new equilibrium that embraces the entire community, as well as the individuals directly involved in the conflict.

> "[T]he settlement [must have] a social and moral character, and restore peace and harmony to the community."[43]

Customary law places a great deal of emphasis on the post-trial phase, and specifically on the restoration of harmony in the community in which the dispute originated (K. von Benda-Beckmann 2003: 238). It is in this social setting that the real outcome of the settlement is negotiated. That is why there is such an emphasis on reconciliation in what might commonly be seen as "civil cases." That is also why reconciliation, compensation, and restitution for damages are considered such crucial elements of such cases. Customary law not only takes the victim's wellbeing into account, it is also concerned with the offender's fate. Therefore, another purpose of customary law is the reintegration of the offender into the community. An additional purpose involves the re-education of the offender. Usually this is done by the current or former *cabildo* members, other *dirigentes*, and elders who provide counsel to the offender. In line with this, a final purpose of customary law is to serve as an example for the community, especially for its younger members. Basically, the objectives can be summarized as follows: an offender is required to reconcile him- or herself with both the victim and the larger community. At the same time, the sentence meted out is meant to serve as an example to the community.

The procedures for settling internal disputes according to customary law are flexible, and different stages are not always discernible. In addition, as is typical of customary law, procedures can vary widely between different regions and communities (Berk-Seligson 2006; Chávez & García 2004). The following exposition represents a typical scenario. First, a dispute has to be reported. In case of a report to a *cabildo*, this is done orally by the victims or

---

42 "[L]a sanción de carácter social, moral y de retorno de armonía y paz entre sus habitantes," acta May 5, 2002, La Cocha.
43 *Acta* May 5, 2002, La Cocha.

their relatives.⁴⁴ Such a report has to be accompanied by a request to resolve the problem under dispute. The authority then proceeds to launch its own independent investigation of the case. In the following stage, the two conflicting parties are brought together in the presence of the authority. First, the authority reports its findings. Then both parties get a chance to provide their versions of what happened. Then other parties (for example, relatives, community elders, or current or former *dirigentes*) are given a chance to speak. Basically, everybody involved or with some sort of status is given time to report findings or express feelings regarding the case. Finally, the chairman of the authority pronounces a sentence, in the company of other members, elders, and ex-leaders. If it is considered necessary, the agreements and/or the sentences are written down in a *libro de actas*.⁴⁵

The indigenous authorities have a wide range of sentences that they can apply, either separately or in combination. For example, they can limit their sentences to nothing more than a warning or advice. Usually this is followed by promises of the offending parties involved never to repeat their offenses.

> "[F]rom this day forward, never again commit an offense and continue to live in peace, respecting one another."⁴⁶

Indigenous authorities can impose a fine or threaten to do so in cases of recidivism or the breaking of an agreement.

> "It is hereby mutually agreed that anyone who makes trouble again will have to pay $1,..."⁴⁷

---

44 In case of a report to a higher authority (for example, to an OSG) this has to be done by the chairman of a *cabildo* (Brandt & Valdivia 2007: 116).

45 Tibán and Ilaquiche (2004: 36–42) have elaborated extensively on these different stages. The first stage in an indigenous trial is called *willachina* (that is, the oral report of the internal conflict to the *cabildo* by the victim or his relatives). The next stage, *tapuykuna*, refers to the investigation done by the *cabildo*. The third stage, the *chimbapurana*, is the public trial at which the defendant and the accuser are brought together face-to-face. The *kuana*, which means "good counsel," is an essential component of this stage. During the last stage of *killpichirina*, a final ruling is issued, the sentence is determined, and the sanctions are imposed (see also Berk-Seligson 2006; Brandt & Valdivia 2006: 31–33; Llasag Fernandéz 2009: 198–199; Simon Thomas 2009: 31–35). A similar description of the different stages can be found in Poveda Moreno (2007: 185). The "Tibán and Ilaquiche Manual" can be found in several offices of legal officials and it is also required reading in a course at the Universidad de los Andes in Ambato (Berk-Seligson 2006). I obtained the Tibán and Ilaquiche Manual on July 23, 2007, at the bookstore of CODENPE in Quito, when I was there to interview Lourdes Tibán, at that time Secretaria Ejecutiva Nacional of that organization.

46 "[D]esde este fecha hacia adelante nunca más volverán a ofenderse de palabra y otra forma y vivirán en marco de paz, respetando uno al otro," *acta* July 10, 2008, Guantópolo.

47 "Se ponen de mutuo acuerdo ingresar de una acta [sic] de sanción de ambas partes de 1.000 dólares americanos, el que diera otra vez problemas," *acta* February 6, 2010, Guantópolo.

In the Rosita vs. Miguel case, a fine of $5,000 was threatened in the event that either party violated the promise not to see or call the other again in the near future. Litigants can be ordered to pay fines to either the victim or to the community.

> "[j]oint compensation of a human and social nature in favor of [the victim], requiring those involved to pay $3,000, which means x thousand dollars per each person involved"[48]

The settlement can also concern an obligation to repair the damage done (in the Rosita vs. Miguel case, Miguel had to pay Rosita's bills), to provide restitution for losses, or to compensate for damages or losses. In Chapter 2, an example was given of a case in which the head of a family was injured because of a fight. The offender might also be ordered to replace the victim in the fields for a specified duration of time. Work on behalf of the community can also be imposed.

> "[s]entencing [the guilty party] to five years of community work"[49]

One of the most severe punishments that can be imposed is temporary or permanent expulsion from the community (Brandt & Valdivia 2007: 143).

> "[e]xpulsion of [the guilty parties] from the community and the Zumbahua parish for two years, and assuming [financial] responsibility for the rehabilitation of the families involved"[50]

And finally, in almost in every case that I studied, the convicted party also had to admit his or her fault, and to apologize before all those present at the time of sentencing.

> "[a] public apology before all those assembled"[51]

In the Zumbahua region, several kinds of physical punishments (although their primary objective usually is not to "punish" in the sense of penance or penalty, but rather to be part of a purification ritual) can also be imposed. One of them is known as the *ortigazo*, which involves rubbing the skin of an

---

48 "*Indemnización de carácter solidario, social y humano a favor de [víctima] consistente en que los involucrados tienen que cancelar la cantidad de 3x mil dólares, que comprende x mil dólares cada involucrado,*" acta May 5, 2002, La Cocha.
49 "*Sentenciar en trabajo comunitario por el tiempo de 5 años,*" acta May 23, 2010, La Cocha.
50 "*Expulsión de [los culpables] durante dos años de la comunidad y la parroquia Zumbahua así como responsabilizarse de la rehabilitación por parte de los familiares involucrados,*" acta May 16, 2010, La Cocha.
51 "*El perdón público ante la asamblea,*", acta May 16, 2010, La Cocha.

offender with stinging nettles (*ortigas*). Its purpose is to purify and heal the offender. It is believed that these plants, which are provided by *Pachamama* (Mother Earth), extract "evil spirits" from the convicted person's body. The rubbing is typically combined with a shower of ice-cold water, although the shower can be applied by itself. In combination, the rubbing and shower provide the ultimate purification, resulting (according to the authorities) in the immediate expulsion of evil spirits.

> "[A] true punishment [...] with all of the materials provided by Mother Earth [consists of] a bath with healing plants [that is, the rubbing of the skin with stinging nettles and a shower with cold water]."[52]
> "a 30-minute bath with cold water and stinging nettles"[53]

This purification ritual is usually conducted by women.[54] In severe cases, the offender can be whipped. Whippings are carried out by *cabildo* members or elders. Another physical punishment involves making offenders walk a certain distance (for example several times around the main plaza), barefooted while carrying a sack filled with rocks or soil for a specified duration of time.

> "[T]he [offender] has to carry a quintal of earth from the place where he killed [the victim]."[55]

During this walk, the person who has been convicted is given warnings or counsel by one of the members of the *cabildo*. At times, the offender is required to show some piece of evidence, or the weapons with which they fought.[56] In the La Cocha murder case in 2002 (Simon Thomas 2009), one of the convicted men carried the pipe with which he had beaten the victim, while another had to walk carrying a screwdriver as well as a cardboard sign dangling around his neck that read "I killed someone with this screwdriver." In another case, the offender had to walk with a sign that indicated the name of the person that he had killed.[57]

Authorities also must decide upon the intensity of particular punishments. There are a lot of contextual circumstances an authority has to take into account, and the specific rulings vary among indigenous communities (Brandt

---

52 "[E]l castigo auténtico [...] con todos los materiales existentes en la Pachamama [...] el baño de plantas medicinales," *acta* May 5, 2002, La Cocha.
53 "[C]on el baño de agua con ortiga por el tiempo de 30 minutos," *acta* May 16, 2010, La Cocha.
54 See *acta* May 5, 2002, La Cocha, *acta* May 16, 2010, La Cocha, and Berk-Seligson (2006).
55 "[E]l [culpable] vendrá cargando un quintal de tierra desde el sitio donde mató a," *acta* November 5–7, year unknown, Guantópolo.
56 *Acta* May 5, 2002, La Cocha.
57 *Acta* November 5–7, year unknown, Guantópolo.

& Valdivia 2007: 124–128). Obviously, the sort of crime or infraction and its severity are important factors that determine sentencing. So does the damage that occurred as a result of the offense. The age, gender, and social status of both victims and perpetrators are also taken into consideration. Usually men are punished harder than women for the same crime. So are young and strong people, compared to their old and weak peers. *Dirigentes* and other persons with high status in the community also tend to be punished more severely. This is because it is felt that such persons have failed to set a good example. In addition, married persons are less likely to be expelled from the community, given that this would involve separation of offenders from their nuclear families. Every conceivable personal or contextual circumstance is taken into account in determining a sentence, which is typically the product of the results of the authorities' own investigation, combined with what has been said during the trial.

The teniente político *and the police*

The *teniente político*'s juridical role in general, and specifically in the parish of Zumbahua, will be discussed in detail in the next chapter. Briefly, a *teniente político* functions like a *juez de paz*. The *teniente político* receives complaints directly from aggrieved citizens, or he is informed by *dirigentes* from neighboring communities about citizen complaints. He is responsible for recording the reports of citizens who come to his office, and also for assigning cases beyond his own jurisdiction to the competent authorities. According to national law, he is only allowed to hear small civil cases or penal cases involving minor infractions. However, the *teniente político* in fact sometimes rules on cases that, strictly defined, lie outside his legal jurisdiction. He is required to apply national law but, as shown in the next chapter, the *teniente político* of Zumbahua typically issues rulings in accordance with customary law. Therefore, most people in Zumbahua look upon him as an indigenous authority or local authority, rather than as a state official (Brandt & Valdivia 2006: 137; Brandt & Valdivia 2007: 117).

The *teniente político* is also head of the local police force, which in the parish of Zumbahua consists of three officers who work shifts of six to nine days, which should result in at least two officers always being on duty. However, my personal observation was that there was generally no more than one officer on duty at any given time.[58] The Zumbahua police work out of a brand new police station near the center of town.[59] The station contains three medium-sized rooms of about 16 square meters each (one used as the office, one as the

---

58 This was explained to me by one of the *sargentos* (sergeants) as being a result of holidays and other days off; interview on October 28, 2010.
59 In the time between my first visit to Zumbahua on August 7, 2007, and a subsequent one on October 23, 2009, the old police station had been replaced by a new one.

sleep/living room, and one used for storage), a kitchen and two closets (one used as such and one used as an archive). Because rural police officers are not allowed to imprison anyone, the police station lacks a jail. The sleep/living room contains two beds, a small wardrobe, a side table, a television, and an ironing board with an electric iron. These furnishings are intended for the use of on-duty officers. On the morning that I first visited one of the officers at the police station, he was resting on his bed, watching television. The holster containing his handgun was on the side table, along with some other personal items like shaving gear. His tie and his policeman's cap were hanging on a hat rack. The sleep/living room is at the back of the building, as is the kitchen, a small space consisting of a sink, a stove, and a small table. It soon became clear to me that the kitchen mostly was used to make coffee and eat some bread.[60] For more substantial meals, the officers typically go to one of the many small places to eat in the village.

The office is in the front of the police station, and contains only three chairs, a table, and a computer. On those occasions that I visited the office, I never actually saw the computer being used. In fact, my distinct impression was that the office as a whole was not often used. On the one occasion when I was allowed to take a look at recently reported cases, these files were fetched from a closet that is used to store files. It was also noteworthy that the police station lacked a fax machine, a phone, and internet service. Like the *teniente político*, the police officers of Zumbahua only have cellular phones. They do have one vehicle at their disposal, a Chevrolet LUV D-Max pickup truck, which is used for patrolling. As the officers admitted to me on a number of occasions, two on-duty officers (usually only one) and one police car are hardly sufficient to cover the whole parish, an area of about 171 square kilometers with an estimated population of 13,500 inhabitants.

The daily routine of the policemen consists of patrolling, responding to calls for assistance, providing security for local officials and functions, writing reports, and occasionally moving criminals or suspects to the prison in Latacunga. Theoretically, the police are responsible for the prevention and detection of crime, the apprehension of criminals, and the maintenance of public order (Manning 1977: 199). In practice, the daily routine of the policemen in Zumbahua has less to do with fighting crime than it does with maintaining order. The police usually patrol at night, between 10:00 pm and 2:00 am, accompanied by either the *teniente político*, a member of the Junta Parroquial, or a local *dirigente*. Most of their patrol work is done in and around the communities in the parish (rather than in the village of Zumbahua), and mostly during weekends and fiestas. I was told that the main purpose of such patrols – which are done by car – is to prevent robberies or the disturbance of social order, and also to assure that minor quarrels don't become violent disputes.

---

60 For example, on October 28, 2010, in the lead up to November 2nd (*El dia de los Difuntos* – All Soul's Day), I was offered the traditional *colada morada* (cooked liquid grains that are colored purple) with *guaguas de pan* (small pieces of bread).

Another part of their job is to provide assistance to local authorities. For example, the *teniente político* requests that police provide security during trials (as we will see in the Rosita vs. Miguel case) or when he has to visit communities. The Junta Parroquial usually asks the police to provide security for the weekly Saturday markets. Their assistance could also be requested by the *cabildo*s of parish communities, and they are sometimes called upon to be present at fiestas and other public occasions. This is not to say that the police are present at all such occasions. The officers I spoke to know that a lot of things happen in the parish of which they are unaware. In part, this results from their being understaffed and in part from them not being informed of any possible incident that might require their intervention. They are also occasionally asked by a superior at the district level, the Fiscal or the Court of Justice to provide written reports under certain circumstances. On those few occasions when they capture a suspect, he or she has to be immediately transported to Latacunga for imprisonment. Finally, everything they have done, where they have been, who they have spoken to, and what they have seen, has to be reported in a logbook (and this included the interviews that I conducted with them).

Instances in which their assistance is requested, or which unfold during their patrols, concern a wide range of conflicts, such as family disputes, physical violence, robberies, traffic accidents, the discovery of a stolen car, the use of counterfeit money, drunk driving, driving without a license, and so on. The selling or drinking of alcohol is legally prohibited on Sundays, but this is one of the few things they mostly turn a blind eye to, particularly during fiestas. Although the police officers admit that alcohol is one of the main causes of aggression, they are unable to enforce the Sunday liquor prohibition due to their lack of manpower. As Glebbeek (2003: 54–55) argues, a good relationship between police and the community is essential for the success of police work. Whether or not a police officer is accepted by the community, especially in culturally divided countries, depends largely on how the police approach a community's values and norms. Given this important consideration, it is probably wise of them not interfere in local drinking habits. Glebbeek also argues that, in cases of indigenous communities, it is ideal to employ policemen from the surrounding region. In Ecuador, however, this is not the policy.[61] In the parish of Zumbahua, only one of the police officers lives in the neighboring parish of Chugchilán, while the other two live in faraway Ambato. These policemen display what could be called a neutral attitude regarding customary law. Whenever asked about it, they refer to the Constitution, they admit that the boundaries between customary law and national law are not clear, and they condemn violence and the violation of human rights. They do not express an opinion one way or the other regarding the

---

61 However, since the police revolt of September 30, 2010, attempts have been made to gradually reduce the number of police officers that are stationed in a province other than that where they reside (*El Comercio* 2010a; *El Comercio* 2010c).

importance of customary law, but they do point to the fact that some inhabitants of the parish are prejudiced against national law. So, if the occasion arises, they explained to me, it is their task to mediate as regards which legal system best suits a particular case.[62]

Overall, one could say that the daily routine of the local police force in the parish of Zumbahua is more reactive than proactive. Thus, when the police are informed of some disturbance (whether impending or in progress) it is typically via the *teniente político*, a member of the Junta Parroquial or one of the local *dirigentes*. In cases of conflicts, people do not turn directly to the police, and this considerably decreases its role in settling disputes.

Provincial authorities

Civil Court

Zumbahuan citizens who seek to resolve a civil matter (for example, a divorce, a quarrel between neighbors, or a labor dispute) in accordance with national law, must turn to a Civil Court. For the people living in the parish of Zumbahua, the closest Civil Court is the one in the town of Pujilí, the capital of the canton. By bus, it takes about two hours to get from Zumbahua to Pujilí. The small Juzgado Quinto de lo Civil de Pujilí (Fifth Civil Court of Pujilí) is located in the center of town, at Calle Juan Salinas y Calle Simón Bolívar, a side street near the market place. Many small law offices and notary offices can be found in the surrounding area. Currently, there is a plan to construct a new Fiscalía office just one block away. The Civil Court is always bustling with activity during its official hours. Besides those people working at the court, lawyers walk in and out, and there are typically at least one or two persons in the waiting room. On one occasion, I found the waiting room crowded with ten adults, two children, and a crying baby. The only judge working in Pujilí is Edwin Palma Herrera.

The court building consists of two floors. On the ground floor are the waiting-room, the archives, and the office of the secretary, Beatriz Neto Loja; it is in this office where most of the cases are dealt with. On the first floor are three other offices, including the office of the judge. Compared to the *teniente político*'s office or the police station in Zumbahua, the Civil Court in Pujilí is well equipped. There are several telephones, a fax machine, and typewriters in every office, and there are also computers on the desks of the secretary and the judge. However, there is no internet access. Besides the judge and his secretary, an assistant is also employed in the court. He is responsible for filing cases, making copies, and maintaining the archives. The secretary deals with all administrative matters and the content of case files, and she is the

---

62 These sections on the police are based on data I gathered during several visits to the police station (participant observation) and two more formal interviews I had with two different officers on October 20 and October 28, 2010.

first point of contact for those who visit the court. Visitors to the court are required to report to the assistant before being seated in the waiting-room. They then must wait (sometimes for hours) before being invited into the secretary's office. The secretary serves as a gatekeeper for the judge. However, as is common in Ecuador, this does not apply to lawyers and notaries, who are part of what I call the "legal elite" in Ecuador (Simon Thomas 2007),[63] who are free to walk in and out of the office, and even to have an impromptu chat with the judge. A clear distinction is thus drawn between those who belong to this legal elite and their clients, who do not.[64]

As a Civil Court, the Juzgado Quinto de lo Civil in Pujilí deals with civil disputes (mainly regarding financial matters between individuals). During several hours of archival research,[65] a general picture emerged of the number of cases that the court hears, and of the content of those cases. Nowadays, the court deals with over 500 cases on a yearly basis. There has been a yearly increase in the number of cases since 2003.[66] This is the result of the broadening of the legal jurisdiction of cantonal courts that year.[67] Many cases, about 40 percent, concern people living in the town of Pujilí. The remaining 60 percent of the cases concern people living in communities or villages in the canton, such as Tigua and Zumbahua. Because the number of litigants residing in Pujilí is so vastly disproportionate to their weight in the parish as a whole, one could suggest that distance is an important factor in determining if one turns to the Civil Court in Pujilí. The judge himself did not confirm this. However, the practical hindrance of distance (in terms of time and costs) is a complaint that I often heard, and it seems to offer at least a partial explanation of why rural indigenous people do not to turn to the national

---

63 My position was somewhat intermediate between an outsider and an insider. I did not have to wait in the waiting-room, like clients, but I could not move as freely as members of the "legal elite" either. I was usually seated in one of the offices on the first floor, where I was provided the files I had requested, and where I could conduct research in the archives by myself. As was my experience in other courts in Ecuador, I was surprised by the cordial assistance I received from the people working at this court.
64 Lawyers and notaries do not only walk freely in and out of the office (instead of having to wait). They also deal with the judge and other court employees on a friendly and informal basis. Those who belong to this "legal elite" can be identified by their clothes: suits and ties vs. jeans and ponchos. This is also the case in other Latin American countries. During earlier research on two courts in Guatemala, I encountered similar behavior and differences in dress (see also Simon Thomas 2007).
65 I conducted research (participant observation, talking to people, and conducting archival research) at the Civil Court in Pujilí on October 14, 19, and 26, 2010.
66 Based on the *libro de ingresos de documentas* (Registration Book); 2000: 221 cases, 2001: 188 cases, 2002: 144 cases, 2003: 172 cases, 2004: 225 cases, 2005: 330 cases, 2006: 388 cases, 2007: 429 cases, 2008: 415 cases, 2009: 532 cases, and 2010: 521 cases (until October 19).
67 Interview Judge Herrera on October 19, 2010.

courts. It is noteworthy that the three "international" cases that I mentioned in Chapter 3 were heard by the Pujilí court.[68]

The majority of the cases concern family issues: typically disputes over alimony or paternity. Another frequent source of disputes concerns land, although the majority of land property cases concerned people living in (or near) Pujilí. This confirms what has been said previously: that a good many rural, communal quarrels between neighbors over land are settled by a *cabildo*. Still other cases concern disputes between individuals and their employers. Usually these latter cases have to do with absenteeism or payment issues. Those who resort to the civil judge are not required to pay the court to initiate a lawsuit.[69] However, in a lot of cases (for example divorce) one has to be represented by a lawyer, and lawyers do cost money. An important exception to the rule that one has to have a lawyer is made in cases of alimony,[70] in which applicants are simply required to complete a special form, which can also be downloaded from the internet.[71] This right is emphatically promoted at the Civil Court, where several posters are glued to the wall with messages like "Alimony cases no longer require lawyers." This simplified procedure has surely resulted in an increase in the number of alimony applications. Three out of the four cases concerning people living in the parish of Zumbahua that I came across in the archives concerned alimony.

Two of these cases were referred to briefly in the previous section on conflicts in Zumbahua. The proceedings described in that section are typical. In most cases, it takes several months before the judge reaches a decision, and a duration of six months to a year or even longer is not uncommon. I did my archival research in October 2010, and I estimated that over 50 percent of the cases that were brought to the court in 2009 had still not been closed by that time. Partly this is due to the variety of third parties that have to be consulted during the process. For example, parties involved in a dispute about alimony have to provide truthful data regarding their financial situation so that the court can properly determine the fair amount of alimony to be paid. As such, certified statements of banks and other financial institutions are required. In cases of paternity suits, a DNA test at the Ecuadorian Red Cross is sometimes required. Other cases require the completion of other kinds of paperwork. Of course, such proceedings take time. Add to this the fact that the Civil Court has a huge backlog of cases.[72] It is thus fair to say that anyone bringing a case before the Civil Court in Pujilí should be prepared to have a great deal of patience.

---

68 One of these cases concerned someone now living in Spain, another case concerned someone living in Italy, and the third case was about someone living in Azerbaijan.
69 Article 75 of the Montecristi Constitution ensures every citizen free access to a court.
70 See articles 2, 4, 5, 15, 16, Title 5, Book 2 of the Código de la Niñez y Adolescencia (Child and Youth Code) (R.O. Nro. 643 del 28 Julio el 2009).
71 See http://www.funcionjudicial-pichincha.gob.ec/pichincha/images/FJP/demanda_dep ensiones. pdf (accessed April 3, 2012).
72 On September 5, 2011, President Correa decreed a national emergency in order – among other reasons – to deal with a backlog of some 1.2 million cases across the country (Correa 2011).

Court of Justice

In penal law cases, people living in Zumbahua depend on the Court of Justice in Latacunga. This court comprises four floors and four Criminal Courts.[73] Several judges hear cases in these courts. The pink and green court building is one of the largest modern structures in Latacunga. It has the same operating hours as the Civil Court in Pujilí, but is less accessible to the general public. One cannot just walk the stairs to one of the courts without being questioned, and the entrance of the building is usually guarded by several heavily armed policemen. Once again, these security measures are not applied to lawyers and other members of the legal elite, who can freely walk in and out of the building. As in Pujilí, there are dozens of small lawyers' offices located near the court, and both the Fiscalía and the Fiscalía Indígena are just one block away. This legal complex forms part of the administrative center of the Cotopaxi province, of which Latacunga is the capital.

The majority of the penal law cases are dealt with by one of the three Criminal Courts situated side by side on the second floor, and their layout is quite similar. Each of them contains a courtroom, a judge's office, an administration room, and an archive. The courtroom in fact serves a number of different purposes. It contains two or three desks, depending on whether the judge has one or two certified secretaries. The remaining desk is occasionally used by lawyers who have business with the court. The courtroom is also of course where sessions of the court are held. Next to its main entrance is a door to the secretary's office, and there is another door leading to the court archives. The judge's chambers of each of the criminal courts are the most impressive of all. They contain large, antique-style wooden desks with a huge leather desk chair, a wooden bookcase (the desks and cases in the other rooms are made of iron), and a number of other adornments, including a sculpture representing Justice. The criminal courts are well equipped: every desk contains a typewriter, and the judge and his or her secretaries also have desktop computers. Every room (except for the archive) has a telephone and a fax machine. And at the Juzgado Segundo de lo Penal and at the Juzgado Tercero de lo Penal, a radio was playing popular songs during one of my visits.

Obviously, the Criminal Courts deal with all kinds of penal law cases. Thumbing through the files, I could not escape the impression of receiving a summary of all crimes mentioned in the Penal Code: insults, threats, fights, sexual abuse, robberies and burglaries, illegal possession of firearms, counterfeiting, drug-related cases, and even murder cases. Complaints can be brought before the court by the public prosecutor or by an individual.[74] However, according to the court registry, less than 10 percent of the complaints end up

---

73 Besides the Criminal Courts it has also three Civil Courts, two Juzgados de Transito (Court of Transit), one Juzgado del Trabajo (Labor Court), and a Superior Court.
74 The latter case is called an *Acción Penal Privada*, see also Chapter 6 on the Toaquiza case.

becoming cases. The majority of the complaints are dismissed as frivolous. Because the Criminal Courts do not have computerized records, and also because litigants are not required to state their place of residence, it is impossible to provide exact figures regarding how many cases heard by the court concern people living in the parish of Zumbahua.[75] According to one of the judges I spoke to, less than 5 percent of the cases concern indigenous people (see also Berk-Seligson 2006). He suggested that, if I wanted to get an idea of the kind and number of conflicts heard by the court, I should go to a *cabildo* and examine its book of minutes.[76]

If a complaint becomes a case, one has to be prepared to wait a long time before the judge issues a ruling. The judge needs to have a file as complete as possible before he or she can decide on a case.[77] For this reason, a judge collects all of the information and evidence provided by the parties involved (that is, by their lawyers). Judges can also summon witnesses or experts to give oral testimony, and ask individuals or institutions to provide written statements or evidence. During trials everybody present stands, except for the certified secretary, who takes notes. The judge and the lawyers always have their books of legal codes with them, from which they cite regularly. The lawyers usually have their paper files with them as well. In contrast to trials according to customary law, sessions of the national courts do not last a long time. Fifteen minutes is the average, with the longest sessions lasting half an hour. Although the paper files might contain all sorts of writings, evidence, and other possible relevant information, the oral sessions stick to the legally relevant facts of the case. Contrary to customary law, every complaint is narrowed down to a strict juridical case; and this puts a greater emphasis on the role of lawyers and affords fewer opportunities to the parties involved to actively participate (see also Chávez & García 2004: 31). Similar to what I witnessed at the Civil Court in Pujilí, the judges and the lawyers are on an

---

75 Every complaint is filed and, when it becomes a case, it subsequently is filed on two more occasions. Initially, it is manually registered in a registration book. Date, name of the accuser, and short description of the case is written down on one line, and a file number is assigned. This is done by the secretary. When a complaint becomes a case, a computerized file is created. This is done by the certified secretary. Court documents are stored in this file. One can search this system by date, file number, description of the case, or by name. Everything that is produced on the computer is printed, and these hard copies, accompanied by all other file information, are placed in a paper file. When a case is closed, these paper files are stored in the archive. This is done by the secretary. Every Criminal Court has the same filing procedures, but there is no combined or linked database. Thus, if I had wanted to know exact figures of how many people living in Zumbahua went to a criminal court, I would have had to sift through three different sets of paper files in the archive. Such an endeavor simply proved impractical for the present study.
76 Interview with Judge José Luis Segovia Dueños on September 22, 2010.
77 Libro II: La Prueba (the evidence) of the Código de Procedimiento Penal addresses what kind of evidence a judge can use. Basically, the following evidence is accepted: written statements of suspects, witnesses, and experts, and other written documents.

equal footing, and sometimes even seem to be friends. Those who are parties to the case, however, typically act with a high degree of deference. In sum, those parties whose cases are heard at the Criminal Court in Latacunga need to have patience, and need also to be prepared to take no more than a small role in their own cases.[78]

The Fiscalía and the Fiscalía Indígena

Just one block away from the Court of Justice stands the blue building of the Fiscalía Provincial de Cotopaxi (Public Prosecutor of the Cotopaxi province). This building has four floors, each of which contains several small offices of prosecutors. According to the law,[79] the main purpose of this institution is to prosecute criminal actions (on its own initiative or when asked to on behalf of the state or an individual). The prosecutors act as investigators. In general, Ecuadorians do not turn to a public prosecutor to resolve their conflicts, and neither do people from Zumbahua. Indigenous people, however can have recourse to a special department of the Public Prosecutor in Latacunga, situated on the ground floor, the Fiscalía de Asuntos Indígenas de Cotopaxi (Public Prosecutor for Indigenous Affairs in the Cotopaxi province). This entity is more commonly known in its abbreviated form: Fiscalía Indígena.

On the initiative of CODENPE, in collaboration with the Public Prosecutor, the Fiscalía Indígena was created in November 2007. The main purpose of this entity is to provide indigenous people a place to go within the national legal system, but with a very low barrier (Tibán 2008). To illustrate, at the Fiscalía Indígena people can speak their own local indigenous language. In addition, in its handling of cases,[80] the Fiscalía Indígena respects local norms and practices. Besides the increase of access to national justice, its purpose is also to provide indigenous people an alternative to dealing with local indigenous authorities or a *teniente político* (Hoy 2007). As an official institution, it has to apply national law. However, contrary to national judges, who are inclined to narrow a case down into strict juridical terms, a Fiscal Indígena typically takes a much broader view of a case, including a consideration of local norms and customs (Tibán 2008). The difference between a Fiscal Indígena and a *teniente político* is that the former's competence is less limited (for example, a Fiscal Indígena is not restricted to minor infractions, but is allowed to deal with more serious crimes as well).

---

78 These sections on the Court of Justice in Latacunga are based on participant observation during several visits to the Court (especially to the three Criminal Courts) and on several informal conversations and more formal interviews I had with the people working there.
79 Ley Organica del Ministerio Público (Codificación 2, Registro Oficial 250 de 13 de Abril del 2006), Capítulo IV.
80 Berk-Seligson (2006, 2008) argues that language is one of the most important reasons that indigenous persons do not to turn to the national courts. Therefore, one can argue that the Fiscal Indígena fills an important gap.

Conflicts, authorities, and procedures 133

One prosecutor works out of the Fiscalía Indígena in Latacunga: José Segundo Jami Llumitasig,[81] and he has one secretary, Miriam Umajinga. Both these individuals hold formal law degrees. The secretary explained that their main purpose is to hear complaints in Kichwa of indigenous people living in the provinces and, in cases involving conflicts, to mediate between the parties. The offices of the Fiscalía Indígena have a telephone, a fax machine, a typewriter, and a desktop computer. They also have copies of Ecuadorian legal codes. The Fiscalía is open from 8:00 am to 12:00 pm, and from 2:00 to 6:00 pm, from Monday to Friday. However, the office does close when Llumitasig and his secretary visit communities in the region to assist local *dirigentes*. Because they are a fairly recent institution, they actively have to educate the public regarding their existence and purpose. They do so when they visit communities, but they also make use of radio advertising. This appears to be successful, because over the last six years, their caseload has increased.[82]

Many of the cases tried by the Fiscalía Indígena concern injuries. In cases of accidents or fights, sometimes people need certified doctors' bills or other official declarations in order to make reimbursement claims. For example, in the Rosita vs. Miguel case described in the next chapter, at one point it seemed as if the legitimacy of every bill was going to be disputed. The *teniente político* cut off that discussion by accepting the legitimacy of all bills immediately, in order to enable the proceedings to continue. The *teniente político* warned the parties that the only alternative was for them to have the bills certified at the Fiscal Indígena, which would involve a long delay. Both Rosita and Miguel decided to continue the proceedings at the *teniente político*'s office, but as the files at the Fiscalía Indígena show, in several other cases, people have chosen to have bills verified. On one occasion, I even witnessed some people who had been involved in a car accident just a couple of hours ago visiting the Fiscalía Indígena immediately after they had been to the hospital. Their clothes were torn and blood-stained, and one of the victims had his arm in a cast. They made their declarations in Kichwa, and photos were taken to be used as evidence. Another important category of litigation involves "criminal cases," ranging from robberies to burglaries to kidnappings. Some such cases are handled by the Fiscal Indígena, some cases are referred back to a local *cabildo*, and the most serious cases are referred to the Court of Justice.

The services of the Fiscalía Indígena in Latacunga are free, and they proceed quickly (I was told by the secretary that most of the cases are settled within one or two weeks), although the most serious cases can take longer. On the average, the parties involved have to make several appearances in

---

81 José Segundo Jami Llumitasig's official title is Fiscal (prosecutor), but he actually functions more like a mediator.
82 In 2007 (they opened in December): 20 cases; in 2008: 169 cases; in 2009: 237 cases; in 2010 (through October): 219 cases.

court, and sometimes third parties (for example, witnesses, expert witnesses, or the police) are also summoned. No appointment is necessary for the first visit, and people are seen on a first-come, first-serve basis. I noticed that, during opening hours, there were always people in the waiting room. Every declaration is recorded in a registry in which the date, names of the parties, short description of the case, and whether or not third parties (like the police) have been involved are all indicated. In addition, each declaration is entered by the secretary on a desktop computer. After all of the relevant data are entered into the computer, the plaintiff is asked to read his or her statement one last time before a certified copy is provided to him or her. Each case typically results in a file containing the Investigation Plan of the prosecutor, correspondence, and declarations of witnesses and/or the police. In cases involving injuries resulting from a fight, a form detailing what happened is also attached. The prosecutor's final settlement is included. At first glance, the indigenous prosecutor's files and procedures do not differ much from those of a regular prosecutor or a judge. Yet there is one important difference: this specific institution was created to serve indigenous people. This is mainly achieved because Kichwa is spoken, and because of the relatively short time it takes to settle the majority of the cases.[83]

Whom to turn to?

The kinds of conflicts, and the authorities available to deal with them, present a rather complex picture. Several indigenous authorities can be distinguished (that is, the *cabildo* and the *asamblea general*). Several authorities applying national law can also be discerned (for example, the Civil Court and the Criminal Court), and Zumbahuans also have recourse to "in-between" authorities (that is, the *teniente político* or the Fiscal Indígena). Since the boundaries between jurisdictions are not always clearly defined, and because some authorities deal with a wide range of different conflicts, a one-on-one relationship between authorities and conflicts cannot be provided. The introduction of this chapter already hinted at this. Actually, it is only in cases of national law, with its specific rules, written down in laws, and regulations, that one can distinguish between civil and criminal law (and, within the latter category, between infractions and serious crimes), defining which court one has to turn to, and what procedure would be applicable. Within customary law, such strict rules do not exist. And, because Ecuador has formally embraced a situation of formal legal pluralism, but lacks coordinating rules, the personal, territorial, and material jurisdiction of customary law in relation to national law is especially unclear.

In the absence of clear and firm rules, one might think that certain patterns of behavior could be distinguished in terms of particular kinds of cases being

---

83 These sections on the Fiscal Indígena in Latacunga are based on several visits to the office, and on two formal interviews I had with the secretary on November 12, and November 24, 2010.

brought before certain authorities. It will be shown that such is not the case. During my initial literature research on legal pluralism, my first impression was that indigenous people nearly always prefer local authorities who apply customary law instead of national courts who apply national law. For an outsider, this might not come as a surprise. The picture depicted by the scholarly literature provides insight as to why indigenous people prefer to turn to customary law (Assies 2001; García 2009a; Sieder 1997; Yrigoyen Fajardo 2000). Their reasons can be divided into two broad categories. The first of these can be termed a favorable bias toward customary law, which basically means that many indigenous persons consider customary law to be more efficient, legitimate, and cost-effective than national law. The second category can conversely be termed an unfavorable bias toward national law, resulting from real and perceived difficulties of access to the national courts. However, the same authors, as well as others (Berk-Seligson 2006; Chávez & García 2004; García 2002), also hint at the possibility that there are exceptions to the rule. This suggests a more complicated reality. It is this second line of thought, which has been on the research agenda of other scholars too, that is confirmed by more in-depth research.

Research on forum shopping reveals that there are many factors that influence people's decision-making behavior. As von Benda-Beckmann and von Benda-Beckmann (2006: 25) argue, "a complex set" of personal characteristics, self-interest, the particular features of the available systems or the authorities within those systems, the nature of the conflict, the relationship between the parties, and the interest of other parties concerned, are relevant factors. Other important considerations in this regard include power relations and other factors involving social dependency. This means, for example, that indigenous people do not always turn to indigenous law merely because it is part of their tradition (Sierra 1995b: 233; Spiertz 1991).[84] Nor do they always reject national law for purely procedural reasons.[85] This does not mean that positive bias toward customary law and negative bias toward national law are of no importance all. The point here is that specific reasons for people's choices in particular instances – reasons that go beyond pre-existing biases – *also* exist. As the Rosita vs. Miguel case in Chapter 6 will suggest, social pressure (that is, of certain *dirigentes*) can play a role here as well.

---

84 Examples of such perceived "tradition" are as follows: customary law is orally administered and places a heavy emphasis on both reconciliation and providing compensation and restitution to the victim, instead of doling out punishment to the perpetrator. Additional reasons in favor of customary law are that it is more physically accessible, cheaper, faster, and is administered in the people's own, indigenous language.
85 Examples of such procedural reasons are: state law is expensive; its institutions are distant from the places where many indigenous inhabitants live; its procedures take a long time and are recorded in a Spanish that is filled with legal jargon that is often incomprehensible to indigenous persons who speak a different native language; and is administered by judges and lawyers suspected of being corrupt and biased (Berk-Seligson 2008; Chávez & García 2004: 169; García 2002: 58).

Additionally, in Chapter 7, the Toaquiza vs. the community case provides an example of how local power relations can constitute yet another important factor. Finally, in Chapter 8, the La Cocha-Guantópolo murder case will show that even national politics can influence decision-making behavior.

Based on these case studies, as well as the empirical data cited in this chapter, it can be argued that the favorable–unfavorable bias distinction is far too simplistic to accurately reflect the daily reality of legal decision-making behavior. The archives of both the Civil Court in Pujilí and the Criminal Court in Latacunga reveal that there are several "national law cases" in which indigenous people have voluntarily participated. In matters involving civil law (divorces, alimony, custody of children, etc.) such a choice might be explained by people needing to obtain essential documentation. Indigenous people are very well aware of the fact that in some cases they are simply not able to avoid recourse to state law. Yet, even in some criminal cases, indigenous people sometimes resort to national law instead of customary law.[86] This suggests that, at least in certain circumstances they are not always biased against national law. Berk-Seligson (2008: 12) even argues that many ordinary indigenous people prefer national law,[87] but because of their limited access to it, they are forced to turn to customary law. However, notwithstanding several cases in which indigenous people turned to national law, the majority of the cases end up being resolved according to customary law.

These findings are in line with a recent study by the Ecuadorian anthropologist Fernando García, research that was conducted as part of a larger project on the relationship between customary law and national law in four Andean countries (Cóndor Chuquiruna 2009). García's (2009a) data offer a profound insight into indigenous people's legal decision-making processes. On the face of it, García's findings point to a limited knowledge of national law on the part of indigenous people. However, his respondents are very well aware of the fact that in some cases they are simply not able to avoid recourse to state law. This suggests that some indigenous persons are more knowledgeable about national law than is apparent at first glance, at least on the part of some of the informants. Even more telling is the fact that, if the respondents do express knowledge of state law, and if they are biased against it, they are opposed to the use of it because of how it is applied rather than because of any disagreement in principle with its content. In other words, they do not have that much difficulty with the rules as such, but are instead wary of state officials, who are supposed to be professional and impartial, but who

---

86 Jackson and Warren (2005: 563) have even argued that "specific rulings employing customary law are sometimes disputed within indigenous communities themselves, resulting in individuals *appealing* their sentence by turning to Western courts [emphasis mine]".
87 Similarly, Sierra (1995b: 233), in her research among the Nahuas in Mexico, shows that indigenous people sometimes "even think that 'justice' is better provided in the city [national law] than in the village [customary law]."

are, in the eyes of many indigenous persons, corrupt and biased (see also Chávez & García 2004: 31).

An even more striking finding in the study of García (2009a) is the critical attitude displayed by many indigenous persons against their own traditional authorities. Thus, some informants complained (in a way that reflected their view of national law officials) about the indigenous authorities and the enforcement of indigenous law, rather than about the rules of customary law as such. Among the most commonly heard criticisms: the authorities are mostly older persons; the authorities put too much emphasis on parties' records, rather than on the facts of individual cases; sometimes the authorities are biased; and sometimes the authorities misuse their power when they administer overly harsh punishment (see also Berk-Seligson 2006; García 2002: 83–84).

Another circumstance in which indigenous people turn to national law is when customary law seems unable to provide adequate remedies in particular circumstances (see also García 2002: 60). A case of a Tiguan woman who was beaten and robbed by fellow community members can serve as an illustration.[88] The woman, who was living in the Tigua-Chimbacucho community, presented a complaint against six members of the same community concerning severe injuries,[89] as well as the theft of a cellular phone, a hat and $500 in cash ($300 belonging to the community and $200 of her own). Interestingly, in a letter to the judge, she refers to earlier threats and assaults, which had been settled within the community with "Agreements of Mutual Respect." However, even though this agreement stipulated that any recidivism would result in a fine of $5,000, neither customary law nor the local authorities inspired fear in the six defendants. Consequently, the victim saw no other option than to resort to national law.

To summarize, in line with what von Benda-Beckmann and von Benda-Beckmann (2006) argue, both insights of García (2009a) (that is, that indigenous people don't have that much trouble with national laws *per se*, and are sometimes critical of local authorities), combined with cases in which customary law appears not to be adequate, paint a much more nuanced picture of the daily practice of indigenous decision-making behavior than that which is discernible from a distance, and one very different from a clear bias *in favor* of customary law. Such a state of affairs might lead one to resort to the concept of "forum shopping" to explain what is going on. "Forum shopping" refers to any party to a dispute deliberately choosing to pursue litigation among different authorities according to generally pragmatic and rational criteria. However, with the examples cited in this chapter in mind (for example, Rosita and Miguel feeling social pressure, the Tiguan women seeing no other option) it

---

88 Caso 2009–1216 Juzgado Tercero de lo Penal de Cotopaxi.
89 In a letter to the judge, the Tiguan woman (or rather, her lawyer) referred to article 463 of the Penal Code which penalizes such injuries with the maximum penalty of thirty days and a fine; Caso 2009–1216 Juzgado Tercero de lo Penal de Cotopaxi, exhibit 1.

can clearly be seen that people's actions are not always or entirely intentional, conscious, or pragmatic in the way that the verbs "to shop" or "to choose" suggest. Examples of other cases in the following chapters underscore this reserve with regard to the picture of people just picking an authority that they believe will produce the outcome they consider desirable.

Conclusion

This chapter's main conclusion is that, because a workable categorization of conflicts is untenable, and also because there are no strict boundaries between the jurisdictions of different authorities, there is no one-to-one correspondence between particular kinds of conflicts and the authorities resorted to in order to resolve them. The daily practice of conflict resolution in Zumbahua appears to be highly complex. It is for this reason that legal pluralism from an empirical perspective cannot be seen as a dichotomy between customary law and national law. De Sousa Santos' (2002) concept of interlegality sheds considerable light on these findings. Thus, if conflicts, as well as jurisdictions of authorities and their procedures overlap, where should the line between customary law and national law be drawn in the first place? De Sousa Santos' theory of interlegality suggests that, given such a state of affairs, it is hardly surprising that people don't conceptualize the different legal jurisdictions in terms of clear categories or clear-cut rules (de Sousa Santos 2002: 437).

For analytical purposes, however, a distinction between different kinds of conflicts and different authorities has proven useful. For example, it has been shown that different kinds of conflicts do not occur in isolation, but rather in connection with one another. And a description of the various available authorities and their procedures has shown that strict rules regarding an authority's jurisdiction can only be provided if a case is brought to the state's legal system. Compared to the situation that prevailed in the past, it appears that not much has changed regarding local conflicts, on the one hand, and available authorities and their procedures (except for the number of authorities Zumbahuans can turn to), on the other.

What has changed, however, is the scope of these conflicts, mainly as a result of contextual developments that were discussed in Chapter 4, such as an increasing state presence, emerging indigenous movements, and changing legal and political attitudes regarding diversity and pluralism. For example, because the hacienda has been abolished, and Zumbahua has become a parish, the state has become more visible. The parish has *comunas, cabildos*, a *teniente político*, a small police force, and a Junta Parroquial, to name just a few authorities. Each of these, in their own way, have become objects in the settlement of internal conflicts – and sometimes have even become subjects in such conflicts. Another example of the increasing state presence is the creation of the Fiscalía Indígena in the provincial capital. Additionally, the power of indigenous movements has become more tangible. As will be shown in Chapter 8, the national indigenous movement CONAIE, its provincial branch

MICC, and its local division UNOCIC in La Cocha, all had an influence on the settlement of a number of internal conflicts. But the most important contextual development was the progressive 1998 Constitution (and its successor, the Montecristi Constitution), in which Ecuador's multicultural nature was recognized, and a situation of formal legal pluralism was created.

In terms of the legal-anthropological understanding of disputes, transformations in the scope of the conflict, in dispute institutions (Felstiner et al. 1980–81), or even in the rules as such, all have their influence on the development of a conflict. For the people living in the parish of Zumbahua, the legal playing field now offers more options, while the rules of the game are not always that clear (that is, coordinating rules that make customary law and national law compatible are absent). Based on case studies in the following three chapters, this book will show how ordinary Indians, local authorities, and even national politics deal with this varied and unclear legal context, and what kinds of effects this has on the settlement of internal conflicts.

6 Interlegality at the *teniente político*'s office

After almost two hours of heated debates that had at one point escalated to blows, a final agreement was reached. Miguel's wife and Rosita's husband promised not see or call one other again in the near future, and each agreed to pay a fine of $5,000 should they violate this agreement. This was written down by the *teniente político*'s secretary in the *libro de actas* and was read out loud by her. Everybody present in the small *teniente político*'s office mumbled or nodded their approval. Only one *dirigente* suggested an additional stipulation: that the two people involved promise not to turn to national law in case they should have a problem with the decision at some later point. Although some other *dirigentes* seemed to initially approve of that comment, it was quickly rejected by the police officer, who explained that such a statement was unnecessary considering the fact that the *teniente político* happens to be a state official, which meant that the legal case in question already had formal status. This reminder was recognized by everyone, and the original text of the *acta* was approved. Subsequently, it was signed by the two parties before being stamped and signed by the *teniente político*. Finally, Miguel's wife and Rosita's husband apologized in public for their bad behavior, and then the case was closed. Measures had been taken to prevent infidelity in the future, and harmony was restored between the parties.

Introduction

This vignette describes part of the outcome of a trial held at the *teniente político*'s office in Zumbahua. Although this dispute appeared to be complicated, it actually serves as a good example of the kinds of conflicts that the *teniente político* has to deal with. As will be shown in this chapter, the *teniente político* in Zumbahua is an appointed political official who, in his juridical role, is not only confronted with the breach of local customary norms, rules, and procedures but who, when asked to resolve the subsequent conflicts, makes use of customary law as well. As such, it illustrates legal pluralism in practice – the general aim of this chapter, which should be read as an empirical elaboration of Chapter 5. In particular, the material here will reinforce the key point made there: that the daily practice of legal pluralism in Ecuador should *not* be seen as a dichotomy between two different legal systems, but rather as interlegality. In order to get an idea of how customary law and national law interrelate on a local level, this chapter describes the role of the *teniente político* and shows how he settles local disputes.

Throughout the chapter, the Rosita vs. Miguel trial will be used as an illustration of daily practice at the *teniente político*'s office. The dispute that had to be settled in that trial had to do with marital infidelity (Rosita's husband had an affair with Miguel's wife), a physical altercation (between Rosita and Miguel over the affair), and money (the doctor's bills resulting from the injuries caused by that fight). The story of the trial will be told in three stages: initial preparations, the procedure, and the settlement. The above vignette represents part of that settlement.

We will begin by explaining the ambiguous role of the *teniente político*, with an emphasis on the self-ascribed role of the *juez de paz* of the *teniente político* in Zumbahua. As will be shown later in more detail, the procedure at the *teniente político*'s office reflects many features of customary law. One such feature is giving everybody present a chance to speak (toward the end of reaching a settlement acceptable to both parties). The suggestion of one of the *dirigentes* to ask the people involved to promise not to turn to national law is also typical of proceedings conducted according to customary law.[1] The disagreement itself, which involves a combination of infidelity, a fight, money, and potentially more fighting, is an example of both the diversity and overlapping of local conflicts in the parish of Zumbahua.

This chapter ends with a suggestion of how to interpret the Rosita vs. Miguel trial. Besides providing an example of interlegality, and as such offering insight into the daily practice of legal pluralism, the concluding section also highlights the *teniente político*'s role as state official. It will be shown that the ambiguous role of this official is not fundamentally different from that of his predecessors in the nineteenth and twentieth centuries. The *teniente político* could then be seen as functioning as a mediator between the state and rural indigenous communities, a role that is central to Chatterjee's (2004) concept of a political society. In Zumbahua, at any rate, the *teniente político* still appears to be carrying out such a role.

The *teniente político*

When it comes to the settlement of disputes on a local level in the Ecuadorian Andes, *tenientes políticos* are important and powerful state officials. In this respect, the situation in the parish of Zumbahua does not differ from that in many other places in the Ecuadorian highlands. The only remarkable thing

---

1 This *dirigente*'s suggestion is based on what is actually quite often done in *actas* (which are typically drafted by a *cabildo* or an *asamblea general*). See for instance an *acta* from La Cocha dated May 5, 2002, expressly prohibiting any later recourse to national law (Simon Thomas 2009: 66). Jackson and Warren (2005: 563) have shown that indigenous people sometimes try to appeal an indigenous sentence by turning to national law.

about this office in Zumbahua is that it has only existed since 1972 (that is, the year that Zumbahua ceased being a hacienda). In several other places, *tenientes políticos* have a much longer history, in some even going back to the 1830s. However, it will be shown that there is a striking similarity between the present-day ambiguous juridical role of the *teniente político* in Zumbahua and that of his predecessors elsewhere. To provide a basic understanding of this similarity, this section starts with the introduction and the development of *tenientes políticos* in general, and ends with some remarks on the functioning of the office in Zumbahua. As such, it provides insight into the development of the ambiguous role of the *teniente político* at the local level. But above all, this historical background will serve as a foundation for understanding the present powerful, juridical role of the *teniente político* in Zumbahua.

Historical overview

The office of *teniente político* was introduced in Ecuador in 1830, when the former Spanish colony became an independent republic and enacted its first organizational laws (Guerrero 1989: 328). One of the effects of its first constitution and of this new office was that customary law gradually became illegal. Before that time, the use of customary law had been tolerated to a certain extent in the *Repúblicas de Indios*, and so it was during the first half of the nineteenth century (Guerrero 1997: 585).[2] Basically, this appointed political officer was assigned two duties; one political (protecting the state's interests) and one juridical (the adjudication of minor offenses in indigenous communities). As political officers, *tenientes políticos* served as interpreters of national politics for indigenous persons on the one hand, while reporting on indigenous affairs to same-state authorities, and thus acting as gatekeepers of indigenous affairs and autonomy, on the other (Baud 2007: 87). To use the terms of Chatterjee (2004: 64), *tenientes políticos* are mediators in a political society. In general, they attempt to ensure a convergence of the claims of rural, indigenous people and the state's own interests. In other words: "they mediate between those who govern and those who are governed" (Chatterjee 2004: 66).

As juridical officials, these *tenientes políticos* had to enforce national legal regulations. They were responsible for settling local, minor disputes, but for major crimes they were only the first link in the legal chain (Cervone 2012: 168). In practice, however, they did not always follow the letter of the law. Nor did they always determine legal matters within the community. Some even argue (for example, Cervone 2012: 169) that in some instances in which they knew that major cases had been settled at the community level by local authorities,

---

2 Guerrero (1997) points to two periods of "ethnic administration" following independence: during the years 1830–1857, the Indian population was administered as a public entity, following the model of the *Repúblicas*. From 1957 on, when the "Indian tributes" were eliminated, rural indigenous people legally obtained the status of citizens, like all Ecuadorians.

they could feign ignorance and not bring this to the attention of higher-ranked state officials. Here too, *tenientes políticos* acted like mediators, functioning in the gray area between national and customary law (or, to use the term of Chatterjee (2004: 74), engaging in "paralegal processes"). In this context, many rural indigenous communities in actual practice followed their own political traditions and customary law within their communities whenever possible. Thus, a situation of *de facto* legal pluralism prevailed. However, a great deal of facilitating power remained in the hands of the *tenientes políticos*, since they could decide whether they wanted to function in any given case as protectors of indigenous legal autonomy, or as enforcers of national law.

The most important, albeit hidden, agenda behind the creation of the office of *teniente político* was to break the local rural elite's power, in particular that of the *curacas* (Guerrero 1989) during the early days of the Republic. As previously indicated in Chapter 3, the colonial division into two *Repúblicas* was abolished and any sign of the "indigenous world" had to be removed. The national government set out to break the power of these *curacas* – who were "*indios*" – and they used *tenientes políticos* to do so. The success attained in pursuit of this goal, particularly with respect to the juridical authority attached to the position, was considerable. Although their sphere of jurisdiction was limited to minor offenses,[3] in practice they settled more disputes than they were officially allowed to rule upon. By alternately applying formal law as well as customary norms and procedures as circumstances dictated (Guerrero 1989: 342), *tenientes políticos* effectively managed to undermine the power of the *curacas* that had existed for centuries (Guerrero 1989: 336). Their "mixed" procedures were highly valued by local, indigenous populations because of their oral and personal character, and also because of their relatively greater efficiency (Guerrero 1989: 343).

With the end of the tributary system in 1857, when power from the state-centered administration transferred to local landowners and power brokers (Guerrero 1997), the power of *tenientes políticos* concomitantly increased. "Free" indigenous communities in the countryside effectively came under the control of these nominally political officers, who collaborated with hacienda owners and Catholic priests to advance their interests (Korovkin 2001: 45). This kind of dynamic can be viewed as the dark side of mediators acting in a political society (Chatterjee 2004: 75). The period of *de facto* rural power in the hands of "the holy trinity" had begun. The termination of the tribute system removed indigenous peoples from the jurisdiction of the government and made them subordinate to the private authority of *hacendados* and other local power holders, rendering them administratively invisible (Guerrero

---

3 By referring to the Ley Orgánica del Poder Judicial of 1843, Guerrero (1989: 336) illustrates this limited jurisdiction of *tenientes políticos*. They were allowed to settle claims related to injuries and small offenses not exceeding a monetary value of 16 pesos, and the maximum penalties they were allowed to impose were imprisonment of eight days and a fine of 12 pesos.

1997). Consequently, rural indigenous communities had no official administrative or territorial status (Korovkin 2001: 45), and thus little access to the use of state resources to defend any threats to their interests that might arise. Of course these communities could turn to informal lawyers (locally known as *tinterillos*) but most of these individuals had a well-deserved reputation for being corrupt (Becker 2011b; Berk-Seligson 2006; García 2002),[4] which meant that rural indigenous people were, in the end, at the mercy of the "holy trinity." However, within this power struggle, indigenous authorities succeeded in maintaining some degree of autonomy.[5] Therefore, customary law continued to be practiced, and *tenientes políticos* continued to apply formal law, as well as customary norms and procedures.

Following the Liberal Revolution of 1895, when General Eloy Alfaro became president, the power of *tenientes políticos* was affected because the formal position of indigenous people fundamentally changed. After being largely neglected by the state since the time of the Spanish conquest, the rural indigenous population was no longer viewed by ruling elites as being in need of protection, but rather as needing to be incorporated into the state. It is in the late nineteenth and early twentieth century that liberal mediators began to rise in defense of the rights of rural indigenous people, presenting them as an oppressed group whose way of life needed to be protected (Guerrero 1997: 588). Guerrero (1997) introduced the term "ventriloquists" to characterize the liberal intermediaries who mediated between the dominant elite and the marginalized rural indigenous population. As a result, the power position of *tenientes políticos* appeared to decrease. During the period 1895–1911 large numbers of petitions and files were presented at courts to protest the unjust behavior of local elites like hacienda owners and *tenientes políticos* (Baud 1996: 220).

As soon as the liberal period ended in 1911, things returned to the *status quo ante*: the "holy trinity" re-emerged and once again obtained control of the rural areas (Baud 1996: 220) and *tenientes políticos* reacquired their previous power. The dark side of that power also resurfaced. Unwarranted labor demands and other abuses were not only the work of large landowners, but also of *tenientes políticos*. This of course does not mean that all of them behaved badly at all times. Sometimes *tenientes políticos* belonged to the

4 Until recently (Cervone 2012: 177; García 2002: 71), *tinterillos* were frequently hired by indigenous people to handle the legal paperwork required by courts. Since the people who hired them could not read or write Spanish sufficiently, these *tinterillos* – who were bilingual in Spanish and Kichwa – provided services to those who had cases in Ecuador's national courts. As such, *tinterillos* could easily take advantage of their poor, illiterate peers; and obviously they often did, because contemporary historical writings generally portray them in an unflattering light (Berk-Seligson 2006: 14; Cervone 2012: 298, note 12).
5 Cervone (2012: 45) shows that *hacendados* appointed indigenous authorities (*alcaldes*) within the hacienda, who were in charge of the administration of justice in the communities.

white/*mestizo* elite (and were sometimes even large landholders), but just as easily, they could be indigenous leaders (Baud 1996: 227). Often they acted as an extension of oppressive local elites, while at other times defending the interests of rural indigenous people and the villages where they resided. It is for this reason that the actions of *tenientes políticos* resist easy characterization. The ambiguity of this role did not change after 1937, when, as a result of the Ley de Comunas, several *comunas* (that is, legally recognized indigenous communities) arose, with their own authorities, or *cabildos*. *Tenientes políticos* succeeded in retaining their control over these *comunas*, even when in some cases former *curacas* once again assumed power (Korovkin 2001: 46).

So far, one might well infer that *tenientes políticos* exercised the same level of power in the rural areas where they functioned. Such a generalization, however, neglects important local differences. For example, areas with a lot of "free" indigenous communities (where *tenientes políticos* did exercise a good deal of power) differ from areas with many large haciendas (where they exercised very little). As a metaphor, the image of the holy trinity is useful for portraying power relations in the Andean highlands as a whole. But locally, or even regionally, actual relations could vary. Sometimes *tenientes políticos* held sway, and sometimes, as Kaltmeier (2007) rightly stresses, in areas with many large haciendas, *de facto* power was in the hands of *hacendados* and their *mayordomos*. A few examples will suffice to give an indication of how variable the level of power exercised by *tenientes políticos* actually was. Guerrero (1989, 1997) describes the Otovalo region in the nineteenth and early twentieth century, and Baud (1996) refers to the area around the town of Cuenca in the early twentieth century. Neither of these regions had a large number of extensive haciendas, and therefore local power remained for the most part in the hands of *tenientes políticos*. Kaltmeier (2007), on the other hand, describes the situation surrounding the village of Saquisilí in the province of Cotopaxi, which during the period 1930–1980 was home to a great many large haciendas. He mentions *tenientes políticos* who actually had no power at all (Kaltmeier 2007: 79).

A similar situation seemed to hold true for the parish of Zumbahua. For centuries, Zumbahua had been a large hacienda that bordered other large haciendas (for example, Tigua and Chugchilan). As Weismantel (1988) stresses in her historical section on the parish of Zumbahua and its surroundings, only a few "free" communities survived into the twentieth century. And a lot of inhabitants of such "free" communities earned their living as laborers (*yanapos*) at haciendas. Consequently their position ultimately differed little from that of the indigenous population living at the hacienda (Weismantel 1988: 62). With the nearest *teniente político* in the parish of Pilaló (five hours away on horseback) (Becker 2007: 162), the indigenous workers on the Zumbahua hacienda were at the mercy of the landlord and his *mayordomos*. This state of affairs reflected the fact that the state had largely been absent from the region for about 150 years.

This brief historical overview portrays an ambiguous picture of the office of *tenientes políticos*. This ultimately resulted from their having been assigned the dual task of representing the state (both politically and juridically), and acting at the same time as protectors of local and indigenous autonomy. While strategically managing the performance of their tasks – sometimes acting against the interests of rural indigenous people, sometimes as their representatives – *tenientes políticos* gained a great deal of local power. But, for the purpose of this book, the most important conclusion that can be drawn from this complex picture is that *tenientes políticos* played an important role on the local level as a mediator in, or settler of, disputes. Appointed as state officials required to apply formal law, they themselves at times both applied customary norms and procedures in practice, and facilitated indigenous authorities in their role of settling local disputes. In Zumbahua, however, a nearby *teniente político* had been absent until the second half of the twentieth century, meaning that local power was almost completely in the hands of the landlord. Therefore, it is striking to note that the present *teniente político* nowadays plays a quite similar ambiguous role, at least in terms of his juridical duties. As part of his daily work, he carries out a lot of juridical tasks himself (whether or not these conform to the strict letter of the law), while at other times he unofficially assists indigenous authorities in settling local disputes. All of this reflects the daily routine of his predecessors in Zumbahua and elsewhere in the Ecuadorian Andes.

The *teniente político* in Zumbahua

In 1972, when the parish of Zumbahua was established, the first (*mestizo*) *teniente político* was appointed almost immediately (Umajinga 1995: 258). But his authority was limited. This situation continued through the first half of the 1980s, when Mary Weismantel conducted her research on food and gender. She mentions that the *teniente político*'s influence on affairs in the village of the parish seemed greater than his influence on surrounding communities. She observed that, from the perspective of people living in the outlying communities, the primary if not exclusive priority of the *teniente político* in Zumbahua was the settlement of disputes (Weismantel 1988: 56, note 13).

Today's *teniente político* in Zumbahua, Jaime Rodrigo Pallo, plays a rather more varied role. He is a man of medium height, thirty-six years old, born in the community of La Cocha, who currently resides for the most part in Latacunga. His office is centrally situated on the main road of the village of Zumbahua, very close to the central Plaza Rumiñahui. It is made of concrete, with a corrugated iron roof; and the following text is written in large yellow letters on the mint green outside wall: "*Teniente Político de la Parroquia Zumbahua.*" Its opening hours are 9:00 am to 5:00 pm, Saturday through Wednesday.[6] Most of the office space is occupied by a consulting room

---

6   Jaime Rodrigo Pallo considers Thursday and Friday, when his office is closed, as his "weekend." The office has to be open on Saturday because it is market day, and on Sunday because so many parties are held on that day.

measuring only four square meters, which is also used as courtroom. It has one street door and a rather large window that looks out onto the main road. Inside, there are two more doors, one for a broom closet and another for a storage room. This storage room, however, is almost empty; it only contains an iron filing cabinet in which a handful of different *libros de denuncias* and *libros de actas* are stored. The consulting room contains an iron desk and chair, with six additional chairs placed against the wall. A number of items are glued to the wall: two campaign posters of President Rafael Correa, one newspaper article about the nomination of Correa, a calendar and three *art naïf* prints portraying indigenous life – one of which depicts an indigenous trial.[7] The office has a typewriter, but no computer, internet access, telephone, or fax machine. If *Teniente Político* Jaime Rodrigo Pallo wants to make a call, he has to use his mobile phone. When he is in, Jaime Rodrigo Pallo usually is seated at his desk, either attending visitors or performing administrative duties.

When I met Jaime Rodrigo Pallo for the first time,[8] he had served six months as *teniente político* after having been appointed to that office by the governor of the province.[9] Because his appointment is a political one, it is unclear how long he will continue to serve. His role is still both political and juridical in nature, and is characterized by the same ambiguity as that of his predecessors. In his own words, he is working as a representative of the Governor and he is the *juez de paz* of the parish.[10] Officially,[11] he is responsible for quite a few tasks involving political coordination and representation, and also serves as the head of the local police force. According to that same law,[12] however, many of his political tasks have been officially transferred to the Junta Parroquial. In practice, the abolition of the *teniente político*'s political role has not yet taken full effect (Cervone 2012: 302, note 18; Vintimilla & Andrade 2003: 58–62). In Zumbahua, both the *teniente político* and members of the Junta Parroquial told me that they had coordinating and representation tasks regarding the administration of the parish and its *comunas*, but the real

7 It is that painting that is featured on the cover of this book.
8 August 29, 2010.
9 His predecessor was Pablo Umajinga, from Guantópolo.
10 This is a self-designated role; officially he is not a *juez de paz*. The position of *juez de paz* is described in article 189 of the Montecristi Constitution. Basically, this article characterizes the *juez de paz* as a kind of mediator, who uses processes of conciliation and dialogue to settle local conflicts. He has to be elected by the community he is living and working in. His exact role is defined in the Proyecto de Código Orgánico de la Función Judicial and approved by the Comisión de Legislación y Fiscalización (Andrade 2009a, 2009b: 266–268; Vintimilla & Andrade 2003). There is some debate as to how a *juez de paz* can or should cooperate with a *teniente político* serving in the same community (http://dspace.ups.edu.ec /bitstream/123456789/ 299/2/Anexos.pdf). Until today no *juez de paz* has been appointed yet.
11 Articles 85 and 86 Ley Organica de la Funcion Judicial, and articles 8 and 9 of the Registro Oficial No. 12 (31 de Enero de 2003), Acuerdo No. 0018; Ley Orgánico Funcional del Régimen Seccional del Gobierno.
12 Ley Orgánica de las Juntas parroquiales (Registro Official No. 193, 27 de Octubre 2000).

division of labor between the Junta Parroquial and the *teniente político* is not at all clear to me.

In his juridical role, which is actually quite limited according to the law, he is responsible for recording the complaints presented to him by citizens, and he is also required to keep his superior informed about any conflict in the parish. He is required to delegate cases transcending his jurisdiction to the competent authorities. This means that he functions as a gatekeeper between citizens and the law. However, in most cases he and his police officers depend on information provided by others, thus limiting the scope of events that he has knowledge of.[13] In addition, and as previously indicated, he can feign ignorance in other cases or decide not to interfere. When he is asked to settle disputes, he is only allowed to rule in matters involving minor civil disputes and family matters, especially those involving violence toward women, whenever no official commissioner is available to deal with such cases.[14] In practice, the *teniente politico* of Zumbuahua rules on more disputes than he officially is allowed to (see also Brandt & Valdivia 2007: 118–119). It is therefore fair to say that the *teniente politico*'s present-day juridical role in the parish of Zumbahua is just as ambiguous as the role of his predecessors in other places. He too acts as a mediator within the gray area between customary law and national law (Simon Thomas 2015), as do the police officers working in Zumbahua.[15]

It remains to be seen what will happen to the *teniente político* if the limitations of his formal role are legally enforced. In her research in an indigenous parish in Chimborazo province, Emma Cervone (2012) offers some interesting insights in this regard. She found that the *teniente político* did not generally enjoy the trust of local people, and this led to the emergence of an informal indigenous organization called Inca Atahualpa. This organization began taking an active role in the administration of justice, thus drastically limiting the juridical role of the *teniente político*. The changes in the law that were discussed above suggest that a similar fate is in store for Zumbahua. It remains to be seen what will happen in practice with regard to the introduction of the *juez de paz* in relation to the juridical role of the *teniente político* (Berk-Seligson 2006: 16; Vintimilla & Andrade 2003: 58–62). As far as I have seen, and as will be shown in the next sections, today's juridical role of Jaime Rodrigo Pallo in Zumbahua continues to be relevant.

---

13 Interview I had with a police officer on October 21, 2010, in which the officer explained to me that a lot of events in the parish take place beyond their scope; this due to the fact that they are – deliberately or not – not always informed of several events in advance.
14 Article 9, section 19, of the Registro Oficial No. 12 (31 de Enero de 2003), Acuerdo No. 0018; Ley Orgánico Funcional del Régimen Seccional del Gobierno refers to the Ley contra le Violencia a la Mujer y la Familia.
15 In Chapter 5 (in the section on "Local Authorities") I have shown that a *teniente político* is head of the local police force. The policemen in Zumbahua explained to me that one of their actual tasks is to mediate as regards which legal system is best suited to a particular conflict.

Rosita vs. Miguel trial: getting started

As part of my daily routine during the course of my fieldwork, I would often take an early morning walk to the office of the *teniente politico* in Zumbahua, just to see if there might be something interesting going on that day. Sometimes the office was not open yet. Sometimes (and without any explanation) it stayed closed all day. Sometimes people were already lined up outside, waiting for their turn to present their complaints. But just as frequently, nothing important was going on. At such times, I could chat with Jaime Rodrigo Pallo, or with his secretary Eloisa. And during several of those conversations, they offered me the use of one of the office desks so that I could examine the *libros de denuncias* and the *libros de actas*.

The chilly Wednesday morning of December 1, 2010 seemed to be one such uneventful day. Wearing a gray winter coat and a blue, woolen shawl, Jaime Rodrigo Pallo was sitting behind his desk attending a number of different visitors simultaneously. To an outsider, the situation might have looked a bit chaotic, but Jaime Rodrigo Pallo, with his natural calmness and his moral authority, had everything completely under control. Just as he had done on several previous occasions, he explained to me that he did not have much time for me, but he suggested that I return in a couple of hours because two trials were scheduled for later that day.

When I returned at 10:30 am, I was quite surprised to see a number of large and small trucks parked in the street, and about a hundred indigenous people waiting outside. When I entered the office, it was full of people. When I took a seat at the desk that had been assigned to me, I noticed that Jaime Rodrigo Pallo and Eloisa were sitting behind the desk, and that a uniformed police officer was standing next to me, near the door to the storage room. I had never seen so many state officials in the office at the same time, and I therefore suspected that something important was going on. Pallo courteously escorted most of those present outside before beginning the first trial, which concerned a case of marital infidelity. In about an hour and a half, the *teniente politico* managed to settle the case. Promises were made and apologies were offered – par for the course in terms of what I had witnessed previously. But as soon as the litigants left the office at the conclusion of the trial, a group of more than twenty people came storming in. Everybody seemed to be very excited, arguing loudly and shouting, and there seemed to be even more people outside the office who were making just as much of a commotion. When I went over to the window, I noticed that the crowd had grown to more than 200 people. The crowd began to push closer to the outside door and window and the tension became palpable. At that point, I knew this second trial was going to be an interesting one.

The crowd consisted of members of the two extended families of Rosita and Miguel who had gathered in Zumbahua to follow the proceedings. For a moment, it seemed as if they all wanted to be inside the office, but with help of the police officer, who had repositioned himself at the entrance, Jaime

150   *Interlegality and the teniente político*

Rodrigo Pallo began to gently guide people out the door. Obviously, with an office of only about four square meters that contained a desk and a couple of chairs, there is not much space for anyone other than the parties directly involved with the case. Clearing the building took a while, as most of those asked to leave initially refused to do so. Pallo first tried to persuade people to leave by explaining that this case was only the concern of Rosita and Miguel, but that did not have much of an effect. Several different family members continued to leave and enter the office, just as they had before. At one point, it became evident from his body language that the *teniente político* was losing his patience. Initially seated behind his desk, at some point he decided to show his authority by standing up. Raising his voice, he presented a simple choice: either resolve the case or continue arguing. Finally, he suggested that those assembled exercise their constitutional rights under article 171 by going to their local indigenous authority to resolve the dispute. The police officer proceeded to recite article 171 of the Montecristi Constitution verbatim to the crowd before sternly concluding as follows: "Either you listen to the *teniente político* or leave and go to your own *cabildo*." Apparently, "going to the *cabildo*" was not considered a viable option, because ultimately most of the people left the office. When Rosita, Miguel, and their closest relatives finally were separated from the rest of their families and other spectators, the trial finally got underway, behind closed doors.

Rosita vs. Miguel trial: the procedure

Six persons other than *Teniente Político* Pallo, his secretary, the police officer, and myself were present. These were Rosita, her husband and her daughter, Miguel and his wife, and a male relative of theirs. It was readily evident that these persons of very humble means were all wearing their Sunday best. And of course, all of them were wearing hats (Pallo and I were the only persons present lacking headgear). Before the *teniente político* started talking, both Rosita and Miguel had handed over the bills for doctor visits and the receipts for medicine that had been purchased. Pallo then provided an explanation of the procedure, emphasizing that solving the matter was preferable to continuing to fight. He then called upon Miguel's wife, at which point a tiny and sad looking woman stepped forward and, directly facing the *teniente político*, began to explain her side of the story.

As soon as Miguel's wife started talking, Rosita became hysterical. Screaming and crying at the same time, she slapped her rival in the face and delivered a forceful kick to her husband's shin. Within seconds, the four litigants were involved in a chaotic brawl. The police officer jumped in to restore order. It took him a few minutes to separate them and meanwhile the *teniente político* had stood up again. He opened the small window and called out to a number of *dirigentes* to come and help out. Thus, we ended up with four more people in the office, all of them wearing a poncho and a hat, whose task it was to separate the four spouses from one another. These four *dirigentes* helped convince the parties to stop fighting and to concentrate instead on resolving the problem. Rosita and her daughter especially seemed to question the *teniente político*'s authority, but as one of the *dirigentes* explained, "There is no other authority," and so they had no choice other than to recognize his competence to try the case.

After separating the parties, the police officer had ordered that both Rosita's husband and Miguel's wife be locked up separately: Rosita's husband in the broom closet and Miguel's wife in the storage room. With the *dirigentes* present, it was now safe to release them and to continue the proceedings. For reasons of safety, the four *dirigentes* stood between the parties involved and the *teniente político*. Meanwhile, Rosita continued to cry loudly, but as soon as Jaime Rodrigo Pallo started talking again, she stopped sobbing. The *teniente político* was obviously not amused. Shaking his head in disapproval, he angrily questioned the propriety of continuing the procedure. One of the *dirigentes* then asked for permission to speak and explained to the two couples that they had no option than trying to reach a settlement. Another *dirigente* added that "none of us is a saint" and that a settlement had to be reached. Without further ado, the parties calmed down and the *teniente político* was able to proceed.

During the more than two hours that the hearing lasted, everyone present had a chance to say a few words, some speaking in Spanish and others in Kichwa. Rosita and Miguel got a chance to explain their version of the fight and to blame their spouses. Each of their spouses proceeded to play down what had happened; emphasizing that it had not meant anything. Rosita took the longest. Sometimes angry, sometimes sad, but always long-winded, she tried to convince the *teniente político* that Miguel should pay her medical expenses, and emphasized the fact that her husband had been unfaithful. Rosita's husband responded by offering apologies. Neither Miguel nor his wife said more than was strictly necessary. It seemed to me that Rosita used the forum provided by the trial to exact her revenge. But in fact it was the four *dirigentes* who stole the show. Skilled public speakers, they took the opportunity to repeatedly emphasize local values such as harmony, forgiveness, and reconciliation. And the *teniente político* did basically nothing but facilitate the process and work toward a solution.

During the entire hearing, some people outside the office attempted to follow the proceedings by pushing their ears to the door and window. Those who succeeded in doing so conveyed updates to the rest of the crowd. At several points, we could hear the people outside shout their approval or disapproval of what had just been said inside. At a certain point, one of the *dirigentes* went outside while the trial proceeded in order to cool heated tempers. After the proceedings had continued uninterrupted for almost two hours, Teniente Político Pallo indicated that, in his opinion, enough had been said. He abruptly called an end to all discussion by declaring that minutes (an "*acta*") would be drawn up in which a ruling would be issued and sentences imposed. After some additional discussion, this suggestion was approved by the majority, with only Miguel's wife dissenting. When she persisted in her refusal, everybody turned against her, even the *teniente político*. Although he was supposed to be impartial, he snapped at her: "You are the one that's the problem here!" This made it obvious yet again that not reaching an agreement was not an option. Finally, Jaime Rodrigo Pallo instructed his secretary to type the *acta*. While the police officer dictated the names of everybody present, Eloisa started typing. A final settlement of the dispute appeared to be imminent.

Rosita vs. Miguel trial: the settlement

Finally, three decisions to settle the dispute were made by the *teniente político*, in dialogue with the four *dirigentes*, and with approval of the two married couples. First, it was concluded that Miguel was responsible for starting the fight. Therefore, he had to pay Rosita's bills after deducting his own costs. To calculate the amount of money he had to pay, both he and Rosita had to hand over the relevant bills. Rosita handed over three bills and Miguel just one. At one point, it seemed that the legitimacy of every bill was going to be disputed by both couples, but Jaime Rodrigo Pallo quickly cut off that discussion by directing the parties to go to the Fiscal Indígena in Latacunga to get the bills certified if they refused to acknowledge their authenticity right then and there. This dictate promptly ended any further discussion. Rosita's expenses added up to $163.50 and Miguel's bill amounted to $20. So Miguel was ordered to give Rosita $143.50, an amount of cash that he did not have on hand. He was therefore allowed to leave the office for a couple of minutes to collect the needed money from his family members outside.

Meanwhile, the *teniente político*'s secretary had finished the *acta*. As soon as Miguel returned with the money, she read the text out loud. It stated that Rosita's husband and Miguel's wife agreed to not see or call each other in the near future. It also stated that, in the event that this agreement was violated, they would each be fined $5,000. Both Rosita's husband and Miguel's wife (the latter grudgingly) signed the *acta*, as did the four *dirigentes* as witnesses, and finally it was stamped and signed by *Teniente Político* Jaime Rodrigo Pallo. Now it was time for apologies. Rosita's husband was the first to apologize. He seemed quite relieved that the case was over, because while saying he was sorry, he tried to hug and kiss his wife. Rosita in turn seemed to relish her last moment in the spotlight, refusing his advances with the theatrical air of a woman scorned, but signaling her acceptance of the apology with a nod of her head. Then Miguel's wife had to apologize to her husband. She did so while looking at the ground, and in a very soft voice. Just as Rosita had done, Miguel accepted the apologies with a nod.

After the money was paid, the *acta* was signed, and the apologies were made, Rosita and her husband went outside. Accompanied by two of the *dirigentes*, they explained to their family members what had taken place inside the office and what had been agreed. Miguel and his wife stayed inside and

Pallo invited their family members into the office. He too, explained what had happened and what had been agreed. He emphasized the importance of the apologies exchanged between Rosita and her husband and Miguel and his wife, and the reconciliation between the two couples. Everybody seemed to be satisfied with the settlement, as the crowd parted without incident. The conflict had been settled, violence prevented, and harmony restored.

Analysis: the *teniente político*'s juridical role

This account of the Rosita vs. Miguel trial provides insight into the role of the *teniente político* of Zumbahua. Although not officially appointed as such, he functions like a *juez de paz*. In his juridical role, he hears cases involving domestic disputes, petty theft, traffic accidents, public drunkenness, property damage, and other minor offenses that have disrupted social harmony – or that have threatened to do so. Whether he is dealing with simple civil cases or with small penal cases like *contravenciones*, his freedom of action is limited. As he explained to me, he is only competent to adjudicate cases that involve monetary amounts of $120 or less. Or in his own words, he is "competent to deal with the theft of a cell phone, but not of a computer."[16] And, above all, he has to apply national law. However, Jaime Rodrigo Pallo does not always observe these rules. In addition, on the numerous occasions that I observed him at work in his office, I have never seen him using a law book or any kind of legal code. This is striking, because everywhere else where national law is applied, I observed a prominent use of law books.[17] This naturally raises the question of what kinds of norms, rules, and procedures he is applying. As will quickly become clear, in his daily routine, the *teniente político* falls back on customary law rather than on national law.

I will start this analysis with a brief discussion of the pre-trial phase of the Rosita vs. Miguel case. During the trial at the *teniente político*'s office, it became clear that infidelity preceded the fight which had caused a dispute over money. And the whole thing now had the potential to escalate into an outright war between the two families. It is obvious that this domestic dispute had not been successfully resolved within the sphere of the family. Neither the parties' own efforts or that of their families worked, and thus it was necessary to resort to a third party in search of mediation, arbitration, or adjudication. In this way, an initially dyadic disagreement had become a triadic trial. In their search for a third party, Rosita, Miguel, and their relatives apparently could not turn to an indigenous authority. Both couples live in Quilotoa, and this community does not have a *cabildo* capable of applying customary law in this specific case. So they had to look for an authority outside their community. They could have gone to the Court of Justice in Latacunga, but that

---

16 Interview November 14, 2010.
17 For example at the Civil Court in Pujilí, at the Penal Court in Latacunga, but also at the Constitutional Court in Quito.

would not have been very practical. In addition to issues of cost, time, and distance (remember that they did not even want to go to the Fiscal Indígena in Latacunga to get the doctor's bills certified), this probably would have resulted in the case being considered in strictly legal terms. Infidelity is not a crime or a violation according to penal law, and is also not mentioned in family law, so such a disagreement would probably not have been resolved in the court room. It also is possible that the authorities in Latacunga would have reacted to the kind of physical altercation that broke out during the trial by dismissing the case and arresting the offenders. Consequently, the "narrowing" into legal terms of this whole issue would have meant that, in a best-case scenario, only the issue of the initial fight and its economic consequences would have been dealt with.[18] The *teniente político*, on the other hand, was able to deal with the total scope of the conflict. The choice of going to the *teniente político* thus not only transformed the scope of the conflict, but also redefined the parties involved (Felstiner et al. 1980–81: 639–642).[19] This meant that Rosita and Miguel were not the only parties in this case. Their spouses were as well.

This lack of a competent *cabildo*, combined with the apparent limitations of national law, led Rosita and Miguel to seek justice in the office of *Teniente Político* Pallo. Although he is a political official bound by national law, in his self-designed role as *juez de paz*, he was able to deal with this case from a rather broad perspective. As a matter of fact, everybody I spoke to about his juridical competence mentioned examples similar to the Rosita vs. Miguel trial. Whether it was the Fiscal Indígena, a member of the Junta Parroquial, a police officer, or my friend Sergio, they all emphasized the *teniente político*'s role in settling family affairs and small fights – a combination of trust and authority provided him local legitimacy to settle conflicts. And that is what he did. More specifically: that is what he was asked to do.[20] Although one could argue that, in a strictly legal sense, this case exceeded his financial competence and as a state official he was not able to deal with infidelity, this did not seem to bother anyone present on that Wednesday in December. Nobody inside or outside the office referred to Jaime Rodrigo Pallo's limited jurisdiction. On the contrary, because infidelity is a serious offense according to customary

18 A similar example is used in Felstiner et al. (1980: 641). The authors refer to a hypothetical case which involves a man's wife and his lover. The wife has been fighting with the lover, and the latter has complained to the police. The discussion there initially focuses on the fight and then expands to include the infidelity. The scope of the incident is thus complicated by the confrontation between the two women. Narrowed to that incident alone, it could be handled by the police and court. But the broader issue of the battle for the man's affections required the help of a mediator.
19 Such transformations have been elaborated on in Chapter 4, in the section "Understanding Disputes."
20 In an interview on November 17, 2010, Jaime Rodrigo Pallo explained to me that if he was acting like a *juez de paz*, it would always be because people had asked him to do so.

norms, it was expected that he would deal with it. And he had to deal with that aspect of the dispute before resolving the financial matter.

A couple of procedural issues in this case are of particular interest. First, the whole procedure was oral. This is interesting, because one of the characteristics of customary law, as was explained in Chapter 2, is its prominent oral component (Assies 2001: 88–89; Sieder 1998: 107). Of course, a trial at a formal court would have had an oral component too, but written documents and records would have held far greater importance. This is what Felstiner et al. (1980–81: 642) refer to when they argue that the choice of institution influences the course of the dispute. Other than the doctor's bills and the *acta*, at the trial at the *teniente politico*'s office and in his final settlement, no written records or documents were used at all. In a way, this de-emphasis on written records on the part of customary law makes logical sense, given that a lot of people living in the Ecuadorian countryside do not know how to read or write. To give an example, most *actas* that I studied – those of *cabildos*, as well as those at the *teniente politico*'s archive – were "signed" with fingerprints rather than actual signatures. It therefore should not come as a surprise that the *teniente politico*, in his role as *juez de paz*, as well as the people concerned in the Rosita vs. Miguel case, relied heavily on the spoken word.[21]

Additionally, everybody got a chance to express his or her point of view. This too is exemplary of customary law (Sieder & Sierra 2010: 17). In the Zumbahuan context, this aspect is an important phase in customary procedures. It is during this phase that the perpetrator and his or her victim are publicly brought face to face (Brandt & Valdivia 2007: 31–33; Tibán & Ilaquiche 2004: 36–41). In a customary procedure, first the victim or prosecuting party is allowed to illustrate what happened, and why a third party's help was needed. Then it is the turn of the suspect or defendant to tell his or her side of the story. The general idea behind such a proceeding is to provide a stage on which everything can and should be said, not only by those most directly concerned, but by anybody who is entitled in some way or another to have a say, including relatives, godparents, community elders, and both current and former *dirigentes* (Simon Thomas 2009: 62). And, with the exception of the absence of village elders, this is precisely what happened at the Rosita vs. Miguel trial. Rosita, Miguel, their spouses and relatives, as well as the present

---

21 This, however, is not to say that everything is done orally in customary law procedures and that no written texts are used at all. On the contrary, it has been emphasized by André Hoekema (2004) among others that agreements and settlements are nowadays often written down in *actas*, contrary to what was typically done thirty years ago. This has its consequences for the functioning of customary law and its authorities. The *acta* resembles a written sentencing of a formal court. When the ruling is called into question, the parties involved tend to rely on what is written down rather than consult, for instance, the *cabildo* members or elders and their memory (Hoekema 2004: 19; Simon Thomas 2009: 7). This is, according to Hoekema, an example of the process of interlegality. The point I want to make is that, besides the doctor's bills and the *acta*, no *other* written pieces of paper (such as law books) were used.

dirigentes, got a chance to express their thoughts. Rosita seemed to be most in need of expressing herself. As illustrated, the *dirigentes* took their time to elaborate on local norms. This would not have been possible during a formal law suit. During every formal trial I have witnessed – as well as at the Civil Court in Pujilí, at the Penal Court in Latacunga, and at the Constitutional Court in Quito – it was mostly the attorneys, the Fiscal or the judge who did the talking. It is also beyond question that the judge would have cut off any discussion bearing no direct relationship with the core issue under dispute. This is what Felstiner et al. (1980–81: 645–647) mean when they highlight the influence of representatives and officials during a trial. Just as attorneys, the Fiscal, or the judge affect the course of a formal trial, so did the *dirigentes* at the *teniente politico*'s office. Their influence manifested itself in a number of important ways: they emphasized the need to settle the case that day, they provided counsel to the parties, they acted as guardians of social norms, and they assisted Pallo throughout the proceedings. In the words of Felstiner et al. (1980–81: 645), "the essence of [their] professional job" was to do so, and as such they produced a transformation.

Comparison with a formal procedure brings me to the issue of representation. During the Rosita vs. Miguel trial, everyone spoke for him- or herself. Contrary to national law, one cannot be represented by a lawyer in customary law. Spanish as well as Kichwa was spoken. And, as far as the proceeding itself was concerned, time did not seem to matter. This too is typical of customary law in the Ecuadorian Andes, where one's ability to reason, argue, and engage in dialogue is highly valued. Also striking was the role of the *dirigentes*. They not only had a role in cooling tempers in the *teniente politico*'s office, they also were active in resolving the core dispute. First, their help was instrumental in getting the parties to acknowledge the *teniente politico*'s authority and in convincing them to continue to settle the matter that day. Secondly, the *dirigentes* took their time, not only to emphasize local norms, but also to provide the parties with so-called *kuana*, which means "good counsel" in Kichwa (García 2005: 2–3; Simon Thomas 2009: 63). The *dirigentes* gave expression to the timeless wisdom that "no one is a saint" and "nobody is pure." And finally, they too, urged Miguel's wife to cooperate in reading a final settlement.

In the end, it was obvious that the settlement was not the *teniente politico*'s decision alone, but was a collectively reached compromise. This aspect of collective consensus is also one of the characteristics of customary law. After all, customary law is strongly related to reconciliation, compensation and restoring harmony. As such, everyone's cooperation is needed. A final point regarding the procedure that merits attention is the fact that the whole trial – although it took place behind closed doors – showed unmistakable signs of a public hearing. Almost every move and every word said inside was passed through to the audience outside by those with their ears and faces pressed against the outside door and window. At one point, one of the *dirigentes* attending the proceedings had to go outside in order to calm the crowd by explaining what was happening inside the office. Openness is also a common and highly valued element in customary procedures in the Ecuadorian Andes.

Finally, a brief comment is in order regarding the solution of the dispute. It was agreed that Miguel had to pay Rosita's costs. This form of compensation or restitution, monetary or otherwise, is typical for customary law, which values compensation and restitution to the victim much more than punitive measures.[22] This also accounts for the fact that the two unfaithful spouses were required to make public apologies. These apologies are considered essential for the restoration of harmony.

Conclusion

This chapter initially posed the question of how to interpret the Rosita vs. Miguel trial. A day at *Teniente Político* Jaime Rodrigo Pallo's office (or in my case: several days of participant observation) leads to the conclusion that the daily practice of settling disputes on a local level could rightly be characterized as an instance of "interlegality" (see Chapter 2). The observation that the *teniente político* in Zumbahua (an appointed state official charged with applying national law), frequently makes use of customary law, forms the basis of the argument that the line between customary law and Ecuadorian national law is in practice quite blurred.

As explained in Chapter 2, by using the term interlegality (that is the mixing of different legal spaces in people's actions and minds (de Sousa Santos 2002)), this book aims to underscore the fact that the living reality of legal pluralism in the Andean highlands shows that there is no such thing as a dichotomy between customary law and national law. An in-depth analysis of both the procedure and the final settlement of the Rosita vs. Miguel trial points to the use of several elements of customary law by a state official. This situation clearly stems from a mixing of different legal systems in practice. A notice glued on the window of the *teniente político*'s office seemed perfectly emblematic of the social values of customary law: "All who uphold the values of respect, harmony, open communication, a dynamic approach, and positive thinking are welcome here."[23] Another reflection of these values, and of the mixing of national and customary law, was that *Teniente Político* Pallo once described his juridical role to me as being a *juez de paz* (which officially he is not), stressing his role in enabling parties to come to a solution themselves rather than that of enforcing the law. The most striking feature of the proceedings in this regard was the fact that one of the *dirigentes* present seemed to have forgotten that Jaime Rodrigo Pallo was a state official. This is also a reflection of the mixing of the two systems among the indigenous population of Ecuador in general.

22 In some cases, "punishment" in the form of sanctions in relation to the damage is imposed. For example, if the head of the family is injured because of a fight, the offender might be ordered to replace him in the fields (Simon Thomas 2009: 22). This kind of sanction also has unmistakable elements of compensation, restitution, and aid.
23 "*En este dependencia está bienvenido con: Respeto – Armonia – Comunicacion, Dynamica y Positivismo.*"

Thus, the present chapter has illustrated the specific application of what was described at an abstract level in Chapter 5. On the one hand, the Rosita vs. Miguel case shows that different elements in conflicts in Zumbahua cannot be viewed apart from their relationship with the other elements. Family norms and community norms interrelate, and so do written and unwritten norms, and serious and less serious cases. And this mixing reflects the murkiness involved in resolving local conflicts. The daily practice at Jaime Rodrigo Pallo's office in general, and the Rosita vs. Miguel case in particular, provide insight into how a situation of legal pluralism works in daily practice, and also into how it is perceived by the parties involved. From an ordinary Indian's perspective, one cannot speak of a dichotomy of two different legal systems. Instead, one must draw upon the notion of interlegality, in which "law" is a "network of legality" (Goodale 2009: 33).

Seen in historical perspective, Jaime Rodrigo Pallo's role is just as ambiguous as that of his predecessors in other areas of rural Ecuador that have a longer history of dealing with the power of a *teniente político*. His political role might be decreasing, since several communities now have *cabildos* of their own and the parish as a whole has a Junta Parroquial, but his juridical role is still important. *De facto* local sovereignty, especially when it concerns the settlement of conflicts, remains for the most part in his hands (the other part lies in the hands of *cabildos*). Sometimes he is the first link in the formal chain of law and sometimes he facilitates the application of customary law by *cabildos* in their own communities, but he himself adjudicates most of the cases that come to his attention. And while settling such cases, he not only frequently transcends his formal competence, but also primarily makes use of customary law. The principle of subsidiarity (that is, lowest-level authorities settle as many conflicts as they possibly can, while the state becomes involved only in the event that resolution cannot take place at lower levels) seems to naturally mesh with the juridical practices of a *teniente político*.

Drawing on the idea of subsidiarity, Jaime Rodrigo Pallo's functioning as an official who resolves conflicts could be characterized as that of a mediator between the state, on the one hand, and rural, indigenous people, on the other (Chatterjee 2004). Within a situation of formal legal pluralism, but without rules that define any strict boundaries between the jurisdictions of different authorities available, a *teniente político* is an important local official who applies both customary and national law in a pragmatic manner. Sometimes acting on behalf of the Zumbahuan residents, sometimes as a representative of national law, but often acting like a self-defined *juez de paz*, a *teniente político*'s functioning could be seen as a powerful low-level authority, who shapes on a "bottom-up" basis the *de facto* enforcement of formal legal pluralism. As such, his activities bring rural, indigenous people into a certain political relationship with the state (what Chatterjee (2004: 38–40) calls a political society), in which the daily reality of legal pluralism seems to be negotiable. At any rate, this seems to be the case at the local level in Ecuador.

7   Trouble in Tigua

Tiguans now have a distinctive art tradition, and for those who know anything about the western parishes of Cotopaxi province, Tiguans are also known for their infighting.

(Colloredo-Mansfeld 2009a: 204)

[The resolution of disputes] is a political process whereby divisions are created or overcome.

(Nader 1990: 7)

Introduction

This chapter describes an internal conflict in the parish of Zumbahua that was taken to the Court of Justice in Latacunga. And it also concerns the members of one specific community, the Tiguans, who have a reputation for being easily offended. The previous empirical chapter might give the reader a false impression that disputes in the parish of Zumbahua are typically settled quickly and easily. This chapter will show that this is not always the case. In the Rosita vs. Miguel case, everybody involved seemed satisfied with both the settlement and the role of the *teniente politico*, despite the fact that his authority had been challenged during the initial phase of the trial. The previous chapter on conflicts, authorities, and their procedures already made the general point that criticism of local authorities is not uncommon, and that indigenous people do not invariably advocate recourse to customary law. The present chapter aims to offer insight into what happens when such discontent becomes manifest, resulting in recourse to the national courts of Ecuador.

The present chapter should therefore be read as an expansion of Chapters 5 and 6, which provide a thorough description of possible disputes, as well as a specific example of how one particular conflict was settled locally. Here, we will move beyond the locality of the parish of Zumbahua to the larger territorial units of the canton of Pujilí and the province of Cotopaxi. The dispute that will be examined here arose between two members of the well-known Toaquiza family, on the one hand, and some of their fellow community-members, on the other. This chapter addresses three important issues. First, it explores what happens when a case never previously heard by local indigenous authorities comes before the provincial Court of Justice. Second, it examines what can be learned from this case concerning the differences between customary law and national law. Finally, we will see what this case has to teach us about the daily practice of formal legal pluralism.

This chapter focuses on a single legal case, which will be used as an illustration of how legal disputes can be settled in the national courts. There are a number of reasons why I have chosen to examine the present case, in which the initial conflict arose in a small indigenous community and in which the matter under dispute was eventually settled in national courts located in the province's capital. First, Tigua is considered one of the most important communities in the Zumbahua parish, both within and outside Ecuador. It is famous for being the "heart" of *art naïf* paintings. In fact, Tigua's fame has brought with it certain adverse consequences (for example, excessive immigration to the town and economic disputes). As such, it provides a good example of how no indigenous community is without frictions. Second, the authority involved is the Criminal Court in Latacunga, one of the authorities people from Zumbahua can turn to if they want to settle a dispute according to national law.

"Toaquizas vs. the community" will be related in three different parts: the charge, the verdict, and the appeal. This chapter begins, however, with a section providing some essential background information about the town of Tigua. The chapter will conclude with an in-depth analysis of the differences between traditional and national legal procedures that will shed light on how legal pluralism works in practice in the country of Ecuador.

Tigua: a bird's eye view

The first time I drove through Tigua on my way from Latacunga to Zumbahua, the village made no impression on me at all. That day,[1] the weather conditions were fine, so that could not have been the reason why I failed to notice it. Maybe I missed it because I was distracted by either my fellow passengers in the overcrowded bus, or by the reckless maneuvers of the bus driver. But a more likely reason is that I was simply sitting on the wrong side of the bus to see the billboards for the Galeria de Artes y Artesanias de Tigua on the right-hand side of the road – the only obvious sign of the existence of Tigua and its painters in the rural highlands.[2] It is difficult to see any of Tigua's

---

1 August 7, 2007.
2 As a matter of fact, there are two billboards on the right-hand side of the road. The first one contains the word "*Galería*," accompanied by three large pictures of painters at work in the countryside (Magdalena Toaquiza, Julio Toaquiza-Primer Pintor, and Luzmila Toaquiza). The second one contains the text "*Bienvenidos a la Galeria de Artes y Artesanias del Primer Pintor de Tigua, Maestro Julio Toaquiza Tigasi*" and in English "Welcome to the Gallery of Arts and Crafts of the First Painter de [sic] Tigua, Teacher July [sic] Toaquiza Tigasi." The brightly colored outside walls of the gallery also contain some images of *art naïf*.

communities from the main road. As a matter of fact, after having driven through the area a dozen times (by bus as well as in my own car) I still do not know exactly where the parish of Tigua begins and ends. After a while, I concluded that this is because the small settlements of these communities are dispersed over such a wide area,[3] and because only a few of these settlements are located next to the main road.

The main road from Latacunga to Zumbahua, after passing through the town of Pujilí, begins the ascent into the *páramos* of the Western Cordillera of the Andean mountains in Cotopaxi province. The road meanders through the parishes of Pujilí, Tigua, and Zumbahua, passing the highest point at 4,100 meters above sea level near the Tigua Art Gallery, before a slight descent into the village of Zumbahua (3,700 meters). From Pujilí to Tigua is a drive of some 40 kilometers, and takes at least an hour and a half due to the road's innumerable twists and turns (and because of obligatory stops to allow flocks of sheep to cross the road, as well as delays resulting from getting stuck behind slow-moving trucks). The views over the fields in the mountains can be breathtakingly beautiful but, during the rainy season, low clouds can make visibility very poor. Tigua was concealed by fog on many of the occasions that I passed through or visited it, and therefore my recollection of it is mainly as a wet and chilly place. A visitor playing very close attention will notice that the first indication of the existence of Tigua is a small white sign near the road advertising a hostel two kilometers further down the road. One subsequently discovers that this information is grossly inaccurate. After considerably more than two kilometers, there is another small, green sign announcing the Hacienda Tigua Centro. And a few turns further on, a blue sign directs tourists to the right, 800 meters below the Pujilí–Zumbahua road which leads to the hostel. The main road continues uphill, and finally, after three more kilometers, you cannot miss (as long as you are seated on the right side of the bus) the Tigua Art Gallery and its billboards. Every time I took this route, I was struck by the pristine beauty of the fields, the widely dispersed houses, and the relative absence of human beings. Although every single, small piece of land was clearly under cultivation, it seemed to me as if the area was virtually uninhabited. How was it possible that Tigua, which to a certain extent is well known, could seem so desolate? Part of the answer obviously lies in the fact that a lot of Tiguan communities are not situated close to the main road. Another reason is that these settlements are so widely dispersed.

Weismantel (1988: 60) and Colvin (2004: 17) both believe that the area of Tigua was uninhabited before the Spanish arrived. As a result, its history started when the Spanish expanded their initial trading business in previously

---

3   The communities I visited all had a plaza, a church, a school, or a community building, as well as some houses built next to the plaza. Most families, however, build their homes near their fields, which thus are scattered up or down the hillside, far from what could be considered the central areas of such communities (Colvin 2004: 14).

established towns to include agriculture and livestock breeding in the Andean highlands (Simon Thomas 2009: 55). It was in 1639 that an Augustinian hacienda bought the land (which later came to be known as the Zumbahua and the Tigua haciendas) in order to raise sheep, and workers recruited from elsewhere formed small communities (Colvin 2004: 18; Simon Thomas 2009: 56). During the years that followed, the land passed through several hands until the early 1900s,[4] when the large hacienda owned by the Riofrío family dominated the Tigua area (Colloredo-Mansfeld 2009a: 35).[5] It was the so-called *huasipungueros* who lived in the communities and worked for the hacienda owner and his *mayordomos* and *mayorales* (field foremen and supervisors). When the last Riofrío owner died in the mid-1950s, the hacienda was bought by the Davalos family, which sold the entire property. At that time, the hacienda consisted of six communities (Colvin 2004: 20–21; Ilaquiche 2004b: 51).[6]

The large hacienda was divided as a result of the land reform laws of 1964 and 1973.[7] Several small plots of land were sold in the early 1970s to the *huasipungueros* that had been working on the hacienda for generations. Just as in the case of Zumbahua, land also passed into the hands of the former *mayordomos* (Colvin 2004: 20; Ilaquiche 2004b: 53). Due to the conflicting interests of certain extended families or local leaders, in subsequent years several of the already existing communities were subdivided into a number of smaller communities. Currently, eight of these are officially recognized in the sense that they have their own *cabildo*, with five members at its head (Ilaquiche 2004b: 54).[8] Only the communities of Rumichaca and Chimbacucho have become part of the parish of Zumbahua, the others forming the neighboring parish of Tigua. In 1984, the communities of Tigua and their *cabildos* united in a local Organization of the Second Degree (OSG), the UNOCAT, which became part of the provincial organization MICC, an affiliate of CONAIE (Colvin 2004: 22–23; Ilaquiche 2004b: 55). Most people who live in the area today are subsistence farmers who hardly harvest enough crops to support their households. The most well-known development in the Tigua area since the 1970s, however, is the emergence of what has become known as "Tigua art." The evolution of this local art has had consequences for the

---

4 See Becker (2007: 162) for the history of take-over of the Zumbahua hacienda.
5 In 1908, the hacienda of Zumbahua was officially transferred to the Junta Central de Asistencia Pública (Public Assistance Coordinating Body), a public body that rented the hacienda out to landlords for eight years at a time (Becker 2007: 162; Simon Thomas 2009: 57).
6 The six communities of workers on the hacienda in those days were: Tigua Centro, Chimbacucho, Yahuartoa, Chami, Sunirrumi, and Anchi Quilotoa.
7 See Chapter 4 for more information on the land reform laws of 1964 and 1973.
8 The eight communities with an official status are: Casa Quemada, Aghsa Loma Grande, Tigua Centro, Rumichaca, Chimbacucho, Niño Loma, Pactapungo, and Ugshaloma Chico (Ilaquiche 2004b: 54). Other communities in Tigua are: Yatapungo, Ugshaloma Grande, Sunirrumi, Chami, Quiloa, Calerapamba, Yahuarto and Yatapungo (Colvin 2004: 17; Ilaquiche 2004b: 54; Jácome 2009: 63).

economic and social wellbeing of the area. Farmers became painters and, as painting artists, they eventually left their communities. Most of them migrated to Quito, where they have earned their living through painting and/or selling paintings.

As Jean Colvin (2004) has so beautifully described, nowadays Tigua is renowned for its colorful *art naif* paintings depicting daily life in the Andean highlands. Originally, farmers in the Tigua area decorated drums and masks for their festivals and fiestas. In the 1970s, local artists began to paint the same simple figures and geometric designs on a flat frame. Since then, these paintings have become more complex, with themes reflecting the history, festivals, legends, politics, and tradition of those living in the area (Colvin 2004: 5). Because, beginning in the early 1970s, folk art collectors and other foreigners showed interest in the painted drums, Julio Toaquiza and two of his brothers, from the Chimbacucho community, began to purchase and sell them to art dealers like Olga Fisch, as well as to cultural centers. Olga Fisch is recognized as being the person who suggested that the drum images be painted on a flat surface (originally, sheep hide stretched over a flat frame),[9] mainly for commercial reasons. Flat, small paintings are easier to transport than large drums, and thus easier to sell to foreign buyers of folk art. Julio Toaquiza is generally regarded as the first painter to work on a flat surface (Bonaldi 2010: 19–31; Colloredo-Mansfeld 2009a: 38–40; Colvin 2004: 26–27; Naranjo 1996: 170–177).

These two-dimensional works of art turned out to be such a commercial success that Julio Toaquiza and his brothers shifted their business from drums to paintings. This proved to yield something of an economic bonanza for them, so they started to teach other family members to paint in order to provide them with the same means to increase their meager income as farmers. Obviously, it did not take long before other people from neighboring communities, such as Quiloa and Chami, also began to create and sell their paintings. Soon, painting offered an economically viable alternative to farming for many people in the area. And especially after the economic crisis of 1982, more and more Tiguans started painting, selling most of their works to tourists in Quito. Initially, Tiguan painters traveled to Quito and back (a trip of more than five hours) to sell their paintings to either a few retail shops, or directly to tourists on the street. Eventually, a lot of them decided to move to Quito to live and paint (and sell) close to their customers (Colloredo-Mansfeld 2009a; Colvin 2004).[10]

Jose Vega, of the Quiloa community, was one of the first to migrate to Quito. During the 1990s, more and more artists from Quiloa as well as from

---

9   Colloredo-Mansfeld (2009a: 40), on the other hand, refers to an interview he had with Julio Toaquiza in which the latter insisted that it was not Olga Fisch who suggested framing his paintings.

10 Colvin (2001, cited in Colvin 2004: 130) for example reports that over 80 percent of the artists from the Quiloa community had migrated to Quito by the end of the 1990s.

other Tigua communities moved to the capital. Most of them tried to sell their wares at the weekend art fair in El Parque Ejido (Ejido Park), in the center of Quito. In order to compete with other non-Tigua artists and art vendors, and to be able to negotiate with the municipality that controlled these sales activities, they started to organize themselves. One of these organizations was the Association of Indigenous Small Traders of Paintings and Handicrafts of Tigua,[11] founded by Jose Vega in 1982. This association primarily was meant to unite artists from Quiloa and their neighboring community Yatapungo. Because the intention of this association was to give a legal voice to those who wanted to sell their artwork in Quito, its jurisdiction was sought in the province of Pichincha (Quito) and not in the province of Cotopaxi. By the end of the 1990s, some ten such associations had been established, and the number of painters allied to them had grown to over 300. This expanding group of Tiguan artists in turn led to the emergence of a new class of businessmen: so-called *negociantes* (intermediaries or dealers) who earned their living as middlemen between the painters and their customers. These developments had the general effect of increasing the quantity while reducing the quality and prices of the paintings. Tigua art in Quito blossomed into a real business, with all the competitiveness and tensions that this implied (Bonaldi 2010; Colloredo-Mansfeld 2009a; Colvin 2004).

Meanwhile in Tigua, in the Chimbacucho community to be exact, Julio Toaquiza and his family members continued to paint in their rural hometown. Especially Julio and his eldest son, Alfredo, became nationally and internationally renowned, exhibiting their work in Ecuador, as well as in the United States and Europe.[12] In 1989, the artists of Chimbacucho, just like their peers in Quito, organized themselves into the Association of Autonomous Workers on Indigenous Culture of Tigua-Chimbacucho.[13] Julio Toaquiza was its first president and, after a few years, he was succeeded by his son Alfredo. Due to both political tensions in the community and the desire of some to live near the main road (in order to get easier access to potential buyers like passing tourists), the community split. Most of the painting families from Chimbacucho moved up the mountain and settled in the Turupata sector. It was there that, in 1991, the Galeria de Artes y Artesanias de Tigua was constructed (Bonaldi 2010: 48; Colvin 2004: 127) – the gallery that I completely missed the first time I passed through Tigua on a bus.

11 In Spanish: Asociación de Pequenos Comerciantes Indígenas de Cuadros y Artesanías de Tigua.
12 Their first exhibition was held in Quito in 1979 (Colvin 2004: 29). International exhibitions were held for instance in Washington, D.C. (1981 and 1994), San Francisco (1994), Berkeley (1997), and San Diego (1997) in the United States, and in Europe in, for instance, Potsdam, Germany (1994), and Paris, France (1997) (Bonaldi 2010: 35; Colvin 2004: 6–7, 30, 33).
13 In Spanish: Asociación de Trabajadores Autonomos de la Cultura Indígena de Tigua-Chimbacucho.

Initially, the gallery was operated by the association, but when the envisaged masses of art-buying tourists did not materialize, forcing many artists from Chimbacucho and Turupata to migrate to Quito, the Toaquiza family began managing the gallery (Bonaldi 2010: 48; Colvin 2004: 127). As a matter of fact, the few tourists that visit the area actually come to see the crater lake of Quilotoa. Most of them just drive through Tigua-Turupata, and only a small minority stop to visit the gallery. An unforeseen consequence of the majority of tourists going directly to Quilotoa is that, in the community of Ponce-Quilotoa, near the crater lake, a new cooperative of artists has formed who paint and sell paintings "in the Tigua-style" (Noroña Salcedo 2006: 13). Because these artists are not natives of the Tigua area, this development has caused great dismay among painters from the original Tigua art communities (Colvin 2004: 140).

This bird's eye view of Tigua's history thus far depicts an originally isolated and remote area that, during the past three decades, has witnessed many of its inhabitants turning from farming to painting and selling art as a means of earning a living. The majority of such individuals ended up moving to Quito. With the exception of a few other artists, only the Toaquiza family has remained in the Tigua area (Bonaldi 2010; Colloredo-Mansfeld 2009a; Colvin 2004). No wonder the area itself gives such a desolate impression, even though its fame might lead one to expect otherwise. Besides explaining its desolation, my brief research on the history of Tigua revealed another insight to me, namely that of Tiguans being unhappy with, and resistant to, existing power relations. Colloredo-Mansfeld (2009a: 210) explains that this "taking on outsiders" is one of the two meanings of what he calls "fighting like a community," and that this can be considered typical for Tiguans. Or as Colvin (2004: 23) states: "Over the years, Tigua gained a reputation for open resistance and assertive indigenous leaders."

Let me give just a few examples of this willingness to fight, starting from the first half of the twentieth century. In 1929, in reaction to their miserable working conditions, the *huasipungueros* of the Tigua hacienda began to organize and protest. Their protest, however, was broken up by the provincial authorities, leaving nine indigenous workers dead (Colloredo-Mansfeld 2009a: 35; Colvin 2004: 19). But this did not prevent them from organizing several more strikes and protests, led by Agustín Vega (Fiallo 2000, cited in Colvin 2004: 19). Fifteen years later, the same Agustín Vega participated in founding the FEI (Becker 2007: 177), the first significant organization in the countryside. Half a century later, people from Tigua still continued to fight large landowners. In the early 1990s, for example, they (including several of the better known artists) tried to appropriate land from the Hacienda Tigua Centro. The Tiguans claimed that, because they were indigenous inhabitants, the land was rightfully theirs. It was only the intervention of the Church that resulted in this issue being peacefully solved. More recently, people from Tigua were active in the overthrow of the Mahuad government in 2001 (Colvin 2004: 23).[14] Colloredo-Mansfeld (2009a) writes extensively

---

14 They did so through the local UNOCAT and the provincial MICC (Colvin 2004: 23).

about Tiguan artists in Quito who have challenged the authorities during the last decade, in order to obtain more rights (and space) to sell their paintings.

"Fighting like a community" also has another meaning, namely "fighting each other" (Colloredo-Mansfeld 2009a: 210). Jackson and Warren (2005: 566) observed that "any indigenous community will be riddled with conflicts," and this generalization certainly applies to the Tiguan artists. While artistic developments brought relative prosperity, these same developments also caused (or aggravated) internal disputes and other tensions. For example, the literature provides several examples of conflicts between painters and their associations or intermediaries. In addition, associations fight with each other and so do intermediaries (Colloredo-Mansfeld 2009a: 145; Colvin 2004: 134, 156). However, most conflicts arise among painters themselves.

The most intense conflicts are between the rural painters of Tigua and Chimbacucho and the urban painters of Quito. On the one hand, it is the relative commercial success of the urban painters that threatens the business of those who remained in the countryside. Therefore, the rural painters, led by Julio Toaquiza and his son Alfredo, are on bad terms with people who originate from Tigua-Quiloa but now live and paint in Quito, criticizing the latter for what they characterize as the "inferior" quality of their paintings. They claim that the real Tigua paintings come from Tigua, and not from Quito. On the other hand, the painters and dealers in Quito blame the Toaquiza family for being selfish, claiming that the Toaquizas attract most of the attention, and receive important financial benefits, neither of which they seem willing to share with their neighbors. This caused envy among the painters in Quito (Colloredo-Mansfeld 2009a: 59, 143, 154; Colvin 2004: 135–136). This urban–rural controversy between the rival groups of artists apparently dates back to at least the early 1990s.[15]

The rural painters themselves, however, also have their internal disputes. The Tiguan *libros de actas* that I was allowed to examine showed a long series of conflicts about land, robberies, and so on (in other words, the same kinds of conflicts described in Chapter 5).[16] In the archives of the Criminal Court in Latacunga, I also came across several cases that involved residents of Tigua (including one that concerned the theft of a computer from the communal

---

15 Interview with Alfredo Toaquiza on December 1, 2010. I asked him about the details of a painting that showed him as a prisoner behind bars. The title of this painting is "Prisión de Alfredo Toaquiza en el Penal García Moreno" (and is also available as a postcard). He explained to me that it was painted in 1995, when he had been falsely accused of theft and other criminal activities by members of "a gang of urban painters" from Quito, which resulted his being jailed for a couple of days. His daughter Sisa Toaquiza has recorded a song, titled *La Carcél* (the prison), about this incident (Toaquiza 2009). In an earlier interview, on October 28, 2010, he also referred to existing tensions between Tigua-Chimbacucho and Tigua-Quiloa.
16 Visit to Alfredo Toaquizo's house in Tigua-Turupata on December 1, 2010.

building).[17] And, as mentioned above, there have been tensions between painters from Tigua and Quilotoa-Ponce, and between inhabitants of the Tigua-Chimbacucho community and the Tigua-Turupata sector situated higher up the hill. And one Tiguan painter even referred to "political tension" between himself and other members of the local painters' association.[18] As is the case with many of the urban–rural controversies, several of the purely rural disputes involve Toaquiza family members against others. That is why I have chosen in the following sections to describe and analyze one of these conflicts between "the Toaquizas" and other parties.

The Toaquizas vs. the community: the charge

It was on Sunday September 23, 2007 that the conflict escalated. At 3:00 pm, a group of people began gathering in the communal building of Tigua-Chimbucacho. Among them were two members of the Toaquiza family, the president of the *cabildo*, and six other community members.[19] Although there were several issues on the agenda that afternoon, the meeting mainly had to do with the administration of a hostel – the Hostería Samana Huasi.[20] This particular hostel had been established in Tigua-Chimbacucho in the early 2000s with help from Jean Colvin. Initially, the purpose of this establishment was to attract tourists and art buyers, in order to promote sales and to offer job opportunities to members of the community. It was supposed to be run by the community, and its revenues were to be shared among all involved parties (Colvin 2004: 157). However, Alfredo Toaquiza had, over the years, arrogated the operations and revenues of the hostel to himself and his family members.[21] Since the number of guests visiting the hostel had declined over the years, the meeting that Sunday afternoon was about the future of the locale. Alfredo Toaquiza's particular concern had to do with how he would be compensated for his past investments in the hostel.[22]

17 I came across this case (that dates back to 2006) the first time I did research in the archives of the Criminal Court, on October 22, 2009. Unfortunately I did not make a note of the file-number that time.
18 One might get the idea from this statement that they had a difference of opinion on politics (in the strict sense of the term), but what this Tiguan painter was suggesting was instead a power struggle between himself and the other members (interview on October 28, 2010).
19 In order to protect the anonymity of the people involved in this legal case, I will not mention their real names, but I will note for the record that the two Toaquiza family members were not Julio and his son Alfredo, although the latter was present at the meeting.
20 Caso 85–2008, Juzgado Segundo de lo Penal de Cotopaxi, exhibit 86–90: Minutes of the meeting of the General Assembly of the Tigua-Chimbacucho community.
21 Conversation with Jean Colvin on August 24, 2010. See also Caso 85–2008. Juzgado Segundo de lo Penal de Cotopaxi, exhibit 86–90: Minutes of the meeting of the General Assembly of the Tigua-Chimbacucho community.
22 Caso 85–2008, Juzgado Segundo de lo Penal de Cotopaxi, exhibit 86–90: Transcribed version of the original (handwritten) *acta* of the meeting of the General

According to the minutes of the meeting, 146 members of the Tigua-Chimbacucho community were present. Several of them spoke about the hostel, and various issues came up in that connection. For example, the involvement of Jean Colvin was mentioned. The Share Foundation, founded by Jean Colvin and her husband to support the building and management of the hostel, was discussed. Several of the persons in attendance pointed out that the hostel had been established as, and remained, a communal undertaking (and was in fact characterized as a *minga* of the association of Tigua-Chimbacucho painters).[23] If the involvement of Alfredo Toaquiza was mentioned by them, it was mostly in reference to him being the project manager, not the owner. When Alfredo Toaquiza spoke at the meeting, he did not deny these statements. However, he did stress all the extra efforts he and his family members had put into the hostel. This was confirmed by relatives of his who were also present at the meeting. When it was their turn to speak, they recalled that the contribution of the association only consisted of the building of the hostel. Everything that had been invested in the hostel over the years, like its inventory or necessary improvements, was done by them. And financed by them, of course. So basically what the Toaquizas were arguing was that, because of their efforts, they had not only been entitled to the minimal revenue that had been generated, but they were entitled to compensation for their investments as well. All of the arguments on both sides were recorded in the minutes. Finally, it was concluded that the conversation with Jean Colvin would continue at a later date, and that the association would deliberate upon its future involvement in the hostel.[24]

A very different version of what happened during that meeting was provided by two Toaquiza family members who were in attendance. These men lodged a complaint with the judge of the Criminal Court in Latacunga, on January 23, 2008. In their letter, addressed to the criminal court judge of Cotopaxi province, they mentioned severe insults and threats that they claimed were expressed by seven attendees at that meeting. When, at a certain point during the meeting, the two Toaquizas felt physically intimidated, they decided to leave. As they approached the door, one of the members of the *cabildo* told them: "Wait, you sons of bitches, assholes, thieves, scoundrels! Why are you leaving?" Then a second man snapped: "Just go. You've stolen money from the hostel. You live from the money you steal from foreigners." Next, a third person, a woman, said, "Let's kill the Toaquizas. Let's break their fucking bones!"[25]

The complaint of the two Toaquizas continued with allegations of still further threats directed toward them at the meeting. They contended that three more

23 *Minga* (Kichwa): communal work that would benefit a group of people or the whole community.
24 Caso 85–2008 Juzgado Segundo de lo Penal de Cotopaxi, exhibit 86–90.
25 According to the letter, the literal abusive language used was: "*ratito hijos de puta, cabrones, ladrones, pillos, por qué no se quedan,*" "*ve, ustedes son los ladrones del dinero de la hostería, viven robando a los gringos,*" and "*les vamos a matar Toaquizas, les vamos a romper los huesos hijos de puta.*" Caso 85–2008 Juzgado Segundo de lo Penal de Cotopaxi, exhibit 1.

men blocked their way and shouted at them like madmen: "Give back the money from the hostel, you thieves! Don't take money from foreigners! You're not getting out of here alive, you sons of bitches!"[26] And then the seventh person entered the scene brandishing a stick with which he threatened them. The rest of the crowd (consisting of more than 120 people, as the Toaquizas remembered it) turned against them as well. They were mainly people from Quito and Ambato (capital of Tungurahua province), who were called to attend this particular meeting, accompanied by some inhabitants of nearby communities. Things seemed to be getting out of hand, but with help from their family members and some others, the two men managed to leave the communal building safely.[27]

After describing what had happened to them, the Toaquizas demanded that the seven people involved be prosecuted and punished to the maximum extent allowed by the Criminal Code. They also filed a civil suit against the seven men, claiming $10,000 for pain and suffering. The two members of the Toaquiza family contended that this money was intended to compensate for diminished prestige "as painters and artists, well-known on a local, provincial, national, and international level," and for future expenses like legal costs and lawyer fees.[28] Finally, they demanded that the summonses be personally delivered to the seven accused by the *teniente político* of the parish of Zumbahua (of the larger political unit to which the community of Tigua-Chimbacucho belongs). The complaint was signed by the two men, as well as by their three lawyers.[29]

The complaint against the seven was brought to the Juzgado Segundo de lo Penal in person by one of their lawyers on January 23, 2008, and it was accepted by the secretary of the Juez Segundo de lo Penal, Judge Jiménez.[30] The judge accepted the case, and in accordance with the law,[31] he considered it a criminal proceeding initiated by an individual instead of by a public prosecutor (a so-called *Acción Penal Privada*). Almost immediately, he initiated the usual formalities. The first thing judge Jiménez did, on February 7, was to send for the two Toaquizas in order to give them an opportunity to vouch for the truth of their previous statements. They did so, and after this declaration was taken down, it was signed by them and the judge, and then it was filed.[32] Next, as the law in cases of private prosecution prescribes, the judge decided on February 12 that the *teniente político* in Zumbahua had to

---

26 Originally: "*devuelvan la plata de la hostería ladrones, no les roben a los gringos, no salen de aquí vivos, son unos hijos de puta.*"
27 Caso 85–2008 Juzgado Segundo de lo Penal de Cotopaxi, exhibit 1.
28 Caso 85–2008 Juzgado Segundo de lo Penal de Cotopaxi, exhibit 1.
29 Caso 85–2008 Juzgado Segundo de lo Penal de Cotopaxi, exhibit 2.
30 This is his real name. I decided to refer to people in public positions with their real names, because this is a matter of public record that can be easily discovered by anyone.
31 Caso 85–2008 Juzgado Segundo de lo Penal de Cotopaxi, exhibit 4: article 371 of the Código de Procedimiento Penal (Code of Criminal Procedures).
32 Caso 85–2008 Juzgado Segundo de lo Penal de Cotopaxi, exhibit 5.

summon the seven accused in order to provide their personal data to the court by February 22.[33]

The *teniente político* only managed to locate family members of three of the seven accused within those ten days. These family members reported to the *teniente político* that the three accused now worked and lived in the town of Pujilí, and that they were not able to travel to Zumbahua.[34] The *teniente político* proceeded to write a letter to the judge on February 27 reporting this information, suggesting that the other four men probably lived outside the province of Cotopaxi, and requesting that the judge himself follow up on the matter.[35] Within two weeks, on March 11, Judge Jiménez received two letters from the Toaquizas, in which they both reaffirmed their willingness to pursue their complaint, and requested that the judge resubmit the initial order to the *teniente político*. Judge Jiménez promptly did so in a letter received by the *teniente político* on March 13.[36]

Meanwhile, Judge Jiménez received other documents that became part of the dossier of the case. Among these was a letter from the Toaquizas and their lawyers in which they requested that only one of them be allowed to represent both in future written communications.[37] The judge also received a copy of a resolution of the Ministry of Agriculture, in which the composition of the *cabildo* of the Tigua-Chimbacucho community was confirmed.[38] Altogether, the file for the case ended up swelling to some 300 pages.

At the same time, the *teniente político* had somewhat more success in his second effort to contact the seven accused parties. The same day he received the letter from the judge, he managed to speak to family members of all of the accused.[39] He was told by them exactly where to find the homes of the accused in Tigua-Chimbacucho, and he went there the next day. Given that he did not find the accused or any of their relatives, he decided to post the formal charge to each of their doors in the presence of a witness.[40] Since this also produced no effect, he repeated this action one more time three days later.[41] By then, it should have been beyond all doubt that the criminal judge was seeking the seven because of the Toaquizas' charge against them. Evidently, this led the Toaquizas to write a letter to the judge on March 28 in which they demanded a date, place, and time be set for a Reconciliation Hearing.[42]

33 Caso 85–2008 Juzgado Segundo de lo Penal de Cotopaxi, exhibits 6 and 9.
34 Caso 85–2008 Juzgado Segundo de lo Penal de Cotopaxi, exhibits 10–12.
35 Caso 85–2008 Juzgado Segundo de lo Penal de Cotopaxi, exhibit 13.
36 Caso 85–2008 Juzgado Segundo de lo Penal de Cotopaxi, exhibits 16 and 22.
37 Caso 85–2008 Juzgado Segundo de lo Penal de Cotopaxi, exhibit 6.
38 Caso 85–2008 Juzgado Segundo de lo Penal de Cotopaxi, exhibit 17; the *cabildo* had been elected on January 21, 2007.
39 Caso 85–2008 Juzgado Segundo de lo Penal de Cotopaxi, exhibits 23–25.
40 Caso 85–2008 Juzgado Segundo de lo Penal de Cotopaxi, exhibits 26–28.
41 Caso 85–2008 Juzgado Segundo de lo Penal de Cotopaxi, exhibits 29–31.
42 Caso 85–2008 Juzgado Segundo de lo Penal de Cotopaxi, exhibit 32; the Toaquizas and their lawyers referred in this letter to article 327 of the Code of Criminal Procedures.

Between March 28 and March 31, Judge Jiménez received letters on behalf of six of the accused.[43] It was clear that these letters were composed by their two lawyers, Wladimir López and Raúl Ilaquiche.[44] The letters were accompanied by copies of the accused's identification cards, which enabled their personal data to finally be entered into the case record. The six men and one woman all appeared to have been born in the parish or the surrounding region, and to range in age between twenty and fifty-six. They indicated that they held the following occupations: *jornalero* (day laborer), *estudiante* (student), *quehacer domésticos* (housewife), *artesano* (artisan), and *pintor* (painter). The purpose of the letters could not be more clear. Referring, among other things, to article 191 of the 1998 Constitution, to the UN Declaration of Rights of Indigenous Peoples, and to ILO Convention 169, they denied everything that the Toaquizas alleged that they had said in the complaint that was filed. The six letters also requested that everything that had happened be considered an internal conflict, and thus they asked that Judge Jiménez: 1) recuse himself; 2) consider the complaint inadmissible; and 3) declare all of the proceedings that had thus far taken place regarding the matter to be null and void. In other words, they stated that this was an internal indigenous matter that had nothing to do with national law.

Based upon the narrative to this point, a number of conclusions can be drawn regarding this case. Most striking of all, especially in light of the previously examined case study, is the role of the *teniente político*. In the Rosita vs. Miguel case, the *teniente político* was clearly the authority in charge. In the present case, however, he only had a minor supporting role. This difference shows how the choice between customary law and national law affects that official's relative power. Most striking of all is the influence of the involvement of national law on the present case. Even before the conflict is brought to the judge, it is framed in juridical terms, and as soon as the judge becomes involved, he dictates the terms of the proceedings. Existing law defines what this case is about (while ignoring other undeniably important factors such as longstanding tensions). Everything is written down and the role of those initially involved seems to fade into the background as their lawyers assume center stage. In addition, the question of whether what happened on September 23, 2007 can legitimately be labeled an internal conflict assumes an importance nearly equal to that of the events of that day. In other words, both article 191 of the 1998 Constitution and the absence of coordinating rules together seem to exercise an important influence on the development of this case.

---

43 Caso 85–2008 Juzgado Segundo de lo Penal de Cotopaxi, exhibit 33–62. The file only contains six such documents, while the complaint concerns seven accused. I assume that a seventh letter was written but never subsequently filed, since it was not in the case files and was never subsequently referred to.

44 Caso 85–2008 Juzgado Segundo de lo Penal de Cotopaxi, exhibit 33–62.

The Toaquizas vs. the community: the verdict

In their aforementioned correspondence of March 28 and March 31,[45] the accused – or rather, their lawyers – formulated their arguments as follows. First, they defined and explained the collective rights of the accused. The first point they made in this regard was that the events had taken place among indigenous people, in an indigenous community which is part of an indigenous parish, and in the presence of an indigenous assembly. Therefore, they argued, the events should be considered an internal conflict. Then, each of the accused referred to his or her identification card, which constituted objective proof that they were indigenous people too because they were born in indigenous communities.[46] Additionally the accused stated that they belonged to the Panzaleo people, an indigenous group that has been legally and constitutionally recognized. As such, they were entitled to certain collective rights (specifically, those mentioned in the 1998 Constitution, in the UN Declaration of Rights of Indigenous Peoples, and in the ILO Convention 169).

With regard to the 1998 Constitution, they referred to article 191 (section 4), which is about the recognition of customary law and local authorities in cases involving internal conflict; to article 84 (section 7), which deals with the conservation and development of traditional social organization; and to article 24 (sections 11 and 12), which concerns the right to be judged by a competent judge in one's own language. With respect to the UN Declaration of Rights of Indigenous Peoples, they referred to the articles 1, 2, 3, 4, 5, 34, and 35 (essentially for the purpose of emphasizing their rights as indigenous people). Finally, with regard to ILO Convention 169, they referred to articles 8 (sections 1, 2, and 3), 9 (sections 1 and 2), and 10 (sections 1 and 2), as the basis for their argument that local customs of the involved parties should be taken into consideration whenever the national legal system adjudicates a case involving indigenous people. They concluded their argument on collective rights by referring once again to the 1998 Constitution, specifically to articles 18, 163, 272, and 273. These articles were used to convince the judge that he was bound by the previously cited laws. Thus, the lawyers for the accused argued that the case had to, in principal, be considered an internal indigenous matter.

The second argument in their letters explicitly referred to the content of the complaint itself, its point of origin, and its condition of admissibility. The argument in this second section was firmly grounded in the objective facts and details of the case. First, the lawyers referred to articles 36 and 371 of the

---

45 Caso 85–2008 Juzgado Segundo de lo Penal de Cotopaxi, exhibit 33–62.
46 For example: Caso 85–2008 Juzgado Segundo de lo Penal de Cotopaxi, exhibit 34. It should be noted in this connection that the national identification cards issued by Ecuador do not indicate whether the bearer is indigenous. However, an indigenous first or last name or one's place of birth can give a clue as to ethnicity. These clues are not conclusive, and probably that is why the defendants made the declaration: "I hereby declare that I am an indigenous person" ("*Justifico que soy un indígena*").

Criminal Procedure Code in relation to article 191 (section 4) of the Constitution. They argued that, in cases involving an *Acción Penal Privada*, one has to be very careful about forming an opinion about whether or not certain words are slanderous, and about the intention behind such words (in terms of the present case, especially in relation to customary law). Basically, the lawyers argued that a national judge is not capable of making such a determination in cases of internal indigenous conflict. Additionally, they contended that parties (in this case, the Toaquizas) formulating a complaint were obliged to be very specific about which law or laws were being violated. In this connection, the lawyers contended that the complaint lacked the required specificity. They made the further point that, in order to allow the determination of whether or not the conduct in question was punishable, it was important to stick to the facts. Thus – the lawyers contended – *every* fact in the case needed to be taken into consideration, and not only some particular facts. In this way, the lawyers accused the Toaquizas of not telling the whole story. To sum up the accused's lawyers arguments so far: they tried to play down the complaint's point of origin. It seems like they were trying to say: whatever happened should not be taken too seriously; and if it somehow does rise to a certain level of seriousness, it still really cannot be judged by a non-indigenous judge.

They continued to state that the complaint did not meet the requirements of admissibility. For example, it did not relate the events to either a crime (*delito*) or an infraction (*infracción*), and this therefore made it difficult to legally assess the events in question. The lawyers further contended that the complaint was not sufficiently specific regarding the exact time, place, and sequence of the events under dispute. Thus, the attorneys cast aspersions on the veracity of the Toaquizas' specific recollection of the events. In addition, the lawyers of the accused asked how, in a gathering of more than 120 people, one could possibly know exactly who said what. In specific reference to the case at hand, the lawyers wondered how the seven accused could have been accurately targeted as having made the alleged insulting and threatening remarks. In any case, the seven denied everything that they were accused of having said. In their words, the allegation itself was "pure fantasy, ridiculous, absurd, illogical, and completely removed from reality." They concluded, based on this second argument, that the events in question could simply not be labeled criminal acts.

In their third and final argument, the former two arguments were used as the basis of the previously mentioned petition to Judge Jiménez in which they requested that he recuse himself, dismiss the complaint, and declare all previous legal proceedings involving the case invalid. In addition, the lawyers said that, in the event that the judge did not honor the previous requests, their clients were on record as denying everything they were accused of. Each of the six multiple-page letters were signed by one of the accused and by both lawyers (who were representing all six of the accused). It was because of these requests (and also because of the earlier demand of the Toaquizas) that Judge Jiménez set April 21, 2008 as the date of the Reconciliation Hearing.

On that same day, at 10:10 am, almost everybody involved in the case was present in Judge Jiménez's office, on the second floor of the Court of Justice in Latacunga. The two Toaquizas and one of their lawyers were present as well. Six of the accused, their lawyer López, and the lawyer for the seventh defendant (who was unable to attend) were all in attendance. The purpose of the hearing, in accordance with the Criminal Procedure Code, was to attempt to get the parties to agree to a settlement regarding the case before it came to trial. López spoke first. In a lengthy monologue, he basically repeated what had been stated in the previous letters. He emphasized that this was an internal indigenous matter and that, consequently, the judge lacked jurisdiction to rule on it. Afterward, the lawyer of the Toaquizas was given time to respond. In a similarly lengthy exposition, and with reference to numerous legal precedents, he opposed López's point of view, basically arguing that it was legally valid for Judge Jiménez to rule on the present case. It was quite obvious that a settlement would not be reached that morning. Finally, Judge Jiménez admitted the complaint as legitimate, stating that he did not agree with López's points of view. He then gave the parties involved fifteen days to provide more evidence, in order to be able to rule on the case. These proceedings were recorded in a six-page document, which was signed by everybody present.[47]

The two Toaquiza men and their lawyers proceeded to write a letter to the judge in which they formally denied everything that had been stated by the accused and their lawyer that could be held against them.[48] In a second letter, they asked the judge to admit the testimony of four witnesses who had been present at the meeting on September 23, 2007.[49] The judge did so on May 6. In four sessions of about half an hour each, at which lawyers of both the plaintiffs and the defendants were present, the four witnesses testified on behalf of the Toaquizas.[50] They all declared that the version of the Toaquizas regarding what had happened that particular Sunday afternoon was true. They stated that they had personally witnessed the insults and the threats that the Toaquizas had recorded in their initial complaint. Additionally, the Toaquizas presented written declarations of character witnesses on their behalf, and they copied every certificate and diploma that they had received over the years as painters (for the purpose of establishing their national and international prominence).[51] This evidence was brought together and, accompanied by a letter, sent to Judge Jiménez.[52]

The seven accused and their lawyers each proceeded in a similar manner. Separately, each of the accused sent a letter to the four criminal judges at the Court of Justice in which they requested the issuing of a statement that they

47 Caso 85–2008 Juzgado Segundo de lo Penal de Cotopaxi, exhibit 63–66.
48 Caso 85–2008 Juzgado Segundo de lo Penal de Cotopaxi, exhibit 69.
49 Caso 85–2008 Juzgado Segundo de lo Penal de Cotopaxi, exhibit 71.
50 Caso 85–2008 Juzgado Segundo de lo Penal de Cotopaxi, exhibit 73–76.
51 Caso 85–2008 Juzgado Segundo de lo Penal de Cotopaxi, exhibit 173–216.
52 Caso 85–2008 Juzgado Segundo de lo Penal de Cotopaxi, exhibit 217.

had no criminal record during the past five years.[53] Each received four such declarations.[54] Then all seven of the accused parties started to collect written statements from character witnesses (employers, unions, committees, or associations that they belonged to, currently or in the past). In the end, each individual collected five or six such declarations (which contained phrases like "an honorable, responsible, hardworking person" or "one whose honorability attracts others"). This was all of course meant to convince Judge Jiménez that the conduct they were accused of by the Toaquizas was entirely inconsistent with the kind of people they were, and therefore highly dubious. To underscore their version of what had happened, they all provided a typed version of the original (handwritten) minutes of the meeting of the General Assembly of the Tigua-Chimbacucho community, and that made no mention whatsoever of any insults directed against the two Toaquizas.

With the help of their lawyers, the seven wrote a second letter to Judge Jiménez. Basically, they repeated their previous six-page long presentation, arguing that the judge should recuse himself and that they were innocent. To underscore that latter claim, they attached proof of clean criminal records, the statements of their character witnesses, and the transcribed version of the minutes of the meeting where the events under dispute took place. One of them also added a copy of an earlier conviction of one of the Toaquizas and another of his family members for robbery[55] in order to demonstrate the "criminal behavior" of the Toaquiza family in general and this Toaquiza in particular. In an additional seventh page, they pled their innocence. They referred to article 24 (section 7) of the 1998 Constitution, which declares that everybody is innocent until proven guilty. In their conclusion, they rejected all charges. Their letter, accompanied by all the aforementioned documents,[56] was received by Judge Jiménez' secretary on May 7 (that is, within the time allotted by the court).[57]

The Toaquizas and their lawyers responded to the statements of the lawyers of the accused to the effect that the complaint did not meet the requirements of admissibility in a letter, in which they once again accused the seven of insults and threats, but now accompanied this accusation with a reference to the Penal Code.[58] They specifically referred to Title VII, Chapter 1, article 491 (which deals with slander against one's personal honor), stating that

---

53 To the Juez Primero de lo Penal de Cotopaxi, to the Juez Segundo de lo Penal de Cotopaxi, to the Juez Tercero de lo Penal de Cotopaxi, and to the Presidente del Tribunal Penal de Cotopaxi.
54 See for example exhibit 77–80 of Caso 85–2008 Juzgado Segundo de lo Penal de Cotopaxi.
55 Juicio No. 756–95 ("95" refers to the year 1995) of the Juzgado Décimo Tercero de lo Penal de Pichincha; exhibits 113–121 of Caso 85–2008 Juzgado Segundo de lo Penal de Cotopaxi.
56 Caso 85–2008 Juzgado Segundo de lo Penal de Cotopaxi, exhibits 99–172.
57 Caso 85–2008 Juzgado Segundo de lo Penal de Cotopaxi, exhibits 218–219.
58 Caso 85–2008 Juzgado Segundo de lo Penal de Cotopaxi, exhibits 222–223.

slanderous insults can be sanctioned with imprisonment of up to six months plus a fine when the insults are expressed during meetings or in public places at which more than ten people are present. The Toaquizas thus framed the events as a crime defined within a legal code that was currently in effect. In seven separate letters,[59] the accused and their lawyers reacted to this, arguing that no insults (as defined by article 491 of the Penal Code) were involved. They also cited the legal literature regarding slander. Reading through the whole file of Case 85–2008, one cannot help avoid the impression that the seven were gradually but inexorably pushed into a defensive position. Obviously, this is what the Toaquizas and their lawyers thought as well, because on June 2, they asked the judge to rule on the case. And so Judge Jiménez did one month later, on July 4, 2008.

In his seven-page verdict,[60] the judge took all the evidence that had been presented into consideration. He then indicated that he did not consider this case to be an internal indigenous affair and therefore he refused to recuse himself or to dismiss the case. He argued that there had been no trial in the community. He comprehensively elaborated on the phases of an indigenous trial according to customary law,[61] pointing out that none of these had taken place. Because of that, he continued, the accusers had the possibility of initiating an *Acción Penal Privada*. He observed that the two Toaquizas had, of their own free will, turned to the national courts of law. Interestingly, the judge – in so many words – recognized the possibility of forum shopping in this particular case. He declared that he never felt incapable of judging this case. He then continued to weigh the evidence provided to him. In a lengthy account of what had happened on the Sunday afternoon in question, he indicated that there was insufficient proof that the seven persons accused were all equally guilty of insults and threats. He acquitted four of them, but passed sentence on the other three. He held these three individuals responsible for what had happened, and consequently sentenced them to six-month prison terms plus a fine of $20. In addition, he ordered the three guilty parties to reimburse the Toaquizas' legal expenses. Each of the seven accused were in turn declared responsible for their own legal expenses.

The Toaquiza vs. the community case focused on two legal questions: 1) Could this case be labeled an internal conflict? (which in turn implied the question of the national court being an appropriate venue); and 2) Could the actual events of September 23 be considered a criminal offense? The way the second

59 Caso 85–2008 Juzgado Segundo de lo Penal de Cotopaxi, exhibits 224–240.
60 Caso 85–2008 Juzgado Segundo de lo Penal de Cotopaxi, exhibits 241–244.
61 Judge Jiménez mentioned the *Willachina* (Kichwa for the phase in which local authorities receive a verbal report about an internal conflict), the *Pushakkuna Rimari* (the moment when the authorities decide to take the case), the *Yachankapak Capuchina* (the investigation done by a local authority), the *Chimpapurachina* (when a perpetrator and his victim confront one another), the *Kishpirina* (when the parties involved make their statements), the *Kishpichina* (when responsibility is taken), and finally the *Paktachina* (when the ruling is issued).

question was dealt with is an example of what happens when a conflict is brought before a national court. Events tend to get increasingly framed in strictly legal terms and, eventually, the judge bases his decision on the written evidence collected in the case file. On the one hand, the judge in this case had to weigh the versions of the events provided by the seven accused, accompanied by a typed version of the minutes of the assembly and clean criminal records and the testimonies of their character witnesses. On the other hand, he had to assess the version of the plaintiffs, taking into account their own criminal records and the testimony of *their* character witnesses, as well as the legal basis of their accusation. Reasoning from the evidence in this case, the judge came to the conclusion that the charge of insults and threats was just, and that three of the seven accused deserved punishment.

For the purposes of this book, the first question the judge had to deal with (that is, whether this was an internal conflict, and thus, whether he was competent to hear the case) is even more interesting. As suggested before, the 1998 Constitution suddenly became relevant. If there had been no constitutional recognition of legal pluralism, or if there had been clear rules coordinating the relative or simultaneous use of customary versus national law, then this would not have become an issue in the first place. However, since article 191 of the 1998 Constitution recognizes the use of customary law in cases involving internal conflicts, and since there are no coordinating rules, the accused took advantage of the opportunity to raise the issue of the judge's competence to hear the case. In a way, they tried to divert the focus of the case from the events in the community building of Tigua-Chimbacucho to a more theoretical discussion of what constitutes an internal conflict. The judge gave this fundamental question a twist by arguing that no indigenous trial had taken place. Judge Jiménez therefore contended that the plaintiffs had legitimate recourse to a national court. There were two natural corollaries to this determination: 1) if there had been an indigenous trial, then he might not have been competent to hear the case (in other words, the rule prohibiting double jeopardy would have come into effect); and 2) since there are no rules that define the personal, material, and territorial jurisdiction of customary law in relation to national law, indigenous people are free to choose the authority to which they recur. If this verdict were to be upheld, then innovative jurisprudence could have resulted. However, the final result of this extended litigation would have to await the results of an appeal lodged by the seven accused parties.

Toaquizas vs. the community: the appeal

Five days after Judge Jiménez's verdict, the seven accused parties lodged an appeal. In an eleven-page letter, each of the seven entered an appeal against the judge's considerations and against his final judgment.[62] They argued that the judge's description of the events at the assembly did not paint a true

---

62 Caso 85–2008 Juzgado Segundo de lo Penal de Cotopaxi, exhibit 245–286.

picture. They repeated their previous argument that it is impossible to recall precisely what had happened in which order, and who had exactly said what. They continued to argue that everything that had happened had to be considered an internal indigenous affair. Once again, by referring to the relevant articles in the Constitution, the UN Declaration of Rights of Indigenous Peoples, and ILO Convention 169, they argued that this event happened among indigenous people and within an indigenous community, and that therefore it could not be judged by a national judge. They also once again disputed the factual correctness and the legal viability of the complaint. Finally, they pointed out a number of inconsistencies and errors in the judge's reasoning, which led them to the conclusion that the final judgment was without proper foundation. They asked the court to dismiss all charges.

The two Toaquizas were also not satisfied with Judge Jiménez' ruling. They stated in a letter that they wanted all seven of the accused to be convicted.[63] They lodged their appeal (on the same day as the seven accused did) with the Special Penal Division of the Court of Appeals of Cotopaxi. On August 25, a plenary session of the Court of Appeals in Latacunga issued a verdict that was brief and to the point.[64] The three judges upheld all of the elements of Judge Jiménez's previous ruling, including the conviction of three of the seven accused. This meant that both appeals – that of the seven accused, and that of the Toaquizas – were dismissed.

But this was not the end of the case, which was appealed by both parties to the National Court of Justice in Quito. On September 24, 2009, almost exactly two years after the events in Tigua-Chimbacucho took place, the First Specialized Penal Court of that national court issued a final ruling on the case. It was asked to do so by both the seven accused and the Toaquizas. Both the defendants and the plaintiffs in this criminal proceeding lodged an appeal for annulment of judgment. This national court would prove to have quite a different view of the situation of legal pluralism and the scope of customary law than the two provincial courts.

In a verdict that ran to sixteen pages,[65] the three judges of the court developed an interesting doctrine regarding the previous rulings in the case. They argued that, when something occurred between indigenous people in an indigenous community, one of the first obligations of national judges was to decide whether they were competent to judge the case. The ruling cited the writings of Carlos Poveda, lecturer at the university and expert in legal pluralism and customary law. Poveda underscores the importance of the formal recognition of customary law, emphasizing that such recognition implies that no limitations apply to the jurisdiction of indigenous authorities, and insisting that national judges have the obligation to defend these rights. However, Poveda continues, since there is no general agreement regarding the authority to be granted

63 Caso 85–2008 Juzgado Segundo de lo Penal de Cotopaxi, exhibit 287–288.
64 Caso 85–2008 Juzgado Segundo de lo Penal de Cotopaxi, exhibit 290–291.
65 Caso 85–2008 Juzgado Segundo de lo Penal de Cotopaxi, exhibits 292–299.

indigenous authorities for the administration of customary law, a legal framework has to be developed which respects multicultural aspects of the situation of legal pluralism. The national court agreed with Poveda's view.

Second, the court referred to an earlier, quite similar, case which had made reference to writings of a Spanish scholar on the subject of the foundations of indigenous penal law.[66] The court maintained that, in addressing the question as to whether or not customary law has been (or can be) applied correctly in a certain case, one has to be informed about its local peculiarities (that is, because customary norms and procedures tend to differ locally) and to be aware of the possibility that it may also be abused. Third, the national court referred to the results of a project of CODENPE which stated that customary law is not subordinate to national law.[67] Fourth, it referred to page 25 of a book called *Jurisdicción Indígena en la Constitución Política del Ecuador*, published by Fundación Hanss Seidel.[68] The cited section of this book defines some broad characteristics of customary law (that is, it is oral, flexible, aims at restoring harmony, etc.). It seems to me that, in these four comments, the national court expressed a certain openness of formal legal pluralism.

After commenting on customary law and the situation of legal pluralism, the national court continued to elaborate on the legal regulations related to the case. It referred to numerous articles in various laws, all of which essentially emphasized the role of customary law in relation to national law, and/or the right of indigenous people to make use of customary law.

As regards the case itself, the ruling declared that the insults had been uttered in an indigenous community, during the meeting of an indigenous assembly, at which indigenous people were present, and that therefore this internal conflict in fact had to be resolved according to customary law. The ruling therefore concluded that both of the previous courts had violated the law by claiming jurisdiction in the case. For that reason, the national court declared the whole case invalid, and ordered both provincial courts to bear all expenses of both the accused and the plaintiffs in all of the previous criminal cases.

With this verdict, which was issued almost exactly two years after the events at the meeting hall of Tigua-Chimbacucho, the case was finally closed. In essence, the argument of the seven accused that the case was an internal indigenous affair that was not within the scope of jurisdiction of national law was upheld. The bad blood between the Toaquizas and the rest of the community has not disappeared. That was made clear to me during talks I had

---

66 The national court referred to a case of the Tercera Sala de la Corte Suprema de Justicia (August 7, 2008) in which that court made reference to the "*Introducción a los fundamentos del derecho penal indígena*" by Emiliano Borja Jiménez of the University of Valencia in Spain.
67 The national court referred specifically to page 7 of a report on a project about the administration of customary law in 2001.
68 *Jurisdicción Indígena en la Constitución Política del Ecuador* (Tibán & Ilaquiche 2008).

with several Tiguan painters. Furthermore, the future of the *Hostería Samana Huasi* remains unresolved. Currently the hostel is closed,[69] and the few tourists that seek it out are redirected to the Posada de Tigua, a couple of kilometers down the road.[70]

Conclusion

This chapter sought to address three separate issues. The first of these (that is, regarding the processing of the case in the provincial courts) has been thoroughly dealt with in the three previous sections of this chapter. To summarize, Caso 85–2008 concerned two Toaquiza family members who accused seven inhabitants of the Tigua-Chibacucho community of insulting and threatening them during a meeting in a community building on September 23, 2007. In their complaint, addressed to Judge Jiménez, Juez Segundo de lo Penal de Cotopaxi, they demanded that the seven be punished to the maximum extent allowed by law. In addition, they sued the seven persons for $10,000 in damages. In response, the accused denied everything they were accused of while also contending that the national courts lacked jurisdiction to adjudicate the case. According to them, this was an internal indigenous conflict that lay outside the scope of national law.

The Criminal Court of Latacunga claimed that it was competent to judge this case. On July 4, 2008, Judge Jiménez convicted three of the seven accused. He sentenced them to six months in prison and a fine of $20 each, and also ordered them to reimburse the legal expenses of the two Toaquiza men. Each of the seven accused were held by the court to be responsible for their own expenses during the process. However, both of the contending parties lodged an appeal of the verdict. On August 25, 2008, the Court of Appeals in Latacunga upheld Judge Jiménez's verdict. The disputants then turned to the National Court of Justice in Quito. This court ruled that earlier decisions in the case should be declared null and void, because the matter in question involved an indigenous internal conflict, and as such the Court of Justice had not been competent to settle this case.

This brings us to the second issue addressed by this chapter: the differences between customary and national law that can be derived from this case. Compared to the Rosita vs. Miguel case presented in Chapter 5, some obvious differences can be discerned between a *teniente político* in Zumbahua using mainly customary law, and a court in Latacunga using national law. These include differences in the duration of proceedings, in the extent of recourse to written documents, and in the role of lawyers. The most striking difference, however, is that the court addressed the conflict in strictly legal terms. This was done by parties (or rather, their lawyers), as well as by the judge. In the

---

69 Interview with a Tiguan painter on October 28, 2010.
70 On December 1, 2010, for example, I witnessed how two tourists driving a rented car were redirected to the Posada.

Toaquiza vs. the community case, the Toaquizas initially described the insults and threats in rather broad terms. But when their opponents criticized that first complaint, the Toaquizas specifically made a reference to article 491 of the Penal Code in a subsequent letter to the judge. The seven accused on the other hand, contested the competence of the judge by referring to several articles in the Constitution and other national laws, and in international law as well. Their argumentation basically read as follows: because we are a legally recognized indigenous people, the incident in question should be considered an internal affair, and consequently a national judge lacks jurisdiction to hear the case.

Of equal importance were the measures the judge took. In accordance with the law, he accumulated information in the case file. For example, he filed all letters and other written evidence, instructed the *teniente politico* to assist him in notifying the accused, scheduled a special session of the court, and heard the testimony of witnesses. He then based his verdict on the information in the case file, referring to relevant articles in the law and the legal arguments presented by the parties. No, he did not consider the incident an internal conflict, and yes, he considered himself competent, and consequently he sentenced three of the accused according to the Penal Code. More than a year later, the National Court of Justice in Quito reasoned in a similar way, although it came to a different conclusion. Evidently, no attention was paid to the pre-trial and post-trial phase; both verdicts were strictly based on what was in the file. The choice to go to court (and, implicitly, the choice to use lawyers, and to conceptualize the case in strictly legal terms) influenced the course of the case (Felstiner et al., 1980–81). How different would it have been if the Toaquizas had decided to turn to another indigenous authority? And how differently might the case have developed if a situation of formal legal pluralism had not existed?

Conceptualizing this case in strictly legal terms allows us to answer the third question, regarding the lessons the case has to teach us about the daily practice of legal pluralism. First, with regard to the selection of an authority (a dynamic inherent in any situation of legal pluralism) I think it is fair to say that it was clear why the Toaquizas turned to the Court of Justice in Latacunga, despite the fact that they had other options. Given the reputation of the members of the Tigua community for being easily offended, conflicts there are far from rare. This is confirmed by what I saw in the *libros de actas*, so from that point of view it would not have been strange if they had relied on the *cabildo*'s experience. But the underlying tensions that caused this specific incident (that is, arguments about money, disagreement over the management of the hostel, and ongoing troubles between rural and urban painters) made the Toaquizas question the *cabildo*'s authority, and especially its impartiality, in this particular case. In this connection, it should be remembered that it had been one of the *cabildo* members who had insulted them during the meeting in September 2007 in the first place. From that point of view, it is understandable that they harbored suspicions about the objectivity of the *cabildo*.

Their decision in favor of national law, while not common, is also not unprecedented. Poveda Moreno (2007: 187) mentions a similar case in Tigua, in which community members specifically asked the First Judge of the Criminal Court of Cotopaxi to intervene in an ongoing conflict because they did not trust the *cabildo* to be impartial. I also came across another case, in which someone specifically asked the judge not to hand over certain suspects to a *cabildo*.[71] The person in question had been the victim of a robbery, and the three suspects of that criminal offense were held at the prison in Latacunga, awaiting their trial for the Juez Tercero de Garantías Penales de Cotopaxi. During that procedure, at a certain point the *cabildo* of the indigenous community where the robbery had taken place asked the judge to hand over the suspects to them, so that customary law could be applied in that case. They argued that these three suspects, as well as the victim, were community members, and based on article 171 of the Montecristi Constitution, they considered this an internal conflict. Almost immediately, the victim refused to cooperate, and instead "continued to pursue the case through legal channels in order to assure that those responsible for what had occurred were punished to the maximum extent possible by the Criminal Code currently in effect."[72] In other words, he showed more faith in national authorities than in the local, indigenous *cabildo*.

Instead of going to court, the Toaquizas could have opted for turning to the *teniente político*. Yet, strictly speaking, this case was beyond his jurisdiction, so he probably would have either referred them back either to their own *cabildo* or advised them to pursue the case in the national courts. Alternatively, they could have turned to either a state prosecutor or an indigenous prosecutor. However, the primary task of those officials is to prosecute alleged criminal events. In the present case, the Toaquizas contended that the insults and threats indeed constituted criminal offenses: this is why they initiated an *Acción Penal Privada* in the first place. Thus, their decision to recur to the national courts is understandable. Although the majority of local conflicts are settled by a local authority according to customary law, there are more examples of indigenous people turning to national law. Dissatisfaction with local authorities, or the need for paperwork (for example, in cases of alimony or paternity), underlie such decisions. It was therefore concluded that indigenous people do not invariably prefer customary law.

The case examined in the present chapter underscores this argument. As in the previous examples, the Toaquizas did not criticize customary law (that is, its norms, values, and procedures). At the very least, no such criticism can be inferred from the case files. Instead, their doubts concerned the capability of the authorities in question. The *cabildo* was considered incapable and biased, and was suspected of even misusing its power, and this is what led the Toaquizas to have recourse to national law in the first place. It is a matter of speculation

71 Caso 489–2009 Juzgado Tercero de Garantías Penales de Cotopaxi.
72 Caso 489–2009 Juzgado Tercero de Garantías Penales de Cotopaxi.

as to what would have happened if they had turned to the *cabildo*, but it is fair to assume that this latter body would have reflected at least some of the prejudices against the Toaquizas that had been voiced at the assembly on September 23. Could their behavior therefore be considered forum shopping? Should it be considered a strictly rational choice, a rational deliberation of the pros and cons of different legal venues (as legal scholars typically characterize forum shopping)? Or should their decision be seen instead as arising from a complex social, cultural, and political context (as legal anthropologists would be inclined to frame it)? Both considerations might be true to a certain extent, but neither entirely captures what this case was about. As far as I am concerned, this case was not primarily about forum shopping at all, for the Toaquizas simply had no other option. If this case was about anything besides the conflict between the Toaquizas and some other community members, then it would have to be about local power. In terms of the present study, I would submit that this case was first and foremost about *de facto* sovereignty: the actual day-to-day governance of a community, including the monopoly over measures to enforce, maintain, and restore order.

The concept of "shopping forums" (that is, a tendency by authorities to actively seek to hear disputes that they feel touch directly upon their interests) does make more sense. This is the second lesson regarding the daily practice of legal pluralism that can be drawn from the Toaquiza case. As Hoekema (2003: 183) has argued, the power that is exercised or aspired to by an indigenous authority depends heavily on the support of the indigenous people represented by that authority. Thus, such an authority not only has to be visible, it has to be decisive as well (Berk-Seligson 2008: 25). And this can only happen when the authority in question has an opportunity to be decisive. Take for example the Rosita vs. Miguel case. One of the reasons why the *teniente politico* in the Rosita vs. Miguel case emphasized the importance of reaching an agreement was to show his authority. His conflict-resolution skills were challenged on a number of occasions (for example, when Rosita's daughter had to be reprimanded by a *dirigente*, or when Jaime Rodrigo Pallo snapped at Miguel's wife). In the Toaquiza case, the plaintiffs turned to national law because they clearly did not want indigenous authorities to be involved. The seven individuals who were accused, who had strong ties to the local *cabildo*, sought recourse to indigenous law for the opposite reason.

One could say that this phenomenon of shopping forums follows logically from the possibility of forum shopping. If such is indeed the case, then one could argue that, just as people can choose between different authorities to settle a conflict, so can different jurisdictional bodies actively lobby to hear cases that they perceive as touching upon their interests. As Keebet von Benda-Beckmann (1981) argued, the showing of initiative by authorities is by no means rare. And I would like to add that such especially is the case when the rules of the game change. This certainly applies in the Ecuadorian context, where customary law has been recently constitutionally recognized (after being formally denied for more than 500 years) but where coordinating rules are still lacking. I would argue that it is this situation of legal uncertainty that has provided the opportunity for the seven accused to challenge Judge Jiménez's competence. After all, if there had been no constitutional recognition of customary law, nobody would have had any legal reason to doubt the judge's competence to hear the case, because the question of whether it had been an internal conflict would not have been relevant.

So, what insights into the situation of formal legal pluralism does this case provide? To put it bluntly, without constitutional recognition of customary law, there would not have been a situation in which this extended legal case could have played out as it did. Judge Jiménez would not have been forced to justify his competence in this case, and the National Court of Justice would not have had any legal ground to declare the case invalid. In general terms, it can be concluded that a situation of formal legal pluralism, in the absence of coordinating rules, creates a legal void which provides opportunities to contest existing power relations. Or, to put it in the terms of Nader (1990:7): the dispute becomes a political process whereby divisions are either created or overcome. It is the legal void with regard to the jurisdiction of indigenous authorities (in this case surrounding the question of whether the events on September 23 could be considered an internal conflict) that gives rise to conflicts over local sovereignty,[73] or that at least makes such conflicts more visible.

---

[73] In a similar way, Lund (2008: 2) argues regarding the situation in Ghana that "the context of legal and institutional pluralism [...] opened a hornet's nest of potential conflict [...] over competing claims as to who had the authority to settle those conflicts."

8 The La Cocha-Guantópolo murder case

> We already have experience with this kind of thing. At this point, we are functioning as judges – just like "official" judges. We deal with all of the community's problems.[1]

Introduction

A third and final case study will be presented in this chapter, which constitutes a continuation of the discussion in the previous two chapters. The first empirical chapter on the "Rosita vs. Miguel case" was about a minor local conflict that was settled locally by the *teniente político*. Building on that local case, the next empirical chapter on the Toaquiza case showed how a local conflict could develop into a national lawsuit. The case examined in the present chapter shows how the "internal" aspect of a conflict becomes one of the legal questions that needs to be addressed by the judge. It is about a homicide in the village of Zumbahua that involved members of the Guantópolo community, and that was initially adjudicated by the *cabildo* of the community of La Cocha. As was the case with a previous murder case in La Cocha (in 2002), this case attracted nationwide attention. That is how an internal conflict that was initially settled locally became the subject of a lawsuit in the national courts, with the provincial Court of Justice as well as the national Constitutional Court in Quito both becoming involved.[2] And, as will be shown, this was also a political case. As such, it provides a perfect illustration of legal and political controversies regarding the contemporary situation of formal legal pluralism.

---

1 "*Nosotros ya tenemos experiencia. Hoy en estos momentos, somos jueces. Somos jueces, como al mismo nivel de los jueces ordinarios. Nosotros tratamos todos los problemas que existen en la comunidad.*" Interview I had with a member of the *cabildo* of La Cocha, on November 13, 2010, in which he was explaining to me how far their competence to apply customary law reached according to his interpretation of the Montecristi Constitution.
2 These two murder cases have been described and compared – however, for different purposes, and less comprehensively – in an earlier publication of mine (Simon Thomas 2012). See also Simon Thomas (2009) for the La Cocha murder case of 2002.

There are two questions that constitute the framework of this chapter. What happens if an initially local indigenous trial becomes of national legal and political interest, and – once again – what does this teach us about the daily practice of legal pluralism? The answers are provided by a description and analysis of what I've referred to in this book as the La Cocha-Guantópolo murder case. This case is told in two sections. The first describes the indigenous trial and the second details the subsequent trying of the case in the national courts. However, before we examine the La Cocha-Guantópolo murder case, we need to first review the La Cocha murder case of 2002. A brief review of that earlier case will provide needed context for a more in-depth understanding of the latter proceedings. Finally, this chapter will reinforce the primary argument of the previous chapter: that the current legal situation with regard to the recognition of customary law has caused a legal void, that it is within this legal void that existing power relations are contested, and that such a dynamic is manifest at both the local and national levels.

The La Cocha murder case of 2002

It all started on the night of Sunday April 21, 2002 at a fiesta in the community of La Cocha, where people were drinking and dancing at the celebration following a baptism. At about 9:30 pm, three men, all living in the nearby Quilapungo sector, got into an argument with Maly Latacunga, a forty-four year old man from La Cocha. After the initial confrontation, it seemed that tempers had calmed but, as the evening progressed, and the three men continued to drink heavily, the dispute flared up once again and grew more and more heated. The three men attacked Maly Latacunga with a screwdriver, a pipe, and a rock, and kept on hitting him until their victim became unconscious.[3] The seriously injured Maly was immediately transported to a hospital in Zumbahua, where he died within twenty-four hours from the effects of the beating.

The death of Maly Latacunga left the small community shaken. That is why, within a few days, the *cabildo* convened to deliberate on the matter. Because it determined that the murder was an "internal matter," and therefore part of their jurisdiction according to the 1998 Constitution, this local body decided to spring into action immediately. The first thing it did was arrest and imprison the three men in the local jail. Subsequently, the *cabildo* arranged a meeting with the other *comunas* of the parish of Zumbahua, who all jointly decided that the three detainees should not be handed over to state authorities, but would instead be adjudicated in accordance with customary law. They also determined that the widow of Maly Latacunga had the right to be compensated for the loss of her husband. Having made those decisions, an *asamblea general* of the OSG UNOCIC was convened only fourteen days

---

3 Caso 43–2002 Juzgado Tercero de lo Penal de Cotopaxi, exhibit 18: testimony of one of the attendants of the party.

after the fatal confrontation had taken place. The OTG MICC was also invited to this meeting. On May 5, 2002, at a public trial held in the main square of La Cocha before an audience of nearly 5,000 indigenous residents of the region, the three accused were found guilty of murder, and each of them received a sentence in accordance with local customary law. First, they were sternly warned by the indigenous tribunal to never again engage in such actions, and ordered to offer a public apology. In addition, the three men were ordered to pay a fine of $6,000 to the widow. Each of the men subsequently received thirteen lashes with a leather whip, was stung with painful nettles, and then was drenched with buckets of ice-cold water.[4] Finally, the men were expelled from the village and ordered not to return for two years. According to the majority of eyewitnesses, justice had been done. The proceedings were all recorded in official minutes and signed by all of the parties (including presidents of the communities involved, and representatives of UNOCIC and MICC).[5] After the indigenous tribunal rendered its verdict, the case was closed and social harmony was restored (García 2005: 151–153; Tibán & Ilaquiche 2004: 60–68).

The case soon began to receive national attention, primarily as a result of a brief nationally televised report.[6] Many Ecuadorians were outraged at what they viewed as the "barbaric" treatment of the three men (*El Comercio* 2002a, 2002b). This led the public prosecutor of the Fiscalía Provincial de Cotopaxi in Latacunga to initiate his own independent criminal prosecution. He began to collect testimonies and evidence, and also decided to exhume the body in order to determine the exact cause of death. An autopsy was performed in the presence of two witnesses.[7] It was determined that Maly Latacunga had succumbed to a combination of head and body injuries. On July 3, 2002, the public prosecutor was satisfied that he had gathered enough evidence to request a preliminary court investigation.[8] Among other things, he requested provisional custody of the three men,[9] on the grounds that they were under suspicion of murder according to article 450 of the Criminal Code.[10] That same day,

---

4   The rubbing of the skin with stinging nettles and then dousing with cold water is intended as a purification ritual.
5   The handwritten *acta compromiso de indemnización* is filed as exhibit 72–74 of Caso 43–2002. A typed version of this *acta* can be found in Ilaquiche (2004b: 68–72).
6   In 2007, I obtained a DVD copy of this three-minute news report from the Ecuadorian television network ECUAVISA.
7   Caso 43–2002 Juzgado Tercero de lo Penal de Cotopaxi, exhibit 33–35.
8   A criminal procedure that is conducted according to national law comprises two phases: the preliminary investigation and the principal court investigation. A criminal procedure starts with a criminal investigation by the police or by the public prosecutor. As soon as a judge gets involved, the preparatory court investigation commences. Both of these elements form part of the preliminary investigation. The principal court investigation takes place at a court, and consists of the court session, the court deliberations and the final judgment. These procedures are laid down in the Code of Criminal Procedures.
9   Caso 43–2002 Juzgado Tercero de lo Penal de Cotopaxi, exhibit 36.
10 Código Penal.

Segovia, Juez Tercero de lo Penal de Cotopaxi, accepted this request.[11] However, the public prosecutor never succeeded in arresting the three men because the policemen from Zumbahua could not find them by themselves, and also because not a single family member turned out to have any clue as to the whereabouts of the suspects. In their final report, the police officers investigating the case alleged that the family members of the accused were uncooperative.[12]

The preparatory court investigation file nevertheless grew, and when, at the end of August, sufficient evidence had been produced, a meeting of the court was scheduled for September 9, 2002. The three men each faced maximum prison terms of sixteen years. By chance, the regular presiding magistrate, José Luis Segovia was absent that particular day, so the case was heard by his colleague, Carlos Poveda. Judge Poveda seemed to be much less convinced of the evidence. In his opinion, a constitutionally recognized indigenous authority had, with regard to its customary law, already settled this *conflicto interno*. Among other arguments, Judge Poveda based his conclusion on article 191 of the 1998 Constitution, and on ILO Convention 169. To the public prosecutor's utter amazement, Judge Poveda argued that, according to the "double jeopardy" rule, he was not competent to adjudicate this particular criminal case. Therefore he declared the public prosecutor's investigation null and void.[13]

Three days later, on September 13, 2002, the public prosecutor wrote to the court that he would not accept the judge's verdict and that therefore he would lodge an appeal at the Court of Justice of Cotopaxi.[14] He also wrote that the verdict had left him with "an unsettling sense of the impotence of the legal system." According to him, it was unacceptable for the kinds of "ancestral practices" evident in the original trial to be conducted within a "civilized" culture.[15] In the meantime, the indigenous authorities of Cotopaxi province were informed about this official protest of the public prosecutor, and subsequently decided to get involved in order to defend not only their specific decision, but also – in general terms – their authority as well. In a letter to the Court of Justice of Cotopaxi dated September 19, 2002, the leaders of the La Cocha community, of UNICOC, and of MICC (the same persons who had signed the *acta*), at this time accompanied by two lawyers (Lourdes Tibán and Raúl Ilaquiche of the law firm FUDEKI) requested that the verdict be upheld.[16] Just as Judge Poveda had done, the indigenous authorities referred

---

11 Caso 43–2002 Juzgado Tercero de lo Penal de Cotopaxi, exhibit 18.
12 Caso 43–2002 Juzgado Tercero de lo Penal de Cotopaxi, exhibit 36.
13 Caso 43–2002 Juzgado Tercero de lo Penal de Cotopaxi, exhibit 60–63.
14 Caso 43–2002 Juzgado Tercero de lo Penal de Cotopaxi, exhibit 64–65.
15 The public prosecutor wrote: "*penoso y escabroso, cuando las costumbres ancestrales vibran haciendo presente un pasado ambiguo y tenebroso superado a medias por la claridad de una cultura civilizada*" ("[it is] awkward and embarrassing when ancestral customs breathe new life into an ambiguous and murky past that has at least been partially superseded by a clear-sighted and civilized culture").
16 Caso 43–2002 Juzgado Tercero de lo Penal de Cotopaxi, exhibit 66–71.

to article 191, section 4, of the 1998 Constitution as well as to ILO Convention 169, but they also referred to articles 1, 83, and 84 of the 1998 Constitution. Their letter can be seen as an elaboration of implicit and explicit references to the constitution and universal human rights that earlier had been made in the minutes of the indigenous proceedings.[17] The handwritten *acta* of May 5, 2002 – which until then had not been an exhibit – was added as piece of evidence to their letter.[18] Nevertheless, their plea was to no avail, because on September 27, 2002, the Court of Justice of Cotopaxi decided to follow the public prosecutor's appeal, and subsequently the Court of Justice referred the case back to the same trial court. Pointing out that, in its view, customary law could only legally be applied to internal family disputes [sic], the Court of Justice not only showed its unwillingness to apply customary law but also its ignorance as to its proper application.[19] According to Tibán and Ilaquiche (2004: 66–67) this was clear evidence of the lack of knowledge of the Court of Justice of Cotopaxi concerning the content and the meaning of article 191 of the 1998 Constitution, the binding legal force of the ILO Convention 169, and of the court's view of customary law as "barbaric."

It was this rather unusual turn of events that led Judge Segovia (the judge initially assigned to the case) to adjudicate the La Cocha murder case. On October 8, 2002, he declared the three accused men guilty and sentenced them to prison terms in accordance with article 450 of the Criminal Code. For their part, as lawyers of the three accused, Lourdes Tibán and Raúl Ilaquiche lodged an appeal of the judge's verdict with the Court of Justice of Cotopaxi.[20] On October 25, 2002, Tibán, Ilaquiche, and the public prosecutor again convened at the Court of Justice of Cotopaxi in Latacunga. As a means of emphasizing the relevance of this case, several important individuals in the indigenous movement attended the court session.[21] Their attempts were to no avail, because the Court of Justice of Cotopaxi did nothing other than confirm its earlier decision.[22] At this court session, fifty police officers were present, allegedly because, as one of them explained, "Indians are dangerous" (Tibán & Ilaquiche 2004: 67–68). This comment illustrates the sociopolitical tensions

---

17 The minutes of the proceedings (*acta*) expressly referred to articles 1, 83, 84, and 191 of the 1998 Constitution. In addition, by referring to the right to due process, the *acta* implicitly appealed to universal human rights.
18 Caso 43–2002 Juzgado Tercero de lo Penal de Cotopaxi, exhibit 72–74.
19 Statement made by Carlos Poveda at a conference on customary law in Latacunga on July 30, 2007.
20 On October 10, 2002, Lourdes Tibán and Raúl Ilaquiche, as lawyers for FUDEKI, became the defendants of two of the convicted men; the third one received legal counsel from a public defender. Caso 43–2002 Juzgado Tercero de lo Penal de Cotopaxi, exhibit 84–86.
21 These included: Luis Macas (president of CONAIE at that time), Leonidas Iza (former president of CONAIE), Patricio Shingri (director of ECUARUNARI), and several leaders of MICC, UNICOC, and the La Cocha community.
22 Caso 43–2002 Juzgado Tercero de lo Penal de Cotopaxi, exhibit 88–90.

surrounding this case. In the end, the defense team decided to accept the decision without offering statements or witnesses.

Murder in Zumbahua

The crime

Similar to the previous murder case of 2002, the La Cocha-Guantópolo murder case of 2010 started at a fiesta.[23] While celebrating Mother's Day at one of the houses near Plaza Rumiñahui in the village of Zumbahua on May 9, 2010,[24] a group of five young men got into an argument with Marco Olivo, who lived in a nearby house with his mother.[25] According to eyewitnesses, they did not get into a fight at the party.[26] But when the corpse of Marco Olivo was found later that day in the Parque Central de Cóndor Cocha,[27] the five young men were immediately suspected of involvement in his death. All five were from the community of Guantópolo – although on weekdays they either attended school or worked in Latacunga, Quevedo, or Quito and they had a reputation among the locals as "troublemakers." The five men formed a small street gang. Everybody knew that, as a group, they had recently been involved in vandalism and fights.

In the days that followed, the five suspects were captured by local residents and handed over to the *cabildo* of La Cocha. One of them was apprehended the following morning on his way to school. Two days later, the other four men turned themselves in to the *cabildo* of Guantópolo. In consultation with *cabildo* members of Guantópolo, and with the Fiscal Indígena of Latacunga (Vicente Tibán, a brother of Lourdes Tibán), they decided to turn themselves

---

23 Because of the similarities between these two murder cases, the Ecuadorian legal anthropologist Fernando García has called the La Cocha case and the La Cocha-Guantópolo case, respectively, La Cocha I and La Cocha II (García 2010b). To avoid confusion, I have chosen not to use La Cocha I and La Cocha II, but to distinguish between La Cocha 2002 and La Cocha-Guantópolo 2010.
24 In Ecuador, Mother's Day is celebrated every second Sunday of May.
25 This is an example of when I am using a subject's real name because it is a matter of public record (see the Ethics section in the Introduction). As a matter of fact, all the names of the people mentioned in this section – unless stated otherwise – are their real names, and for the same reason.
26 My description of on the events of May 9, 2010, and of all of the subsequent events, is primarily based on information I found in the files of the Juzgado Tercero de Garantías Penales de Cotopaxi (Caso 2010–0412) and of the Fiscalía Provincial de Cotopaxi (Caso 10-05-25013). I was able to conduct archival research in these files while the case was still being tried. I was also allowed to copy large sections of these files, which are still in my possession. However, in order not to violate confidentiality, I will not make references to the specific details of these files. In those instances in which my data are based on sources other than these files, I will make references in the usual manner.
27 Marco Olivo, a twenty-one year old student, had been found dead, hanging from a lamp post by his own belt (*El Comercio* 2010g).

in to the *cabildo* of La Cocha (Poveda Moreno 2010). This is an interesting aspect of the case, given that the community of Guantópolo has a *cabildo* of its own. But, those who captured the first suspect probably either knew or suspected that he or one of his friends were related to a member of the *cabildo* of Guantópolo, and therefore might receive preferential treatment in that community.[28] A second reason not to hand the five suspects over to the *cabildo* of Guantópolo was that it had absolutely no experience with serious crimes such as homicide.[29] On the other hand, because of its exemplary handling of the murder case in 2002, the *cabildo* of La Cocha was considered to be the most trustworthy local authority in such a serious legal matter. The president of the Junta Parroquial of Zumbahua kept himself apprised of events in the case during these early days. In this role, he consulted the *cabildo* of Guantópolo, wrote a letter to the *cabildo* of La Cocha in order to request respectful treatment of the suspects, and also went there to meet with them personally.

After the five had been captured and handed over to the *cabildo* of La Cocha, this authority embarked upon an investigation of the case. The investigation and interrogation were concluded in less than a week. During this time, nobody except for the *cabildo* and a few other individuals knew where the five suspects were being held. Meanwhile, a rumor spread that one of the five "troublemakers"(who was the leader of the gang) had had a long-standing dispute with the victim. It was said that this individual, Orlando Quishpe, had been seen clearly threatening the victim shortly before the murder. Whether this rumor had any influence on what happened afterward remains unclear, but as a result of the interrogations, the five suspects confessed that they had gotten into a fight with Marco Olivo, who was later found dead. None of them, however, confessed to having killed him. Nonetheless, according to the *cabildo*, the confessions all pointed to Quishpe as the person who actually killed the victim, since he emerged as the party most involved in the fight.

The cabildo *of La Cocha hears the case – part I*

That is why the *asamblea general* tried four of the suspects one week following the fatal incident, and decided to try Orlando Quishpe separately the following week. The *asamblea*'s sentence of the four men was in accordance with customary law, and contained the following elements: an obligation to make apologies and pay a fine, mandatory submission to a purification ritual and a whipping by members of the ruling *cabildos*, and expulsion from the community. During the purification ritual, the skin of the five men was rubbed with stinging nettles before each of them was doused ice-cold water. This "ritual cleansing" took half an hour. As was subsequently revealed in reports

---

28 An ex-*dirigente* of Guantópolo informed me directly that at least one of the suspects is related to a *cabildo* member (interview, November 1, 2010).
29 Interview with a member of the *cabildo* of La Cocha on November 13, 2010.

on Ecuadorian television,[30] during this purification ritual, the four convicted men were completely nude, and their bound wrists were tied to a rack which held them suspended above the ground. This whole trial was conducted in public. In addition to several indigenous leaders and other officials and local dignitaries, a huge crowd of spectators were present.

The sixteen-page handwritten *acta* not only described what took place during the trial on Sunday, May 16, 2010, it also used a mixture of political, legal, and cultural arguments to support the validity of the proceedings. To start with, the *asamblea general* for this case was a large one, thus underlining its political power. It consisted of members of several *cabildos* of communities within the parish of Zumbahua, and also included the OSGs UNOCIC and UNOCIZ,[31] and several others. Besides the *cabildo* of La Cocha, more than twenty neighboring communities were represented; among them Tigua, Quilotoa, and Guantópolo. The *acta* also mentioned that the following individuals were in attendance: Vicente Tibán (the Indigenous Prosecutor at that time); the *teniente político* of Zumbahua; two police officers of Zumbahua; representatives of the Association of Tigua painters; the Junta Parroquial of Zumbahua; officials the Protestant Church in Zumbahua; as well as representatives of MICC, CODENPE, and CONAIE.[32] According to the *acta*, a crowd of approximately 6,000 persons was present. Such a crowd not only illustrates the importance of the case in the public eye, but also the organizing capacity of the indigenous organizations involved.

The *acta* continued by explaining why the *cabildo* of La Cocha considered itself competent to hear this case: it had been asked to do so by family members of Marco Olivo, it considered itself impartial enough to do so, and it referred to article 171 of the Montecristi Constitution in relation to article 343 of the Organic Code of the Judiciary to establish its formal legal competence. In line with this justification, the *acta* emphasized that from as early as Monday, May 10, 2010, on, there had been a consultation between the *cabildo* of La Cocha and several other persons involved in this case (for example, with a brother of the victim, and with the *cabildo* of Guantópolo). Obviously, the *acta* did so in order to emphasize that the *cabildo* of La Cocha had been conducting itself according to established precedent. Next, the *acta* continued with an extensive description of the interrogations that had taken place, who had been present, and what had been said, denied, and confessed. This resulted in the *cabildo* arriving at the conclusion that customary law had to be used to settle the case.

In referring to customary law, the *acta* once again emphasized that this case should be considered an internal conflict, and that therefore the *cabildo*

---

30 For instance on ECUAVISA, Teleamazonas, GAMA TV, and on MICC TV.
31 UNOCIZ: Unión de Organizaciones y Comunidades Indígenas de Zumbahua (Union of Indigenous Organizations and Communities of Zumbahua).
32 The full name, occupation, and ID number of each individual was recorded in the *acta* (obviously to prove that they had been actually there).

of La Cocha was competent to handle the case. In this instance, events played out in a way that mirrored the "shopping forum" description given by K. von Benda-Beckmann (1981) of how conflict-settling institutions have to actively establish their authority. It also referred not only to one of the central aims of customary law, namely "to seek peace and calm, and to resolve conflicts among ourselves," but also to the rejection of imprisonment as a sentence.[33] The *cabildo* clearly distinguished customary law from national penal law, and thus stressed a cultural justification for recourse to the former. The *acta* explained that the *cabildo* properly followed the several different stages that can be distinguished within a procedure to settle conflicts in accordance with customary law.[34] For example, it referred to *tapuykuna* and *chimbapurana*, Kichwa terms for, respectively, the investigation conducted by a *cabildo*, and the public trial (Tibán & Ilaquiche 2004: 36–42). Interestingly, several interrogations carried out by the *cabildo*, as well as a confession made by Orlando Quishpe, were also recorded on video. Prior to the trial, these video tapes were shown to several people with knowledge of customary law (that is, the Fiscal Indígena Vicente Tibán and a representative of CONAIE, who both confirmed the correctness of the procedure, respect for due process, and the protection of human rights). By doing so, the *cabildo* not only showed its impartiality, but it also established that the procedures were in accordance with article 171 of the Montecristi Constitution. In addition, it also asserted their competence to phrase their decisions in the idiom of national law.

Finally, the *acta* provided a detailed enumeration of what every *dirigente* present believed would constitute a just settlement of the case. They showed a striking unanimity, and thus it was easy to reach an agreement. The final resolution stated that it had been proven that the four men had participated in the fight which had caused the death of Marco Olivo, and that therefore they had to be sentenced in accordance with customary law. Second, they had to pay a fine of $5,000. Third, the *asamblea general* recognized that it was usually gang members who were responsible for disruptive behavior during fiestas, and who were often suspected of vandalism. That is why these specific four *roqueros* (in order to provide an example to others) were forbidden to attend any fiesta in the parish of Zumbahua for a period of two years. Fourth, they were expelled from the parish for two years. Fifth, they underwent the thiry-minute ritual cleansing with stinging nettles and ice-cold water at the central plaza of La Cocha, and then were whipped in the presence of the *dirigentes* of all of the neighboring indigenous communities. Sixth, the five offenders were made to each carry a sack containing 46 kilograms of rocks and soil around the plaza. Seventh, they were obliged to offer a public apology for their crime.

---

33 A *dirigente* in La Cocha told me that they had had previous experience with community members who had been in jail, where they had been subject to "bad influences" (personal interview, November 13, 2010).
34 And in a manner in accordance with the description of an indigenous trial in Tibán and Ilaquiche (2004).

Finally, the *acta* stated that it had been Orlando Quishpe who was directly responsible for the killing of Marco Olivo, and that is why the *asamblea general* decided that there would be a second trial, conducted before another *asamblea general*, which would determine Quishpe's punishment.

The cabildo *of La Cocha hears the case – part II*

So far, what can be understood is that there are basically two parties to this case: the inhabitants of the parish of Zumbahua, on the one hand and, on the other, some of its members, namely the five young men who were suspected of murdering Marco Olivo. The first of these parties, however, can be divided into several different camps, each of them – as will become clear – with different and sometimes even conflicting interests. Through the completion of the first trial, all parties concerned agreed on this case being an internal conflict, and they all seemed to be content with the application of customary law as well as with the sentences in this murder case. These attitudes subsequently changed. In the following phase of the trial, the attitude of one of the camps (that is, the people from the Guantópolo community) did so mainly as a result of additional information about the trial which became public. Additionally, a third party became involved, the Fiscal General del Estado, which was a representative of the state. The change of position of one of the camps, as well as the appearance of a third party, caused transformations in the case that will be described later.

Beginning on May 16, 2010, several meetings between the different parties involved took place, and both confusing and conflicting details were published in the national press. The following day, several of the parties with an interest in the case gathered at MICC's office in Latacunga. In the presence of a police officer, the president and the vice-president of MICC, the president of UNOCIC, the president of the *cabildo* of La Cocha, a representative of the Guantópolo community, the president of the Junta Parroquial of Zumbahua, and Jaime and Vicente Olivo (two brothers of Marco Olivo) all stated that they believed that Orlando Quishpe should receive the maximum sentence allowable by customary law. But, as the police officer reported to his superior, the aforementioned men all agreed that Quishpe should not pay for his crime with his life. This meeting, and the conclusion reached there, was cited in a newspaper article in *El Comercio* (2010g) on May 19. However, that same article mentioned a statement by the *cabildo* of La Cocha on Tuesday May 18 to the effect that Quishpe would receive the death penalty. This forced the Fiscal Indígena, also in the same article, to vociferously deny any such intention. In doing so, he referred to both the Ecuadorian constitution (which does not allow the execution of criminals) and to international human rights standards.

However, troubled by the Fiscal Indígena's report and, especially, the proposed death penalty, Washington Pesántez, Fiscal General del Estado, the highest ranking prosecutor in the nation, decided to go to La Cocha the following day, in order to take Orlando Quishpe into custody in a state prison for his own protection. He was escorted by ten police cars, with a throng of journalists witnessing the scene. He and his escort, however, did not reach La Cocha because community members had erected a roadblock between Zumbahua and La Cocha. In a heated discussion during which community members and policemen almost came to blows, the president of the *cabildo* of La Cocha restated the community's position on the matter. Yes, Orlando Quishpe was still held in detention and he would not tell where, and no, he would not receive the death penalty the following Sunday when sentenced in a public trial. As was shown on television that evening, the president of the community said, "we are going to carry out indigenous justice while providing good treatment, without, uh … taking the man's life." In the end, the community members did not let Pesántez enter La Cocha, so he and his retinue had to return home on Wednesday, May 19 (*El Comercio* 2010e).

The developments that week even captured the attention of Ecuadorian President Correa, who in his weekly televised speech contended that customary law was obliged to respect human rights, and therefore that it could not countenance either torture or a death penalty. Correa further called for Orlando Quishpe's immediate release, threatening to charge those holding him captive with kidnapping if this did not happen (*El Comercio* 2010f, 2010l). Therefore, the first important consequence of the appearance of a third party – the Fiscal General del Estado and with him president Correa – was that this case was drawn into the national legal system. Because the boundaries of legal pluralism were a fundamental component of this murder case, it became a political issue.

Meanwhile, in Guantópolo, family members and other residents were concerned about protecting Orlando Quishpe's right to due process. Specifically, their concern focused on the interrogation practices of the *cabildo* of La Cocha. It was considered unusual that almost nobody knew exactly where Orlando Quishpe was being held throughout the proceedings, and how he was being treated. In the newspaper (*El Comercio* 2010e) they had read that he was being taken to a different location every day, in order to assure that his whereabouts would be unknown. Even his sixty-five year old father was not allowed to see his son or bring him food. "He is innocent," he declared in an interview in *El Comercio* (2010d). In the same newspaper article, Orlando's sister declared: "The only thing he did wrong was have long hair and dress in black. But he hasn't done anyone any harm." She also expressed her displeasure with the role of the Fiscal Indígena. According to her, he had promised Quishpe that, after he had turned himself in to the *cabildo* of La Cocha to explain what had happened, he would be set free. Because this is not what transpired, she called the Fiscal Indígena a liar.

In any event, on Sunday May 13, 2010, the same *asamblea general* convened once again, this time to sentence Orlando Quishpe. In the handwritten *acta* of this meeting, the body expressed its awareness of the controversy that had surrounded the case during the past week. The assembly emphasized that Orlando Quishpe had been treated well by the *cabildo* of La Cocha, both physically and psychologically. It also made reference to the action of the

Fiscal General del Estado and to the words of President Correa, claiming that both were wrong, because everything that had been done so far by the indigenous authorities had been in accordance with the law. In addition, the *acta* referred to a meeting of members of the *cabildos* of La Cocha and Guantópolo with the father and the sister of Orlando Quishpe. It had been agreed by these parties, according to the *acta*, that customary law would be applied in this case and that nobody should turn to national law. Once again, the *acta* underlined the political power of the indigenous authority in charge. Rather than emphasizing the procedures of the trial itself, this second *acta* focused on the testimonies of what had happened on the day of the murder. Although not every detail was clarified, it emerged that the five men had been drinking and smoking marihuana that day. Based on the overall evidence, the *asamblea general* declared Orlando Quishpe guilty of murder.

Orlando Quishpe's sentence was similar to that of his four friends, but with a number of additional elements. He too had to carry a sack containing 46 kilograms of rocks and soil around the plaza, apologize to the family of Marco Olivo and to the *asamblea general* in public, and be "purified" by having his naked body submitted to a ritual cleansing of stinging nettles and ice-cold water, for forty minutes. He also was whipped by several members of the *cabildo*, and he was assessed a fine of $1,250. Additionally, he was sentenced to carry out communal work over a period of five years in each of the twenty-four communities present at the trial. As was shown on television afterwards, the whipping and the ritual cleansing were rather brutal. This explains why, shortly after the public punishment had been administered, he required hospitalization.

In the national legal system

At the Provincial Court

As previously mentioned, the indigenous legal proceedings of four of the men had become the subject of an outcry among many Ecuadorians. This outcry continued after Quishpe's trial, with the media, judges, the government, and many common citizens condemning the punishment as "barbaric." Some dissatisfaction with the procedure as a whole was heard in the parish of Zumbahua as well. Several people I interviewed about this case voiced their disapproval of what they saw as the physical brutality of the treatment. Some residents of Guantópolo in particular expressed concern as to whether the indigenous legal proceedings had been correctly conducted throughout its various stages.[35] Quishpe's sister complained that her brother had not been given anything to eat, and that he had been beaten and tortured (*El Comercio* 2010l). She went on to declare that "24 [community] presidents punished my

---

35 Interview I had with residents of Guantópolo, November 14, 2010.

brother. This is not indigenous justice. This is a beating!" (*El Comercio* 2010l).

Another individual who was also concerned was Washington Pesántez, Fiscal General del Estado. He summoned the Fiscal Indígena, Vicente Tibán for consultation immediately after the conclusion of the trial in La Cocha. On May 24, at the same time as MICC was giving a press conference in Latacunga to clarify what had happened, Vicente Tibán drove to Quito to report to Pesántez. One can only surmise what was discussed at that meeting, since there is no public record of it. However, the next day *El Comercio* (2010o) informed its readers of the dismissal of Vicente Tibán as Fiscal Indígena in Cotopaxi. The reason for the dismissal, according to Washington Pesántez, was that Tibán had acted in disregard of the constitution. "Customary law can be applied in minor offenses, but not in cases of serious crimes like homicide," he explained (*El Comercio* 2010m). In addition, Pesántez announced that he was considering a criminal investigation of the cause of the death of Marco Olivo (in which the five men would obviously be considered suspects), as well as on the role of the *dirigentes* of La Cocha, on account of a possible unlawful detention of Orlando Quishpe over the course of two weeks.

Because of these developments, it became clear that, probably sooner rather than later, the Fiscalía in Latacunga would be ordered to start that investigation. It did not have to wait long, because on Thursday, May 27, 2010 the Juez Primero de Garantías Penales de Cotopaxi demanded preventive custody of Orlando Quishpe within twenty-four hours, in order to be able start an investigation on the murder of Marco Olivo. This meant that the consequences of the involvement of a third party – that is, the state – in the conflict would soon be felt. And so they were. The five suspects turned themselves in to the national authorities (Poveda Moreno 2010) the next day, after which the criminal investigation of the public prosecutor, and the proceedings conducted by the national courts, got underway. As soon as the suspects reported to the Court of Justice, the Juez Segundo de lo Penal de Cotopaxi ordered the Fiscalía to start a criminal investigation on the homicide, and issued an order calling for the preventive detention *cautelares de orden personal*, a prejudgment custody of the five men, who subsequently were moved from the jail in Latacunga to a prison in Quito (Poveda Moreno 2010; *El Comercio* 2010b).

Before the five men were moved to Quito, they denounced the method by which interrogations were conducted during the indigenous trial. They told the public prosecutor that they had been blackmailed and tortured. Subsequently, the public prosecutor initiated a second preliminary investigation, this time of the six members of the *cabildo* of La Cocha. This was of course a novel element of the state intervention that was not part of the original trial. Eventually, this resulted in the arrest of three of the *cabildo* members (the president, the secretary, and the treasurer). But with the assistance of their attorneys, Carlos Poveda, Raúl Ilaquiche, and Alex Alajo, they were released within twenty-four hours. By order of the President of the Provincial Court, who was convinced by the arguments of the attorneys, the three *dirigentes* were set free. What this means is that they were free to go, but that the investigation against them continued. The President of the Provincial Court thus overruled his subordinate, the Juez Tercero de lo Penal, Judge Segovia,[36] who was placed on half pay for three months on the grounds that his decision had caused "a public disturbance." A few weeks later, Judge Segovia wrote a letter to the Constitutional Court asking it to provide a ruling as to whether the decision made by the *cabildo* of La Cocha in this murder case should be upheld.[37] The Tribunal de Garantías Penales (Criminal Guarantees Tribunal of Cotopaxi), which eventually was assigned to deal with the murder, also decided to suspend the proceedings and to submit a consultation to the Constitutional Court.[38] These are all indications that the judiciary was having difficulties with article 171 of the Montecristi Constitution.

Meanwhile in Guantópolo, community members, especially family members of the five suspects, were unhappy with the most recent developments in the case. Initially, they continued to express their reservations regarding the actions of the *cabildo* of La Cocha, thus moving away from the other indigenous camps. But soon it was national law which became the target of their grievances.[39] Initially, on May 31, 2010, a group of protesters held a demonstration in front of the Ministry of Justice in Quito, where they proclaimed the innocence of the five suspects and criticized the *cabildo* of La Cocha: "This wasn't indigenous justice but, clearly, an execution," they stated on television,[40] expressing their concerns over due process in this case. Such criticism is in line with what was shown in Chapter 5,[41] which referred to the critical attitudes of local residents toward indigenous authorities, who were seen as abusing their power and meting out excessive punishment. Their pleas, however, were to no avail: the criminal investigation proceeded and the five suspects continued to be held in preventive custody. On September 24, 2010, sixty Guantópolo community members attended the public hearing where the decision would be announced regarding whether preventive detention of the five suspects would continue. And when the judge finally decided

---

36 Note that Judge Segovia also had been judge in the La Cocha murder case of 2002.
37 Judge Segovia had found a contradiction between the text of article 171 of the Montecristi Constitution and corresponding articles 33 and 117 in the Code of Criminal Procedures.
38 See Ecuadorian Constitutional Court ruling 006–14-SCN-CC, September 11, 2014, https://www.corteconstitucional.gob.ec/sentencias/relatoria/relatoria/fichas/006–14-SCN-CC.pdf (accessed November 30, 2015).
39 Such shifting alliances as a result of new information about, or a redefinition of, a conflict is not that uncommon. See Felstiner et al. (1980: 639).
40 Teleamazonas, May 31, 2010.
41 I am especially referring to García's (2009a) findings about indigenous peoples' legal decision-making process.

to continue custody, there was such an uproar that the judge had to be escorted from the premises by police (La Gaceta 2010c).

In a way, this discontent is understandable. After all, the five suspects had turned themselves in, and they and their supporters in Guantópolo had been promised that the investigation would last less than three months (Hoy 2011; La Gaceta 2010c). So, when the Criminal Court of Justice in Latacunga decided on continuation of the custody and declared itself incompetent to hear the case as long as the Constitutional Court did not issue its opinion on the relevance of the indigenous legal proceedings that had been conducted, it became evident that the case would drag on much longer, much to the consternation of the parties involved. This forced the *cabildo* of Guantópolo into collaborating with the *cabildo* of La Cocha, as well as with MICC, for the purpose of presenting a joint request for both the immediate release of the five men and the suspension of legal proceedings against the three members of the *cabildo* of La Cocha. And that in turn led to an appearance of representatives of these three parties before the Constitutional Court on October 13, 2010.

At the Constitutional Court

The La Cocha-Guatópolo murder case once again entangled the Constitutional Court in politics. The Constitutional Court is the highest court in Ecuador dealing with constitutional matters,[42] and its purpose is to safeguard citizens' constitutional rights. Actually, it is the only state institution to interpret what the Constitution says, and that judges whether laws and procedures are in accordance with that Constitution. Its decisions are final and cannot be appealed. The Court is located in Quito, and it consists of nine judges, each of them serving a maximum nine-year period. The Constitutional Court was created as part of Ecuador's 1996 constitutional reform package, and thus is a fairly new institution.[43] Formally, the Court is apolitical, but in fact it inevitably operates in a political context. To begin with, its judges are appointed by the Congress, which makes them vulnerable to political influence. This susceptibility became evident in 2005, when President Gutiérrez manipulated the Congress in such a way that it decided to replace eight of the nine members of the Court.[44] In addition, the cases the Court has to deal with are usually politically sensitive. In this regard, the La Cocha-Guantópolo murder case was certainly no exception.

President Correa and his administration have had their clashes with the Constitutional Court as well. In March 2007, Correa's project of drafting a

42 This differs from the role of the *Corte Suprema* (Supreme Court), which is the highest judicial authority in Ecuador.
43 See Constitucion Política de la República del Ecuador, Codificación 1996, Ley No. 000.RO/969 de 18 Junio de 1996; initially it was called Tribunal Constitucional.
44 See http://archive.transparency.org/news_room/in_focus/2005/crisis_ecuador1 (accessed September 11, 2012).

new constitution brought him into conflict with the Court for the first time. The Court had warned him that he would be acting illegally if he ignored its ruling that the national referendum that was necessary for such an Assembly was unconstitutional. As soon as the Court ruled against Correa, its headquarters were mobbed by a pro-government demonstration, forcing the judges to evacuate the building under police escort. Because of this, Correa disregarded the Court's ruling, and when, a few days later, the nine judges were dismissed by a pro-Correa majority in Congress, the Court's ruling was officially nullified (Conaghan 2008: 51–52). Another example stems from the aforementioned turmoil regarding the new mining law.[45] Although the Constitutional Court finally approved this mining law, it expressed serious reservations with regard to whether the procedures involved in its drafting and approval were constitutional. Such examples indicate a certain disregard on the part of President Correa and his administration for the Constitutional Court's rulings. It seems that Patricio Pazmiño, President of the Constitutional Court, foresaw another clash coming in the La Cocha-Guantópolo case, because in an interview about the Court's supposed political role in this case, he declared that "this institution will not yield to political pressure."[46]

Thus, on Wednesday October 13, 2010, the Court knew what it could expect. In a hearing that lasted less than an hour, four different attorneys were heard, each of them pleading in defense of one of the parties (and camps within these parties) involved in the La Cocha-Guatópolo case (Simon Thomas 2012). The first speaker was Raúl Ilaquiche, who represented the family of the victim. The second speaker was Carlos Poveda, who represented MICC. Poveda was followed by Alex Alajo, who spoke on behalf of the *cabildo* of the community of La Cocha. Finally, the lawyer representing the five suspects, Bolívar Beltrán, arose and spoke. The five suspects were, at the time of these proceedings, still being held in prison. Although all four attorneys represented different parties – parties that in some respects were in conflict with one another– a striking consensus among them emerged from their oral arguments. In a variety of ways, each of these parties emphasized that the murder case concerned an internal conflict of people living in the parish of Zumbahua and therefore that the hearing of the case by local indigenous authorities had been appropriate. In support of this position, they cited the "double jeopardy" rule. And in line with that argument, they claimed that the decision of the Court of Justice of Latacunga to take the five suspects into preventive custody was unlawful. They all cited relevant articles in the Montecristi Constitution, as well as international rules such as ILO Convention 169, the UN Declaration on the Rights of Indigenous Peoples, and national and international jurisprudence. They all demanded that the five suspects be released immediately, and that the charges against the indigenous authorities be dropped.

45 See Chapter 2 (section on CONAIE) for more details.
46 See http://laminga.radioteca.net/leer.php/2975818 (accessed September 18, 2012).

This session of the Constitutional Court was attended by a group of about forty inhabitants of the La Cocha and Guantópolo communities, who arrived in Quito by bus. Those who could not be admitted to the courtroom because of lack of space were asked to wait outside the building, in the Parque Simón Bolívar, across the street. Indeed, the Sala de Audiencias on the fourth floor of the court building was packed. Besides the people from the parish of Zumbahua, the audience consisted of representatives of the press, and of indigenous organizations like MICC, CONAIE, and Pachakutik. The session started at exactly 10:00 am and, because the four attorneys were each given only limited speaking time, it was over within an hour. Afterwards, the crowd outside was addressed by several speakers, among them Raúl Ilaquiche, Lourdes Tibán, César Umajinga (Prefect of the Cotopaxi province), Marlo Santi (president of CONAIE), and Nina Pacari (at that time one of the nine judges of the Constitutional Court). The crowd was thanked for their support, and the importance of this court session for the *de facto* recognition of indigenous rights in general, and the acceptance of formal legal pluralism in particular was underlined once more. The indigenous leaders expressed their hope that the Court would give its ruling soon. The crowed then erupted in chants of "Long live La Cocha!" and "Long live indigenous law!"

Despite the pleas of the four attorneys and the hopes expressed by the indigenous leaders, the Constitutional Court determined that it was not well-enough informed to issue a ruling. Thus, in December 2010, it ordered that expert testimony be given on the use of customary law in this specific case. This testimony was supplied by the Colombian legal anthropologist Esther Sánchez Botero in January 2011. After conducting fieldwork and interviewing more than twenty people (indigenous people, lawyers, and judges, all of them one way or another parties to the La Cocha-Guantópolo murder case) over the course of two weeks, Sanchéz Botero delivered her expert testimony on January 24, 2011.[47] The following month, the Constitutional Court decided to review the case once again.[48] In May 2011, the Tribunal de Garantías Penales de Cotopaxi ruled that the five men, who had been imprisoned for a year, be set free (*El Universo* 2011a; Hoy 2011). The criminal investigation, however, continued.

It was not until July 30, 2014,[49] and on September 11, 2014,[50] that the Constitutional Court finally decided on this case. It stated that murder is

---

47 This expert testimony, titled "Peritaje en Antropología juridicial: Presentado a la Honorable Corte Constitucional del Ecuador a Solicitud del Doctor Patricio Pazmiño Presidente" was put at my disposal by Esther Sanchéz Botero through personal correspondence.
48 Decision of February 3, 2011, in Case 0006–11-CN of the Constitutional Court.
49 See Ecuadorian Constitutional Court ruling 113–14-SEP-CC, http://www.araujoasocia dos.net/blog/2014/08/01/texto-de-la-sentencia-de-la-corte-constitucional-caso-la-cocha-justicia-indigena/ (accessed November 30, 2015).
50 See Ecuadorian Constitutional Court ruling 006–14-SCN-CC, September 11, 2014, https://www.corteconstitucional.gob.ec/sentencias/relatoria/relatoria/fichas/006–14-SCN-CC.pdf (accessed November 30, 2015).

always part of national law's jurisdiction, and it reversed the constitutional text by adding the condition that customary law can be applied only when "internal affairs" concern "local values." It remains to be seen how this ruling will be interpreted and used in practice.

The ultimate consequence of state involvement in this case took three different forms. First, the initial question of who murdered Marco Olivo was superseded by the question of which court was competent to hear the case. Second, because of the transformed legal perspective, this case became politically sensitive. Third, because of its political sensitivity, legal uncertainty became a reality for those involved directly (that is, the five suspects and the three members of the *cabildo*) until mid-2014.

The two murder cases compared

A comparison of the La Cocha case of 2002 and the La Cocha-Guantópolo case of 2010 is interesting for several reasons. First, there are some striking similarities. In both cases, the indigenous authorities involved considered the homicide in question to be an internal conflict and therefore they determined that it was appropriate that the cases be adjudicated in accordance with customary law. In both cases, it was also decided not to extradite the accused to national legal authorities.[51] Second, both indigenous trials were attended by representatives of indigenous organizations, and all parties concerned approved the use of customary law. Both sentences principally aimed at reconciliation, restoring harmony, and purification, rather than punishment *per se*. In addition, both cases referred – in their written *actas* – to applicable sections of the Constitution and to relevant international jurisprudence. So, at first sight, both cases provide a beautiful example of how customary law is applied by an indigenous authority to settle an internal conflict. Bearing in mind what has been illustrated in previous chapters on customary law, its authorities, and its procedures, almost every detail of these trials is of interest (for example, the major oral component, the public character, the attention to the victim's welfare, and the reintegration of the suspects into the community). As such, these cases could serve as a perfect example of the strengths of customary law. Yet this is something that has not been acknowledged by state law representatives, and that is another interesting aspect of these cases.

Both cases were covered on national television, and consequently, both became subject of a public outcry over the infliction of what was perceived as "barbaric" punishment. The result of this was that both indigenous cases almost immediately were followed by trials in accordance with national law. The public prosecutor, the judges, and the Court of Justice of Cotopaxi all indicated, from their respective points of view, that trying a homicide case according to

51 At one point during the La Cocha murder case of 2002, the *cabildo* seriously considered the possibility of handing the three suspects over to the national legal authorities, but in the end decided not to do so (Simon Thomas 2009: 62–63).

customary law (which according to the Penal Code could be punished by up to sixteen years of prison) was way beyond the limits of the constitutional recognition of legal pluralism. In both cases, the judges and the public prosecutors involved all made explicit reference to the Constitution and to international rules (as did the indigenous authorities). However, while the indigenous authorities and their lawyers did so in order to protect indigenous jurisdiction, the national authorities did so for the purpose of arguing that indigenous customary law conflicts with national law and with individual human rights.

The two murder cases also differ from one another in some respects. One such difference has to do with geography. The La Cocha case of 2002 was about a homicide in the community of La Cocha, and only involved inhabitants of that indigenous community. In the La Cocha-Guantópolo case of 2010, the murder was committed in the village of Zumbahua, the accused were residents of Guantópolo, and the actual trial took place in La Cocha. According to some indigenous authorities involved in the case, the different locations of the crime, residence of the accused, and trial are not particularly important from a legal standpoint. However, it is precisely because the homicide did not occur in an indigenous community, but in a village (one, it should be noted, with a *teniente político*, who could have served as the first link in the legal chain) that this case does not meet the Ecuadorian state's definition of an "internal conflict."

Another point of divergence between the two cases can be found in the application of customary law. The most blatant difference in this regard concerns the physical treatment of the suspects. In 2002, the three men convicted of the crime, after they had been sentenced, all were able to walk away without severe injuries. In 2010, on the contrary, one of the five offenders required hospitalization. Furthermore, in the aftermath of the first indigenous trial, nobody involved complained about denial of due process, while in the second case, such complaints were heard, especially on the part of residents of Guantópolo. These two differences point to the apparent imposition of severe restrictions on freedom in the latter case (Simon Thomas 2012), and as such underscore the warning made in the introduction of this book that one should not unquestioningly accept the use of customary law. It also shows that, at any given moment, residents of the parish of Zumbahua differ among themselves about the proper use of such law. It is such debate that highlights the fact that customary law not only involves the settling of disputes, but local power struggles as well.

A final set of differences between the two cases can be found in the proceedings in the national courts that followed, and in the political reactions. In 2002, the Court of Justice did not prosecute the indigenous authorities, while in 2010 it did. In 2002, the three suspects were not arrested, while in 2010 they were. These points of divergence point to a stronger assertion of state authority in the latter case. The actions of the courts in 2002 can largely be described as resulting from ignorance of and/or unwillingness to submit to customary law, and to the formal recognition of legal pluralism, which can be seen as an illustration of the political views regarding those matters that prevailed at that time (Simon Thomas 2009: 47; Simon Thomas

2012).⁵² In 2010, by contrast, the Court of Justice in Latacunga, whether intentionally or not, assumed a more important role, and even the Constitutional Court became involved. Additionally, the position of the Correa administration seems far more clear than that of the earlier Noboa administration. And finally, the involvement of indigenous organizations was much more pronounced during the latter case. Obviously, the parties involved underscored the political significance of the La Cocha-Guantópolo case, and also felt the need the make their viewpoints more public.

With regard to this increasing political significance and the changing role of indigenous organizations, a final observation can be made regarding the role of certain indigenous leaders. Specifically, the involvement of some specific indigenous organizations, as well as the dual role of Lourdes Tibán and Raúl Ilaquiche, are particularly worthy of mention. It is not a secret that the local UNOCIC, the provincial MICC, the regional ECUARUNARI, and CONAIE have strong ties with one another. I therefore think that it is fair to suggest that the prominent presence of these organizations in both cases from the very beginning influenced the course of events. Whatever the role of these organizations in shaping events, the cases definitely provided them showcases for illustrating the strengths of customary law. At the trial in La Cocha in 2002, Lourdes Tibán, in her role as representative of MICC, had been present as an indigenous leader; and thus may have had an influence on the final text of the *acta*. During the course of the lawsuit within the national legal system, she and her husband Raúl were involved as lawyers, and in this role they made an effort to develop coordinating rules on the basis of case law. Afterwards, in 2004, they published material on the case, framing the use of customary law in rather positive terms. As will become evident in the next section, in the La Cocha-Guantópolo case in 2010, Lourdes Tibán had a more prominent role as politician, while Raúl Ilaquiche retained his role as jurist. Therefore, both cases served several purposes, not only for them personally, but also for the way customary law in Ecuador is represented.

Todo es político

If there is one thing that should be clear by now, it is that the importance of the La Cocha-Guantópolo murder case goes far beyond its mere legal

---

52 The only representative of national law who was satisfied that the 2002 indigenous trial had been fair was Judge Poveda. Because of this stance, he was subject to insults and threats from his colleagues and superiors. This resulted in his resignation as a judge and return to private legal practice (Simon Thomas 2009: 70–71). There was no protest registered in the media or among politicians regarding this railroading of Judge Poveda. This leads me to the observation that the final result of the 2002 case is in its way similar to that of President Noboa's veto in 2002, and National Congress's treatment of two draft coordinating laws in January of that same year. Each of these events clearly reflected the Ecuadorian elite's unwillingness to accord a *de facto* recognition to legal pluralism in the country.

significance. At first glance, one might think that the outcome of the case hinged on an interpretation of the law. Upon further consideration, however, it becomes clear that there is far more going on. We previously saw in the Toaquiza case that the legal questions revolved around the term "internal conflict," but in reality the *cabildo*'s local jurisdiction was at stake. In the La Cocha-Guantópolo case, the interpretation of article 171 of the Montecrsiti Constitution in relation to other relevant articles constituted the fundamental legal question. However, the scope of the personal, material, and territorial jurisdiction of customary law, or in other words, the sovereignty of every indigenous *cabildo* in the country, constituted the transcendent underlying issues. And this made the La Cocha-Guantópolo murder case politically controversial from the very beginning.[53] This controversy became manifest on a local, provincial, and national level. We will soon see how the controversy led to blurring of the boundaries of these three different levels.

I was repeatedly told by many Ecuadorians that I spoke to that "*todo es político*" ("everything is politics") in the country. At the local level, this means not only that "politics" is visible everywhere, but that people's actions often include (or are accused of including) a hidden political agenda. In this connection, "politics" should not be defined in the narrow sense of political parties, party policies, and politicians, but instead as representing power relations in a broader sense (that is, power to strengthen one's position, to affect social relationships, etc.). The visibility of politics (in the strict sense) is best illustrated by the prevalence of political graffiti (that is, political slogans, names of political parties, or names of politicians on walls, signposts, or even on rocks). The dozens of "*Correa Presidente*" or "MPAIS 35" one comes across in Guantópolo and Zumbahua seem to suggest a high degree of impassioned popular support for President Correa and his political party in those places. There are also numerous yellow, blue, and red striped billboards on roadsides proclaiming that "The Citizen's Revolution rolls on," meaning that Correa and his administration are seen as doing good work in improving public infrastructure (roads, schools, clinics, etc.). Even in the offices of the *teniente político* and the Junta Parroquial in Zumbahua, one cannot escape posters glued to the wall that praise Correa and, intentionally or not, suggest at least some links between the officials working in these offices and the Correa administration.

The broader sense of "politics" might be less visible, but that doesn't make it any less real or important. Take for example a Tiguan painter, who spoke of "a political problem" that he was having with some other community members. I have also heard a member of the Junta Parroquial grumble that their work in

---

53   This La Cocha-Guantópolo case should not be seen as an isolated instance of the phenomenon under discussion here, since there are more examples of recent controversial cases. Flores (2011) mentions a case in the El Topo community in the Imbabura province (about the proper use of a cleansing ritual), and the Sarayaku case (which has been brought before the Inter-American Court of Human Rights). See also http://www.corteidh.or.cr/casos.cfm?idCaso=388 (accessed November 29, 2012).

distant communities was hampered because of the negative influence of certain indigenous leaders connected to CONAIE. On the other hand, the members of the Junta Parroquial have in turn been accused by others of conspiracy. "Once they were elected, they just took the money without delivering anything they promised," I heard someone complain. Thus, at least in some instances, there seems to be a thin line between "politics" and corruption. There are elements of the La Cocha-Guantópolo murder case that also show signs of such "politics."

Obviously, there is some sort of a power struggle going on between the leaders of La Cocha and Guantópolo. In and of itself, a struggle of this kind is not surprising, given the fact that the community of La Cocha has had its struggles with Zumbahua (over which was going to be the parish's administrative center), and with Quilotoa (over which would be entitled to receive the tourist revenues of the Quilotoa Lake) before. Now it seems – again, at first glance – that a number of inhabitants of Guantópolo are dissatisfied with the outcome of the trial against five of their fellow community members in general, and with the physical brutality of the sentence in particular. But their underlying discontent included other issues (for example, the non-observance of the agreement with Vicente Tibán, a supposed hidden agenda of the Olivo family, and the strong ties between La Cocha and MICC).[54] My impression was that these inhabitants were afraid of becoming pawns in a political game, and of becoming victims of the alleged bias of the *cabildo* of La Cocha.

Whether the fear of the inhabitants of Guantópolo is justified is open to question. But it cannot be denied that there are clear political ties among certain individuals and parties involved in this case, including the *cabildo* of La Cocha. Just as in the La Cocha murder case of 2002, in the 2010 murder case, the role of MICC (with its affiliations with CONAIE), and of the customary law protagonists Lourdes Tibán and Raúl Ilaquiche, both during the trial as well as afterwards, should not be underestimated. For example, Vicente Tibán, the Fiscal Indígena in 2010, had previously been one of the *dirigentes* of MICC,[55] thus suggesting a personal connection with UNOCIZ and/or the *cabildo* of La Cocha. The victim, Marco Olivo, had been a Pachakutik member. The victim's previously mentioned brothers still appear to have such ties. Victor Olivo is one of the *dirigentes* of MICC, and Jaime Olivo was elected Fiscal Indígena of Latacunga in July 2011. Previously, Jaime Olivo had worked at DINAPIN in Quito,[56] and in that capacity he showed himself to be a vocal

---

54 Interview with the involved parties on November 14, 2010, in Guantópolo.
55 I met Vicente Tibán for the first time on August 7, 2007, when I was visiting MICC's office in Latacunga.
56 DINAPIN: Dirección Nacional de Defensa de los Pueblos Indígenas (National Organization for the Defense of Indigenous People). As a matter of fact, it was at this office in Quito on July 19, 2007, where I met Jaime Olivo in person for the first time. I had a conversation with him about his work at DINAPIN, and he provided me some useful information on the La Cocha murder case of 2002 (on which I was doing research at that time). He also gave me a copy of book written by Ilaquiche (2004b).

advocate of customary law. Imagining the dissatisfaction of the people of Guantópolo with the developments in this case, one could understand their suspicion of personal and political ties among the *cabildo* of La Cocha, family members of the victim, MICC, and other officials. These ties may have led them to accuse the La Cocha *cabildo* of bias.

On a provincial level, the La Cocha-Guantópolo murder case showed some signs of "politics" too, mainly concerning MICC and the judiciary. As we have previously seen, MICC had been involved in the La Cocha murder case of 2002, and it also played a role during several phases of the current murder case. For example, MICC was present when the four suspects were on trial, MICC hosted the meeting of the parties immediately involved, where a decision had been made as to what to do with Orlando Quishpe, and it was present at Quishpe's trial on Sunday May 13. MICC also expressed its dissatisfaction about the dismissal of Vicente Tibán as Fiscal Indígena. During a protest march on June 25, 2010 celebrating the twentieth anniversary of the indigenous uprising, about 3,000 people used the occasion to demonstrate in front of the Court of Justice as part of a protest directed against the appointment of the new Fiscal Indígena. The president of MICC declared that the nomination was political, since the new Fiscal Indígena did not have the support of the thirty-three *cabildos* (*El Comercio* 2010p). In other words, MICC was unhappy that it had been passed over during the selection procedure. The organization is likely more pleased with the recent appointment of Jaime Olivo. Finally, MICC organized the demonstrations at the Constitutional Court on August 25, and October 13, 2010, in Quito, including the transportation of protesters to the event.

The role of the judiciary in Latacunga, whether intended or not, has also become political. Demonstrations were held by the MICC during the indigenous celebration, and by the inhabitants of Guantópolo on September 24, at the time that the judge had to make a decision regarding the preventive custody of the five suspects (a demonstration that got completely out of hand, and where the police had to escort the judge to assure his personal safety). From the point of view of the court, these were clearly unintended consequences. The decision to place the president of the Provincial Court on half pay for three months as punishment for his decision to set free the three members of the *cabildo* (on the supposed grounds that the decision had caused a public uproar) also had unintended consequences. Less unintended was the letter Judge Segovia wrote to the Constitutional Court in order to ask that body to provide a ruling on the use of customary law in the La Cocha-Guantópolo murder case. This not only directly led to the proceedings at the Constitutional Court, but was also an indication that the Court of Justice in Latacunga did not want to bear sole responsibility for trying the case, and was looking for juridical (and perhaps also political) cover.

The involvement of MICC, and especially of representatives of CONAIE and Pachakutik, can be seen as clear indications of the national importance of this case. Similar to what we have seen at a local level, the demands these organizations have made are – at first glance – juridical in nature. Specifically, they want the Constitutional Court to provide rules regarding how article 171 of the Montecristi Constitution should be interpreted. Basically, they try to enforce jurisprudence. The main strategy of the representatives of this organization, with help from lawyers of the parties involved, is a legal one. As part of this effort, they cite pertinent articles in the Constitution and of other national laws and international rules, refer to jurisprudence in neighboring countries (for example, Colombia), and also cite the scholarly literature. One could argue that indigenous organizations are conducting their activities within different arenas: both the legal arena but also (given Lourdes Tibán's drafting of a bill) in the political arena as well. Both efforts aim at attaining legal guarantees of a greater level of autonomy, and thus these efforts are political in nature.

The role of Lourdes Tibán and her husband Raúl Ilaquiche, both dedicated advocates of indigenous rights and customary law, are of special interest in this legal and political maneuvering. It seems like they are involved, one way or another, in almost every legal case concerning customary law in the Cotopaxi province. Tibán, originally from the indigenous community Chirinche Bajo (in Salcedo canton, Cotopaxi) received her academic training in social sciences and law, and for many years has worked for indigenous organizations as well as for the government. She is currently a member of the national assembly, and in that role she drafted the coordination bill of 2011.[57] Ilaquiche, originally from the indigenous community Tigua Yatapungo (Guangaje parish, Pujilí canton, Cotopaxi) also studied law and social sciences. His master's thesis was on customary law in Tigua (Ilaquiche 2004a) and he has worked for indigenous organizations, has political experience, and is currently a lawyer in Latacunga.[58] Together, as well as separately, they have published numerous books, pamphlets, and articles on customary law,[59] of which their *Manual de Administración de Justicia Indígena en el Ecuador* (2004) appears to be the most frequently cited (Berk-Seligson (2006) constantly refers to it as the "Tibán and Ilaquiche Manual"). Tibán and Ilaquiche are thus at the center of the indigenous struggle to secure *de jure* recognition of customary law.

---

57 Lourdes Tibán has a law degree (received in Mexico), as well as a degree in social sciences (received at FLACSO in Quito, Ecuador). She has been *dirigente* of the MICC and also served as national executive secretary of CODENPE. For the past couple of years, she has been a member of the National Assembly representing the party of Pachakutik. In this capacity, she drafted the bill for the Coordination and Cooperation between Customary Law and National Law of December 19, 2011 (see: http://lourdestiban.blogspot.nl/, accessed October 2, 2012).

58 Raúl Ilaquiche has a law degree (received at Universidad Central in Quito), as well as a degree in social sciences (received at FLACSO in Quito, Ecuador). He has been *dirigente* of MICC, vice president of ECUARUNARI, and an assembly member representing Pachakutik. Currently, he is director of the law firm FUDEKI in Latacunga.

59 See for example: Ilaquiche (2001a, 2001b, 2001c, 2004a, 2004b), Tibán (2001a, 2001b, 2003, 2007, 2008, 2010), Tibán & García (2008), and Tibán & Ilaquiche (2004, 2008).

However, the most striking evidence of the fact that the La Cocha-Guantópolo murder case of 2010 is more than a mere legal issue, is the interference in the case on the part of President Correa and his administration. As a reaction to what had happened at the trials in La Cocha, he called customary law "monstrous" (*El Vistazo* 2010), and the events "a degrading spectacle," while adding that "this is torture, this is barbarity" (Caselli 2010), as well as other statements reflecting his own view of the proper scope of customary law (*El Comercio* 2010f, 2010l). Correa's former Interior Minister, Gustavo Jalkh, declared that, in cases of homicide, for example, customary law should not be applied (*El Comercio* 2010q). In using the media as part of his effort to make this case political,[60] Correa has not only tried to influence public opinion and the judiciary, he has also insinuated that his adversaries in the matter are involved in a widespread conspiracy. Newspaper reports of supposed ties between Lourdes Tibán and the American CIA as part of a plot to overthrow the Correa government (*La Gaceta* 2010a) are apparently based on sources tied to the Correa administration.[61] In reaction to the supposed *coup d'état* on September 30, 2010,[62] Correa struck back harshly at one of the police officers involved: namely Marco Tibán, a brother of Lourdes Tibán. Lourdes Tibán expressly accused Correa of getting back at her through her brother (*La Gaceta* 2010b).[63] The fact that the case has led to such actions is a clear illustration of how legal affairs and politics in Ecuador can become inextricably intertwined on national, provincial, local, and even personal levels. The challenge of legal pluralism thus seems to concomitantly include legal, political, and even personal components.

Conclusion

Todo es político, and this includes the law. This would seem to be a fair summary of the preceding sections and would also make the following short

---

60 Referring to a newspaper article, Becker (2010a: 305), wrote that "Pachakutik accused Correa of manipulating the situation and converting it into a political persecution against indigenous leaders."

61 Mijeski and Beck (2011: 118) state that in general there is a "strong tendency by Correa and his administration [...] to intimidate and diminish the independent press and to insult [...] political enemies."

62 On September 30, 2010, elements of the national police went on strike to oppose a government-sponsored law that supposedly would reduce their benefits. This strike culminated in a protest at which Correa was attacked with a tear gas canister and had to be taken to the hospital. He was subsequently prohibited from leaving the hospital by rebellious policemen. This forced the president to declare a state of emergency. By early evening of that same day, the apparent *coup d'état* was successfully repelled after Correa was set free from the hospital by loyal special army forces. The fights that accompanied this rescue operation left several people dead and hundreds wounded.

63 This reflects a broad-based opposition to indigenous leaders, particularly Lourdes Tibán, among the Correa administration and its supporters (Mijeski & Beck 2011: 121).

answer to this chapter's first question possible: the developments in the La Cocha-Guantópolo murder case of 2010, did cause political concern on local, provincial, and national levels. Having analyzed the events in this way, a second observation can be made: this case reveals the current power struggle resulting from the legal void created by a situation of formal legal pluralism in circumstances in which coordinating rules are absent.[64] Neither the Toaquiza case examined in the previous chapter nor the two cases examined in the present chapter would have unfolded as they did had article 171 of the Montecristi Constitution not existed, or if coordinating rules had been drafted. The actual legal situation with regard to the formal recognition of legal pluralism in Ecuador thus provides the opportunity to challenge existing power relations. In the current case, contrary to the Toaquiza case, such conflicts over sovereignty not only became visible on a local level, but also on a national level. This observation leads to a preliminary answer to the second question, the one about the daily practice of legal pluralism. It thus seems as if the question of culpability is made subordinate to the question of which authority is entitled to determine guilt or innocence.

In analyzing the La Cocha-Guantópolo murder case, one thing becomes evident: there is a huge gap between strict legal questions and a number of important practical implications. Initially, this case could be thought of as involving an internal conflict, one about a homicide. The basic "legal" question involved determining who murdered Marco Olivo. However, it soon turned out that there was more at stake. As shown in the former sections, when the question arose as to whether customary law should be applied, the role of the Olivo family, of the Fiscal Indígena, and of MICC in answering that question, cannot be underestimated. The roles of each of these parties constitute an illustration of the importance of local power relations in this case. But what was even more striking was that, after the decision had been made to apply customary law, the *cabildo* of La Cocha seized the opportunity to challenge the boundaries of its local sovereignty. For example, it first explicitly (in interviews, as well as in the *acta*) emphasized its experience and its authority to deal with murder cases (as the quote at the beginning of this chapter shows). Second, with regard to the investigation phase of the case and the interrogations conducted, it took measures to protect itself from unwanted external interference. Thus, community members from Guantópolo, the police, and the Fiscal General del Estado were forbidden both entry to the La Cocha community, as well as access to any information about the proceedings. Third, the *cabildo* of La Cocha, in consultation with several parties involved, and with the support of the *asamblea general*, decided to give maximum sentences to the five suspects. One cannot escape the conclusion that the *cabildo* seized its opportunity to confirm, or even to extend, its status as *the* indigenous community capable of applying customary law in severe cases in the parish.

---

64 K. von Benda-Beckmann (1981: 139) also argued that jurisdictional disputes between institutions and functionaries constitute legal expressions of power.

The legal question as to who could be held responsible for the death of Marco Olivo should also have been of importance to the Court of Justice in Latacunga. However, since it decided to await the ruling of the Constitutional Court as regards the role of the three *cabildo* members, the question of culpability became less of a pressing matter. In strictly legal terms, this second issue implicit in the case is about the scope of article 171 of the Montecristi Constitution. The fundamental question in the case thus revolved around who is in charge of the day-to-day governance of an indigenous community. It is this question that appears to have given rise to the conflict between the *cabildo* of La Cocha and its lawyers, on the one side, and the provincial court, assisted by the Fiscalía, on the other. The protests of Guantópolo community members in the court, and the indigenous demonstrations organized by MICC outside the court, should both be seen in that light.

The subordination of the initial question of guilt to that of jurisdiction and political power continues at the Constitutional Court. At a national level, Marco Olivo's death, as such, played no role whatsoever in the juridical question. The Constitutional Court has been asked to provide a ruling on the question of whether customary law had been applied correctly in this case. And by doing so, it provided case law that can be applied in future cases involving the jurisdiction of indigenous authorities. As was argued here, this is the reason why this case became politically relevant, forcing CONAIE, indigenous politicians like Lourdes Tibán, and even the president himself to become actively involved in it. Political turmoil over the contemporary situation of legal pluralism was the result. The fact that it took the Constitutional Court so long is itself indicative of how politically sensitive a matter it is. We thus see once again that the challenge of legal pluralism is formidable indeed.

What, then, does this case teach us about the daily practice of legal pluralism? The answer to this question can be formulated as follows: cases which challenge the boundaries of legal pluralism become transformed from a consideration of the guilt or innocence of the accused to that of who has a right to determine that guilt or innocence.

9 Conclusion

This book has clearly shown that legal pluralism does not mean the same thing to all people. For some people in urban Ecuador, legal pluralism is seen as a dichotomy between customary law and national law. In the daily reality in the parish of Zumbahua, however, there are a wide variety of interconnected conflicts, as well as a mixture of legal procedures carried out by several different authorities. This study has therefore made the case for a more empirical view of legal pluralism. The main argument of this book is that if we strive to understand what legal pluralism means in the daily reality of those who practice and are affected by it, we have to take such different views into consideration. To paraphrase Goodale (2009: 33), this study tries to bridge the empirical gap between persistent orthodox understandings of legal pluralism and the reality of everyday lived experience.

Ecuador formally recognized its multicultural character in 1998, and as part of that policy it recognized the use of customary law. Thus, a situation of *de jure* legal pluralism prevails in the nation. Because additional rules that would make customary law compatible with national law still had to be developed, this formal recognition led to legal uncertainty for indigenous people regarding how customary law could and should be used in cases involving internal conflicts. It is within this legal void that the *de facto* use of legal pluralism occurs. In several cases analyzed in this book, people's perception and use of different legal systems reflect "interlegality," a situation where there is a general perception that two different legal systems are mixed to such an extent that there they have resulted in the creation of a new system (de Sousa Santos 2002). This illustrates the fact that, on a local level, there sometimes doesn't appear to have been a great deal of change in the actual use of the two systems since the promulgation of the 1998 Constitution (that is, given that there had been *de facto* recognition of customary law ever since the time of the Spanish Conquest). Other cases, however, show some changes in how the two systems are used. In Chapters 7 and 8 of this book, it was shown how, at both the local and national levels, indigenous authorities purposely test the boundaries of the jurisdiction that they were recently granted. The legal void thus provided them a space in which jurisdiction could be asserted. This in turn led the state to implement measures to reassert its own authority.

In this final chapter, the mutually constitutive way in which both indigenous authorities and the state interpret and deal with that legal void, as well as the political tensions to which it gives rise, are viewed within the context of the daily practice of conflict resolution in the parish of Zumbahua. Specifically, an attempt will be made to draw a conclusion here regarding how a jurisprudential understanding of legal pluralism, on the one hand, and the experience of legal pluralism on a local level, on the other, influence one another.

Settlement of internal conflicts

The first part of this book's research question asked how internal conflicts are settled in the parish of Zumbahua. It took seven chapters to answer that question. The internal conflicts that were the subject of this book ranged from disputes over material goods, to social relations, to matters of life and death. It was shown that these conflicts concern different interpersonal levels, from purely domestic disputes to issues of communal power. But what this book has also shown is that there are a number of different authorities employing different legal procedures (which sometimes mix national and customary elements) available to the residents of Zumbahua (that is, a *cabildo*, an *assamblea general*, a *teniente politico*, a Civil Court, a Penal Court, and a public prosecutor). Some of these authorities (for example, several *cabildos*) exploit the recent situation of formal legal pluralism, in the sense that they take advantage of the legal void to extend their local sovereignty. Others (for example, the previously mentioned courts) tend to adhere to the philosophy of legal monism, which served as the basis for the dominant policy throughout most of Ecuador's history. The overall picture of conflict settlement thus appears to be highly complex.

Succeeding the introductory overview, the second chapter of this study presented the debates surrounding this book's main concepts. It showed that both the concept of customary law and legal pluralism have undergone some paradigmatic changes in the legal anthropological literature. Nowadays, legal pluralism often is understood as the coexistence of two legal systems of differential power within the same social field, and its phenomenological counterpart is referred to in the literature as "interlegality" (de Sousa Santos 2002). Chapter 2 also showed that neither of these phenomena can be studied in isolation from their context, and that the state (that is, national law and state agents) has to be taken into account. The state can therefore be analyzed in various ways, but Chatterjee's (2004) notion of a "political society" as a site of ongoing negotiation and debate proved to be most helpful to understand the Indian–state relationship in Latin America and to analyze the phenomenon of legal pluralism in Ecuador.

It was shown in Chapter 3 that, from the time of colonization to the end of the twentieth century, legal monism was official government policy, although customary law continued to be widely applied in the nation's rural areas. The actual day-to-day governance, or "real sovereignty," as defined by Hansen and Stepputat (2006) and Sieder (2011), had been divided among different authorities in rural areas, including those that used customary law. The ways in which this *de facto* legal pluralism was dealt with politically ranged from segregation to assimilation to integration. The longstanding overall policy of juridical monism was replaced by the constitutional recognition of legal pluralism in 1998. Although rights had previously been granted to local rural authorities (for example, by virtue of the Ley de Comunas of 1937 and the land reform laws of 1964 and 1973) the *constitutional recognition* of customary law represented a radical break with the past. For the people concerned, however, the actual practice of several different authorities, and the legal procedures available, did not change all that much. What happened instead was that practices that had long been in effect were constitutionally recognized.

This showed how this formal recognition of legal pluralism could be considered a victory for indigenous people, or more specifically, for the national indigenous movement CONAIE. However, in the context of the absence of coordinating rules that might harmonize customary law and national law, this *de facto* recognition sometimes led to legal uncertainty for persons involved in internal conflicts. The fact that this recognition was ill-defined increased political tensions regarding the actual scope of customary law. One reflection of this tension was President Noboa's refusal to sign two different bills proposing such harmonization into law in 2002, the quashing by the Ministry of Justice of a later attempt to draft such rules, and a highly politicized bill designed by the assemblywoman Lourdes Tibán which, at the moment of this writing, is in the early phases of discussion. Because of both the content of this most recent draft law (for example, it grants indigenous authorities what appear to some to be rather excessive rights), and its provenance (that is, Lourdes Tibán is widely considered a polarizing figure), it seemed all too clear that a legal or political solution to this undesirable situation of legal uncertainty continues to be far off.

Chapter 4 provided a snapshot of the state of affairs at the local level, summarizing the history and socio-political geography of the parish of Zumbahua, the locality that is the focus of this book, and portraying daily life there. Within the framework of a description of a wedding and its subsequent fiesta, important issues of poverty, migration, fighting, and bonding were discussed, all of which have an influence on the sort of conflicts that take place in the parish. One particularly salient fact highlighted in this chapter was the relative absence of the state in the parish ever since the time of Spanish colonization – an absence that has only partially been remedied since Zumbahua ceased being a hacienda in 1972. This has had consequences for the ways indigenous Ecuadorians perceive and navigate the "network of legality" (Goodale 2009: 33) available to them.

But above all, this fourth chapter revealed the harsh reality of life in the parish. Social life was depicted as a fragile balance between cohesion and conflict. The account of the wedding provided a useful metaphor for this. The ceremony and the following fiesta suggest bonding, while a fight between groups of young men at that same gathering was an example of conflict. At the end of that chapter, some local consequences of the recent recognition of legal pluralism were highlighted. It was suggested that, at least in some cases, indigenous organizations have begun to play a larger role than before, and that formal references to the national Constitution had become more frequent in local *actas*. This chapter's conclusion also showed that, in several cases, specifically those in which the scope of competence of indigenous authorities are at stake, the question of jurisdiction can come to assume greater importance than the legal matter being tried.

Chapter 5 served as a bridge between the national and local context and helped set the stage for the subsequent empirical chapters. The implicit question raised in that chapter concerned how people go about choosing an authority to adjudicate their disputes. The main conclusion drawn was that, because conflicts as well as the jurisdictions and procedures of authorities overlap one another, there is no straightforward correlation between particular kinds of conflicts and the authorities resorted to in order to resolve them. For example, in cases of family affairs, litigants turn to different authorities: some go to a *cabildo*, while others turn to the *teniente político*. In practice, there appear to be no clear boundaries between the jurisdictions of different authorities. The same conclusion was reached regarding the overlap of particular kinds of conflicts.

That highly complex and nuanced daily practice of dispute settlement, combined with ordinary Indians' perception of legal pluralism, resulted in the labeling of the legal reality in the parish as "interlegality" (de Sousa Santos 2002). Compared to the situation that prevailed in the past, not much has changed regarding the practice of conflict settlement (except for the number of authorities that Zumbahuans can turn to). What has changed is the scope of these conflicts. Because of the developments described in the preceding chapters (for example, increasing state presence, emerging indigenous movements, constitutional recognition of multiculturalism and legal pluralism, and changing political attitudes regarding these issues), the legal playing field in the parish of Zumbahua now offers more options. For example, in some cases, state authorities became subjects while, in other cases, indigenous organizations played a crucial role in reaching a settlement. Most importantly, because the rules of the game are not always that clear (that is, the actual scope of jurisdiction of the different authorities is poorly defined), the content of conflicts is liable to become transformed.

Chapter 6, the first of three empirical chapters, described the daily routine at the office of the *teniente político* in Zumbahua, focusing on the Rosita vs. Miguel case. This particular case had to do with marital infidelity, a physical altercation between two persons married to different spouses, and money. The *teniente político* was asked to resolve these matters. The Rosita vs. Miguel case showed that different elements in conflicts in Zumbahua cannot be viewed in isolation from one another. Such interconnectedness reflects the complexity involved in resolving local conflicts. Specifically, the case showed how legal pluralism is perceived by the parties involved. They did not look upon legal pluralism as a dichotomy, but instead imperceptibly combined elements of both systems in their actions as well as in their minds, thus reflecting a daily reality of interlegality.

The Rosita vs. Miguel case also highlighted the ambiguous role of the *teniente político*. Although he is an appointed state official, charged among other things with applying national law, in his daily activities he frequently makes use of customary law as well. He does this so often that local residents sometimes seem to forget that he is a state agent. The *teniente político* himself described his juridical role as being a *juez de paz*, which officially he is not. In any case, he is in fact sometimes the first link in the formal chain of law, while at other times he facilitates the application of customary law. But above all, he turns out to be a pragmatic user of both legal systems, often transcending his formal competence. He therefore is a powerful low-level authority, who shapes on a "bottom-up" basis the *de facto* enforcement of formal legal pluralism. He is, as will be shown in more detail later, an Ecuadorian personification of mediators in terms of Chatterjee's (2004) political society.

Chapter 7 described an internal conflict in Zumbahua that was taken to the Court of Justice in Latacunga. The dispute in question had taken place during a meeting at the community building of Tigua Chimbacucho, between two members of the prominent Toaquiza family and seven members of that community. Upon initial consideration, this case was legally framed by the Toaquizas and their lawyers in terms of defamation and intimidation. Underlying these issues, however, was a much longer history of status, local power, money, and the management of a hostel among different *art naïf* painters of that community. But none of this turned out to be of any significance at court. The Juez Segundo de lo Penal mainly concerned itself with the narrow legal question of whether or not this was an "internal conflict" as defined in article 191 of the 1998 Constitution, and thereby determined if this case could, or should, be settled in accordance with customary law by an indigenous authority. That was the question the defense of the seven accused had put forward. As a consequence, the judge had to first decide whether he was competent to judge this case before he could determine culpability.

The case took two years to settle, almost every decision made by the judge was based on written files, and discussion of the conflict at court was framed in strictly legal terms. All of this was in contrast to customary law procedures, as exemplified in the Rosita vs. Miguel case. Additionally, the Toaquiza case showed how what was initially a legal argument over the question of whether or not someone had been threatened or intimidated (and if so, by whom), could become transformed into questions concerning the labeling of the incident (that is, whether it constituted an internal conflict) and the competence of authorities. Finally, it was argued that, because the Toaquizas did not have any option to settle the case other than going to a court, this could not be considered an example of "forum shopping."

Chapter 8 was also about an internal conflict that had initially been settled locally, but that was afterward subjected to the procedures of national law. The La Cocha-Guantópolo case concerned a homicide and, contrary to the case involving the Toaquizas, it was because of this case's gravity and political sensitivity that the state decided to intervene, ultimately leading to the case being heard in the Constitutional Court. Due to the interference of the Fiscal General del Estado, a criminal investigation of both the murder and the role of the *cabildo* of La Cocha in the subsequent indigenous trial soon followed. Both cases were brought to the Court of Justice in Latacunga. The case against the *cabildo* was postponed, but the case against the five young men was brought to the Constitutional Court in Quito. That court had to answer the following fundamental question: exactly how far does the jurisdiction of an indigenous authority reach?

The conclusion of Chapter 8 was that *todo es politico*, and this includes the law, a concept that means different things in different settings. For example, at court (similar to what was concluded with regard to the Toaquiza case), the question of culpability was made subordinate to the question of which authority is entitled to determine guilt or innocence. It also means that the *cabildo* of La Cocha seized its opportunity (provided as a result of the previously mentioned legal void) to confirm, or even extend, its local sovereignty. Similar behavior could be attributed to the *cabildo* of Tigua in the Toaquiza case. But most of all, this chapter provided an example of the politically sensitive nature of the debate regarding the actual scope of jurisdiction of indigenous authorities in Ecuador. After the La Cocha-Guantópolo murder case was brought to the Constitutional Court, both the Correa administration and CONAIE and its affiliates actively tried to influence the course it took. As will be analyzed in more detail in the following section, their different arguments reflected a vision of legal pluralism as a dichotomy.

Legal pluralism revisited

Now that we have answered the question of how internal conflicts are settled in the parish of Zumbahua, these empirical insights can be used to make a contribution to the theoretical understanding of legal pluralism in general. It has been argued that legal pluralism in Latin America is often understood as the dialectical and mutually constitutive relationship between customary law and national law, while taking into account that this relationship is not power-neutral (Merry 1988; Sieder 1997). The use of customary law can therefore be seen as a form of resistance, a strategy of the indigenous people to obtain and maintain their autonomy, and to safeguard it against the hegemony of national law and the state (Collier 1995; Merry 1988; Sieder 1997, 1988). This suggests that people rationally choose to make use of customary law by means of tactics such as forum shopping (K. von Benda-Beckmann 1981). An underlying assumption of such an understanding is that legal pluralism constitutes a dichotomy. This might be true at times at the macro level but, within a local context, legal pluralism can best be understood in terms of interlegality (de Sousa Santos 2002). This book's argument is that legal pluralism does not mean the same thing to everyone, and this is a fact that has consequences for viewing customary law as a form of resistance, and for the applicability of the concept of forum shopping. In order to support this argument, the reader will now be provided a look at legal pluralism from the perspective of both Zumbahuan residents and legal authorities.

The use of legal pluralism: people's practice

This book has argued that, beginning with the Spanish conquest, and continuing during most of the years of independence, indigenous people living in the Ecuadorian Andes have grown accustomed to the fact that there are different authorities using different procedures, thus providing different options to turn to in the event of a legal conflict. Therefore, the experience of highland Indians is not that of the coexistence of two somehow self-contained legal systems (that is, customary law and national law), but rather that of a "network of legality" (Goodale 2009: 33). This "conception of different legal [orders] superimposed, interpenetrated and mixed," which is also known as "interlegality" (de Sousa Santos 2002: 437), seems not to have changed that much over the past fifteen years. This book has shown how, in cases involving internal conflicts, the inhabitants of the parish of Zumbahua will sometimes turn to a local indigenous authority, sometimes to the *teniente político* in the village, and on some occasions even to a court in a nearby town. A similar phenomenon was also observed before the 1998 Constitution of the Republic of Ecuador formally enshrined legal pluralism.

Evidence of interlegality in action in the daily life of Zumbahua can be seen in the empirical findings of this book regarding the variety of conflicts that can occur, and the different authorities and procedures available to the residents of the parish. Cases tended to involve matters that concerned (for example) both "family norms" and "community norms," involved both "minor" and "serious" matters, and addressed both "civil" and "penal" issues. A similar overlap was found in the jurisdictions of local authorities. No strict division can be made among the competences of families, *cabildos, asambleas generales*, and the *teniente político*. Thus, as was argued, if conflicts as well as jurisdictions of authorities overlap, where should the line between customary law and national law be drawn in the first place? Residents of Zumbahua obviously do not conceptualize legal pluralism in terms of well-defined categories or clear-cut rules (de Sousa Santos 2002: 437). Daily activity at the *teniente político*'s office underscored this conceptualization. At his office, the actual mixing of two different normative orders in the actions as well as the minds of Zumbahuan residents was readily evident.

If my conclusion that ordinary Indians do not act or think in terms of a dichotomy between the two systems is correct, then the applicability of the "counter-hegemonic use of customary law," as suggested by Collier (1995),

Merry (1988), and Sieder (1998), at a local level can be questioned. Contrary to what has sometimes been suggested in the literature, Zumbahuans do not typically express either a favorable bias toward customary law or an unfavorable bias toward national law. The findings of the present study point instead to a much more nuanced reality: people living in Zumbahua display a certain skepticism regarding *both* normative systems. More specifically, if they express objections, these are for the most part not aimed at the systems as such, but rather at their application. This is consistent with the earlier observation that the dividing lines between different kinds of conflicts or procedures are not very clear.

This book suggests that the use of legal pluralism be viewed in terms of a continuum (von Benda-Beckmann & von Benda-Beckmann 2006) or a spectrum, as Comaroff and Comaroff (2012) have argued should be done in the case of "resistance."[1] "Pure" customary law cases such as gossip, slander, or witchcraft, which are entirely outside the scope of national law, would define one end of such a continuum, while those cases that are constitutionally excluded from customary law (for example, genocide, war crimes, and other highly serious offenses) would lie at the opposite endpoint.[2] Most routine conflicts, however, fall somewhere between these two extremes. To understand what legal pluralism is about in daily practice, one needs to map this middle ground.[3] It is my contention that the particular position on the continuum occupied by a given conflict depends on the different kinds of issues (that is, territorial, material, and personal), that are at stake. But more important than a case's "exact" position on such a hypothetical continuum, is how the overlap, or mixture, of customary law and national law is dealt with.

How such a mixing of elements of the two systems is dealt with can be drawn from the case studies presented in this book. It can range from a loose approach to national law to mutual influence and understanding, to outright refusal.[4] For example, Rosita vs. Miguel was a local case that was also settled locally. Its particular characteristics define it as more of a customary law than

1 Comaroff and Comaroff's (2012: 393) consider resistance as a spectrum, with "gestures of tacit refusal" on one end, and "organized political protest" on the other.
2 See articles 80 and 233 of the Montecristi Constitution. The exclusion of such cases from the scope of customary law is explicit in the coordination law drafted by Lourdes Tibán.
3 Here I paraphrase Merry's (2006) article "Transnational human rights and local activism: Mapping the middle," in which she argues that, if one wants to understand how transnational ideas such as human rights become meaningful in a local setting, one has to study "the middle" (that is, intermediaries like community leaders, NGOs, or social movement activists) who translate ideas from global to local contexts, and *vice versa*.
4 Here I am indebted to Maarten Bavinck, who informed me of the different understandings and perceptions of legal pluralism on different sociopolitical levels during the course he gave at the international conference *Living realities of legal pluralism* on September 5, 2011, in Cape Town, South Africa.

a national law case. At the very least, it can be said that there are not many conflicting interests regarding differences in procedures or anticipated settlements related to both systems involved in that particular case. The parties involved seemed to be content with the *teniente político* as the adjudicating authority. And as a consequence of that, what we saw in the procedure for resolving that case was a rather loose approach to national law. This was perhaps best illustrated in the conduct of the *teniente político*, who made use of several elements of customary law, although as a state official he was officially required to apply national law. No one present at his office on the morning that the case was heard either noted or complained about this inconsistency.

While portraying the different kinds of legal authorities and procedures, this book has presented, in addition to other examples of a loose approach to national law, illustrations of mutual influence between the two systems: *cabildos* and *asambleas generales* that refer to "penal law" characteristics of a case, or that frequently make use of *actas* written in Spanish can be considered as examples of the influence of national on customary law. Hoekema (2003, 2004, 2005) has characterized such examples as the mixed outcome of interlegality. The reference to relevant articles in the Constitution, and international rules in proceedings characterized by customary law, could both be considered such an influence (Simon Thomas 2009). Examples of "interlegality in reverse" (that is, the assimilation of elements of customary law by national law (Hoekema 2004: 23, 2005: 6–7)) were provided as well. Such examples include the provincial court judge's references to different phases to an indigenous trial (that is, in the verdict of the judge in the Toaquiza case), or the use of expert testimonies of legal anthropologists in such trials (as was done by the Constitutional Court in the La Cocha-Guantópolo murder case). These examples of both a loose approach and of mutual influence suggest a certain mutual accommodation between the two systems. The practice of legal pluralism (accompanied by the perception of Zumbahuan residents reflecting interlegality) can therefore be considered fairly unproblematic in most cases. This highlights the argument that ordinary Indians on a local level do not seem to use customary law as a counter-hegemonic strategy.

A second observation resulting from the acceptance of interlegality can be made with regard to the concept of "forum shopping" (K. von Benda-Beckmann 1981). As was seen in Chapter 2, and then in the descriptions of both the Rosita vs. Miguel and Toaquiza cases, this book challenges the assumption that litigants typically engage in forum shopping. The concept itself suggests a conscious and deliberate choice, and this book argues that such a characterization is inaccurate. Even if people make every choice in a legal dispute process consciously (a rather dubious assertion, as argued in Chapter 7), in many cases there is not much room for choice because of practical reasons related to distance, costs, duration, and social pressure.

If intentional choices are made, it is only done in the more extreme cases. For example, in the La Cocha-Guantópolo murder case of 2010, and also in the earlier La Cocha murder case of 2002, the relatives of the victim expressly chose to turn to a *cabildo*, expressing their wish to settle this case in accordance with customary law. While it seems clear that social pressure played a role in the decisions made in both of those cases, there is no denying that the parties involved had a choice. That is also what the *actas* of those cases reflected. At a certain point in the La Cocha-Guantópolo case, because of changed circumstances, family members of the accused young men, and the five men themselves, reconsidered their initial choice, and chose to appeal to national law courts. Although the behavior in these two cases points to forum shopping, they are exceptions to the rule. Generally speaking, people in Zumbahua do not make such conscious and rational choices, but instead gravitate to one of the available authorities according to circumstances. This book therefore argues that in general, on a local level, the actions taken by Zumbahuans to resolve conflicts cannot rightly be labeled entirely intentional, conscious, or pragmatic in the way that the verbs "to shop" or "to choose" suggest.

The use of legal pluralism: authorities' attitudes

It can be concluded that the behavior of ordinary Indians did not change that much over time. What does seem to have changed since 1998, however, is how indigenous leaders dealt with the constitutional recognition of their legal authority. This is due to fact that there had previously been no general agreement regarding the extent to which indigenous authorities ought to administer customary law. Neither the 1998 Constitution nor the Montecristi Constitution have yet resulted in rules that define exactly how far their territorial, personal, and material jurisdiction reaches. Authorities (that is, both indigenous authorities and national law agents) tend to challenge the boundaries of the new situation of formal legal pluralism. In the case of indigenous authorities, such behavior clearly suggests that customary law has been used as a counter-hegemonic strategy.

Contrary to what was shown on a local level (where legal pluralism is dealt with from a loose approach to national law to mutual influence and understanding of both legal systems), at the national level the way that Ecuadorian jurists deal with legal pluralism mostly equals outright refusal. In the Toaquiza case and in both of the La Cocha murder cases, different interpretations of the scope of legal pluralism on the part of indigenous leaders and state agents led to conflict. What these cases show is that the overlap between two legal systems becomes problematic when the interests at stake become more important (for example, when money, power, life and death, etc., become the subject of a conflict), or when the parties involved think that the division of the two systems is more important than combining them in pragmatic ways. For the most part, such "problems" occur close to the end of the continuum which is considered to be the exclusive province of national law. The two murder cases in La Cocha described in this book can be seen as examples of this. The majority of politicians, jurists, the media, and the general public considered the use of customary law (for example, flogging and ritual cleansing) as "barbaric." According to many indigenous people, however, the exclusive application of national law in cases involving the most serious crimes should not be taken for granted.

In addition to the severity of a conflict, the opinions of the parties to a dispute regarding the division between the two legal systems defines how the situation of legal pluralism is dealt with in practice. In the Rosita vs. Miguel case, the parties seemed to be content with some overlap. Conversely, the parties to the Toaquiza case and the La Cocha murder cases were uncomfortable with the mixing of the two legal systems. In the Toaquiza case, a local conflict had been brought to a provincial court. Because the content of this conflict involved longstanding issues about local power, and because this case was taken to the national courts, the competence of authorities became the main legal issue. For this reason, any mixing of systems was consciously avoided in the final decision of the court. Something similar occurred in the La Cocha-Guantópolo murder case where, in the indigenous trial and settlement, the procedures at the different courts and the debates surrounding them reflected a strict division between customary law and national law. In a way this is understandable, because the much-needed coordinating rules were at stake. On the other hand, it is striking how this dichotomy in the acting, talking, and thinking of indigenous and national authorities involved contrasted with the common practice of legal pluralism by ordinary Zumbahuans. Clearly, the indigenous authorities challenged the hegemony of national law at that point. Especially in a situation of formal legal pluralism, in which the boundaries of different authorities' jurisdictions are not clear, a clash between the two systems seems unavoidable.

The first important thing we can learn when such a clash arises is that an internal conflict can easily become transformed into a case where proper jurisdiction becomes the main point of contention. On a local level, as well as on a provincial and even a national level, different authorities can become involved in a dispute over jurisdiction. In the La Cocha-Guantópolo murder case, for example, the *cabildo* of La Cocha seized its opportunity, while being backed by several indigenous organizations and other protagonists of indigenous rights, to confirm and even extend its ability to apply customary law and as such to protect its local sovereignty. The question of whether or not the *cabildo* and the *asamblea* involved had the right to do so in this case also gained increased prominence at the provincial court. The Court of Justice in Latacunga explicitly challenged the competence of the local indigenous authorities. Finally, at the Constitutional Court in Quito, this particular case was used to ask the more fundamental question of how the recognition of formal legal pluralism in article 171 of the Montecristi Constitution should be interpreted in practice. Strikingly, at all three levels, the parties involved mainly made use of legal arguments (that is, they cited the relevant articles, jurisprudence, and scholarly writings). Their arguments were thus framed in terms of a jurisprudential understanding of customary law vs. national law, and thus in terms of a dichotomy between the two systems.

A second important conclusion of the analysis of both the Toaquiza case and the La Cocha murder cases is that the counter-hegemonic use of customary law is used as a strategy by indigenous leaders and their representatives rather than that of ordinary Indians. Thus, it was the *cabildos* of Tigua Chimbacucho and La Cocha that were parties to the trial at the Court of Justice in Latacunga. Both were represented by lawyers who had direct or indirect ties with CONAIE (that is, Raúl Ilaquiche, Lourdes Tibán, and Carlos Poveda). In the La Cocha murder cases, the *cabildo* was backed by the OSG UNOCIC and the OTG MICC, both affiliates of CONAIE. And at court, the *cabildo* was supported by high-ranking indigenous leaders. The actual involvement of indigenous organizations and other protagonists not only highlighted the political sensitivity of the case, but also showed how the indigenous movement as a whole valued the importance of these cases. It sought to influence the course of the trials in order to secure legal precedents favorable to its cause.

A final observation can be made with regard to the concepts of "forum shopping" and "shopping forums" (K. von Benda-Beckmann 1981). I suggested in Chapter 2 that the concept of "shopping forums" might prove a useful tool for understanding legal pluralism in action. The argument that authorities tend to be selective in the kinds of disputes they agree to hear is illustrated by the three previously mentioned case studies. In the Rosita vs. Miguel case, the *teniente político* emphasized his own importance with regard to the settlement of disputes several times. For example, he provided the parties the choice of going to another authority, although he knew that they were unlikely to do so for practical reasons. He also at a certain point clearly steered the parties towards a settlement, making clear that *not* reaching an agreement was simply not an option. In the Toaquiza case, the plaintiffs turned to national law because they clearly did not want indigenous authorities to be involved. The seven individuals who were accused in that case had strong ties to the local *cabildo* and sought recourse to indigenous law for the opposite reason. In the two La Cocha murder cases, the reference to customary law in the *actas* emphasized that these cases should be considered internal conflicts, and that therefore the *cabildo* of La Cocha was competent to adjudicate them. These and other references to the Consititution clearly showed that the *cabildo* was "claiming" these cases. In the La Cocha-Guantópolo murder case, even the Criminal Court in Latacunga showed "shopping-forum" behavior when it declared itself incompetent to hear the case as long as the Constitutional Court did not issue its own opinion regarding it. I therefore argue that it is the change in the rules of the legal game (that is, the legal void that was created with regard to the actual scope of legal pluralism) that encourages such behavior. Thus, contrary to what has been argued about forum shopping, the concept of shopping forums does seem to be of relevance.

To summarize this section on legal pluralism: what the case studies in this book show is that there is a difference in how indigenous individuals and authorities use and perceive customary law in relation to national law. In many cases, the two legal systems coexist harmoniously. In exceptional cases, mostly when the stakes are high and/or parties (especially the adjudicating authorities) prefer a strict division, legal pluralism is instead seen as a threat. It depends on the level examined whether the use of customary law is perceived as a *means* (that is, to settle a conflict), or as an *end* (that is, to increase power). That is why this book has emphasized that legal pluralism does not mean the same thing to everyone. Ordinary Indians act and think of legal pluralism in terms of interlegality, while authorities do so in terms of a dichotomy.

One of the consequences of this state of affairs is that the "one-size-fits-all" image of customary law being always a form of resistance needs to be more nuanced. This book shows that in minor cases, on a local level, individuals make pragmatic use of legal pluralism to resolve internal conflicts. They do not show any typical bias toward any legal system. If this daily practice is a matter of local, everyday resistance at all (Abu-Lughod 1990), then this is merely the result of a largely unconscious process of the continuation of custom and tradition in daily practice. This contrasts with examples of more severe cases, especially when they become nationally known, in which indigenous authorities and organizations emphatically seize the opportunity to challenge the boundaries of state legal power. The latter implies a more direct and conscious resistance to the dominance of the state (see also Comaroff & Comaroff 2012).

In more theoretical terms, the fact that different perceptions of legal pluralism exist means that the concept itself should be a subject of inquiry. In Chapter 2, it was stated that the focus of research on customary law has shifted from the question of what customary law *is* to how it is *used*. A similar approach to the study of legal pluralism was made in this book as well. If we want to understand how legal pluralism works in daily practice, it is less important to describe and analyze what legal pluralism *is* than find out what it *means* to particular individuals, and where, when, and how it is used. Treating legal pluralism in this way as a dependent variable will facilitate a more profound understanding of state–society relationships from a legal anthropological perspective.

The challenge of diversity[5]

The second aim of this book was to view the contemporary relationship between Ecuador's indigenous population and the state through the prism of formal legal pluralism. This is of specific interest because, during the past twenty years, some remarkable changes in this relationship have taken place. While the political and legal doctrine had for centuries been one of supposed

---

5 Here, once again, I refer to the volume *The Challenge of Diversity*, edited by Willem Assies, André Hoekema and Gemma van der Haar (2000). This is a book that I've gone back to time and again over the course of the past decade and by which I am profoundly influenced. Assies, who died in 2010, in particular has played an important role in my career development, as an inspiring teacher and supervisor.

homogeneity of national identity and of monism, the past two decades have witnessed a formal recognition of ethnic and cultural diversity. An interplay of Indian political activism and a centralized and inefficient state that had to reorganize itself have defined these radical transformations (Pallares 2002; Sieder 2002; Van Cott 2005; Yashar 2005), which elsewhere have been labeled the politics of multiculturalism. With the leftist Correa administration in power for more than five years, this situation calls for an analytical update.

With regard to the Ecuadorian situation, studies of multiculturalism have generally focused on the relationship between indigenous people and the state as this relationship has been redefined by neoliberal changes since the 1990s (Cervone 2012: 236). As part of these neoliberal changes, a policy of decentralization and recognition of plurality could be seen as projects of the state to strengthen its position. Through granting some sort of autonomy to indigenous people (cf. Hale 2002), such a policy sought to deal with a relatively weak control over the countryside and the subordinated position of rural indigenous people, on the one hand, and a centralized and inefficient state system, including a weak and politically compromised judiciary, on the other. It was hoped that these changes would contribute to the empowerment of the indigenous population, which had become a steadily growing demand.

After years of indigenous protest, Ecuador constitutionally recognized its ethnic and cultural diversity in 1998. This *de jure* recognition, however, did not go hand in hand with a *de facto* recognition, let alone a redistribution of resources and power. Ethnic discrimination, exclusionary practices, and racist and anti-indigenous attitudes continue to exist in certain sectors of society, manifesting themselves in social and political conflicts (Baud 2009: 36). This especially seems to be the case as regards the *de facto* recognition of legal pluralism, either by jurists or by the government. What was meant to provide indigenous authorities some sort of judicial autonomy, on the one hand, and to reduce the backlog in the national system, on the other hand, did not end up working in practice. In other words, the much-needed formal redistribution of legal power has not occurred in tandem with the formal recognition of legal pluralism.

The first question that arises when the rather problematic functioning of the situation of formal legal pluralism in Ecuador is considered concerns *what* exactly has been recognized. In retrospect, nobody really knew what was recognized in the 1998 Constitution. As far as I know, no empirical research had been done on what constitutes customary law in Ecuador. Some basic knowledge of this phenomenon might have produced a nuanced definition of it in the Constitution. It is fair to assume that a gap already existed even then between how CONAIE and the state (that is, the judiciary and the government) understood customary law, but that these contrasting viewpoints were not acknowledged then – and have still not been acknowledged. In the case of Bolivia, Goodale (2009: 80) argues that the recognition of legal pluralism in that country was the result of "a fundamentally mistaken account of the reality of law." Second, the Ecuadorian recognition is stated in vague terms and its implementation was not adequately planned. The absence of coordinating rules is illustrative of this. Therefore, it should not have come as a surprise that recognition under such conditions would eventually lead to controversy.

What we have seen so far is that constitutional recognition has actually encouraged local authorities to extend their jurisdiction, while it simultaneously increased local tensions over this increased autonomy. At the same time, it also led to political tensions on a national level over the exact interpretation of relevant articles in the constitution. As soon as local sovereignty becomes the subject of debate, the state (that is, the judiciary, accompanied by the government, both backed by national law) immediately moves to defend its own interests in order to prevent an increase in indigenous authorities' jurisdiction. This top-down politics provokes bottom-up reactions of the indigenous and other social movements. Thus, a first conclusion can be drawn: formal recognition of legal pluralism, as part of a decentralization policy, has worked both in favor of and against the legal-political empowerment of indigenous people in Ecuador.[6]

With regard to the struggle over *de facto* recognition of legal pluralism, CONAIE and its most well-known allies seem to be implementing an essentialist strategy.[7] This manifestation of state power, followed by a counter-reaction that depicts legal pluralism in uncritical terms, appears to be highly politicized in nature. This recent politicized discussion of legal pluralism therefore only seems to widen the gap between persistent notions of legal monism and a position that approaches cultural relativism. As such, it is an impediment to a solution to the challenge of legal pluralism in two different ways. First, it ignores the fact that, in many cases, customary law and national law have coexisted quite well. Over considerable segments of the continuum, the coexistence of two different legal systems takes the form of mutual influence and understanding. Only in exceptional cases do tensions arise.

The discussions concerning the development of "mechanisms of coordination and cooperation" (article 171 of the Montecristi Constitution) seem to target only these exceptional cases. The two bills of 2002 and the recent efforts undertaken by Lourdes Tibán (who developed another draft coordination law) can be seen as examples of this. What is particularly striking is that these proposals consistently emphasize the dividing lines between two legal systems' jurisdictions. If they instead reflected the nuanced and complex reality of daily life, then they would cover the whole continuum (including those cases in which the coexistence of two legal systems is not perceived as problematic). This leads to a second conclusion: the challenge of formal legal pluralism is

---

6 See Lund (2008) for a similar conclusion regarding the situation in Ghana.
7 Their definition of customary law is not only essentialist in nature (that is, a fixed, authentic normative system that always restores harmony), but also ignores the complexity of daily practice, in that it treats legal pluralism as a dichotomy, while ordinary Indians typically perceive it as "interlegality" in the context of their daily lives.

mainly of legal and political concern, and debates concerning its implementation are inappropriately based on consideration of exceptional cases.

Indian–state relationships

We have seen that the present-day policies of recognizing difference (for example, legal pluralism) are in many ways similar to the situation that prevailed when the Ecuadorian state underwent decentralization at the end of the twentieth century. The actual day-to-day governance of the country had previously been divided among different authorities in rural areas, and this *de facto* reality was at last transformed into *de jure* recognition. In this way, customary law became part of the national legal system – in other words, "weak" (J. Griffiths 1986) or "state law" (Woodman 1998) legal pluralism. For example, local *cabildos* now had to "show their administrative capabilities under the watchful eye of other institutions" (Assies 2000b: 12), both within and outside their jurisdictions (Assies 2003). This explanation is consistent with the view of Hale (2002, 2005) who argues that neoliberal recognition of multiculturalism comes with a high price. In real terms, however, the principle of subsidiarity proved to be more useful in this regard (de Benoist 1999). Daily practice proved to be a "bottom-up" dynamic, in which local authorities resolved internal conflicts as much as they could, and under circumstances in which the state only had a subsidiary function. In this conceptualization, it is the lower-level authority that delegates tasks and responsibilities to the state.

Here, a comparison with Chatterjee's (2004) conceptualization of the state–society relationship in terms of a "political society" proves to be helpful. Chatterjee argues that, in the postcolonial world, poor and marginalized people (in Ecuador, the rural indigenous population) do not really belong to civil society. However, since they are not completely excluded or included in the state, they still have to be "looked after and controlled" (Chatterjee 2004: 38), and consequently such populations are brought into a certain political relationship with the state. This results in a situation in which these populations live in a "political society," which has become a site of negotiation and contestation. In such a state of affairs, contacts between the state and its agents, on the one hand, and poor and marginalized people, on the other, are *mediated* rather than direct.

In postcolonial Ecuador, it was the *tenientes políticos* that played an important role in the communication between the Ecuadorian state and its rural population over the course of almost two centuries. From 1830 on, these political officials were assigned two duties, one political and one juridical. In both of these duties, they played an ambiguous role. Sometimes they acted as protagonists of state interests, while at other times they chose the side of the rural indigenous population (Baud 2007; Guerrero 1997). As mediators (in Chatterjee's terminology) in legal affairs they were responsible for settling local and minor disputes. In practice, however, they did not always follow the letter of the law. They often decided which cases had to be brought to court, which cases should be settled within communities, and which cases they could deal with themselves. In terms of the principle of subsidiarity, *tenientes políticos* were the personification of the "bottom-up" dynamic with regards to the application of the law.

In order to be successful in a political society, the state (or, rather, state agencies) must follow "a different logic from that of the normal relations of the state with citizens in civil society" (Chatterjee 2004: 41). It remains to be seen to what extent contemporary *tenientes políticos* will be able to continue to function in the role of mediators between the state and rural indigenous people. First, their political role is decreasing because several communities now have *cabildos*, and parishes as a whole have Juntas Parroquiales. Second, their juridical role is under attack as well, since other state officials (for example, Fiscalías Indígenas or newly built Fiscalías on a cantonal level, as in Pujilí) seem to fulfill the same purpose, and because *tenientes políticos* have to wait and see how their juridical role changes once *jueces de paz* actually assume office. Third, because of the constitutional recognition of legal pluralism, *cabildos* have also been given an administrative role, which undoubtedly also affects the *tenientes políticos*' juridical role.[8] *Tenientes políticos* have not completely lost their role as mediators in a political society, but their role is changing. The fact that the state does not seem to have a clear mediator in rural political society anymore is an important consequence of the formal recognition of legal pluralism. And it is therefore legitimate to ask who will be able to step into this vacant role of low-level state agent.

In addition, the contemporary position of the rural indigenous population must also be considered. We have witnessed that, since 1998, a new mediator has entered the stage. I am referring here to the *cabildos*. The case studies presented in this book demonstrate that some *cabildos* nowadays play quite an active role in settling local disputes: not only in the actual settlement, but also as mediators (in Chatterjee's terminology) in legal affairs.[9] *Cabildos* thus often act as a first link in the legal chain (for example, convincing people to turn to a *teniente político* or to a court) and sometimes they decide to resolve cases themselves. This is comparable to what *tenientes políticos* have traditionally done, and still do, so in a way the responsibilities of these two categories of officials overlap with one another, thus leading to conflicts between

8 Although it can be argued that, in the era preceding the formal recognition of legal pluralism, these *cabildos* already had an important role in the settlement of internal disputes, it has become evident that rural power-relations have unmistakably changed since 1998. The way that some *cabildos* seize their opportunity to make use of the legal void in order to increase local sovereignty is illustrative of this.

9 In the Rosita vs. Miguel case, it was a *dirigente* that convinced the parties involved to accept the authority of the *teniente político*. In the Toaquiza case, the *cabildo* of Tigua Chimbacucho actively tried to defend its local sovereignty. And so did the *cabildo* in both La Cocha murder cases. In the La Cocha-Guantópolo murder case, however, it was another *cabildo* (that is, of Guantópolo) who at one point convinced the five young men accused of murder to turn themselves in to state authorities.

them. Because rules that define the actual jurisdiction of both customary law and national law in cases of internal conflicts have not yet been developed, *cabildos* have relatively more freedom to act as they please than *tenientes politicos*. Although *cabildos* are formal institutions, their legal competence can be characterized as involving a high degree of informal *de facto* sovereignty. Nowadays, it is not only in the daily practice of *tenientes politicos*, but in that of *cabildos* as well, where the "entire set of paralegal arrangements" (Chatterjee 2004: 56) concerning the application of *de facto* legal pluralism is to a large extent negotiated and contested. This is a second important consequence of formal legal pluralism.

The state (that is, the judiciary, accompanied by the government, both backed by the law) only seems to be able to step into this site of negotiation and contestation when internal conflicts touch on issues that the state considers to fall under its exclusive jurisdiction (for example, homicide). This fact, however, is contested by some *cabildos*, especially those who are supported and backed by indigenous organizations and other advocates of customary law. This seems to make matters worse. As soon as indigenous authorities cross the line drawn by those according recognition, the state manifests itself through visible police force, prisons, judges, and courts, or what Hansen and Stepputat (2001) have called the "practical language of governance." This in turn, elicits a legal and political response on the part of indigenous organizations.

Given the highly politicized tensions between the Correa administration and CONAIE about this matter,[10] it is fair to assume that a political and legal solution is not within reach in the near future. Keeping in mind Chatterjee's political society, with its mediators for marginalized populations, and state agencies following a different logic in order to reach solutions, it appears that a viable response to the challenge of diversity is not likely to be initiated by the national government of Ecuador. Given the changing role of *tenientes politicos*, the state does not have a strong representative in political society anymore, while local indigenous people seem to have obtained a strong mediator with *cabildos* instead. But more important than hypothesizing about whether this weakens the role of the state or strengthens the role of indigenous people is the fact that, because legal pluralism is constitutionally recognized, customary law and national law are now legally connected, so their co-existence has to be negotiated on a local level as well as on a national level in order to make the situation of formal legal pluralism work in daily practice – whether the parties involved like this or not. This leads to this book's third conclusion: compared to the prior situation of real legal pluralism, the Ecuadorian state and its indigenous population nowadays are now more interdependent than ever before.

So, what can we learn in general from the Ecuadorian case, where multiculturalism (and consequently legal pluralism) has constitutionally been

---

10 Nowadays, the struggle over jurisdiction only tends to sharpen boundaries (Simon Thomas 2012).

recognized, but where implementation of this recognition leaves much to be desired? Multiculturalism, as described in this book's theoretical section, could best be seen as a political project, an effort of liberal democratic governments to embrace ethnic differences (Cowan 2006; Postero 2007). Consequently, a society's acceptance of ethnic diversity calls for changes in its legal arrangements (Parekh 2000). Some theorists have argued for a politics of redistribution, with a focus on transforming the political and economic structure of society (Almeida et al. 2005; Rawls 1971). Others instead have favored a politics of recognition, with a focus on the cultural nature of an injustice which requires state intervention to undo cultural domination (Taylor 1994). Both lines of thought have received pointed criticism (Benhabib 2002), leading to a contemporary view that a strict distinction between a politics of redistribution and a politics of recognition cannot be maintained, and that they should instead be integrated (Postero 2007).

With regard to one specific aspect of multiculturalism, the dilemma of individual vs. collective rights, it has been suggested that, besides an integration of the politics of redistribution and the politics of recognition, mutual dialogue, and understanding between those advocating different points of views is needed. Parekh (2000) suggested that acceptance of difference requires changes in actions as well as in thinking. Assies et al. (2000) and Sieder (2002) also noted that the full recognition of a situation of legal pluralism required a profound adjustment in legal thinking and practice, combined with an open dialogue in cases in which legal pluralism is seen as a dichotomy and perceived as a threat. Such an open dialogue, however, is not what we have witnessed thus far in the Ecuadorian case. Instead, we have seen indigenous organizations and authorities clashing with the state over actual interpretation of the formal recognition of legal pluralism.

The recognition of multiculturalism as part of a decentralization policy in essence aims to strengthen the state. The result has been the opposite. The politics of recognition seems to have weakened the state (or at least the dominant role of national law) because it increased *de facto* as well as *de jure* local sovereignty to a certain extent because of the formal recognition of legal pluralism. This is in line with what this book has argued about the principle of "subsidiarity" being an accurate term to describe local legal practices. However, the actual scope of jurisdiction granted to local authorities is contested, both internally as well as externally. Not only are indigenous people internally divided over the use of customary law, but the actual use of it in cases involving serious matters such as homicide has led to legal, political, and social disapproval among Ecuadorians in general. In some instances, this has resulted in a strong state response. Formal recognition of legal pluralism can thus work both in favor of and against the legal and political empowerment of indigenous people.

It also remains to be seen what the negotiations and contestations over the actual scope of legal pluralism will lead to in the near future. Terms like "weak" or "strong" do not seem to capture the complexity of the current situation (Clark & Becker 2007: 6). Given the long history of continuing negotiation and contestation (Chatterjee 2004) between the Ecuadorian state and its indigenous population, after such a profound political and legal break with the past, it is perhaps too soon to define this new situation of formal legal pluralism in such terms. One thing that can be observed, however, is that the constitutional recognition of legal pluralism has led indigenous people and the state to discuss the coexistence of customary law and national law in a different way than they had previously. They are now forced to deal with the *reality* of legal pluralism, rather than merely state their opinions about its desirability. Formal recognition of diversity influences an indigenous population's position in political society.

Finally, the fact that legal pluralism does not mean the same thing to everyone is not only helpful in understanding the daily practice of dispute settlement, but also in shedding light on discussions regarding the actual scope of the recognition of legal pluralism. On the one hand, we have seen that a lot of minor internal conflicts are settled more or less smoothly at a local level to the satisfaction of all parties involved. The way customary law in relation to national law is treated in such cases shows signs of a loose approach to national law, as well as mutual understanding and influence. The perception of legal pluralism reflects interlegality in action. In such cases of legal pluralism, the acceptance of difference, along with mutual dialogue and understanding, appears to be the rule. On the other hand, in instances of more severe internal conflicts involving cases that touch upon the presumed exclusive province of national law, the differences between customary law and national law are magnified, and legal pluralism is understood as a dichotomy. It is in such circumstances where the absence of coordinating rules is bound to manifest itself. In sum, the challenge of formal legal pluralism is mainly of legal and political concern, while the daily reality at a local level reveals that the actual practice of it is not perceived as an *a priori* legal problem. Legal pluralism in fact manifests its problematic nature only on a national level. In the daily practice of local society, however, legal pluralism is simply perceived and assimilated as a part of ordinary life.

Bibliography

Abrams, Philip. 1988. "Notes on the Difficulty of Studying the State (1977)." *Journal of Historical Sociology* 1:58–89.
Abu-Lughod, Lila. 1990. "The Romance of Resistance: Tracing Transformations of Power Through Bedouin Women." *American Ethnologist* 17:41–55.
Almeida, Ileana, Nidia Arrobo Rodas, and Lautaro Ojeda Segovia. 2005. *Autonomía Indígena: Frente al Estado nación y a la globalización neoliberal.* Quito: Abya-Yala.
Anderson, Benedict. 2006. *Imagined Communities: Reflections on the Origin and Spread of Nationalism – Revised Edition.* London: Verso.
Andolina, Robert. 2003. "The Sovereign and its Shadow: Constituent Assembly and Indigenous Movement in Ecuador." *Journal of Latin American Studies* 35:721–750.
Andrade, Santiago. 2009a. "Justicia de Paz." Pp. 471–478 in *La transformación de la Justicia*, vol. 7, edited by S. Andrade and L. F. Ávila. Quito: Ministerio de Justicia y Derechos Humanos.
Andrade, Santiago. 2009b. "La función judicial en la vigente constitución de la República." Pp. 239–268 in *La nueva Constitución del Ecuador: Estado, derechos e instituciones*, vol. 30, edited by S. Andrade, A. Grijalva, and C. Storini. Quito: Andina Simón Bolivar.
Assies, Willem. 2000a. "About This Book." Pp. ix–xii in *The Challenge of Diversity: Indigenous Peoples and Reform of the State in Latin America*, edited by W. Assies, G. Van der Haar, and A. J. Hoekema. Amsterdam: Thela Thesis.
Assies, Willem. 2000b. "Indigenous Peoples and Reform of the State in Latin America." Pp. 3–22 in *The Challenge of Diversity: Indigenous Peoples and Reform of the State in Latin America*, edited by W. Assies, G. Van der Haar, and A. J. Hoekema. Amsterdam: Thela Thesis.
Assies, Willem. 2001. "La oficialización de lo no oficial: ¿(re)encuentro de dos mundos?" *Alteridades* 11:83–96.
Assies, Willem. 2003. "Indian Justice in the Andes: Re-rooting or Re-routing?" Pp. 167–186 in *Imagining the Andes: Shifting Margins of a Marginal World*, edited by T. Salman and A. Zoomers. Amsterdam: Aksant.
Assies, Willem, Luis Ramírez Sevilla, and María del Carmen Ventura Patiño. 2006. "Autonomy Rights and the Politics of Constitutional Reform in Mexico." *Latin American & Caribbean Ethnic Studies* 1:37–62.
Assies, Willem, Gemma Van der Haar, and André J. Hoekema. 2000. "Diversity as a Challenge: A Note on the Dilemmas of Diversity." Pp. 295–315 in *The Challenge of Diversity: Indigenous Peoples and Reform of the State in Latin America*, edited by W. Assies, G. Van der Haar, and A. J. Hoekema. Amsterdam: Thela Thesis.

Baud, Michiel. 1993. "Indiaans overleven in de Andes: 1530–1930." Pp. 181–201 in *Campesinos: kleine boeren in Latijns-Amerika (vanaf 1520)*, edited by A. Ouweneel. Amsterdam: Thela Publishers.

Baud, Michiel. 1996. "The Huelga de los Indígenas in Cuenca, Ecuador (1920–1921): Comparative Perspectives." Pp. 217–239 in *Indigenous Revolts in Chiapas and the Andean Highlands*, edited by K. Gosner and A. Ouweneel. Amsterdam: CEDLA.

Baud, Michiel. 2007. "Liberalism, Indigenismo, and Social Mobilization in Late Nineteenth-Century Ecuador." Pp. 72–88 in *Highland Indians and the State in Modern Ecuador*, edited by A. K. Clark and M. Becker. Pittsburgh: University of Pittsburgh Press.

Baud, Michiel. 2009. "Indigenous Politics and the State: The Andean Highlands in the Nineteenth and Twentieth Centuries." Pp. 19–42 in *Indigenous Peoples, Civil Society, and the Neo-liberal State in Latin America*, edited by E. F. Fischer. New York: Berghahn Books.

BBC News. 2007. "Ecuador Swears in New President." *BBC News*. January 16.

Becker, Marc. 1999. "Comunas and Indigenous Protest in Cayambe, Ecuador." *The Americas* 55:531–559.

Becker, Marc. 2007. "Indigenous Struggles for Land Rights in Twentieth-Century Ecuador." *Agricultural History* 81:159–181.

Becker, Marc. 2008. *Indians and Leftists in the Making of Ecuador's Modern Indigenous Movements*. Durham, NC: Duke University Press.

Becker, Marc. 2010a. "The Children of 1990." *Alternatives* 35:291–316.

Becker, Marc. 2010b. "Review of 'Fighting Like a Community: Andean Civil Society in an Era of Indian Uprisings'." *Bulletin of Latin American Research* 30:106–107.

Becker, Marc. 2011a. "Correa, Indigenous Movements, and the Writing of a New Constitution in Ecuador." *Latin American Perspectives* 38:47–62.

Becker, Marc. 2011b. "'Gonzalo Oleas, Defensor': Cultural Intermediation in Mid-Twentieth-Century Ecuador." *Journal of Latin American Studies* 43:237–265.

Benhabib, Seyla. 2002. *The Claims of Culture: Equality and Diversity in the Global Era*. Princeton, NJ: Princeton University Press.

Berk-Seligson, Susan. 2006. "Access to Justice for the Kichwa of the Ecuadorian Sierra." Pp. 5–8, 44–76 in *Indigenous and State Justice Systems in the Ecuadorian Sierra*, edited by S. Berk-Seligson, W. Partridge, and Y. Redero. Report to USAID Ecuador.

Berk-Seligson, Susan. 2008. "Judicial Systems in Contact: Access to Justice and the Right to Interpreting/Translating Services Among the Quichua of Ecuador." *Interpreting* 10:9–33.

Bernard, H. Russel. 2006. *Research Methods in Anthropology*. Oxford: AltiMira Press.

Biezeveld, Renske. 2004. "Discourse Shopping in a Dispute over Land in Rural Indonesia." *Ethnology* 43:137–154.

Boeije, Hennie. 2010. *Analysis in Qualitative Research*. London: SAGE Publications.

Bohannan, Paul. 1989 [1957]. *Justice and Judgement Among the Tiv (with a new Preface)*. London: Oxford University Press.

Bonaldi, Francesca. 2010. *Entre dos culturas: Los pintores Andinos de Tigua*. Quito: Abya-Yala.

Brandt, Hans-Jürgen and Rocío Franco Valdivia. 2006. *El Tratamiento de Conflictos, Un estudio de actas en 133 comunidades*, vol. 1. Lima: Instituto de Defensa Legal (IDL).

Brandt, Hans-Jürgen and Rocío Franco Valdivia. 2007. *Normas, valores y procedimientos en la justicia comunitaria*, vol. 2. Lima: Instituto de Defensa Legal (IDL).

Brysk, Alison. 2000. *From Tribal Village to Global Village: Indian Rights and International Relations in Latin America*. Stanford: Stanford University Press.

Canessa, Andrew. 2006. "Todos somos indígenas: Towards a New Language of National Political Identity." *Bulletin of Latin American Research* 25:241–263.

Canessa, Andrew. 2012. "Conflict, Claim and Contradiction in the New Indigenous State of Bolivia." Working Paper Series, No. 22, desiguALdades.net. Berlin.

Caplan, Pat. 1995. "Introduction: Anthropology and the Study of Disputes." Pp. 1–10 in *Understanding Disputes: The Politics of Argument*, edited by P. Caplan. Oxford: Berg Publishers.

Caselli, I. 2010. "Ecuador's Indigenous Justice System on Trial." *BBC Mobile News*. July 27.

Cervone, Emma. 2010. "Celebrating the Chagras: Mestizaje, Multiculturalism, and the Ecuadorian Nation." *The Global South* 4:94–118.

Cervone, Emma. 2012. *Long Live Atahualpa: Indigenous Politics, Justice, and Democracy in the Northern Andes*. Durham, NC: Duke University Press.

Chatterjee, Partha. 2004. *The Politics of the Governed: Reflections on Popular Politics in Most of the World*. Delhi: Permanent Black.

Chaves, Margarita and Marta Zambrano. 2006. "From Blanqueamiento to Reindigenización: Paradoxes of Mestizaje and Multiculturalism in Contemporary Colombia." *European Review of Latin American and Caribbean Studies* 80:5–23.

Chávez, Gina and Fernando García. 2004. *El derecho a ser: diversidad, identidad y cambio. Etnografía jurídica indígena y afroecuatoriana*. Quito: FLACSO.

Clark, A. Kim. 2007. "Shifting Paternalisms in Indian–State Relations, 1895–1950." Pp. 89–104 in *Highland Indians and the State in Modern Ecuador*, edited by A. K. Clark and M. Becker. Pittsburg: Pittsburg University Press.

Clark, A. Kim and Marc Becker. 2007. "Indigenous Peoples and State Formation in Modern Ecuador." Pp. 1–21 in *Highland Indians and the State in Modern Ecuador*, edited by A. K. Clark and M. Becker. Pittsburgh: University of Pittsburgh Press.

Collier, Jane. 1995. "Problemas teórico-metodológicos en la antropología jurídica." Pp. 45–76 in *Pueblos indígenas ante el derecho*, edited by V. Chenaut and M. T. Sierra. Mexico, D.F.: CIESAS.

Colloredo-Mansfeld, Rudi. 2002. "'Don't Be Lazy, Don't Lie, Don't Steal': Community Justice in the Neoliberal Andes." *American Ethnologist* 29:637–662.

Colloredo-Mansfeld, Rudi. 2009a. *Fighting Like a Community: Andean Civil Society in an Era of Indian Uprisings*. Chicago: University of Chicago Press.

Colloredo-Mansfeld, Rudi. 2009b. "The Power of Ecuador's Indigenous Communities in an Era of Cultural Pluralism." Pp. 86–106 in *Indigenous Peoples, Civil Society, and the Neo-liberal State in Latin America*, edited by E. F. Fischer. New York: Berghahn Books.

Colson, Elizabeth. 1995. "The Contentiousness of Disputes." Pp. 65–82 in *Understanding Disputes: The Politics of Argument*, edited by P. Caplan. Oxford: Berg Publishers.

Colvin, Jean G. 2004. *Arte de Tigua: A Reflection of Indigenous Culture in Ecuador*. Quito: Abya-Yala.

Comaroff, Jean and John Comaroff. 2012. "Introduction to *Of Revelation and Revolution*." Pp. 308–321 in *Anthropology in Theory: Issues in Epistemology*, edited by H. L. Moore and T. Sanders. Malden, MA: Blackwell Publishing.

Comaroff, John Lionel and Simon Roberts. 1981. *Rules and Processes: The Cultural Logic of Dispute in an African Context*. Chicago: University of Chicago Press.

Conaghan, Catherine M. 2008. "Ecuador: Correa's Plebiscitary Presidency." *Journal of Democracy* 19:46–60.

Cóndor Chuquiruna, Eddie. 2009. *Estado de la reación entre justicia indígena y justicia estatal en los países andinos: Estudio de casos en Colombia, Perú, Ecuador y Bolivia.* Lima: Comisión Andina de Juristas.

Correa, Rafael. 2011. "Decreto 872: 'Declararse el estado de excepción en la Función Judicial'." R.O. No. 531. September 19.

Cowan, Jane K. 2006. "Culture and Rights after Culture and Rights." *American Anthropologist* 108:9–24.

Crain, Mary. 1990. "The Social Construction of National Identity in Highland Ecuador." *Anthropological Quarterly* 63:43–59.

de Benoist, Alain. 1999. "What is Sovereignty?" (Translated by Julia Kostova from "Qu'est-ce que la souveraineté?" in Elements 96:24–35.) Available at: https://neweuropeanconservative.files.wordpress.com/2012/11/what-is-sovereignty.pdf (accessed May 3, 2016).

de la Cadena, Marisol. 2000. *Indigenous Mestizos: The Politics of Race and Culture in Cuzco, Peru, 1919–1991.* Durham, NC: Duke University Press.

de la Peña, Guillermo. 2002. "Costumbre, ley y procesos judiciales en la antropología clásica: apuntes introductorios." Pp. 51–68 in *Antropologia juridica: Perspectivas socioculturales en el estudio del derecho,* edited by E. Krotz. Mexico: Anthropos.

de Sousa Santos, Boaventura. 1987. "Law: A Map of Misreading. Toward a Postmodern Conception of Law." *Journal of Law and Society* 14:279–302.

de Sousa Santos, Boaventura. 2002. *Toward a New Legal Common Sense: Law, Globalization, and Emancipation.* London: Butterworths.

de Zaldívar, Víctor Bretón Solo. 2012. *Toacazo: En los Andes equinocciales tras la Reforma Agraria.* Quito: FLACSO/Abya-Yala.

Dembour, Marie-Bénédicte. 2001. "Following the Movement of a Pendulum: Between Universalism and relativism." Pp. 56–79 in *Culture and Rights: Anthropological Perspectives,* edited by J. K. Cowan, M.-B. Dembour, and R. A. Wilson. Cambridge: Cambridge University Press.

DeWalt, Kathleen M. and Billie R. DeWalt. 2002. *Participant Observation: A Guide for Fieldworkers.* Lanham, MD: Rowman & Littlefield Publishers.

Díaz-Polanco, Héctor. 2009. *La diversidad cultura y la autonomía.* Mexico: Nostra Ediciones.

Douglas, Mary. 1975. "Deciphering a Meal." Pp. 249–275 in *Implicit Meanings: Essays in Anthropology,* edited by M. Douglas. London: Routledge & Kegan Paul.

Douglas, Mary. 1987. "A Distinctive Anthropological Perspective." Pp. 3–15 in *Constructive Drinking: Perspectives on Drink from Anthropology,* edited by M. Douglas. Cambridge: Cambridge University Press.

El Comercio. 2002a. "La Cocha quiere aumentar el castigo en caso de muerte." *El Comercio.* May 10.

El Comercio. 2002b. "No hay confianza en la ley." *El Comercio.* May 10.

El Comercio. 2007. "Hoy Correa, Chávez y Evo en el Cotopaxi." *El Comercio.* January 14.

El Comercio. 2009. "Correa lamenta la muerte de un indígena y llama al diálogo." *El Comercio.*

El Comercio. 2010a. "3,497 policías irán a sus lugares de origen." *El Comercio.* November 11.

El Comercio. 2010b. "Ajusticiados de La Cocha se entregaron a justicia ordinaria." *El Comercio.* May 28.

El Comercio. 2010c. "El 41% de policías, inconforme con los pases." *El Comercio*. October 11.
El Comercio. 2010d. "El domingo se definirá la suerte de Orlando Q." *El Comercio*. May 21.
El Comercio. 2010e. "Fiscal Pesántez no pudo entrar ayer a La Cocha." *El Comercio*. May 20.
El Comercio. 2010f. "La Cocha juzgaría hoy a Orlando Q." *El Comercio*. May 23.
El Comercio. 2010g. "La comuna La Cocha ratificó aplicar la pena de muerte a un joven." *El Comercio*. May 19.
El Comercio. 2010h. "La Constitución es clara respecto a la justicia indígena, según el ministro Jalkh." *El Comercio*. May 5.
El Comercio. 2010i. "La Juntas generan más críticas." *El Comercio*. August 17.
El Comercio. 2010j. "Las Juntas Campesinas demandarán a la Cedhu." *El Comercio*. August 19.
El Comercio. 2010k. "'Las Juntas del Campesinado no son legales' (entrevista Raúl Ilaquiche)." *El Comercio*. August 17.
El Comercio. 2010l. "Orlando Q. ne será procesado por la justicia común." *El Comercio*. May 24.
El Comercio. 2010m. "Tibán renunció tras avalar juicios por 43 muertes indígenas en Cotopaxi." *El Comercio*. May 26.
El Comercio. 2010n. "Un accidente fatal en la vía a Zumbahua." *El Comercio*. August 18.
El Comercio. 2010o. "Vicente Tibán quedó fuera de la Fiscalía." *El Comercio*. May 25.
El Comercio. 2010p. "Protestas indígenas contra la Justicia." *El Comercio*. June 26.
El Comercio. 2010q. "La Corte Constitucional todavía no decide sobre el caso La Cocha." *El Comercio*. August 26.
El Vistazo. 2010. "Correa: Justicia Indígena es un monstruosidad." *El Vistazo*. May 26.
En Marcha. 2010. "La justicia indígena no es una ficción." *En Marcha*May 28–June 3, p. 3.
Eriksen, Thomas Hylland. 2002. *Ethnicity and Nationalism: Anthropological Perspectives (Second Edition)*. London: Pluto Press.
Fawcett, J.J. and J.M. Carruthers. 2008. *Cheshire, North & Fawcett: Private International Law (Fourteenth Edition)*. Oxford: Oxford University Press.
Felstiner, William L.F., Richard L. Abel, and Austin Sarat. 1980–81. "The Emergence and Transformation of Disputes: Naming, Blaming, Claiming …" *Law & Society Review* 15:631–654.
Fish, Stanley. 1997. "Boutique Multiculturalism, or Why Liberals are Incapable of Thinking about Hate Speech." *Critical Inquiry* 23:378–395.
FLACSO. 2006. *Ecuador: Las cifras de la migración internacional*. Quito: FLACSO.
Flores, Daniela. 2011. "La justicia indígena y sus conflictos con el derecho ordinario." INREDH, August 3. Available at: http://inredh.org/index.php?view=article&catid=74:inredh&id=422:la-justicia-indigena-y-sus-conflictos-con-el-derecho-ordinario&option=com_content&Itemid=29 (accessed May 3, 2016).
García, Fernando. 2002. *Formas indígenas de administrar justicia*. Quito: FLACSO.
García, Fernando. 2004. "Estado de la cuestión de la antropología jurídica en Ecuador." In *Constitución y pluralismo jurídico*, edited by F. F. Giménez. Quito: Corporación Editora Nacional.
García, Fernando. 2005. "El Estado del Arte del Derecho Indígena en Ecuador." *Revista IIDH* 41:151–170.
García, Fernando. 2008a. *Identidades, etnicidad y racismo en América Latina*. Quito: FLACSO.

García, Fernando. 2008b. "Los retos del pluralismo juridico." *Íconos* 31:11–13.
García, Fernando. 2009a. "Estado del relacionamiento en Ecuador." Pp. 105–170 in *Estado de la reación entre justicia ind'gena y justicia estatal en los países andinos: Estudio de casos en Colombia, Perú, Ecuador y Bolivia*, edited by E. Cóndor Chuquiruna. Lima: Comisión Andina de Juristas.
García, Fernando. 2009b. "La jurisdicción indígena: del monismo jurídico a la interlegalidad." Pp. 479–498 in *La transformación de la Justicia*, vol. 7, edited by S. Andrade and L. F. Ávila. Quito: Ministerio de Justicia y Derechos Humanos.
García, Fernando. 2010a. "El proceso de coordinación y cooperación entre los sistemas de derecho indígena y el sistema de derecho ordinario ecuatorianos." In VII Congreso Internacional, RELAJU. Lima, Peru.
García, Fernando. 2010b. "Retos de la diversidad: el reconocimiento y aplicación de los sistemas de derecho indígenas ecuatorianos." *Íconos* 38:9–16.
García, Fernando, Gina Chavéz, María Moreno, and Mariana Marín. 2005. *Cuaderno de Derecho Indígena: El sistema de derecho de los pueblos Kichwas de la Sierra del Ecuador*. Quito: FLACSO.
García, Fernando and Mares Sandoval. 2007. *Los pueblos indígenas del Ecuador: derechos y bienestar. Informe alternativo sobre el cumplimiento del Convenio 169 de la OIT*. Quito: FLACSO.
Geertz, Clifford. 1973. *The Interpretation of Cultures: Selected Essays*. New York: Basic Books.
Geertz, Clifford. 1983. *Local Knowledge: Further Essays in Interpretive Anthropology*. New York: Basic Books.
Gilissen, John. 1971a. "Introduction a l'etude comparee du pluralisme juridique." Pp. 7–17 in *Le pluralisme juridique*, edited by J. Gilissen. Bruxelles: Editions de l'Université de Bruxelles.
Gilissen, John. 1971b. *Le pluralisme juridique*. Bruxelles: Editions de l'Université de Bruxelles.
Giraudo, Laura. 2008. *Derechos, costumbres y jurisdicciones indigenas en la America Latina contemporanea*. Madrid: Centro de Estudios Politicos y Constitucionales.
Glebbeek, Marie-Louise. 2003. *In the Crossfire of Democracy: Police Reform and Police Practice in Post-civil War Guatemala*. Amsterdam: Rozenberg.
Gluckman, Max. 1955. *The Judicial Process Among the Barotse of Northern Rhodesia (Zambia)*. Manchester: Manchester University Press.
Goldstein, Daniel M. 2012. *Outlawed: Between Security and Rights in a Bolivian City*. Durham, NC: Duke University Press.
Goodale, Mark. 2009. *Dilemmas of Modernity: Bolivian Encounters with Law and Liberalism*. Stanford: Stanford University Press.
Griffiths, Anne. 2002. "Legal Pluralism." Pp. 289–310 in *An Introduction to Law and Social Theory*, edited by R. Banakar and M. Travers. Oxford: Hart Publishing.
Griffiths, John. 1986. "What is Legal Pluralism?" *Journal of Legal Pluralism* 24:1–55.
Guerrero, Andrés. 1989. "Curagas y tenientes politicos: La ley de la costumbre y la ley del estado (Otavalo 1830–1875)." *Revista Andina* 7:321–365.
Guerrero, Andrés. 1991. *La semántica de la dominación: el concertaje de indios*. Quito: Libri Mundi.
Guerrero, Andrés. 1997. "The Construction of a Ventriloquist's Image: Liberal Discourse and the 'Miserable Indian Race' in the Late 19th-Century Ecuador." *Journal of Latin American Studies* 29:555–590.

Guevara Gil, Armando. 2011. *El derecho y la gestión local de agua en Santa Rosa de Ocopa, Junín, Perú*. Lima: ARA editores.

Gulliver, P.H. 1997 [1969]. "Case Studies of Law in Non-Western Societies: Introduction." Pp. 11–23 in *Law in Culture and Society*, edited by L. Nader. Berkeley: University of California Press.

Gutmann, Amy. 1994. *Multiculturalism: Examining the Politics of Recognition*. Princeton: Princeton Universitu Press.

Hale, Charles R. 2002. "Does Multiculturalism Menace? Governance, Cultural Rights and the Politics of Identity in Guatemala." *Journal of Latin American Studies* 34:485–524.

Hale, Charles R. 2005. "Neoliberal Multiculturalism: The Remaking of Cultural Rights and Racial Dominance in Central America." *PoLAR: Political and Legal Anthropology Review* 28:10–28.

Handy, Jim. 2004. "Chicken Thieves, Witches, and Judges: Vigilante Justice and Customary Law in Guatemala." *Journal of Latin American Studies* 36:533–561.

Hansen, Thomas Blom and Finn Stepputat. 2001. "Introduction: States of Imagination." Pp. 1–38 in *States of Imagination: Ethnographic Explorations of the Postcolonial State*, edited by T. B. Hansen and F. Stepputat. Durham, NC: Duke University Press.

Hansen, Thomas Blom and Finn Stepputat. 2006. "Sovereignty Revisited." *Annual Review of Anthropology* 35:295–315.

Harper, Erica. 2011. *Working with Customary Justice Systems: Post-Conflict and Fragile States*. Rome: International Development Law Organization (IDLO).

Herrera, José Israel. 2011. *Unveiling the Face of Diversity: Interlegality and Legal Pluralism in the Mayan area of the Yucatan Peninsula*. Amsterdam: PhD dissertation.

Hess, Carmen G. 1990. "'Moving up – Moving down': Agro-Pastoral Land-Use Patterns in the Ecuadorian Paramos." *Mountain Research and Development* 10:333–342.

Hoekema, André J. 2003. "A New Beginning of Law Among Indigenous Peoples: Observations by a Legal Anthropologist." Pp. 181–220 in *The Law's Beginnings*, edited by F. J. M. Feldbrugge. Leiden: Martinus Nijhoff Publishers.

Hoekema, André J. 2004. *Rechtspluralisme en interlegaliteit*. Amsterdam: Vossiuspers UvA.

Hoekema, André J. 2005. "European Legal Encounters: Cases of Interlegality." *Journal of Legal Pluralism* 51:1–28.

Holleman, J. F. 1973. "Trouble-cases and Trouble-less cases in the Study of Customary Law and Legal Reform." *Law & Society Review* 7:585–609.

Hooker, Barry. 1975. *Legal Pluralism: An Introduction to Colonial and Neo-colonial Laws*. Oxford: Clarendon Press.

Hoy. 2007. "Indígenas tendrán su Fiscalía." in *Hoy.com.ec*. December 13.

Hoy. 2011. "Están libres cuatro involucrados en caso La Cocha." in *Hoy.com.ec*. May 14.

Ilaquiche, Raúl. 2001a. "Administración de Justicia Indígena en la Ciudad: Estudio de un caso." *Revista Yachaykuna* 1:104–121.

Ilaquiche, Raúl. 2001b. "Administración de justicia indígena: estudio de caso: 'Reclamo de competencia a favor de una autoridad indígena'." *Boletin ICCI-RIMAI* 3.

Ilaquiche, Raúl. 2001c. "Autonomia y Desarrollo de los Pueblos Indigenas." *Boletin ICCI-RIMAI* 3.

Ilaquiche, Raúl. 2004a. *La Administración de Justicia Indígena, su evolución y práctica actual*. FLACSO, Quito: Master's Thesis.

Ilaquiche, Raúl. 2004b. *Pluralismo jurídico y administración de justicia indígena en Ecuador: estudio de caso*. Ecuador: Fundación Hanns Seidel.

Jackson, Jeane E. 2002. "Caught in the Crossfire: Colombia's Indigenous Peoples during the 1990s." Pp. 107–133 in *The Politics of Ethnicity: Indigenous Peoples in Latin American States*, edited by D. Maybury-Lewis. Cambridge, MA: Harvard University Press.

Jackson, Jeane E. and Kay B. Warren. 2005. "Indigenous Movements in Latin America, 1992–2004: Controversies, Ironies, New Directions." *Annual Review of Anthropology* 34:549–573.

Jácome, César Enrique. 2009. *Monografía del Canton Pujilí*. Quito: Abya-Yala.

Jameson, Kenneth P. 2011. "The Indigenous Movement in Ecuador: The Struggle for a Plurinational State." *Latin American Perspectives* 38:63–73.

Jokisch, Brad and Jason Pribilsky. 2002. "The Panic to Leave: Economic Crisis and the 'New Emigration' from Ecuador." *International Migration* 40:75–101.

Just, Peter. 1992. "History, Power, Ideology, and Culture: Current Directions in the Anthropology of Law." *Law & Society Review* 26:373–412.

Kaltmeier, Olaf. 2007. "La Universidad terrateniente: Biopolítica, poder soberano y resistencia indígena-campesina en las haciendas de la Universidad Central en la provincial de Cotopaxi, 1930–1980." *Procesos Revista Ecuatoriana de Historia* 26:73–96.

Kennemore, Amy and Gregory Weeks. 2011. "Twenty-First Century Socialism? The Elusive Search for a Post-Neoliberal Development Model in Bolivia and Ecuador." *Bulletin of Latin American Research* 30:267–281.

Koenig, Matthias and Paul de Guchteneire. 2007. *Democracy and Human Rights in Multicultural Societies*. Aldershot, Hampshire: Ashgate.

Korovkin, Tanya. 2001. "Reinventing the Communal Tradition: Civil Society in Rural Ecuador." *Latin American Research Review* 36:37–67.

Kottak, Conrad Phillip. 2008. *Anthropology: The Exploration of Human Diversity – Twelfth Edition*. Boston, MA: McGraw-Hill.

Kritzer, Herbert M. 2011. "The Antecedents of Disputes: Complaining and Claiming." *Oñati Socio-Legal Series* 1(6). Available at: http://scholarship.law.umn.edu/cgi/viewcontent.cgi?article=1005&context=faculty_articles (accessed May 3, 2016).

Kyle, David. 2000. *Transnational Peasants: Migrants, Networks, and Ethnicity in Andean Ecuador*. Baltimore: The John Hopkins University Press.

Kymlicka, William. 1995. *Multicultural Citizenship: A Liberal Theory of Minority Rights*. Oxford: Clarendon Press.

La Gaceta. 2010a. "Lourdes Tibán niega tener vínculos con la CIA." *La Gaceta*. October 7.

La Gaceta. 2010b. "Pueden llevarme presa a mí, pero no a mi hermano." *La Gaceta*. October 28.

La Gaceta. 2010c. "Violencia en la Corte Provincial de Justicia de Cotopaxi." *La Gaceta*. September 25.

Lévi-Strauss, Claude. 1972. *The Savage Mind (La pensée sauvage)*. London: Weidenfeld and Nickolson.

Llasag Fernandéz, Raúl. 2009. "La jurisdicción indígena en el contexto de los principios de plurinacionalidad e interculturalidad." Pp. 179–209 in *La nueva Constitución del Ecuador: Estado, derechos e instituciones*, edited by S. Andrade, A. Grijalva, and C. Storini. Quito: Universidad Andina Simón Bolivar.

Lucero, José Antonio. 2003. "Locating the 'Indian Problem': Community, Nationality, and Contradiction in Ecuadorian Indigenous Politics." *Latin American Perspectives* 30:23–48.

Lucero, José Antonio. 2007. "Barricades and Articulations: Comparing Ecuadorian and Bolivian Indigenous Politics." Pp. 209–233 in *Highland Indians and the State in Modern Ecuador*, edited by A. K. Clark and M. Becker. Pittsburgh: Pittsburgh University Press.

Lund, Christian. 2008. *Local Politics and the Dynamics of Property in Africa.* Cambridge: Cambridge University Press.

Lyons, Barry J. 2001. "Religion, Authority, and Identity: Intergenerational Politics, Ethnic Resurgence, and Respect in Chimborazo, Ecuador." *Latin American Research Review* 36:7–48.

Malinowski, Bronislaw. 1985 [1926]. *Crime and Custom in Savage Society.* Totowa, NJ: Helix Books.

Manning, Peter Kirby. 1977. *Police Work: The Social Organization of Policing.* Cambridge, MA: MIT Press.

Martínez Novo, Carmen. 2004. "Los misioneros salesianos y el movimiento indígena de Cotopaxi, 1970–2004." *Ecuador Debate* 63:235–268.

Martínez Novo, Carmen. 2014. "Managing Diversity in Postneoliberal Ecuador." *The Journal of Latin American and Caribbean Anthropology* 19(1):103–125.

Merry, Sally Engle. 1988. "Legal pluralism." *Law & Society Review* 22:869–896.

Merry, Sally Engle. 1995. "Resistance and the Cultural Power of Law." *Law & Society Review* 29:11–26.

Merry, Sally Engle. 2002. "Ethnography in the Archives." Pp. 128–142 in *Ethnography in Law: New Dialogues, Enduring Methods*, edited by J. Starr and M. Goodale. New York: Palgrave MacMillan.

Merry, Sally Engle. 2006. "Transnational Human Rights and Local Activism: Mapping the Middle." *American Anthropologist* 108:38–51.

Migdal, Joel S. 1988. *Strong Societies and Weak States: State–Society Relations and State Capabilities in the Third World.* Princeton: Princeton University Press.

Mijeski, Kenneth J.andScott H.Beck 2011. *Pachakutik and the Rise and Decline of the Ecuadorian Indigenous Movement.* Athens: Ohio University Press.

Modood, Tariq. 2007. *Multiculturalism.* Cambridge: Polity Press.

Moore, Sally Falk. 1978. *Law as Process: an Anthropological Approach.* London: Rouledge & Kegan Paul.

Moore, Sally Falk. 2005. *Law and Anthropology: A Reader.* Malden, MA: Blackwell Publishers.

Nader, Laura. 1990. *Harmony Ideology: Justice and Control in a Zapotec Mountain Village.* Stanford: Stanford University Press.

Nader, Laura. 1997. *Law in Culture and Society (with a new Preface).* Berkeley: University of California Press.

Nader, Laura. 2002. *The Life of the Law: Anthropological Projects.* Berkeley: University of California Press.

Nader, Laura and Harry F.ToddJr. 1978. *The Disputing Process: Law in Ten Societies.* New York: Colombia University Press.

Naranjo, M. 1996. *La cultura popular en el Ecuador: Tomo II Cotopaxi.* Ecuador: Cidap.

Noroña Salcedo, Maria Belén. 2006. *Seizing the Lake: Tourism, Identity and Power of the Indigenous Peoples of Quilotoa, Ecuador.* University of Texas, Austin: MA thesis.

Ochoa García, Carlos. 2002. *Derecho Consuetudinario y Pluralismo Jurídico.* Guatemala: Cholsamaj.

Okin, Susan Mollier. 1999. *Is Multiculturalism Bad for Women?* Princeton: Princeton University Press.
Oomen, Barbara. 2005. *Chiefs in South Africa: Law, Power & Culture in the Post-Apartheid Era.* Oxford: James Currey.
Orellana Halkyer, René. 2004. *Interlegalidad y Campos Jurídicos: Discurso y derecho en la configuración de órdenes semiautónomos en comunidades quechuas de Bolivia.* Cochabamba, Bolivia: Huella Editores.
Ouweneel, Arij. 1993. "Het 'verhaal' van de boerensamenleving: Een commentaar." Pp. 389–416 in *Campesinos: Kleine boeren in Latijns-Amerika, vanaf 1520*, edited by A. Ouweneel. Amsterdam: Thela Publishers.
Ouweneel, Arij. 2012. "Us and Them: Researching Deep Roots of Andean Culture." Pp. 107–129 in *Andeans and Their Use of Cultural Resources: Space, Gender, Rights & Identity*, Cuadernos del CEDLA, vol. 25, edited by A. Ouweneel. Amsterdam: CEDLA.
Ouweneel, Arij and Rik Hoekstra. 1993. "Corporatief Indiaans grondgebied in vogelvlucht (Mexico, 1520–1920)." Pp. 97–137 in *Campesinos: kleine boeren in Latijns-Amerika vanaf 1520*, edited by A. Ouweneel. Amsterdam: Thela Publishers.
Pallares, Amalia. 2002. *From Peasant Struggles to Indian Resistance: The Ecuadorian Andes in the Late Twentieth Century.* Norman: University of Oklahoma Press.
Parekh, Bhikhu. 2000. *Rethinking Multiculturalism: Cultural Diversity and Political Theory.* Basingstoke: MacMillan.
Perafán Simmonds, Carlos César. 1995. *Sistemas Jurídicos Paez, Kogi, Wayúu y Tule.* Bogotá: Instituto Colombiano de Antropología-COLCULTURA.
Plan de Desarrollo. 2006. *Plan de Desarrollo Parroquial (Zumbahua-Pujilí-Cotopaxi).*
Platt, Tristan. 1982. *Estado boliviano y ayllu andino: Tierra y tributo en el norte de Potosí.* Lima: Instituto de Estudios Peruanos.
Pospisil, Leopold. 1958. *Kapauku Papuans and Their Law.* New Haven: Department of Anthropology, Yale University.
Postero, Nancy Grey. 2007. *Now We Are Citizens: Indigenous Politics in Post-multicultural Bolivia.* Stanford: Stanford University Press.
Poveda Moreno, Carlos. 2007. "Jurisdicción indígena: Reconocimiento de derechos, exigibilidad de obligaciones." *FORO Revista de Derecho* 8:179–189.
Poveda Moreno, Carlos. 2009. "Reflexiones básicas e ideas iniciales sobre el Proyecto de Ley Coordinación y Cooperación entre los Sistemas Jurídico Ordinario e Indígena." Pp. 473–501 in *Derechos Ancestrales: Justicia en Contextos Plurinacionales*, vol. 15, edited by C. Espinosa Gallegos-Anda and D. Caicedo Tapia. Quito: Ministerio de Justicia y Derechos Humanos.
Poveda Moreno, Carlos. 2010. "La Cocha: 2002–2010 retrocesos en un estado constitucional de derechos y justicia, social, democrático, soberano, independiente, unitario, intercultural, pluricultural y laico." *Novedades Jurídicas*, pp. 6–14.
Rabinow, Paul. 2007. *Reflections on Fieldwork in Morocco.* Berkeley: University of California Press.
Radcliffe, Sarah A. and Sallie Westwood. 1996. *Remaking the Nation: Place, Identity and Politics in Latin America.* London: Routledge.
Rawls, John. 1971. *A Theory of Justice.* Cambridge, MA: Harvard University Press.
Salgado Álvarez, Judith. 2002. *Justicia indígena: Aportes para un debate.* Quito: Abya-Yala.
Sánchez Botero, Esther. 2000. "The Tutela-system as a Means of Transforming the Relations Between the State and the Indigenous Peoples of Colombia." Pp. 223–241

in *The Challenge of Diversity: Indigenous Peoples and Reform of the State in Latin America*, edited by W. Assies, G. Van der Haar, and A. J. Hoekema. Amsterdam: Thela Thesis.

Sánchez-Parga, José. 2002. *Crisis en torno al Quilotoa: Mujer, cultura y comunidad.* Quito: Centro Andino de Acción Popular – CAAP.

Selverston-Scher, Melina H. 2001. *Ethnopolitics in Ecuador: Indigenous Rights and the Strengthening of Democracy.* Coral Gables, FL: North-South Center Press.

Serrano Pérez, Vladimir. 2002. *El Derecho Indígena.* Quito: Abya-Yala.

Shahar, Ido. 2013. "Forum Shopping Between Civil and Shari'a Courts: Maintenance Suits in Contemporary Jerusalem." Pp. 147–164 in *Religion in Disputes*, edited by F. Von Benda-Beckmann, K. Von Benda-Beckmann, M. Ramstedt, and B. Turner. London: Ashgate.

Sieder, Rachel. 1997. *Customary Law and Democratic Transition in Guatemala.* London: Institute of Latin American Studies.

Sieder, Rachel. 1998. "Customary Law and Local Power in Guatemala." Pp. 97–115 in *Guatemala After the Peace Accords*, edited by R. Sieder. London: Institute of Latin American Studies.

Sieder, Rachel. 2001. "Rethinking Citizenship: Reforming the Law in Postwar Guatemala." Pp. 203–220 in *States of Imagination: Ethnographic Explorations of the Postcolonial State*, edited by T. B. Hansen and F. Stepputat. Durham, NC: Duke University Press.

Sieder, Rachel. 2002. *Multiculturalism in Latin America: Indigenous Rights, Diversity and Democracy.* Houndsmills, Basingstoke: Palgrave MacMillan.

Sieder, Rachel. 2011. "Contested Sovereignties: Indigenous Law, Violence and State Effects in Postwar Guatemala." *Critique of Anthropology* 31:161–184.

Sieder, Rachel and María Teresa Sierra. 2010. *Indigenous Women's Access to Justice in Latin America.* Bergen: Chr. Michelsen Institute (CMI).

Sierra, María Teresa. 1995a. "Articulaciones entre ley y costumbre: estrategias jurídicas de los Nahuas." Pp. 101–123 in *Pueblos Indígenas ante el derecho*, edited by V. Chenaut and M. T. Sierra. México: Centro de Investigaciones y Estudios Superiores en Antropología Social, CIESAS.

Sierra, María Teresa. 1995b. "Indian Rights and Customary Law in Mexico: A Study of the Nahuas in the Sierra de Puebla." *Law & Society Review* 29:227–254.

Sierra, María Teresa. 2004. "Introducción: Hacia una interpretación comprensiva de la relación entre justicia, derecho y género: los procesos interlegales en regiones indígenas." Pp. 11–56 in *Haciendo Justicia: Interlegalidad, derecho y género en regions indígenas*, edited by M. T. Sierra. Mexico: Centro de Investigación y Estudios Superiores en Antropología Social, CIESAS.

Sierra, María Teresa and Victoria Chenaut. 2002. "Los debates recientes y actuales en la antropología jurídica: las corrientes anglosajonas." Pp. 113–170 in *Antropología jurídica: perspectivas socioculturales en el estudio del derecho*, edited by E. Krotz. Mexico: Anthropos.

Simon Thomas, Marc. 2007. "Elite onder de loep: balanceren tussen algemeen en eigen belang." *MensenStreken* 8:21–24.

Simon Thomas, Marc. 2009. *Legal Pluralism and Interlegality in Ecuador: The La Cocha Murder Case*, Cuadernos del CEDLA, vol. 24. Amsterdam: CEDLA.

Simon Thomas, Marc. 2012. "Legal Pluralism and the Continuing Quest for Legal Certainty in Ecuador: A Case Study from the Ecuadorian Andes." *Oñati Socio-Legal Series* 2(7). Available at: SSRN: http://ssrn.com/abstract=2009450 (accessed May 3, 2016).

Simon Thomas, Marc. 2013. *The Challenge of Legal Pluralism: Local Dispute Settlement and the Indian–State Relationship in Ecuador*. Amsterdam: PhD dissertation.
Simon Thomas, Marc. 2015. "Lokale rechtspraak in de hooglanden van Ecuador. Een bijzonder mooi voorbeeld van inclusieve mediation." *Nederlands-Vlaamd tijdschrift voor mediation en conflictmanegement* 4.
Skocpol, Theda. 1985. "Bringing the State Back in: Strategies of Analysis in Current Research." Pp. 3–43 in *Bringing the State Back In*, edited by P. B. Evans, D. Rüschemeyer, and T. Skocpol. Cambridge: Cambridge University Press.
Snyder, Francis G. 1981. "Anthropology, Dispute Processes and Law: A Critical Introduction." *British Journal of Law and Society* 8:141–180.
Spiertz, H.L.J. 1986. "Vreemde gasten: een casus uit Bali." Pp. 111–132 in *Recht in ontwikkeling: Tien agrarisch-rechterlijke opstellen*, edited by W. Brussaard. Deventer, Netherlands: Kluwer.
Spiertz, H. 1991. "The Transformation of Traditional Law: A Tale of People's Participation in Irrigation Management on Bali." *Landscape and Urban Planning* 20:189–196.
Starr, June and Jane Collier. 1989. *History and Power in the Study of Law: New Directions in Legal Anthropology*. Ithaca: Cornell University Press.
Starr, June and Mark Goodale. 2002. *Practicing Ethnography in Law: New Dialogues, Enduring Methods*. New York: Palgrave MacMillan.
Stavenhagen, Rodolfo. 2002. "Indigenous Peoples and the State in Latin America." Pp. 24–44 in *Multiculturalism in Latin America: Indigenous Rights, Diversity and Democracy*, edited by R. Sieder. Basingstoke: Palgrave Macmillan.
Stern, Steve J. 1982. *Peru's Indian Peoples and the Challenge of Spanish Conquest: Huamanga to 1640*. Madison: University of Wisconsin Press.
Stikwerda, L. 2012. *Inleiding tot het Nederlands international privaatrecht*. Deventer, Netherlands: Kluwer.
Striffler, Steve. 2002. *In the Shadows of State and Capital: The United Fruit Company, Popular Struggle, and Agrarian Restructuring in Ecuador, 1900–1995*. Durham, NC: Duke University Press.
Tamanaha, Brian Z. 1993. "The Folly of the Social Scientific Concept of Legal Pluralism." *Journal of Law and Society* 20:192–212.
Tamanaha, Brian Z. 2008. "Understanding Legal Pluralism: Past to Present, Local to Global." *Sydney Law Review* 30(3): 375–411.
Taussig, Michael. 1978. *Destrucción y resistencia campesina: El caso del Litoral Pacífico*. Bogota: Punta de Lanza.
Taylor, Charles. 1994. "The Politics of Recognition." Pp. 25–73 in *Multiculturalism: Examining the Politics of Recognition*, edited by A. Gutmann. Princeton: Princeton University Press.
Tenesaca, Pedro. 1995. "Testimonio del pueblo indígena de 'La Merced' (Chimborazo)." Pp. 273–306 in *Identidades Indias en el Ecuador Contemporáneo*, edited by J. A. Vinueza. Quito: Abya-Yala.
Tibán, Lourdes. 2001a. *Derechos colectivos de los pueblos indígenas del Ecuador: Aplicabilidad, alcances y limitaciones*. Quito: INDESIC.
Tibán, Lourdes. 2001b. "La ruptura del 'Ventriloquismo' y el establecimento de Normas propias de representacion: El caso del pueblo Kichwa de Cotopaxi." *Revista Yachaykuna* 1:38–55.
Tibán, Lourdes. 2003. *El sistema de representación y la participación política del pueblo Kichwa de Cotopaxi*. FLACSO, Quito: Master's thesis.

Tibán, Lourdes. 2007. *Legislación Indígena.* Quito: CODENPE.
Tibán, Lourdes. 2008. El derecho indígena y su relación con la justicia ordinaria. *ALAI.* Available at: http://www.alainet.org/es/active/26016 (accessed May 3, 2016).
Tibán, Lourdes. 2010. *Estado intercultural, plurinacional y derechos colectivos en el Ecuador.* Quito: Fundación Hanns Seidel.
Tibán, Lourdes and Fernando García. 2008. "De la oposición y el enfrentamiento al diálogo y las alianzas: La experiencia de la Conaie y el MICC en Ecuador." Pp. 271–304 in *Gobernar (en) la diversidad: experiencias indígenas desde América Latina. Hacia la investigacion de co-labor,* edited by X. Leyva, A. Burguete, and S. Speed. México: Centro de Investigaciones y Estudios Superiores en Antropoloia Social (CIESAS).
Tibán, Lourdes and Raúl Ilaquiche. 2004. *Manual de Administración de Justicia Indígena en el Ecador.* Quito: NINA Comunicaciones.
Tibán, Lourdes and Raúl Ilaquiche. 2008. *Jurisdicción Indígena en la Constitución Política del Ecuador.* Ecuador: Fundación Hanns Seidel.
Toaquiza, Sisa. 2009. *Florcita Andina.* CD, track 3.
Trujillo, Julio César, Agustín Grijalva, and Ximena Endara. 2001. *Justicia indígena en el Ecuador.* Quito: Universidad Andina Simón Bolivar.
Turner, Bryan S. 1993. *Citizenship and Social Theory.* London: SAGE Publications.
Ubink, Janine. 2008. *In the Land of the Chiefs: Customary Law, Land Conflicts and the Role of the State in Peri-Urban Ghana.* Leiden: Leiden University Press.
Umajinga, Baltazar. 1995. "Zumbahua." Pp. 247–271 in *Identidades Indias en el Ecuador Contemporáneo,* edited by J. A. Vinueza. Quito: Abya-Yala.
UN Women. 2011. *2011–2012 Progress of the World's Women: In Pursuit of Justice.* Available at: http://www.unwomen.org/~/media/headquarters/attachments/sections/library/publications/2011/progressoftheworldswomen-2011-en.pdf (accessed May 3, 2016).
El Universo. 2007. "Evo, Chávez y Correa en ceremonia indígena en Zumbahua." in *El Universo.* January 14.
El Universo. 2011a. "5 detenidos en caso La Cocha salen en libertad." in *El Universo.* May 13.
El Universo. 2011b. "AP dividió a Zumbahua en ceremonia indígena." in *El Universo.* April 24.
Valdivia, Franco Rocío and María Alejandra González Luna. 2009. *Las Mujeres en la justicia comunitaria: Víctimas, sujetos y actores.* Justicia Comunitaria en los Andes: Perú y Ecuador, vol. 3. Lima: Instituto de Defensa Legal.
Van Cott, Donna Lee. 2000. *The Friendly Liquidation of the Past: The Politics of Diversity in Latin America.* Pittsburgh: University of Pittsburgh Press.
Van Cott, Donna Lee. 2005. *From Movements to Parties in Latin America: The Evolution of Ethnic Politics.* New York: Cambridge University Press.
Van Cott, Donna Lee. 2008. *Radical Democracy in the Andes.* Cambridge: Cambridge University Press.
van de Sandt, Joris. 2007. *Behind the Mask of Recognition; Defending Autonomy and Communal Resource Management in Indigenous Resguardos, Colombia.* Published in-house.
Vanderlinden, Jacques. 1971. "Le pluralisme juridique: essay de synthèse." Pp. 19–56 in *Le pluralisme juridique,* edited by J. Gilissen. Bruxelles: Editions de l'Université de Bruxelles.
Vertovec, Steven. 2001. "Transnational Challenges to the 'New' Multiculturalism." Available at: http://www.transcomm.ox.ac.uk/working%20papers/WPTC-2K-06%20Vertovec.pdf (accessed May 3, 2016).

Vintimilla, Jaime. 2003. "Ausencia del Estado, violencia, derecho y justicia comunitaria: El caso de las Juntas Campesinas." Pp. 62–70 in *Los Métodos Alternativos de Manejo de Conflictos y la Justicia Comunitaria*, edited by J. Vintimilla and S. Andrade. Quito: CIDES.
Vintimilla, Jaime, Milena Almeida, and Remigia Saldana. 2007. *Derecho indígena, conflicto y justicia comunitaria en comunidades Kichwas del Ecuador*, vol. 4. Lima: Instituto de Defensa Legal (IDL).
Vintimilla, Jaime and Santiago Andrade. 2003. *Los Métodos Alternativos de Manajo de Conflictos y la Justicia Comunitaria*. Quito: CIDES.
von Benda-Beckmann, Franz. 2002. "Who's Afraid of Legal Pluralism?" *Journal of Legal Pluralism* 47:37–82.
von Benda-Beckmann, Franz and Keebet von Benda-Beckmann. 2006. "The Dynamics of Change and Continuity in Plural Legal Orders." *Journal of Legal Pluralism* 53–54:1–44.
von Benda-Beckmann, Keebet. 1981. "Forum Shopping and Shopping Forums: Dispute Processing in a Minangkabau Village in West Sumatra." *Journal of Legal Pluralism* 19:117–159.
von Benda-Beckmann, Keebet. 2001. "Legal Pluralism." *Tai Culture International Review on Tai Cultural Studies* 6:18–39.
von Benda-Beckmann, Keebet. 2003. "The Environment of Disputes." Pp. 235–245 in *The Dynamics of Power and the Rule of Law: Essays on Africa and beyond*, edited by W. van Binsbergen. Leiden: Africa Studies Centre.
Waters, William F. 2007. "Indigenous Communities, Landlords, and the State: Land and Labor in Highland Ecuador, 1950–1975." Pp. 120–138 in *Highland Indians and the State in Modern Ecuador*, edited by A. K. Clark and M. Becker. Pittsburgh: University of Pittsburgh Press.
Weismantel, Mary J. 1988. *Food, Gender, and Poverty in the Ecuadorian Andes*. Philadelphia: University of Pennsylvania Press.
Weismantel, Mary J. 1991. "Maize Beer and Andean Social Transformations: Drunken Indians, Bread Babies, and Chosen Women." *MLN* 106:861–879.
Weismantel, Mary J. 1997. "White Cannibals: Fantasies of Racial Violence in the Andes." *Identities: Global Studies in Culture and Power* 4:9–43.
WhittenJr., Norman, E., Dorothea Scott Whitten, and Alfonso Chango. 1997. "Return of the Yumbo: The Indigenous Caminata From Amazonia to Andean Quito." *American Ethnologist* 24:355–391.
Wilson, Patrick C. 2008. "Neoliberalism, Indigeneity and Social Engineering in Ecuador's Amazon." *Critique of Anthropology* 28:127–144.
Wilson, Thomas M. 2005. "Drinking Cultures: Sites and Practices in the Production and Expression of Identity." Pp. 1–24 in *Drinking Cultures: Alcohol and Identity*, edited by T. M. Wilson. Oxford: Berg.
Wiltink, Nancy. 2005. *Achter de bergen: Een jaar met mijn gezin in Ecuador*. Amsterdam: Pimento.
Woodman, Gordon R. 1998. "Ideological Combat and Social Observation: Recent Debate About Legal Pluralism." *Journal of Legal Pluralism* 28:21–59.
Yashar, Deborah J. 2005. *Contesting Citizenship in Latin America: The Rise of Indigenous Movements and the Postliberal Challenge*. Cambridge: Cambridge University Press.
Yin, Robert. 2003. *Case Study Research: Design and Methods*. Thousand Oaks, CA: SAGE Publications.

Yrigoyen Fajardo, Raquel Z. 2000. "The Constitutional Recognition of Indigenous Law in Andean Countries." Pp. 83–96 in *The Challenge of Diversity: Indigenous Peoples and Reform of the State in Latin America*, edited by W. Assies, G. Van der Haar, and A. J. Hoekema. Amsterdam: Thela Thesis.

Yumbay, Mariana. 2007. "El ejercicio de la administración de justicia indígena en el Ecuador." Llacta! Available at: http://www.llacta.org/notic/2007/not0621b.htm (accessed May 3, 2016).

Index

Abrams, P. 34, 42
Abu-Lughod, L. 5, 224
aculturados/aculturacion 98–9, 104, 114
adultery 111, 118; *see also* Rosita vs Miguel case
agrarian reforms 37–8, 48, 51, 52–4, 56, 214; Zumbahua 83, 162
Alajo, Alex 197, 200
alcohol 78, 92–3, 94, 99–101, 104, 115, 117, 126
Alfaro, Eloy 51, 144
alimony 112, 129, 136, 182
Almeida, I. 39, 57, 230
ama killa (do not be lazy) 110, 119
ama lulla (do not lie) 110, 119
ama shua (do not steal) 110, 119
Anderson, B. 103
Andolina, R. 6, 55, 61
Andrade, S. 147
anti-forum shopping 31–3
apology, public 120, 122, 152–3, 157, 187, 191, 193, 196
art naïf see Tiguan art
asamblea general 54, 107, 118–24, 134, 220; La Cocha murder case (2002) 186–7; La Cocha-Guantópolo murder case (2010) 191–4, 195–6, 210, 222
Assies, W. 5, 6, 7, 22, 37, 38, 40, 41, 42, 43, 50, 55, 62, 63, 73, 135, 155, 224, 227, 230
assimilationist model 50, 214
authorities 138–9, 221–4; local *see separate entry*; provincial *see separate entry*; whom to turn to 134–8, 215
autonomy 3, 29, 37, 41, 43, 52, 53, 54, 56–7, 144, 208, 217, 225, 226; CONAIE 55; Constitution of 1998 61, 62; Correa 66

baptism 75, 78, 99–100
Baud, M. 6, 35, 37, 49, 50, 51, 54, 59, 60, 142, 144, 145, 225, 227
Bavinck, M. 219
Becker, M. 6, 7, 18, 52, 53, 56, 60, 66, 79, 82, 83, 103, 106, 119, 144, 145, 162, 165, 209
Beltrán, Bolívar 200
Benhabib, S. 39, 41, 230
Berk-Seligson, S. 64, 72, 110, 118, 119, 120, 121, 123, 131, 132, 135, 136, 137, 144, 148, 183, 208
Bernard, H.R. 10, 11, 14, 15
bias 1–2, 42, 137, 181–3, 193, 206–7
Biezeveld, R. 32, 33
Boeije, H. 13
Bohannan, P. 25
Bolívar, Simon 50
Bolivia 6, 50, 225
Bonaldi, F. 77, 99, 163, 164, 165
Brandt, H.-J. 13, 22, 32, 107, 110, 111, 112, 113, 114, 115, 116, 117, 118, 119, 121, 122, 123–4, 148, 155
bricolage 30
Brysk, A. 6, 55

cabildo 19, 22, 54, 86, 118–24, 133, 134, 138, 213, 220, 227; *comunas* 48, 52, 85; family disputes 107, 118; historical overview 49; impartiality 181–3, 193, 206–7; La Cocha murder case (2002) 186, 191, 220–1, 223; La Cocha-Guantópolo murder case (2010) 190–6, 197–8, 199, 200, 202, 205, 206–7, 210, 211, 217, 220–1, 222, 223; land disputes 129; mediator 228–9; police 126; requirements for service as 119; social norms 116; *teniente político* 145, 150, 153, 154, 158, 228–9; Tigua

162; Toaquiza vs the community 167, 168, 170, 181, 182–3, 205, 217, 223; violent crime: medical bills 115
campesinos or small-scale agriculturalists 9, 85, 96
Canessa, A. 9
canton of Pujilí 81, 82, 84–5, 101
Caplan, P. 108
Caselli, I. 69, 209
Catholic Church 50–1, 53, 54, 55, 73, 77–8, 84, 99, 143
centralization 55, 225; *see also* decentralization
Cervone, E. 9, 31, 43, 50, 94, 99, 100, 119, 142, 144, 147, 148, 225
Chatterjee, P. 20, 35, 36, 37, 38, 42, 43, 45, 141, 142, 143, 158, 213, 216, 227, 228, 229, 231
Chaves, M. 9
Chávez, G. 22, 64, 120, 131, 135, 137
Chávez, Hugo 83
citizenship: real and formal 35–6, 37
Civil Court in Pujilí 127–9, 134, 136, 156; duration of cases 129; land disputes 114–15; sexual violence 107, 112
civil law/cases 117, 119–20, 124, 134, 148, 153, 218
Clark, A.K. 33, 34, 43, 51, 52, 82, 230
class 5, 6, 56
cohesion and conflict in Zumbahua 79, 94, 101, 102–5, 214–15
coincidence of conflicts 116–17
collective rights: individual rights vs 38, 40–2, 43–4, 45–6, 230; Toaquiza vs the community 172
collectivity 110, 116, 119, 156
Collier, J. 25, 26, 29, 217, 218
Colloredo-Mansfeld, R. 9, 18, 36, 43, 79, 98, 102, 103, 110, 162, 163, 164, 165–6
colonialism 49–50, 81, 102, 161–2, 212
Colson, E. 109
Colvin, J.G. 58, 76, 99, 110–11, 161, 162, 163, 164, 165, 166, 167, 168
Comaroff, J. 5, 219, 224
Comaroff, J.L. 25, 26, 108
compensation 16, 22, 23, 120, 122, 135, 156, 157, 168; La Cocha murder case (2002) 186
comuna structure 48, 52–3, 54, 83, 85, 89–90, 102, 138, 145, 186
Conaghan, C.M. 66, 200
CONAIE 6, 9, 55–61, 65, 84, 138–9, 162, 206, 214, 223, 225, 229; essentialist strategy 226; founded 57; harmonization project 63; La Cocha-Guantópolo murder case (2010) 192, 193, 201, 204, 207–8, 211, 217, 223
Cóndor Chuquiruna, E. 136
conflict and cohesion in Zumbahua 79, 94, 101, 102–5, 214–15
conflict and conflict resolution in Zumbahua 106–7, 110–17; authorities *see separate entry*; coincidence of conflicts 116–17; disputes, understanding 107–9; family affairs 110–11, 117; property 113–15; sexual violence 111–13; social norms 116; violent crime 115; *see also* La Cocha murder case (2002); La Cocha-Guantópolo murder case (2010); Rosita vs Miguel case; Toaquiza vs the community
Constitution (1998) 4, 47, 54–5, 61–2, 73–4, 104, 203, 212, 221; compared with 2008 Constitution 67–9; CONAIE 58–9; cultural diversity 5, 59, 61, 64, 225; customary law, recognition of 61, 183–4; formal legal pluralism 6, 48, 59, 73, 104–5, 139, 184, 214; internal conflicts 19, 61, 104, 172–3, 177, 178, 184, 186, 188–9, 202, 216; Junta Parroquiale or parish board 85; lack of coordinating rules 62, 63–4; language 172; Toaquiza vs the community 171, 172–3, 177, 178, 183–4, 216; traditional social organization 172
Constitution (2008) 7, 48, 65–7, 71, 73–4, 104, 150, 221, 226; collective rights 66, 67; compared with 1998 Constitution 67–9; death penalty 194; formal legal pluralism 66, 73, 104–5, 139, 210, 222; internal conflicts 19, 69, 182, 202; Junta Parroquiale or parish board 86; La Cocha-Guantópolo murder case 192, 193, 198, 200, 203, 205, 208, 211, 222; meaning of 'indigenous person' 69; multinationalism 59, 66; territory where indigenous authorities are to hold jurisdiction 69
Constitutional Court 69, 72, 156; La Cocha-Guantópolo murder case 198, 199–202, 204, 207, 211, 217, 220, 222
coordinating rules 6–7, 43–4, 45–6, 48, 62, 63–4, 73, 104, 134, 139, 214, 222, 226, 231; lawyers: effort to develop 204; legal void: formal legal pluralism

and lack of 183–4, 186, 210; proposed Law of Coordination and Cooperation between Customary Law and National Law 69–73, 214, 226; Toaquiza vs the community 171, 177, 183–4
Córdova, Gonzalo 51
Correa, Rafael 7, 59–60, 65–6, 69, 70, 74, 83–4, 88, 95, 97, 129, 195, 196, 199–200, 204, 205, 209, 217, 225, 229
corruption 137, 144, 206
costs: legal representation 129; living 95; medical 117, 120, 122, 133, 141, 150, 151, 152; Toaquiza vs the community 179
Cotopaxi, province of 57, 82, 84–5; poverty 95; transnational migration 98
counter-hegemonic use of customary law 3, 29, 33, 217–20, 221, 223, 224
Court of Appeals 177–8, 180
Court of Justice of Cotopaxi 188–90, 202–3
Court of Justice in Latacunga 11, 84, 107, 126, 130–2, 133, 134, 136, 153–4, 156, 166–7; La Cocha-Guantópolo murder case 196–9, 200, 203–4, 207, 211, 217, 222, 223; shopping forums 223; Toaquiza vs the community 159, 160, 167–84, 216, 223
courts 135, 229; Civil Court in Pujilí *see separate entry*; Constitutional Court 69, 72, 156, 198, 199–202, 204, 207, 211, 217, 220, 222; Court of Appeals 177–8, 180; Court of Justice of Cotopaxi 188–90, 202–3; Court of Justice in Latacunga *see separate entry*; length of court sessions 131; National Court of Justice 178–80, 181, 184; written evidence 171, 177, 180, 181, 216
Cowan, J.K. 38, 230
Crain, M. 50, 51
criminal law/cases *see* penal law/cases
cultural relativism 21, 41, 42, 46, 226
curacas 49, 50, 83, 143, 145
customary law 1–2, 20, 21–4, 45, 54, 110, 142, 159; characteristics of 22–3, 155, 179, 193; civil and criminal law 134; Constitution: internal conflicts 19, 61, 69, 104, 172–3, 177, 178, 182, 184, 186, 188–9, 192, 202, 216; counter-hegemonic use of 3, 29, 33, 217–20, 221, 223, 224; favorable–unfavorable bias toward 135–6, 137, 219; harmony 120, 151, 153, 156, 157, 187, 202;

indigenous 21–2, 39; murder 201–3, 209, 221–2; mutual influence: national law and 220, 226, 231; not subordinate to national law 179; police 126–7; power differences 41–2, 136; procedures 120–1, 141, 150–2, 155–6, 176, 193; reasons for choice of national law or 134–8, 181–3; studying 24–7, 45; *teniente político* 153, 155–6, 157, 158, 216, 220; understanding disputes 107–9; *see also* coordinating rules

de Benoist, A. 44, 227
de facto legal pluralism 6, 47–8, 61, 73, 214, 225, 229; colonial period 49, 212; 'long nineteenth century' 50–1, 143
de la Cadena, M. 9
de la Peña, G. 24
de Sousa Santos, B. 4, 16, 21, 29–30, 31, 33, 45, 138, 157, 212, 213, 215, 218
de Zaldívar, V.B.S. 53, 60, 82, 84, 85
death penalty 194–5
decentralization 21, 28, 36–7, 43–4, 46, 48, 55, 74, 225, 226, 227, 230
Dembour, M.-B. 38
democratization 37, 43, 55
Depression (late 1920s and 1930s) 52
DeWalt, K.M. 8, 10, 13, 14, 15, 17
Díaz-Polanco, H. 73
dirigentes 15, 16, 112, 116, 119, 121, 127, 133; La Cocha-Guantópolo murder case 193, 197, 198; national law 141; patrol work 125; politics 206; punishment 124; re-education of offenders 120; Rosita vs Miguel case 1–2, 141, 150–1, 152, 156, 157, 183; social pressure 135
discourse shopping 32
discrimination 24, 225; *see also* bias
divorce 129, 136
DNA tests 112–13, 129
domestic violence 100, 110–11, 148
double jeopardy rule 68, 109, 177, 188, 200
Douglas, M. 94, 100, 101
drinking 78, 92–3, 94, 99–101, 104, 115, 117, 126
due process 68, 193, 195, 198, 203
Durkheim, E. 24

equality/inequality 39, 54, 56, 58, 82, 95; unequal division of land among former hacienda workers 83, 102
Eriksen, T.H. 41

essentialism 39, 41, 226
ethics 17–18
experts 68, 131, 134, 201, 220
expulsion from community 122, 124, 187, 191, 193

family as an authority 117–18
family disputes 110–11, 118, 126, 189; *cabildos* 107, 118; Civil Court in Pujilí 129; coincidence of conflicts 117; nuclear and extended family 118; Rosita vs Miguel case *see separate entry*; *tenientes políticos* 107, 140–1, 148, 149–57
Fawcett, J.J. 32
FEI (Federación Ecuatoriana de Indios) 56, 165
FEINE (Consejo de Pueblos y Organizaciones Indígenas Evangélicas del Ecuador) 60
Felstiner, W.L.F. 108, 139, 154, 155, 156, 181, 198
FENOC (Federación Nacional de Organizaciones Campesinas) 56
FENOCIN (Confederación Nacional de Organizaciones Campesinas Indígenas y Negras) 60
fiestas: and drinking 92–3, 94, 99–101, 104, 126; police 125, 126; Zumbahua 75–9, 92–4, 98, 99–101, 102–3, 104, 125, 193
fines 121–2, 137, 152, 187, 191, 193, 196
Fiscal General del Estado 194–5, 196, 197, 210, 217
Fiscalía 11, 12, 84, 130, 132, 156, 228; La Cocha murder case (2002) 187–8, 189
Fiscalía Indígena 11, 12, 84, 115, 126, 130, 132–4, 138, 182, 228; free service 133; La Cocha-Guantópolo murder case (2010) 190, 192, 193, 194, 195, 197, 206, 210; medical bills 133, 152; MICC 207
Fisch, Olga 163
Fish, S. 42
FLACSO (Facultad Latinoamericana de Ciencias Sociales (Sede Ecuador)) 64, 97–8
floggings 123, 187, 193, 196, 221–2
Flores, D. 205
forum shopping 31–3, 109, 135–8, 176, 183, 216, 217–18, 220–1, 223
Foucault, M. 34

Galeria de Artes y Artesanias de Tigua 160, 164–5
García, F. 22, 62, 63, 64, 69, 70, 107, 110, 112, 113, 115, 116, 118, 135, 136, 137, 144, 156, 187, 190, 198
Geertz, C. 10, 23
gender 15, 23–4, 41, 94, 101, 110, 124, 148
Gilissen, J. 27, 28
Giraudo, L. 22
Glebbeek, M.-L. 126
Gluckman, M. 25
godparents 76, 78, 118, 155
Goldstein, D.M. 9, 30, 31
Goodale, M. 2, 22, 29, 31, 158, 212, 214, 218, 225
gossip 116, 219
Gramsci, A. 34
Great Depression 52
Griffiths, A. 4, 25, 28
Griffiths, J. 2, 28, 47, 227
Guerrero, A. 50, 99, 142, 143–4, 145, 227
Guevara Gil, A. 22
Gulliver, P.H. 25
Gutiérrez, Lucio 59, 65, 199
Gutmann, A. 39

hacienda system 8–9, 37, 48, 50–1, 52–3, 54, 56, 73, 143–4, 145; Tigua community 162, 165; Zumbahua 53, 79, 81–3, 96, 102, 103–4, 138, 145, 162, 165
Hale, C.R. 7, 225, 227
Handy, J. 23
Hansen, T.B. 33, 34, 35, 42, 43, 44, 213–14, 229
harmony 120, 151, 153, 156, 157, 179, 187, 202
Herrera, Edwin Palma 127
Herrera, J.I. 22, 31
Hess, C.G. 91, 92
historical overview 44, 47–50, 73–4; colonialism 49–50, 81, 102, 161–2, 212; CONAIE 57–9; emergence of indigenous movements 55–7; 'long nineteenth century' 50–2, 142–5, 227; *tenientes políticos* 50–1, 52, 53, 54, 73, 142–6; Tigua 161–2, 165; twentieth century land reforms 52–4; Zumbahua 81–4
Hoebel, E.A. 25, 26, 107
Hoekema, A.J. 4, 21, 28, 29, 30, 31, 33, 47, 63, 73, 155, 183, 220
Holleman, J.F. 26

homicide 110, 209, 229; murder *see separate entry*
Hooker, B. 28
huasipungo system 53, 81, 83, 102, 104, 162, 165
human rights 6, 40–2, 55, 62, 64, 110, 126, 189, 193, 194–5, 203

idiom shopping 32
Ilaquiche, Raúl 22, 57, 58, 107, 110, 118, 119, 162, 171, 187, 188, 189, 197, 200, 201, 204, 206, 208, 223
incomes 95, 96, 103; remittances 97
Indian–state relations 36–8, 45, 213, 225, 227–31
indigenous rights 5, 7, 38, 66, 104; CONAIE 6, 9, 55–61; human rights 6, 55, 62; ILO Convention No. 169 6, 55, 62, 64, 71; *indigenismo* 51; Ley de Comunidades (1937) 52, 56; twentieth century land reforms 52–4
individual rights vs collective rights 38, 40–2, 43–4, 45–6, 230
inequality/equality 39, 54, 56, 58, 82, 95; unequal division of land among former hacienda workers 83, 102
integrationist political model 51, 54, 214
Inter-American Court of Human Rights 72
interlegality 4, 16, 29–31, 45, 46, 104, 138, 212, 213, 215, 218–21, 224, 231; at *teniente político*'s office 140–58; colonial period 50; 'long nineteenth century' 51; Rosita vs Miguel case 140–1, 157–8, 215–16
International Labour Organization (ILO): Indigenous and Tribal Peoples Convention 1989 (No. 169) 6, 55, 62, 64, 171, 172, 178, 188, 189, 200
International Monetary Fund (IMF) 43, 65

Jackson, J.E. 9, 24, 30, 103, 109, 136, 141, 166
Jácome, C.E. 80, 81, 82, 83, 84, 85, 98, 162
Jalkh, Gustavo 209
Jameson, K.P. 65
Jokisch, B. 97
Juntas Parroquiales or parish boards 85–6, 87, 116, 125, 126, 127, 138, 191, 192, 194; politics 205–6; *teniente político* and 147–8, 158, 205, 228

jurisdiction 69, 72, 107, 134, 138, 154, 211, 215, 217, 218, 221, 222, 226; *cabildos* 229; Toaquiza vs the community 177, 178, 179, 182, 183–4, 205
Just, P. 26

Kaltmeier, O. 145
Kelsen, H. 21
Kennemore, A. 66
Kichwa language 59, 77, 85, 119, 133, 134, 151, 156
Kichwa nationality 9, 85
Koenig, M. 40, 43–4
Korovkin, T. 6, 49, 54, 55, 115, 143, 144, 145
Kottak, C.P. 9
Kritzer, H.M. 109
Kyle, D. 81, 97
Kymlicka, W. 40, 41, 42

La Cocha 83, 85, 89, 206
La Cocha murder case (2002) 16, 58, 64, 68, 115, 123, 185, 186–90, 191, 206, 207, 210, 221–2, 223; forum shopping 220–1, 223; two murder cases compared 202–4
La Cocha-Guantópolo murder case (2010) 42, 58, 60, 66, 70, 72–3, 115, 185–6, 209–11, 217, 221–3; *cabildo* hears case 191–6, 220–1; comparison of two murder cases 202–4; Constitutional Court 198, 199–202, 204, 207, 211, 217, 220, 222; crime 190–1; forum shopping 220–1, 223; internal conflict 200, 202, 203, 223; national legal system 196–202; political issue 136, 195, 199, 200, 202, 204–10, 211, 217, 223; provincial court 196–9
Lake Quilotoa 90, 165, 206
land 102; disputes 113, 114–15, 118, 129, 165, 166; fragmentation of 96; hacienda system *see separate entry*; reforms 37–8, 48, 51, 52–4, 56, 83, 162, 214
language: Constitution 172; Fiscalía Indígena 132, 133; Kichwa 59, 77, 85, 119, 133, 134, 151, 156; Spanish 85, 119, 151, 156
Latacunga 11–12, 57, 84, 85, 97, 101, 125; Court of Justice in *see separate entry*
Law of Coordination and Cooperation between Customary Law and National

Index

Law, proposed 69–73, 214, 226; internal conflicts 71; territory which is commonly inhabited by indigenous peoples 71–2
lawyers 128, 156, 204; Civil Court in Pujilí 129; Court of Justice 130, 131–2, 171, 172–6; customary law 156; informal 144; national law 82–3, 171, 180, 200
legal anthropology and pluralism 27–9
legal monism 21, 28, 46, 48, 54, 61, 64, 73, 213, 226
legal pluralism, definition of 2–3
Lévi-Strauss, C. 30
libros de actas 11, 12–13, 23, 111, 117, 121, 147, 149, 166, 181
Llasag Fernandéz, R. 121
Llewellyn, K.N. 25, 26, 107
Llumitasig, José Segundo Jami 133
local authorities 159, 182, 213, 218, 221, 222, 226, 227; *asamblea general* see separate entry; *cabildo* see separate entry; family 117–18; *teniente político* see separate entry; whom to turn to: provincial or 134–8, 215
López, W. 171
Lucero, J.A. 52, 60, 65
Lund, C. 47, 184, 226
Lyons, B.J. 54

Macas, Luís 58, 59, 65
Mahuad, Jamil 65, 165
Maine, Henry 24
Malinowski, B. 24, 25
Manning, P.K. 125
market days 87–8, 89, 96, 101; police 126; rules 116
Martínez Novo, C. 58, 79, 83, 104
mediator between state and rural indigenous communities: *teniente político* 141, 142–3, 148, 158, 216, 227–9
medical costs 115; Fiscalía Indígena 133; Rosita vs Miguel case 117, 120, 122, 133, 141, 150, 151, 152
Merry, S.E. 3, 10, 11, 28, 29, 217, 219
MICC (Movimiento Indígena y Campesino de Cotopaxi) 57–8, 116, 119, 139, 162; La Cocha murder case (2002) 187, 188, 207, 223; La Cocha-Guantópolo murder case (2010) 192, 194, 197, 199, 200, 201, 204, 206–8, 210, 211, 223

Migdal, J.S. 37
migration 57; crime and 113–14; *minifundios* 79; returning home for weddings, baptisms and annual fiestas 76–7, 78, 99–100, 102–3; Tigua 160, 162–4, 165, 166; transnational 97–8; Zumbahua 76–7, 78, 79, 81, 89, 96–100, 102–3, 160
Mijeski, K.J. 57, 59, 60, 66, 209
modernity and tradition 60, 104, 110, 113, 116
Modood, T. 40, 41
monism, legal 21, 28, 46, 48, 54, 61, 64, 73, 213, 226
Montecristi Constitution *see* Constitution (2008)
Moore, S.F. 3, 24, 26, 27, 28
Morales, Evo 83
multiculturalism 20–1, 38–9, 42, 43, 45–6, 55, 59, 225, 227, 229–30; Constitution of 1998 61, 62, 139
murder 118–19, 130; La Cocha murder case (2002) 16, 58, 64, 68, 115, 123, 185, 186–90, 191, 202–4, 206, 207, 210; La Cocha-Guantópolo murder case (2010) *see separate entry*

Nader, L. 22, 24, 25, 26, 30, 184
Naranjo, M. 76, 163
National Court of Justice 178–80, 181, 184
national law 2–3, 4, 6, 9, 16, 21, 27, 28–30, 41, 44, 45, 193; civil and criminal law 134; Constitution of 1998 62; corrupt and biased officials 136–7; courts *see separate entry*; customary law not subordinate to 179; double jeopardy rule 109; Fiscalía Indígena 132; hacienda system 37, 82–3; jurisdiction 107; knowledge of 136; murder 201–3, 209, 221–2, 229; mutual influence: customary law and 220, 226, 231; police 126–7; social norms 116; *tenientes políticos* 124, 141, 142–3, 144, 148, 153, 154, 157, 158, 171, 216, 220; unfavorable bias toward 135–6, 137, 219; *see also* coordinating rules
ne bis in idem principle or double jeopardy rule 68, 109, 177, 188, 200
neoliberalism 6, 7, 21, 36–7, 43, 48, 55, 65, 74, 96, 225, 227
Noboa, Gustavo 62, 63, 65, 204, 214
normative paradigm 24–5

norms 126; family and community 158, 218; Fiscalía Indígena 132; social 116, 118, 156; umbrella 110, 119
Noroña Salcedo, M.B. 83, 90, 96, 165

Ochoa García, C. 22
Okin, S.M. 41, 42
Oleas, Gonzalo 82–3
Olivo, Jaime 206–7
Oomen, B. 29, 33
Orellana Halkyer, R. 22, 31
ortigazo (nettles and ice-cold water) 122–3, 187, 191–2, 193, 196
Ouweneel, A. 9, 49, 50, 79, 102

Pacari, Nina 59, 65, 201
Pachakutik Party or MUPP 58–9, 65, 70, 72, 84, 201, 206, 207–8
Palacio, Alfredo 65
Pallares, A. 5, 9, 55, 225
Pallo, Jaime Rodrigo 146, 147, 148, 149–58, 183
páramos 80, 90–2
Parekh, B. 38, 39, 42, 230
parroquias or parishes 52; Juntas Parroquiales or parish boards *see separate entry*; Zumbahua 9, 53, 83, 85–6, 87, 89, 94–101, 104, 116, 125, 126, 129, 131, 162
paternity suits 112–13, 129, 182
Pazmiño, Patricio 200
penal law/cases 117, 120, 124, 134, 136, 153, 218, 220; Court of Justice in Latacunga *see separate entry*; Fiscalía *see separate entry*; Fiscalía Indígena *see separate entry*;
Perafán Simmonds, C.C. 22
Pesántez, Washington 194–5, 197
Platt, T. 37, 49–50
pluralism and legal anthropology 27–9
police 130, 134, 189, 209, 210, 229; local 124–7, 138, 147, 148, 188, 192
political society 20, 35–6, 42, 45, 213, 229, 231; *teniente político* as mediator 141, 142–3, 148, 158, 216, 227–9
politics and legal affairs 136, 195, 199, 200, 202, 204–10, 211, 217, 223, 226–7
politics of recognition 21, 39, 45, 230
politics of redistribution 21, 39, 45–6, 230
positive law 2, 21, 23, 24, 28
Pospisil, L. 25–6, 107
post-trial phase 108–9, 120; National Court of Justice 181

Postero, N.G. 9, 38–9, 230
Poveda, Carlos 178–9, 188, 197, 200, 204, 223
Poveda Moreno, C. 121, 182, 191, 197
poverty 9, 35–6, 54, 95; *minifundios* 79; theft and 114; Zumbahua 78, 79, 89, 94–6
power relations 45, 47, 205–6, 210, 224; agrarian reform 53; bringing the state in 33–6; choice of local or provincial authorities 135; fiestas 99–100; historical background 50, 143–4; 'holy trinity' 50–1, 53, 54, 143–4, 145; legal void: formal legal pluralism and lack of coordinating rules 184, 186; Toaquiza vs the community 42, 136, 165, 183, 184, 216, 223; within groups or cultures 41–2; Zumbahua 79, 82, 83, 102, 104, 203; *see also* hacienda system
prison 125, 126, 186, 193, 197, 198–9, 200, 203, 229
procedures 187; disputes and customary law 120–1, 141, 150–2, 155–6, 176, 193; judges and national law 171; Rosita vs Miguel case 150–2, 155–6
process-oriented paradigm 25–6
ProJusticia 63, 64
property disputes 113–15
Protestant Church in Zumbahua 192
province of Cotopaxi 57, 82, 84–5; poverty 95; transnational migration 98
provincial authorities 213; Civil Court 107, 112, 114–15, 127–9, 134, 136, 156; Court of Justice *see separate entry*; Fiscalía *see separate entry*; Fiscalía Indígena *see separate entry*; whom to turn to: local or 134–8, 215
public sector 43, 55
Pujilí canton 81, 82, 84–5, 101
Pujilí town 11, 12, 80, 81, 85; Civil Court in Pujilí *see separate entry*
punishment 23, 41, 42, 135, 137, 157, 210; *cabildo* and *asamblea general* 121–4, 187, 191–2, 193, 196, 198, 202, 221–2; family 118
purification rituals 118, 122–3, 187, 191–2, 193, 196, 202, 221–2

Rabinow, P. 15, 16
Radcliffe, S.A. 79, 88, 102
Radcliffe-Brown, A.R. 24–5
Rawls, J. 39, 40, 230
reciprocity 24, 100, 110, 116, 119

recognition, politics of 21, 39, 45, 230
reconciliation 2, 16, 22, 23, 119–20, 135, 151, 153, 156, 202
redistribution 100, 225; land 53–4; politics of 21, 39, 45–6, 230; Zumbahua 91, 100
restitution 16, 22, 23, 120, 122, 135, 157
rituals, purification 118, 122–3, 187, 191–2, 193, 196, 202, 221–2
robberies 113, 114, 126, 130, 133, 137, 166; Juntas del Campesinado 119; livestock 119
Rodríguez Lara, Guillermo 53–4
Rosita vs Miguel case 1–2, 117, 120, 140–1, 149–50, 171, 183, 219–20, 222; analysis: *teniente político*'s juridical role 153–7, 215–16, 223; fine threatened 122; interlegality 140–1, 157–8, 215–16; medical bills 117, 120, 122, 133, 141, 150, 151, 152; police 126; procedure 150–2, 155–6; settlement 152–3; social pressure and customary law 135, 137
rule-centered or normative paradigm 24–5

Salgado Álvarez, J. 63
Sánchez Botero, E. 62, 201
Sánchez-Parga, J. 96, 97
Santi, M. 201
Selverston-Scher, M.H. 55, 60
semi-autonomous social fields 26–7, 28
sentencing under customary law 23, 135, 137, 157, 210; *cabildo* and *asamblea general* 121–4, 187, 191–2, 193, 196, 198, 202, 221–2
Serrano Peréz, V. 22
sexual violence 111–13; Civil Court in Pujilí 107, 112
Shahar, I. 32
shopping forums 33, 109, 183, 193, 223
Sieder, R. 3, 4, 5, 6, 7, 15, 22, 23, 24, 29, 37, 41, 42, 43, 135, 155, 214, 217, 219, 225, 230
Sierra, M.T. 4, 25, 27, 30, 31, 136
Simon Thomas, M. 6, 10, 16, 21, 22, 30, 39, 42, 48, 55, 64, 68, 73, 76, 85, 121, 123, 128, 141, 148, 155, 156, 157, 162, 185, 200, 202, 203–4, 220, 229
Skocpol, T. 30, 33
small-scale agriculturalists or *campesinos* 9, 85, 96
Snyder, F.G. 108
social norms 116, 118, 156

social pressure 24, 135, 137, 220, 221
social rights 53–4
sociopolitical geography of Zumbahua 84–92; *communas* 89–90; *páramos* 90–2; province, canton and parish 84–6; village 86–9
solidarity 110, 116, 119
Solórzano, Carlos 65
sovereignty 21; and subsidiarity 42–5, 46, 158, 227, 230
Spain 97, 98, 129; colonialism 49–50, 81, 102
Spiertz, H. 32, 33, 135
Starr, J. 17, 18, 26
state 57, 106, 138, 226; conceptualization of 33–6; counter-hegemonic use of customary law 3, 29, 33, 217–20, 221, 223, 224; nineteenth century 50–1; sovereignty and subsidiarity 42–5, 46, 158, 227, 230; *teniente político*: mediator between rural indigenous communities and 141, 142–3, 148, 158, 216, 227–9; twentieth century, end of 54–5; –Indian relations 36–8, 45, 213, 225, 227–31
Stavenhagen, R. 40
Stern, S.J. 37, 50
Stikwerda, L. 32
Striffler, S. 52
subsidiarity and sovereignty 42–5, 46, 158, 227, 230
subsistence farming 9, 53, 95, 162

Tamanaha, B.Z. 7, 21, 41, 49
Taussig, M. 98, 99
Taylor, C. 39, 230
Tenesaca, P. 76
teniente político 73, 85–6, 87, 138, 205; family disputes 107, 148; Fiscalía Indígena vs 132; historical overview 142–6; interlegality 140–58; La Cocha-Guantópolo murder case 192, 203; mediator between state and rural indigenous communities 141, 142–3, 148, 158, 216, 227–9; monetary limit: juridical role 153, 154; national law 124, 141, 142–3, 144, 148, 153, 154, 157, 158, 171, 216, 220; nineteenth century 50–1, 142–5, 227; and the police 124–7; role of 124, 141–8, 153–8, 171, 227–8, 229; Rosita vs Miguel case *see separate entry*; Toaquiza vs the community 169–70, 171, 182; twentieth century land

reforms 52, 53, 54; violent crime: medical bills 115, 117, 133
theft 113–14, 118, 137, 153, 166–7
Tibán, Lourdes 22, 49, 57, 58, 70, 72, 73, 121, 132, 155, 179, 187, 188, 189, 193, 201, 204, 206, 208, 209, 211, 214, 219, 223, 226
Tibán, Marco 209
Tibán, Vicente 190, 192, 193, 197, 206, 207
Tiguan art 147, 160, 162–6, 167, 205; urban–rural controversy 166
Toaquiza, Alfredo 164, 166, 167, 168
Toaquiza, Julio 163, 164, 166
Toaquiza, Sisa 166
Toaquiza vs the community 159–60, 180–4, 210, 216, 217, 220; appeal 177–8; background information on Tigua 160–7; charge 167–71; internal conflict 171, 172–3, 176, 177, 179, 180, 184, 216; National Court of Justice 178–80, 181, 184; power relations 42, 136, 165, 183, 184, 216, 223; verdict 172–7, 180
torture 195, 196, 197, 209
tourism 86–7, 90, 91, 114, 163, 164–5, 167, 180, 206
tradition and modernity 60, 104, 110, 113, 116
traffic accidents 117, 126, 133, 153
Trujillo, J.C. 63, 64, 73
Turner, B.S. 39

Ubink, J. 47
Umajinga, B. 83, 85, 91, 98, 146
Umajinga, César 58, 83–4, 201
uncertainty 48, 73–4, 184, 202, 212, 214; political sensitivity 202
unemployment 113, 114
United Kingdom: colonial Ghana 47
United Nations 70; Declaration on the Rights of Indigenous Peoples 55, 71, 171, 172, 178, 200
United States 97
UNOCAT (Unión de Organizaciones y Cabildos de Tigua) 116, 118–19, 162
UNOCIC (Unión de Organizaciones y Comunidades Indígenas de La Coc) 116, 118–19, 139, 186–7, 188, 192, 194, 204, 223

Valdivia, F.R. 13, 15, 22, 41, 117
Van Cott, D.L. 6, 37, 38, 44, 54–5, 56, 60, 225

van de Sandt, J. 22
vandalism 100, 113, 114, 193; social norms 116
Vanderlinden, J. 27
Vega, Agustín 165
Vega, Jose 163, 164
Vertovec, S. 38
Vintimilla, J. 13, 22, 87, 111, 113, 116, 118, 119, 147, 148
violence 83, 93–4, 99, 100, 101, 115, 126, 137; *asamblea general* 118; Court of Justice 130; domestic 100, 110–11, 148; fighting: medical costs 117, 120, 122, 133, 141, 150, 151, 152; Fiscalía Indígena: injury form 134; homicide *see separate entry*; sexual 111–13; social norms 116; *see also* Rosita vs Miguel case
von Benda-Beckmann, F. 4, 21, 28, 33, 135, 137, 219
von Benda-Beckmann, K. 4, 27, 28, 31, 32, 33, 47, 108, 109, 120, 183, 193, 210, 217, 220, 223

Waters, W.F. 53
weddings in Zumbahua 75–9, 92–4, 98, 99–100
Weismantel, M.J. 76, 77, 79, 81, 82, 83, 84, 85, 89, 90, 91, 95, 96, 97, 99, 100, 101, 102, 104, 106, 119, 145, 146, 161
whippings 123, 187, 193, 196, 221–2
Whitten Jr, N.E. 58
Wilson, P.C. 43, 55
Wilson, T.M. 100
Wiltink, N. 114
witnesses 131, 134, 174–5, 177, 201, 220
women 15, 94, 101, 110, 123, 124, 148
Woodman, G.R. 27, 28, 227
World Bank 43, 55, 63, 95, 97

yanapo system 53, 83, 102, 104, 145
Yashar, D.J. 5–6, 52, 53, 54, 55, 58, 225
Yin, R. 8
Yrigoyen Fajardo, R.Z. 23, 49, 50, 61, 62, 135
Yumbay, M. 110

Zumbahua 1–2, 7–11, 206; abolition of hacienda of 53, 83, 102; alcohol 78, 92–3, 94, 99–101, 104, 117, 126; bus journey from Latacunga to 79–81; climate 85, 91; cohesion and conflict in 79, 94, 101, 102–5, 214–15; *comuna* structure 53, 83, 85, 89–90, 102, 138,

186; conflict and conflict resolution in *see separate entry*; establishment of *parroquia* of 53, 83; fiestas 75–9, 92–4, 98, 99–101, 102–3, 104, 125, 193; fighting at fiestas 93–4, 99, 100; hacienda 53, 79, 81–3, 96, 102, 103–4, 138, 145, 162, 165; history 81–4; internal tensions/conflicts 83, 86, 93–4, 102–4; Junta Parroquiale or parish board 85–6, 87, 116, 125, 126, 127, 138, 147–8, 158, 191, 192, 194, 205–6; land reform (1964 and 1973) 83, 162; life in the parish 94–101; location 79–80; methodology 11–13; migration 76–7, 78, 79, 81, 89, 96–100, 102–3, 160; *páramos* 80, 90–2; parish or *parroquia* of 9, 53, 83, 85–6, 87, 89, 94–101, 104, 116, 125, 126, 129, 131, 162; past and present 79–92; police 124–7, 138, 147, 148, 192; population 85, 91–2, 125; poverty 78, 79, 89, 94–6; 'remote' 79; sociopolitical geography 84–92; *teniente político* see separate entry; village of 86–9, 104, 125; *see also* La Cocha murder case (2002); La Cocha-Guantópolo murder case (2010); Rosita vs Miguel case; Toaquiza vs the community